was set in Helvetica Light by York Graphic Ser-
and printed and bound by Murray Printing. Editor:
ara. Designer: Eileen Thaxton. Production Man-
ne Ingrao. Cartoons by Arthur Vergara. Cover by
kton.

1977, by John Wiley & Sons, Inc.

rved. Published simultaneously in Canada.

s book may be reproduced by any means, nor
or translated into a machine language with-
n permission of the publisher.

ngress Cataloging in Publication Data

ard P J
etoric and handbook.

edition of two separately published books—
toric and the second edition of The little
book.''

language—Rhetoric.   I. Title.
4   .808'.042   76-45189

17232-4

United States of America

5 4 3 2

PUTTING IT ALL TOGETHER (pp. 133–183)

SPECIAL KINDS OF WRITING ASSIGNMENTS (pp. 184–270)

WRITING THE RESEARCH PAPER, LETTERS, AND THE RÉSUMÉ (pp. 271–350)

D0609155

The Little Rhetor
And Handbook

Edward P. J. Corbett
The Ohio State University

John Wiley & Sons, Inc.
New York / Santa Barbara / Londo

This b
vices, |
Arthur
ager: S
Eileen

Copyrigh

All rights

No part
transmitt
out the w

Library d

Corbett,
The litt

''Comb
The Little
English h
1. Eng
PE1408.C
ISBN 0-4

Printed in

10 9 8 7

A Double Dedication

—to Aristotle, who taught me most of what I know about rhetoric.

—to all my students over the years, whose written prose sometimes mystified me, often enlightened me, and invariably beguiled me. Bless them all.

Vocabulary Development Aid

The rhetoric section of *The Little Rhetoric and Handbook* features the Wiley Vocabulary Development Aid, which is designed to help

(1) the student who approaches the study of English (and other subjects) without an adequate vocabulary; the Vocabulary Development Aid gives brief definitions of about 750 words of probable difficulty.
(2) the student who wishes to acquire a larger and more varied vocabulary; this student can use the Vocabulary Development Aid to learn new words or to stimulate the use of words known but neglected.

How it works

The Wiley Vocabulary Development Aid is easy to use: you merely glance down to the bottom of the page to find the number and the meaning corresponding to the numbered word in the text that puzzles you. Pass by those numbered words in the text whose meanings you don't need to check out; the numbers are small and should not interfere with your reading.

E.P.J.C.

Preface

The Little Rhetoric and Handbook is a combined edition of two separately published books—*The Little Rhetoric* and the second edition of *The Little English Handbook: Choices and Conventions.*

The rhetoric portion of this combined edition represents my efforts to deal, in a brief and sometimes schematic way, with the process of effective writing. Basically, the approach is the traditional, familiar one—a step-by-step sequence, beginning with the assignment and moving progressively through the stages of Fixing on a Subject, Finding Something to Say, Selecting and Arranging the Material, and Expressing What Has Been Discovered, Selected, and Arranged. In Chapter Six, entitled Putting It All Together, a hypothetical subject is carried through all of those stages, from initial assignment to final product. Chapter Seven deals with four special kinds of writing assignments: writing about literature, writing essay examinations, writing formal reports, and writing abstracts. Chapter Eight deals with some additional special writing assignments: the research paper, business and familiar letters, and the résumé. I have incorporated into this commonplace approach to the writing process several of the traditional and recent techniques of invention or discovery

Preface

and a variety of imitative and sentence-combining exercises in style. By suggesting a variety of methods of "composition," I hope that writers will find a method—or combination of methods—that works for them.

In the handbook section, I concentrate on those matters of grammar, style, paragraphing, punctuation, and mechanics that from years of experience in reading student papers and responding to telephone queries from businessmen and secretaries I know to be the most common and persistent problems in the expressive part of the writing process. Nothing that was in the first edition of the handbook has been dropped, but a few additions and changes have been made in the second edition. A new item (**90**) on capitalization has been added to the mechanics section. Item **40** has been expanded to include a discussion of faulty predication. Item **62,** which deals with the omission of the comma in pairs of words, phrases, and dependent clauses joined by a coordinating conjunction, has been expanded to include an exception to that convention in the case of "suspended constructions." Item **89** (about numbers) has been expanded to include more than merely the rule not to begin a sentence with an Arabic number. A complete paradigm of the tenses of regular and irregular verbs and the verb *to be* has been added in an unnumbered section at the back of the book. A list of the official two-letter postal abbreviations of all the states has also been added at the back of the book. Although I adhered to my original decision not to include a Glossary of Usage, I did add a brief section on Puzzlers, which deals with some common problems of phrasing. Throughout the handbook, I have added or substituted new examples wherever the previous examples did not seem to cover all the varieties of error, and here and there, I have revised some of my inanities.

● Preface

The rhetoric part of this book has benefited immeasurably from the criticism and suggestions of a number of experienced teachers of writing: Elizabeth Wooten Cowan and Greg Cowan of Texas A & M University, Richard Lloyd-Jones of the University of Iowa, Joseph F. Trimmer of Ball State University, Betty Renshaw of Prince George's Community College, James Raymond of the University of Alabama, W. G. Schermbrucker of Capilano College in British Columbia, Caroline Eckhardt of Pennsylvania State University, Margaret Blickle of Ohio State University, Elizabeth K. Burton of Montclair High School, and C. Jeriel Howard of Bishop College.

Both the first and the second editions of the handbook have benefited from the criticisms of a number of teachers: James T. Nardin of Louisiana State University, Gary Tate of Texas Christian University, William F. Irmscher of the University of Washington, James Karabatsos of Creighton University, Marinus Swets of Grand Rapids Junior College, Richard Lloyd-Jones of the University of Iowa, Mina P. Shaughnessy of City College of New York, Kirby L. Duncan of Stephen F. Austin University, Nancy Dasher of Ohio State University, Betty Renshaw of Prince George's Community College, Raymond Liedlich of Portland Community College, W. G. Schermbrucker of Capilano College in British Columbia, Maureen Waters Osers of Queens in New York, Sarah M. Wallace and her colleagues at Volunteer Community College in Tennessee, Peter T. Zoller of Wichita State University, Robert C. Fox of St. Francis College, Paul Sorrentino of the Pennsylvania State University, and Nancy Bandez of John Wiley and Sons.

I am heavily indebted to the editorial and production staffs at John Wiley, especially to Thomas O. Gay for his persistent faith and encouragement during the many months I worked on the book. My debt to Arthur Vergara, my development

Preface

editor, is incalculable. In addition to his expert editing of both the rhetoric and the handbook, he contributed the cartoons and the definitions of words in the rhetoric. I also want to thank my colleague Andrea Lunsford and her husband, Steve, for their help in proofreading. Heaven will forgive me, I hope, for failing to name the many other people—colleagues, students, and authors of other rhetorics and handbooks— who have contributed to whatever merit this book may have.

Edward P. J. Corbett

Contents

The Rhetoric

Contents

Contents

Chapter 8
Writing Research Papers, Letters, and Résumés 271

The Handbook

Contents

Format of Manuscript 10–16

Grammar 20–32

Style 40–49

● Contents

Contents

THE
RHETORIC

Chapter 1
What is Rhetoric?

What is rhetoric? One definition is that rhetoric is the *art of effective communication.* That brief, rather general definition demands explanation. First of all, to say that rhetoric is an *art* means that it is a skill—one that enables us to make wise choice of the means to achieve a desired end.

Choice is a key term in rhetoric. When there is no choice available, we are probably in a realm where we have to do something in a single, invariable[1] way. For instance, if we want to produce water chemically, we must fuse two parts of hydrogen with one part of oxygen; we have no choice in the matter. But in the realm[2] of art, we do have the choice of two or more means to achieve the desired end, and throughout this book, you will be made aware of these choices and will be shown how to make the best choice of the means available to you.

The word *communication* in our definition derives from two Latin words that together mean "making one with." When we say that we communicate with someone, we are suggesting that through words or some other set of symbols or actions,

---

[1] Not varying; unchanging; constant. [2] A region; area.

What is Rhetoric?

we are, in a sense, making that person at-one with us. We are using symbols or actions to make someone understand or appreciate our thoughts and feelings. When that state of at-oneness is not completely achieved, we are still "at odds" with one another. In other words, our communication has not been wholly *effective*. In some way, we have failed to make the right choice of the means of transmitting our message to someone.

There are of course many symbol systems that we can use to convey our message. We can, for instance, use gestures or facial expressions or pictures or sounds or black squiggles on a piece of paper. The most efficient system of symbols that man has devised for conveying most messages is the system of words—either spoken words or written words. This text will deal almost exclusively with effective communication through the medium of written words.

Most of the communicating you will do during your lifetime will be through the medium[1] of spoken words. But occasionally you will have to resort[2] to written words. If you find it difficult to communicate with written words, remember that most people also find it difficult. One reason for this difficulty is that they have had much more practice in speaking than in writing. They probably speak more words in a single month than they will ever write in a lifetime. No wonder they feel so much more at ease in speaking than in writing: frequent practice in any skill is bound to improve the skill.

Another reason why speaking words is easier than writing words is that in speaking, we usually have to produce only short bursts of words—perhaps only a word or phrase at a time, at most only two or three consecutive[3] sentences. And we usually don't have to search for something to say, nor do

---

[1] A means of conveying, communicating, or effecting something. [2] To make use of; to rely on; to go to for help. [3] Following in uninterrupted order.

2

we have to arrange the order of sentences. Our grasp of the vocabulary and the grammar of our native language has been so internalized after years of oral[1] practice that we have only to open our mouths and the words trip off our tongues.

But the written medium is another matter. Except for short notes we sometimes dash off or tack up on a bulletin board, most writing demands an extensive, uninterrupted sequence[2] of sentences—two or three or ten pages of words with a beginning, a middle, and an end, which must have a certain measure of unity and coherence.[3] It is that kind of sustained[4] writing that is difficult for most of us and that this text will mainly deal with.

This text will try to help you *compose*—that is, *put together*—an extended piece of writing—the kind of writing that requires many words, many sentences, many paragraphs, many divisions.

● The rhetorical interrelationships

What might help you at the outset to grasp the art of effective writing is some understanding of the interrelationships that are involved in any act of communication with words. The rhetorical act—the kind of act we are concerned with here—involves *someone* saying *something* to *someone else.* As you can see, there are three distinct elements—a *writer,* a *message,* and a *reader.* These three can be put in pronoun terms—an *I,* an *it,* and a *you.* (Although a singular noun or pronoun is used here for the third element—*reader, you*—most of the time in a sustained piece of writing, the writer is

---

[1] Spoken. [2] Series. [3] Logical and harmonious connection of parts. [4] Kept in being; kept in motion; prolonged.

What is Rhetoric?

addressing a *group* of readers. A word that carries this idea of plurality[1] is *audience,* and it is this word that we will most often use for the third element.)

But there is another, fourth, term that should now be introduced into this rhetorical set of relationships. We will use the word *universe* for this fourth element. The *universe* is the "world out there" in which the writer and the audience exist and about which the message is perhaps talking; but sometimes the message may not be talking about the "world out there." Occasionally, it may be talking only about the thoughts and feelings within the private self of the writer. When a writer says, "The sun is shining today," he is obviously saying something about the condition of the "world out there." But when he says, "I am happy today," he is saying something about the condition of the "world within." Diaries and journals are examples of this latter kind of writing, especially when they are mere recordings of the thoughts, reactions, and feelings of the writer. Eventually, of course, some journals and diaries are read by an audience, and so they take on a communicative aspect that they did not have when they were first composed; but still what they record is primarily the inner world of the writer rather than the outer world that can be perceived by both the writer and the audience. Sometimes this kind of writing is called "expressive discourse"—discourse[2] that "pushes out" what is inside the mind of the writer.

There is a value to, and a place for, expressive writing. We are all richer because of the "personal" writing that has come down to us from the past, whether in elegant prose or in lyric verse. But the writing that most of us have to do in the real world deals with the "world out there." We have to give

[1] The state or condition of being more than one. [2] Spoken or written treatment of a subject at length.

4

information about, or urge a course of action in relation to, an object, a situation, or an idea that exists in that world. The response of readers to this kind of writing will partly depend on how accurately the writer's description or interpretation corresponds with the reality that the readers know or perceive. The writer's view of the world will be rejected if readers say to themselves, "That just isn't so." For that reason alone, the communication will be judged as something less than *effective.*

The four elements of *writer, audience, message,* and *universe* not only shed light on the communication process and the rhetoric that governs effective communication but also provide reference points to help us make a wise choice of options.[1] A diagram may help us see how the four elements serve as reference points:

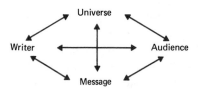

The two-way arrows in this diagram suggest the reciprocal[2] relationships among the four elements.

As a result of the relationships in the communication process, the writer has a number of standards to help him make wise choice of the means at his disposal. He decides, for instance, to adopt one kind of approach in his message instead of another kind (1) because he feels that this approach is closer to *reality* as he sees it in the universe than the other is or (2) because he senses that this particular

---

[1] Things that may be chosen. [2] Existing on, or shared by, both sides.

What is Rhetoric?

audience is likely to accept this approach rather than the other or (3) because this approach fits better (than the other) with the *other approaches* already in the message or (4) because this approach better suits his own *value system.*

The writer may not always, or even often, consciously make his choice in reference to the other elements, but if he is to be effective, he must at least *unconsciously* or *subconsciously* do so. His writing will hang together and do its job to the extent that he deliberately or intuitively[1] makes his choices in relation to the audience, the message, the universe, and himself. And of course if he is to weigh these relationships accurately, he must know something about the disposition of his audience, the nature of the universe, the structure of his message, and his own disposition.

These reference points also work when choices have to be made among units as small as the word or the sentence. Why does a writer choose a certain word rather than another, synonymous, word? He might explain that this word rather than the other is more consistent with his personality ("I don't like big, pretentious words"). Or he might choose the one over the other because he senses that it will be better understood by the particular audience he is addressing. Or he might choose it because it fits better with the level of speech that he has been using or because it more precisely conveys the comment he wants to make about the "world out there." His choice of sentence structures for his message will also be guided by his conscious or unconscious consideration of one or other of the above four elements. But along with those features of style that represent more or less conscious choices, there will be others that represent *habit.* A writer's style is therefore a combination of habitual and chosen features.

[1] Knowledgeably but without conscious reasoning.

6

The art of rhetoric had its beginnings with Greek and Roman practitioners of the art (called *rhetoricians*), such as Aristotle, Cicero, Quintilian, and Seneca. Rhetoric, with them, dealt primarily with persuasive public speaking. It presented theoretical principles and practical suggestions for composing and delivering speeches that would confirm or change an audience's mind or that would induce[1] an audience to act or not to act. As rhetoric developed throughout the Middle Ages and the Renaissance, its principles and practices were extended to written, and other than just persuasive, kinds of expression. By the third quarter of the eighteenth century, George Campbell, the Scottish rhetorician, could define rhetoric as ''that art or talent by which the discourse is adapted to its end,'' the ends of discourse being reducible to four: ''to enlighten the understanding, to please the imagination, to move the passions, or to influence the will.'' Thus rhetoric

[1] Lead (someone) by persuasion or influence.

7

What is Rhetoric?

had been expanded to embrace a wide range of functions: *instructing, informing, entertaining, persuading,* and *moving to action.* This text also regards rhetoric as applicable to a wide range of functions and to the full range of traditional kinds of discourse that serve such functions: *exposition, argumentation, narration, and description.*

So we return to our definition of rhetoric as the *art of effective communication;* but now we have a better understanding of all that is included in that broad, general definition. We see that effective communication involves a concern for the interrelations among the writer, the audience, the message, and the universe, that it depends on wise choices being made from among the available means, and that it embraces a wide range of functional types of written prose. We must now move on to the particulars of this *art of effective communication.*

Chapter 2
Fixing on a Subject

Sometimes when you have to write something, the choice of a subject will be entirely your own. You may feel the urge to write a letter to the editor of the local newspaper about the miserable condition of the city streets. You may be moved to write to the manager of an appliance store to complain about the repeatedly unsatisfactory work that his service department has done on your TV set. You may have to write a letter to a friend to explain why you didn't stop by for a visit on your trip West. In each case, the choice of *whether* or not to write was your own, and the choice of *what* to write about was your own. Under such circumstances, you usually experience little or no difficulty in composing the letter. The words just seem to flow onto the page.

But it seems safe to say that on at least ninety percent of the occasions when you have to write something, either in school or on the job, both the decision to write and the choice of a subject are *not* yours to make. Someone requires you to write something and determines, at least in a general way, the subject you are to write about. A teacher requires you to write a paper on the history of progressive income tax;

Fixing on a Subject

an employer asks you to prepare a written report on annual sales patterns for the forthcoming[1] board meeting; an editor commissions you to write an article on predatory[2] sharks at resort beaches. You can of course refuse to write, but for your refusal, you may have to pay the penalty of failing the course, losing your job, or forgoing[3] a royalty[4] check.

Even when you don't have a choice of subject to make, many choices about the *treatment* of the subject will be left up to you. One of the most crucial decisions you will have to make—even when the choice of subject is up to you—is what *aspect* of the subject you are going to treat. Almost always, you will have to put some limitations on the subject, because usually you will not be able, or even required, to treat it exhaustively.

Let us set forth in outline form some of the considerations that can help you limit your subject:

1 **The amount of wordage you are allotted.**
2 **The purpose of the writing.**
3 **The occasion of the writing.**
4 **The nature of the audience for whom you are writing.**
5 **The extent and depth of your knowledge of the subject.**
6 **The thesis or central point you want to make about the subject.**

Other considerations may help to limit the subject, but these are the common ones.

Let us take a subject and show how these considerations might help you to fix the limits of your treatment. Suppose that you were asked to write about the subject of *capital*

---

[1] Coming or approaching in time. [2] Preying upon other animals. [3] Giving up. [4] Payment to the owner of a patent or copyright for the use of it.

punishment.

(1) Usually when you are assigned a subject, some **word limit** is suggested: a 500-word theme, a 3000-word research paper, a 6000-word article, a 10,000-word pamphlet, a 70,000-word book. Obviously, the amount of wordage allotted[1] to you will greatly influence how much you have to restrict your subject. If you have only 500 words to work with, you may have to treat only one aspect of the subject, and your treatment of that one aspect will have to be more general than if you had 6000 words to work with.

(2) What (besides doing an assignment) is your **purpose** in writing about capital punishment? Do you wish merely *to inform* your audience about the present status or the past history of capital punishment in your state? Or do you wish *to argue* for a particular position on the issue of whether capital punishment should be continued? Your answers to the question of purpose will have some influence on the aspect or aspects of your subject that you will write about.

(3) The **occasion** of your writing will also suggest some limitations. If, for instance, you were writing a letter to the editor about capital punishment, a subject that was being hotly debated in your state legislature, you would choose a smaller portion of the subject than if your were writing a term paper about capital punishment. For one thing, the letter would not require any extensive review of the situation or any definition of key terms, for these would be familiar to newspaper readers from reports about the debate. And, of course, a letter treating the subject in 150 words would have a better chance of being published than would a letter of 500 or more words.

(4) The **audience** for whom you are writing will have a great influence on the limits you set for your subject. For

[1] Assigned.

11

Fixing on a Subject

whom *are* you writing? For your sociology teacher? For a group of concerned university students? For the general public? For the state legislators? For a group of clergymen gathered at a national convention? Once you have determined who your main audience will be, you will have to estimate the extent of that audience's *knowledge* of the subject and its *attitude* toward the subject. Those estimates will help determine what should be included in, and what excluded from, your treatment. For a group of lawyers, you might want to concentrate on the legal aspects of capital punishment; for a group of clergymen, you might decide to concentrate on the moral issues.

(5) Obviously, the extent and depth of your **knowledge** of the subject will help to determine what aspects you will select to write about. As the old saying goes, "You can't give what you don't have." A professional penologist[1] has a wider range of aspects of capital punishment at his command than the ordinary citizen has. You can extend and deepen your knowledge of the subject by research, of course, but you will still probably have less knowledge of the subject than the professional penologist has. You will tend to select that segment of the subject which you know most about or feel most strongly about.

(6) Determining the **thesis** or central point of your discourse is one of the best ways to establish the limits of a subject. The very nature of a thesis statement—a single declarative[2] sentence in which the predicate[3] asserts[4] or denies something about the subject—sets severe limits on a subject. The subject "capital punishment" covers a vast territory. But as soon as you predicate something of that subject—as in the

---

[1] One who teaches or practices penology, the science of prevention of, and punishment for, crime; also the science of prison management. [2] Making a statement or declaration. [3] The part that expresses what is said about the subject. [4] States positively.

● Applying the Six Considerations to a Topic

thesis statement "Capital punishment is not an effective deterrent to crimes of violence"—you fence off a portion of that territory, a manageable part of the subject for purposes of writing. The thesis statement "Capital punishment is morally indefensible"[1] stakes out another manageable portion of the vast territory. **The mere formulation of a thesis statement helps you to define your subject more narrowly.**

●

Applying the six considerations to a specific topic

Having been shown in a general way how the six considerations might help you to narrow your subject to manageable proportions, let us now take the broad subject of capital punishment and show how an application of these six considerations might help you to treat a specific aspect of it. It should be emphasized that the considerations need not be explored in the same order in which they are laid out above, nor need all six of them be explored. But by way of illustration, we will explore all six considerations and take them in the order in which they occur above.

1 You are asked to write a twenty-minute speech on capital punishment to be delivered to the members of an upper-division Speech course you are taking. At a normal speaking rate, eight double-spaced typewritten pages (2000–2500 words) can be delivered in approximately twenty minutes. So you have a fair idea of **how long** a speech you have to write.

2 You are told that the **purpose** of your speech is to inform your audience about the history of capital punishment in the state.

[1] Cannot be defended.

Fixing on a Subject

3 The **occasion** of your speech is a classroom exercise. You recognize that this is a rather artificial situation, so you know that the information you convey will not serve any real function, except perhaps to educate the audience to some extent. (On another occasion, such a historical survey might serve a real function—for instance, as background information for your fellow-legislators who are faced with the decision of whether to reinstate capital punishment for certain crimes.) The artificiality of this occasion, however, might help suggest to you the particular aspect of the subject you should concentrate on in your speech.

4 Your **audience** will be classmates with a wide variety of backgrounds and academic, social, religious, and political viewpoints. Almost anything you tell this audience about capital punishment in your state will be news to them, so the historical details you present will not seem trite.

5 As for your **knowledge** of the subject, you are not an expert on capital punishment; in fact, the only thing you know about capital punishment in your state is something you recall hearing or reading recently: that no one has been executed in the state penitentiary in the last four years. So almost everything you tell your audience about the history of capital punishment in your state will have to be found out from the research you do between now and the time of your speech. You decide that in the time available you can research only the history of the laws about capital punishment passed in your state.

6 You may not be able to formulate[1] a **thesis** until you have done your research, but let us suppose that you tentatively[2] set the following as the thesis of your speech: "The

[1] To set forth in a formula or definite, systematic statement. [2] Experimentally; not in a final manner.

laws about capital punishment in our state have become progressively more lenient.'' Your research will then turn up evidence either to support your thesis or to change it.

After running through these six considerations, you have a clearer idea of the kinds of limitation you must put on your treatment of the assigned subject. You know that you have to limit your speech to eight pages. Accordingly, you know that you can give more details than you could if you had to write an 800-word essay on the subject but fewer details than if you had to write a 6000-word term paper. You will have to touch on only the landmarks[1] in the 150-year history of capital punishment in your state. Since the most natural arrangement for your speech will be to take events as they occurred over the years, perhaps you can present your history in a sequence of 25-year segments—about a page for each segment, leaving some space for an introduction and a conclusion. You realize that your audience will be your classmates, but since the speech is a classroom exercise for a grade, you will have to impress the instructor, who is likely to be impressed in proportion to how well you hold the interest of your audience. You are not likely to hold their interest if you merely recite facts and statistics; so in your research, you will have to look out for human-interest details. Your tentative thesis too will help you to set limits on those aspects of your general subject that you will explore in your speech.

You begin to see now the dimensions of your treatment of the subject. You have reduced the once sprawling subject to a manageable area. The fences are staked out now around it. You know now what aspects of the subject you are going to talk about and what aspects you are *not* going to talk about.

---

[1] Events that mark turning-points.

Fixing on a Subject

In 2000 to 2500 words, you are going to inform your class-mates about the progressively lenient laws passed by the state legislature over the last 150 years.

You are now ready for the next stage in the writing process: finding something to say about your delimited[1] subject. But before we go on to that, let us review the considerations that may help to fix limits to the subject you are going to write on:

---

1 The specified **length** of your paper (how many words are you allotted?).

2 The **purpose** of your paper (what are you seeking to accomplish with this piece of writing? informing? instructing? persuading? entertaining?).

3 The **occasion** of your paper (are there any special circumstances in this occasion that have a bearing on your treatment of the subject?).

4 The nature of the **audience** for whom you are writing (what will your audience be? will it be fairly uniform?[2] what is likely to be its temperament? what is likely to be the extent of its knowledge about your subject?).

5 The extent and depth of your **knowledge** of the subject (how much do you know about this subject? how much more will you have to learn? how much research can you do in the time available?).

6 The **thesis** or central point you want to make about the subject (can you now formulate a thesis statement that will help you fix limits to your subject?).

---

[1] Marked by limits or boundaries. [2] Having the same characteristics, manner, or form; conforming to one pattern.

16

Chapter 3
Finding Something To Say

Once you have fixed the limits of your subject, you face the most difficult part of the composition process: *finding something to say about the subject.* This is the stage that the classical rhetoricians called *invention,* which meant "discovery through a process of search or inquiry." Their texts dealt at great length with this crucial stage of the composing process and suggested a system for generating something to say about a subject. This text will present a simplified form of the classical system and will suggest some other systems for generating ideas. But first let us consider further the problem of finding something pertinent and significant to say about a subject once it has been delimited.

The really hard part of the writing process is, paradoxically[1] enough, the prewriting stage—all those things you have to do before you put a single word down on paper. But if you do a thorough job in the prewriting stage, you will find that writing the paper becomes, if not easy, certainly easier. You have probably had the experience, at one time or another, of writing that simply flowed onto the paper. What happened in that case is that you had gained a firm grasp on what you wanted to say even before you sat down to write. You had assembled all the bricks, and all you had to do was

[1] In a manner that goes against common sense and yet is true.

Finding Something To Say

lay them out in a neat pattern and put mortar between them. If all writing were that easy, many people would try to make their living by writing for publication. But writing never becomes easy; it may, however, become easier. As with any other skill, writing becomes easier if you practice it and if you develop a "discovery" procedure that works for you most of the time.

As we saw in the previous chapter, you will rarely have the opportunity of picking the subject you are going to write about, although you may have the opportunity of delimiting it. If you had the choice of subject, you would naturally write about what you knew best or what you felt compelled to write about. But often when you are handed a subject, you cannot simply write about it off the top of your head. You have to think about it for a while, meditate about it, ponder it, perhaps read something about it. Experienced writers, who necessarily write frequently, develop some system for generating ideas. What works for one writer may not work for another, so you will have to find or devise[1] a system that works for you. What this text will do is acquaint you with some of the systems of search and discovery that have worked for others and invite you to try them out to see if they work for you.

Some common informal methods of search and discovery

(A) BRAINSTORMING

One of the systems that have worked for many writers is a system that might be called *brainstorming.* This is the system

---

[1] To invent; to plot.

of taking a subject and listing, in random,[1] rapid-fire fashion, anything you can think of that has even the remotest relation to the subject. The listing can be done in the form of words or phrases or sentences. Relying on the process of free association,[2] you write down as many ideas as come to your mind. You will often be surprised at how many usable ideas about the subject can be turned up by this brainstorming technique.

Suppose that you were assigned to write a paper on "The Influence of Music on My Life." If you put your mind in gear, you might come up with a random list like this:

First hooked on music by the "singing commercials" on TV

Memories of sing-alongs around the family piano

A prisoner of piano-practice on Saturday mornings

My tone-deaf music teacher

My first piano recital

The folk-song hootenannies[3] on TV

The "big-deal" on my first record-player

My Bob Dylan phase

Beatlemania

Into "hard-rock"

Music and my first date

Family crisis about the loudness of my recordplayer

Protest songs of the late 60s

Hooked on Earl Scruggs and Doc Watson

My bluegrass phase

Strumming a friend's guitar

Buying my first guitar

Pilgrimage[4] to Grand Ole Opry in Nashville

Jam-sessions[5] at parties

My growing record library

Three-finger picking

Music for my lonely hours

---

[1] In no particular order. [2] Reporting whatever comes to mind, regardless of how impractical or irrelevant it may seem. [3] A gathering at which folk-singers entertain. [4] Journey by a pilgrim or devoted person to a shrine or place of deep significance to him. [5] Spontaneous, unrehearsed performance of music, usually by jazz-players.

Finding Something To Say

The list could go on and on, but almost any young man or woman could produce a list that long in ten or fifteen minutes of scribbling "off the top of one's head."

The brainstorming technique works best, of course, with subjects you know something about just from your own experiences. (You probably couldn't come up with a very long list on the subject of nuclear fission.) You may not be able to use all, or even most, of the items you compiled on the subject of music, especially if you had been told to confine your essay to 500–800 words. You will have to do some selecting and grouping. But at least you have discovered more than enough material for the writing assignment.

(B) MEDITATION

Closely allied[1] to brainstorming is the technique of meditation. You may be aware that the practice of meditation has had a long tradition in monasteries and seminaries[2] in the West, beginning in the Middle Ages and continuing to the present day; and the practice is still prevalent in many Asian religions. Ignatius of Loyola, the founder of the Jesuit order in the sixteenth century, wrote a training manual called *The Spiritual Exercises,* in which he gave detailed instructions about the technique of meditation. In general, the technique consists in taking a short passage from the Scriptures or from the text of the day's Mass and, in an atmosphere of silence and freedom from distraction, thinking about it in a serious, persistent way, trying to see the relevance[3] of that passage to one's own life and spiritual growth. If engaged in conscientiously, meditation can be a wonderfully effective way of discovering one's self and one's relations with other people and with God.

[1] Joined; united.   [2] Educational institutions for training in religious professions.
[3] Relatedness; applicability.

● Informal Methods of Search and Discovery

In recent years, there has been a tremendous growth of interest in transcendental meditation in this country. Transcendental meditation—or TM, as it is sometimes called—was first introduced into the United States in 1959 by a monk from India named Maharishi[1] Mahesh Yogi.[2] At first it appealed mainly to young people in the counterculture,[3] but in recent years, it has gained over a half-million adherents among professional people, businessmen, housewives, athletes, musicians, military men, and congressmen. Teachers of TM claim that one cannot learn the technique on one's own; one has to be formally trained in a series of nine meditative sessions taught by authorized teachers. In general, the technique consists of sitting in a relatively quiet place, closing one's eyes, and for a period of about twenty minutes, mentally reciting one's *mantra,* a meaningless sound or word that is assigned to each meditator by the TM instructor. Those who have conscientiously practiced transcendental meditation say that they have realized many psycho-physiological[4] benefits—relaxation of physical and mental tensions, renewal of energy, and general sharpening of awareness and alertness. Transcendental meditation is different from some of the other meditative systems in that the meditator is not encouraged to engage in productive thinking during the period of "withdrawal"; the productive thinking may come *after* the period of meditation.

What all the meditative systems have in common, however, is that they are designed to put people in an atmosphere and a disposition that lead to a heightening[5] of consciousness. For that reason, meditation can be an effective way of turning up ideas for writing about a subject. It differs from brain-

[1] A Hindu teacher. [2] A person who practices yoga. [3] A culture, especially of young people, with values contrary to those of the established society. [4] Psycho[logical]: functional processes of the mind; physiological: functional processes of the body. [5] An increasing or raising.

storming in that it is a more systematic way of pondering[1] the subject. It will work, however, only if you remove yourself from an atmosphere of noise and distraction. An ideal setting[2] is a small, quiet room, with a moderately comfortable chair facing a blank wall, where you can't gaze out the window. In that kind of setting, put your mind in gear and let it run freely. Some people find that jotting down notes on a pad of paper interrupts their meditation, and they prefer to wait until they have finished the meditation before recording their thoughts.

Meditation requires disciplined concentration, and you probably won't find it very productive the first two or three times. But if you persist,[3] you may find that it is an unusually productive method of search and discovery. Like the other systems reviewed in this chapter, it is a way of cultivating the mind and thereby generating ideas.

(C) RESEARCH

One of the commonest methods of search and discovery is research. But since research includes a variety of procedures, we will break it down into various categories and discuss each separately.

(1) Observation

The usual way we learn things about the world outside ourselves is by observation through our senses of sight, hearing, taste, touch, and smell. It is an especially useful method when we have to narrate or report events or when we have to describe some physical object or scene.

---

[1] Weighing in the mind. [2] An environment or background. [3] Continue despite difficulties or opposition.

● Informal Methods of Search and Discovery

Sometimes you may be assigned to attend a certain event and write a report of what happened. In that case, you will have to observe carefully and perhaps take notes on what you observe. What you see and hear will depend partly on your keenness[1] of observation and partly on your physical and psychological point of view. It is well known that three people can witness the same event and report three different versions of it. One reason for the differences is that one of the observers may have developed keener powers of observation. Another reason is that one observer may have a better vantage point than the others, a better physical position for observing what happened. Another reason is that the various observers may have a certain mental attitude toward the event that influences what they see and hear. They tend to select those details of an event that confirm the attitudes they brought with them and to ignore or forget those details that do not agree with their attitudes.

If observation is the most suitable method of search and discovery for your writing assignment, you will have to force yourself to observe more closely than you normally do. Productive observation doesn't just happen; it is a skill that needs to be practiced and refined.

(2) Interviews

Another form of research is the face-to-face interview with a person or group. You can turn to this device when you are assigned to gather and report information or opinions from one or more people, whether they are experts on the subject or simply laymen.[2] The usual technique of interviewing is to ask a series of prepared questions and to record the answers on tape, in a notebook, or in the memory.

[1] Sharpness; alertness. [2] Nonprofessionals.

Finding Something To Say

There is a real art to conducting the kind of interview that will yield significant information or opinion. Some of the moderators of talk-shows, like Johnny Carson, Barbara Walters, Merv Griffin, and Mike Wallace, have brought this art to a highly refined level. Such authors of "profiles"[1] of prominent people as Truman Capote, Tom Wolfe, Gay Talese, and Rex Reed have also perfected the art of the interview.

Even when conducted on an amateur level, however, the interview can turn up useful material for a writing assignment. But it is extremely important to select and to phrase questions so that they get at the kind of information or opinion you are seeking and to record as accurately and as fully as possible the answers you receive. The person you interview may be able to recommend a local restaurant or two, but this information won't be useful if your assignment is to gather opinions about a tax proposal coming up for a vote. And nothing can make the person you interview angrier than to be quoted inaccurately or "out of context." **Listen carefully, record accurately, and report fairly.**

(3) Questionnaires

Another device for gathering information and opinions is the written questionnaire. The questionnaire is like the interview in that it presents a series of carefully prepared questions to several people who have been selected either randomly or deliberately. It differs from the interview in that whereas the interview is conducted face to face, the questionnaire is usually distributed in a written form and often by mail.

The questionnaire is a less reliable way than the interview for gathering material because while the personal interviewer

---

[1] Biographical sketches.

is almost guaranteed some kind of response to his questions, the distributor of a written questionnaire must depend on the goodwill and diligence of the interviewees in filling out and returning the questionnaire. The distributor will be glad if he gets even a fifty-percent return. Normally, the shorter the questionnaire and the easier it is to respond to (check-off answers, for instance, rather than written responses), the higher the percentage of returns. Another significant difference is that the personal interviewer usually has to deal with only a few respondents,[1] but the distributor of the questionnaire may have to deal with hundreds. Consequently, the distributor has to tabulate[2] a great number of responses and then must try to make valid generalizations from the accumulated responses.

(4) Experiments

The controlled experiment is a common technique used in the hard sciences,[3] and it is becoming increasingly common in the social sciences[4] too. Scientists, doctors, sociologists, and political scientists regularly conduct experiments to discover facts or to confirm theories and assumptions. The data provided by the experiment become the basis then for a written report.

Whereas experimenters in the hard sciences most often deal with inanimate[5] elements or with animals, experimenters in the social sciences most often deal with people. A political scientist, for instance, may want to test a theory about how people respond to a persuasive message in various media. So he will assemble a group of people, often by random

[1] Persons making a response. [2] To summarize and arrange in definite and compact form for ready reference. [3] The natural/physical sciences such as physics, chemistry, biology, geology. [4] Such as economics, sociology, psychology. [5] Lacking the qualities of living things.

choice, and expose each member to the same persuasive message delivered successively in writing, in a cassette recording, in a videotape presentation, and in live speech, and then he will try to measure the impact of the message as presented in the various media.

Even simpler experiments could yield material for a fascinating essay. Suppose that you want to test your theory that those who bet on the horses haphazardly[1] do as well as, or better than, those who pick the horses after carefully studying the *Racing Form.* You select six of your friends who claim that they pick their horses ''scientifically'' and six others who know nothing about racehorses at all. Over a five-day period you present each group with the daily racing sheet and ask them to pick the winner in each of the eight races each day. Your tabulations, at the end of the week, of the studied picks and the random picks will confirm or negate your theory and might yield some interesting material for an essay.

(5) Reading

Reading is a great source for discovering facts, opinions, insights, and interpretations, because for centuries, writing or printing was the principal way of recording and transmitting information or judgments. For some writing assignments, books, articles, and other printed matter provide the only, or the main, source of the material you need. The main repository[2] of printed matter is the library. The final chapter of this book carries a section that tells you how to make use of various reference sources in the library in order to find pertinent[3] books and articles for a writing assignment. Once you find the pertinent books and articles, you have to extract from

---

[1] By chance; aimlessly; in no order. [2] A place where something is deposited or stored. [3] Relating to the matter at hand.

them what may be usable. You may want to take notes as you read or after you read. From your handwritten notes, you may later want to summarize, paraphrase,[1] or quote some of the material in your own piece of writing.

●
Some formal, systematic methods of search and discovery

The Journalistic[2] Formula

1 **Who?**   4 **Where?**
2 **What?**   5 **Why?**
3 **When?**   6 **How?**

This formula was once widely used as a guideline for reporters about the key questions that the "lead" part of a news story—the first sentence or the first paragraph—should answer. The formula is less closely followed now than it once was, but it is still useful for suggesting the main points that should be covered in certain types of writing, especially the reporting of an event.

The six questions do not all have to be answered in a single part of the essay, as they are in this "lead" sentence from a news story:

John Proxmire [**who**] was critically injured [**what**] in an auto accident [**how**] because of a malfunctioning stoplight [**why**] at the intersection of Maple and Sycamore [**where**] during the evening rush-hour traffic on Friday [**when**].

[1]To say something in different words. [2]Of or pertaining to newspaper writing.

● Formal Methods of Search and Discovery

Nor do all six questions always have to be answered. The formula does suggest to you, however, those aspects of a happening that you might want to concentrate on and develop in different parts of your narrative. In one part of the narrative, you might want to concentrate on the person (**who**) involved in the happening, supplying details about the person's biography, personality, and achievements; in another part, you might want to concentrate on the causes (**why**) of the event; in other parts, you might want to concentrate on the time (**when**), the setting (**where**), the manner (**how**), or the nature (**what**) of the event.

The journalistic formula is similar to a formula that Kenneth Burke called the "dramatistic pentad"[1]:

1 **Action** (**What** happened?)
2 **Agent** (**Who** did it?)
3 **Means** (**How** did he do it?)
4 **Purpose** (**Why** did he do it?)
5 **Scene** (**Where** and **when** did it happen?)

The journalistic questions and the pentad bear some relation to the four traditional modes[2] of discourse: **exposition, argumentation,**[3] **description,** and **narration.**[4] Although the journalistic questions are especially useful generating devices for reporting events (the narrative mode), they also have a bearing on the other modes. Concentration on the *where* or *when* (to give readers a sense of the "climate of the times") engages you primarily in the descriptive mode. *What* or *how* might lead you into the expository mode. *Why* might lead you into the argumentative mode. But just as there are mixtures of the modes in a single piece of writing (rarely is a

---

[1] Dramatistic: relating to drama; pentad: a group of five things. [2] Particular forms or styles. [3] The art of formal discussion. [4] Telling the details of, as a story.

piece purely expository or purely argumentative), so there could be interchanges between the six questions and the four modes.

The Classical Topics

You are probably familiar with the word *topic* as a synonym for *subject.* But we shall use the term here in a much different sense. *Topic* derives from the Greek word *topos,* meaning "place." Used metaphorically[1] in rhetoric, it came to mean "a place where one went to hunt for arguments." In a more literal sense, *topics* were "suggesters or generators of lines of argument." They were formulated from the typical ways in which the human mind thinks about something. When you probe a subject, especially an unfamiliar one, you typically ask questions like these:

1 "What is it?" (**definition**).
2 "What is it like or unlike?" (**comparison**).
3 "What caused it?" (**relationship**).
4 "What is said about it?" (**testimony**).

These typical mental operations, arranged as headings or categories, serve to suggest to you how you might go about developing a subject.

Let us first outline the topics, and then see how they might be used to find something to say about a subject.

DEFINITION—"What is it?"

Types of definition:

[1]"On loan" from its usual sense to name or describe something else, suggesting a likeness or resemblance between the two.

● Formal Methods of Search and Discovery

Synonym—shortest form of definition.

Formal definition—putting the thing in a general class (*genus*) and then distinguishing it from other members of the class (*differentiation*).

Extended definition—an amplified[1] form of the one-sentence definition.

Stipulative definition—"What *I* mean by. . ."

Classification—division into distinct groups.

Examples—giving concrete instances of an abstraction.[2]

COMPARISON—"What is it like or unlike?"

Results of comparing things:
Similarity in kind
  metaphor and simile[3]
  analogy[4]
Difference in kind
  antithesis[5]
  contrast
Similarity or difference in degree
  more, less, or the same

RELATIONSHIP—"What caused it?"

Types of relationship:
Cause and effect
  this produced *that* (cause to effect)
  that was produced by *this* (effect to cause)
Antecedent[6] *and consequence*[7]
  this followed from *that*

---

[1] Expanded; fuller. [2] Idea, characteristic, or quality apart from a particular instance or example. [3] A figure of speech in which two unlike things are compared by use of *as* or *like*. [4] A likeness in one or more ways between things otherwise unlike. [5] A direct opposite or contrast to a given idea. [6] A preceding event or cause. [7] A following event or result.

Finding Something To Say

TESTIMONY—"What is said about it?"

When you need:
    facts
    precedents[1]
    statistics
    testimonials[2]
    opinions
    documents

What you turn to:
    books
    magazines
    newspapers
    manuscripts
    records
    reports
    interviews
    questionnaires
    observation

Where you go:
    libraries
    private agencies
    government agencies
    museums
    computer centers
    experts
    man-in-the-street
    the scene itself

---

[1] Something said or done that establishes a rule for, or justifies, later words or acts of the same or a similar kind. [2] A statement testifying to the character or worth of someone or something.

● Formal Methods of Search and Discovery

(A) DEFINITION

One line of development that is always open to you is to explain the *nature* of something to someone. Natural human curiosity prompts us to try to define something and to pass the resulting clarification on to others. Definition is the basic line of development behind *exposition,* which presents information about, or an explanation of, something. An entire essay might be devoted to defining a concept (what is justice?) or a process (how to file for bankruptcy or how to program a computer) or an operation (how a digital[1] watch works). But definition is also a line of development for *parts* of an essay. You might want to offer definitions of some key terms that will figure prominently in the essay.

Here are some common types of definition:

(1) Synonym

The simplest and briefest way to clarify the meaning of a word is to supply a word of similar meaning—e.g. *amnesty–pardon, reiterate–repeat, parsimonious–stingy.* There are three things to keep in mind when you are defining by synonym:

1 Most synonyms are *approximate,*[2] rather than exact, equivalents of the other word.

2 The synonym you supply must be the *same part of speech* as the other word—a noun for a noun, a verb for a verb, etc.

3 The synonym you supply must be *more familiar* to the audience than the word for which it stands.

[1] Relating to the figures 1 to 9 and 0.   [2] Nearly correct or exact.

Finding Something To Say

Dictionaries often supply synonyms for some words, and there is a book (called a *thesaurus*) that supplies nothing but synonyms.

(2) Formal Definition

A formal definition is the kind supplied by a dictionary—although instead of quoting verbatim[1] from a dictionary, you could supply a formal definition in your own words. A formal definition is usually presented in a single sentence. A common way of defining concrete and abstract nouns is to put the thing to be defined into a general class (called the *genus*) and then to distinguish it from other members of the class (called the *differentiation*)—e.g. "An automobile is a *vehicle* [genus] with four wheels, propelled by an internal-combustion engine [differentiating details]"; "Democracy is that *type of government* [genus] in which the ultimate source of rule resides with the people [differentiating details]."

(3) Extended Definition

An extended definition is simply an amplified form of the one-sentence definition. It could take up an entire essay; more commonly it occupies several sentences. You often resort to extended definitions when you are dealing with unusually strange, complicated concepts or processes.

(4) Stipulative Definition

A stipulative definition is a definition decided by the speaker or writer. Knowing that a particular term may have a variety of meanings, the speaker or writer tells the audience what *he* means when he uses the term. The audience may

[1] Word for word.

not accept the stipulated definition, but at least they know what meaning the author attaches to the term.

(5) Classification

Classification is another way of clarifying the meaning of something. It consists in dividing something into distinct groups according to a common basis. There are a number of ways, for instance, of classifying college students: (1) on the basis of sex—male and female; (2) on the basis of geographical origin—in-state and out-of-state; (3) on the basis of their year-standing—freshman, sophomore, junior, senior; (4) on the basis of the college in which they are enrolled—Arts and Sciences, Business Administration, Law, Medicine, etc.; (5) on the basis of their religious affiliation[1]—Baptist, Methodist, Catholic, Jewish, etc. There are many other categories, of course, into which students could be classified, but the important point is that classification is a means of *clarifying the nature of something.*

(6) Examples

One of the best ways to define an abstraction is to supply one or more concrete examples. The ungrammatical formula "Justice is when . . ." is an instance of this kind of definition. Charles Shultz's "Happiness is a warm puppy" is another instance. The example could be something from real life or it could be an invented fable or story.

(B) COMPARISON

Another process for unfolding a subject is comparison. Especially when probing a new subject, you tend to compare

---

[1] Association with a group or organization.

it with something that you and your audience are more or less familiar with. And when you compare things, you discover one of the following: *similarity* or *difference* in kind or *similarity* or *difference* in degree.

(1) Similarity

Similarity is the basic principle behind such figures of speech as *metaphor* and *simile* and behind all development of a subject by *analogy.* Bringing two things together, you note their likenesses. If two things were alike in all respects, you would have *identity* rather than *similarity.* But they are alike in just enough respects to cast some light upon each other.

You can resort to analogy for purposes of *description* ("The apartment complex is laid out in the shape of the letter H") or of *exposition* ("A knee operates like the hinge on a door") or of *argumentation* ("If division of labor works efficiently in a beehive, we can expect the same kind of efficiency in a society where various groups of people are assigned to perform specific tasks").

One caution to observe in the use of analogy for purposes of description or exposition is that the thing with which something else is being compared must be familiar to the audience. (Comparing the layout of an apartment complex to the shape of a Maltese cross[1] would probably not convey a clear picture to most people.) A caution to observe in using analogy for purposes of argumentation is that the similarities found between two things must not be overweighed by some crucial[2] differences. (There might be just enough significant differences between bees and human beings to make the analogy of the beehive invalid and therefore unpersuasive.)

[1] Consult an illustrated dictionary under *cross*. [2] Severe; decisive.

● Formal Methods of Search and Discovery

The two questions that are likely to generate a line of development for a subject are **what is this like?** and **in what way are the two things similar?**

(2) Difference

Another possible result of comparison is the detection of differences. Differences disclose the *antitheses* and *contrasts* between things. Pointing out differences can often be as illuminating as pointing out similarities, whether for purposes of description, exposition, or argumentation. To say "Whereas a football game is completed when a specified number of minutes of play have expired, a baseball game is completed when a specified number of innings have been played, no matter how long that takes" certainly gives us an idea of a crucial difference in the structure of these two sports.

Another question that is likely to generate a line of development is **in what significant ways does this thing differ from something else?**

(3) Degree

Sometimes when you compare things, you don't find similarities or differences *in kind*—that is, in the *basic nature or structure* of things—but rather you find similarities and differences *in degree.* Democracy and monarchy are two forms of government that differ *in kind;* but the democracies of two countries might differ only *in degree*—for instance, just in the degree of real power that the people have in determining how and by whom they are governed. Often you have to make a choice not between a *good* and an *evil* (a difference in kind) but between one good and another good or between one evil and another evil (a difference in degree).

In general, when you make a judgment about *more or less, better or worse,* you do so on the basis either that one thing is *inherently*[1] *more worthy or valuable* than another or that one thing is *more advantageous* (it brings more benefits) than another. In that case, you usually have to establish for yourself and reveal to your audience more specific criteria[2] for making the judgment than those two general ones.

The topic of *degree* suggests another line of development that might be used when you are faced with the task of writing about some subject.

(C) RELATIONSHIP

Like the topic of *comparison,* the topic of *relationship* invites you to bring things together and to note the light that is cast by one thing on another. But whereas comparison results in the detection of similarity or difference in kind and degree, relationship may expose a *causal* or *conditional*[3] link between two things.

(1) Cause and Effect

One of the kinds of relationship that may be revealed by juxtaposing[4] things is the *cause-and-effect* relationship. One thing may be seen to be the *cause* of something else or to be the *effect* of something else. In essence, the *cause-and-effect* relationship seeks to establish one or the other of these two kinds of link between two things:

1 *This* produced *that.*

2 *That* was produced by *this.*

[1] In its innermost, essential nature: [2] Standards on which judgments and evaluations are based. [3] Serving as a condition for something else. [4] Placing side by side.

● Formal Methods of Search and Discovery

If you see a rock lying under a recently broken window, you naturally suppose that the rock is the "cause" of that broken window (the effect). And if you were looking for someone to pay for that broken window, you would have to search for a further cause—the culprit[1] who heaved the rock through the window. If you detect[2] the presence of a *potential*[3] *cause* in a particular situation, you may be able to predict the *probable effect* if that potential cause is not removed. Thus, a candle burning dangerously close to some curtains is recognized as a potential cause of an undesirable effect—curtains on fire.

There are certain logical principles that govern cause-and-effect relationships—or at least the arguments that are based on cause-and-effect relationships. For instance, when you are trying to argue that one thing is the probable cause of another (the effect), you may have to establish:

1 That the cause is *capable* of producing the effect.
2 That other causes similarly capable were absent.

If you don't suspect a four-year-old of strangling Lord Carruthers, it is not merely because the child is physically incapable of such an act, nor is it simply because there is the butler to be accounted for. What about the 250-pound gardener? He attracts at least as much suspicion as the butler—perhaps more. And yet unless he is absolutely the last link in the chain of *capable* and *present* probable causes, you cannot point the accusing finger at him. You cannot *assume,* but must *prove,* that the gardener strangled Lord Carruthers.

(2) Antecedent-consequence

Another kind of relationship is the *antecedent-conse-*

[1] The accused or guilty party. [2] Discover or find out the presence, existence, or fact of (someone or something). [3] Existing in possibility; capable of becoming actual.

quence relationship, which is not so much causal as it is conditional. A consequence, for instance, of reaching a certain age in certain societies is that one becomes eligible[1] to vote. The presence of conjunctions[2] like *because, since, for* in a sentence may signal that the writer is claiming either a cause-and-effect relationship or an antecedent-consequence relationship, and you must be able to discriminate between the two. If someone says, ''The water in the birdbath froze because the temperature dropped to twenty degrees above zero,'' he is claiming that the dropping of the temperature *caused* the freezing of the water. If, however, someone says, ''Jim voted this year because he turned eighteen,'' he is not claiming that turning eighteen *caused* Jim to vote. Rather, turning eighteen was the necessary antecedent for any voting Jim might do; and with the antecedent condition satisfied, Jim consequently *did* vote.

It may not always be easy to determine whether a relationship is causal or conditional. Fortunately, in a writing situation, the determination will not always be crucial and will hardly affect[3] how you proceed in your demonstration. It will be sufficient, in other words, to demonstrate that there is some kind of *connection* between things. (On the other hand, the fate of a person on trial for murder might very well depend on whether the alleged[4] connection was causal or conditional.)

(D) TESTIMONY

Whereas the topics of *definition, comparison,* and *relationship* suggest ways of developing a subject from the *inside,* the topic of *testimony* suggests ways of developing a subject

---

[1] Qualified to be chosen or to participate. [2] Words that join together sentences, parts of sentences, or words. [3] To produce an effect on; to influence. [4] Given as a fact without proof.

from the *outside.* Testimony includes all the material you have to find in sources outside your subject—all such supporting material as facts, precedents, statistics, testimonials, opinions, documents. To find such material, you have to go to sources such as books, magazines, and newspapers and to such places as libraries, agencies, museums, computer centers, and the scene itself. Data gathered from interviews, questionnaires, experiments, and observation can also be said to come from *outside* the subject and can also be used in developing the subject.

You simply have to develop a sense of:

1 What kind of outside material can be used in developing your subject.
2 When such material will be pertinent to the development of your subject.
3 Where to go to find such material.

Although formal education cannot provide you with the answers to all of your questions, it should at least acquaint you with the *possible sources* of those answers. Because of the great reverence that our society has for "facts," you have more and more occasion to discover and to make use of "facts" in writing about the "world out there."

Topical Questions

The classical topics were derived from observation of the typical ways in which the human mind thinks about something. But because they are posed in the form of static[1] labels, they don't work as well for some people in turning up usable material for a writing assignment as some of the other

[1] Inactive; not moving.

Finding Something To Say

methods of search and discovery do. When the topics are posed in the form of *questions,* however, they seem to work better as generating devices for some writers. You saw such a list of questions in the *journalistic formula.* If you found the six questions of the journalistic formula too limited, you may find this fuller list, grouped according to different categories of subjects, more helpful.*

(A) ABOUT PHYSICAL OBJECTS

1 What are the physical characteristics of the object (shape, dimensions, materials, etc.)?
2 What sort of structure does it have?
3 What other object is it similar to?
4 How does it differ from things that resemble it?
5 Who or what produced it?
6 Who uses it? for what?

(B) ABOUT EVENTS

1 Exactly what happened? (who? what? when? where? why? how?)
2 What were its causes?
3 What were its consequences?
4 How was the event like or unlike similar events?
5 To what other events was it connected?
6 How might the event have been changed or avoided?

* This list of topical questions has been adapted from a list of 116 questions proposed by Richard L. Larson in his article "Discovery Through Questioning: A Plan for Teaching Rhetorical Invention," *College English,* 30 (November, 1968), 126–134.

● Formal Methods of Search and Discovery

(C) ABOUT ABSTRACT CONCEPTS (*e.g., democracy, justice*)

1 How has the term been defined by others?
2 How do *you* define the term?
3 What other concepts have been associated with it?
4 In what ways has this concept affected the lives of people?
5 How might the concept be changed to work better?

(D) ABOUT PROPOSITIONS (*statements to be proved or disproved*):

1 What must be established before the reader will believe it?
2 What are the meanings of key words in the proposition?
3 By what kinds of evidence or argument can the proposition be proved or disproved?
4 What counterarguments must be confronted[1] and refuted?[2]
5 What are the practical consequences of the proposition?

These are not the only questions, of course, that can be asked in each of the four main categories, but there are enough here to help you overcome your inertia[3] and to get you moving in the development of your subject. From practice with a system of topical questions like this, you may devise other questions that work well for you.

Problem-solving

In recent years, a number of rhetoricians have explored problem-solving as another fruitful method of search and

---

[1] Faced; opposed.   [2] Disproved; proved to be false.   [3] Inactivity; sluggishness.

Finding Something To Say

discovery. It is a rare person who has not had to engage in problem-solving at one time or another, and in some professions and occupations, problem-solving is the principal concern. A TV repairman, for instance, constantly has to trouble-shoot[1] defective[2] sets; he may have to run through a regular sequence[3] of checks to discover what is wrong with the set so that he can repair it. A lawyer agrees to accept a case whose nature confronts him with the problem of how best to present it so that he can get a favorable ruling for his client. A student has difficulty in reading, and he comes to his teacher for help in discovering the source of his difficulty and for suggestions of how he can overcome the difficulty.

The process of problem-solving, by its very nature, is a process of discovering, of "finding out," something. The "something" that is discovered can, in turn, become usable material for a writing assignment. Many articles in professional journals,[4] for instance, are simply reports of someone's engagement in problem-solving.

In every problem, there are some things that you know or can easily find out, but there is something too that you don't know. It is the *unknown* that creates the problem. When confronted with a problem, you have to take note of all the things you *do* know. Then, by a series of inferences[5] from the known, you try to form a hypothesis[6] about what the unknown is. Finally, you test your hypothesis to determine whether your tentative theory leads you to discover the unknown that is causing the problem.

How is the process of solving a problem similar to the process you have to go through in trying to find something to say about a subject? Imagine the following situation. When

---

[1] To use skills in locating trouble or disrepair and correcting it. [2] Faulty. [3] Series; succession. [4] Periodical publications. [5] Conclusions drawn from facts or statements. [6] An assumption made in order to account for known facts and to test for accuracy of reasoning.

you first check into your motel room in the evening, you notice that when you flip the light-switch near the door, the light in the ceiling, the lamp near the bed, and the light on the desk all go on. After dinner that evening, you come back to your room, intending to write a letter. You flip the light-switch, and the ceiling-light goes on, the bed-lamp goes on, but the desk-lamp doesn't go on. Nuts! That's the light you need if you are going to write that letter. You could call the manager, but you are an inquisitive[1] and a resourceful[2] type, and you decide to investigate the problem and see if you can get the desk-lamp working again.

So you have a problem. Let us set up a sequence of procedures that can be used in solving *any* problem—including that of finding something to say about a subject you have to write about—and, by way of illustration, apply the procedures to the problem of the burned-out desk-lamp.

(A) SPECIFY WHAT THE PROBLEM IS

The desk-lamp doesn't go on when I flip the wall-switch, and I need that light if I am to write a letter.

(B) ANALYZE THE PROBLEM

(1) What Do I Know for Sure?

The wall-switch controls three lights, yet only two went on. I know, then, that the wall-switch works, the fuse is sound,[3] and two of the lights are in good working order. Either the electricity is not getting to the lamp, or something is wrong with the lamp itself.

---

[1] Given to questioning; eager for knowledge. [2] Able to handle situations; knowing (or possessing) what is needed, where to get it, and how to use it. [3] In good condition.

Finding Something To Say

(2) What Is the Unknown?

I suspect that the trouble is with the desk-lamp. It worked earlier. Why doesn't it light now, when I flip on the wall-switch? That's the unknown that needs to be known before the problem can be solved.

(C) FORMULATE ONE OR MORE HYPOTHESES ABOUT THE UNKNOWN

I'm not an electrician, but commonsense yields[1] some hypotheses: (1) the lamp-switch is not in the "on" position; (2) the bulb could be burned out; (3) there's a loose connection somewhere that is preventing the electricity from getting to the bulb.

(D) TEST THE HYPOTHESES

Turning the on–off switch several times doesn't make the lamp go on; so my first hypothesis is wrong. Putting in a good bulb doesn't make the lamp go on; so my second hypothesis is wrong. It seems then that the electricity is not getting to the bulb. Shaking the lamp several times to see if it has a loose connection, I find that it still doesn't work. But then I notice the trailing lamp cord. Pulling it from behind the desk, I see that it was not plugged into the wall socket. So my third hypothesis proves to be correct, for there *was* a "loose" connection that prevented the electricity from getting to the bulb. The *unknown* is discovered, and the problem is solved.

What you have traced out here is the solving of a mechanical problem, by a process of observation, inference, guess-work, and testing of guesses. If you were asked to write an

[1] Produces, supplies.

account of the problem-solving, you would have no difficulty about having something to say. Your written document would simply be a narration of the steps you took.

But writing in general can also be approached in terms of problem-solving. Faced with the assignment, for instance, of writing a speech to persuade the members of your sorority to stop smoking, you might go through the steps outlined above—specifying the problem, analyzing the known and unknown elements in the problem, proposing some tentative solutions, and testing the tentative solutions to discover which one might work best for this particular situation.

You might determine that the main problem is to find arguments that will be convincing to the really confirmed smokers in this group. You might want to tote up[1] first the things you know about the situation. Having lived for several months now in the same house with this group, you know that some of them have never smoked, some have recently stopped smoking, some of them would like to stop smoking and have made efforts to stop, and some are so addicted that they have no will to break the habit. Almost any arguments you could present would serve to confirm the nonsmokers in their resolution not to smoke. The *unknown* in this situation is the kind of argument that will work on the wavering[2] smokers and the confirmed smokers. You decide that you are going to appeal to only three of the four groups: those who have never smoked, those who have recently quit smoking, and those who would like to stop smoking. You won't make a special effort to convince the confirmed smokers, but if some of them are persuaded by your arguments, so much the better.

In your efforts to discover the unknown—the kinds of argument that might appeal to your selected audience—your formulation and testing of hypotheses might take the form of

---

[1]To total. [2]Swinging back and forth; showing doubt or indecision.

Finding Something To Say

rehearsing[1] various arguments and then selecting those that seem likeliest to appeal to that audience. The crucial segment of this selected audience is the group of those who still smoke but who genuinely want to stop. This segment has probably been influenced by some of the warnings about the dangers of smoking. But what will push this group over the edge? After reviewing some of the standard arguments against smoking, you finally decide that what is needed is some actual testimonies about the practical benefits—physical, psychological, and economic—of breaking the smoking habit. You can gather this testimony from friends and acquaintances who were once heavy smokers but who broke the habit.

You have approached your writing assignment as a problem, and you discovered something to say by specifying and analyzing your special problem. Then, by rehearsing several possible solutions, you finally settled on a strategy[2] that seemed likely to solve the problem. You know now where you have to go to find the material for your speech: to friends and acquaintances for their testimony about the practical advantages of breaking the cigarette habit. The final test of your strategy will, of course, be the effect of the speech on the audience.

The First Draft As Search and Discovery

All of the systems reviewed so far may be considered part of the prewriting stage. But paradoxically, many writers find that the writing of the first draft is still a part of the prewriting stage for them. For those writers, the composing of a rough draft turns up additional material to be incorporated into the final product. The writing of a sentence or a paragraph sug-

[1] Repeating. [2] A plan or method to achieve something.

gests to them other things that need to be put into the essay, matters that were not turned up by whatever system of search and discovery they may have used before they sat down to write. As one writer has said, "I don't know what I want to say until I have said it." And it is surprising how much additional material is turned up in the act of writing.

Verbalizing[1] your thoughts on paper may suggest a direction or a line of development that you did not foresee when you began to write. Robert M. Gorrell uses two terms to describe this phenomenon[2]: *commitment* and *response.* In speaking about the development of a paragraph, he proposes that some sentence you write—often the lead-off topic sentence—sets up a commitment between you and your readers. If you are to deliver on that commitment, you must make some response to it. In a sense, you make a "promise" to your reader, and you must fulfill that promise.

Take a declarative sentence like this one: "In those circumstances, a concerned citizen has three courses of action open to him." The commitment and response implicit[3] in that sentence should be obvious. Having made that declaration, you have committed yourself to *naming* three courses of action open to a concerned citizen. In addition, you may find that you are also committed to proving that those three courses of action are available to concerned citizens and to showing that other courses of action are not feasible[4] or productive.

Similarly, larger units of the discourse—a cluster[5] of related paragraphs, for instance—may establish a commitment that you have to respond to. In defending an idea, for instance, you may feel that your next step should be a rebuttal[6] of

---

[1] Expressing in words. [2] A fact or occurrence that appears or is observed. [3] Understood or implied, but not directly stated. [4] Capable of being carried out. [5] A group; a bunch. [6] A reply by counterargument or contradiction.

Finding Something To Say

possible counterarguments or the removal of possible suspicions that you are prejudiced or have a vested[1] interest. Once you actually begin writing, you may find that the development of your essay gathers its own momentum.[2] You begin to see many directions that your essay might take. After a while, so many of these may present themselves to you that you will have to pause and gain control once again of your movement. Some directions may take you too far afield, and if you follow them, you will blur your focus; consequently, the bonanza[3] of things to say that you discovered in the act of writing may prove to be more of a disadvantage than an advantage. But at least you will have overcome your inertia and have discovered more than enough to say.

If the use of some of the systems of search and discovery reviewed in this chapter does not turn up ample[4] material for a writing assignment, don't despair. Try sitting down at your desk or typewriter and begin to write. You may be pleasantly surprised, as other writers have been, to find that the minimal[5] material you discovered begins to blossom and ramify.[6] One word will generate another word; one sentence will generate another sentence; one paragraph will generate another paragraph. You may soon find yourself in the happy position of having to *cut* material rather than having to pad it out.

---

[1] Held with personal and strong commitment. [2] The force a moving body has. [3] A source of rich and ready supply. [4] Large; full; abundant. [5] Relating to the least amount. [6] To branch out.

Chapter 4
Selecting and Organizing What You Have Discovered

Discovering something to say about a subject is the most difficult and often the most crucial stage in the writing process. The various systems of search and discovery discussed in the previous chapter may help you in this stage. But once you have discovered something to say, you are faced with the next stage in the writing process: *selecting and organizing what you have discovered.* It is here that you first begin to give some shape and form to your discourse. You have to make some decisions about what you want to include in your paper and about the order in which you will arrange the parts.

In making selections from the material available, you will derive[1] some help from the same set of considerations that you used in fixing on a subject in Chapter 2:

1 **The number of words you are allotted.**
2 **The purpose of your writing.**
3 **The occasion of your writing.**

[1] Receive; obtain.

Selecting and Organizing

4 **The nature of the audience for whom you are writing.**

5 **The extent and depth of your knowledge of the subject (to which might be added here the amount of material you were able to gather in the discovery stage).**

6 **The thesis or central point you want to make about the subject.**

You already put some limits on your treatment when you used these considerations to fix[1] the subject you were going to write about. But some, if not all, of them will come into play again when you decide which of the available materials you will use and which you will discard. Your allotted wordage, for instance, may show that although you have enough material to treat five aspects of your subject, you have space to treat only three. You will then have to decide which three they will be. In making that decision, you might derive help from some of the other criteria,[2] such as your *purpose* or the *occasion* or the *audience* for whom you are writing. Considering *audience,* for instance, you might make your choice simply on the grounds of which three of the five available aspects are likely to be most interesting or most impressive to your readers. Or a consideration of your *purpose* might help you make your choice. If your purpose is to win acceptance of your point of view on a controversial[3] subject, you will tend to exclude material that is mainly explanatory and use only the material that presents arguments.

Of the six considerations, however, the one that will invariably[4] come into play in helping you make selections from the available material is the sixth: the *thesis* or *central point* you want to make about the subject you are writing about. While some of the considerations will not always be helpful, a

---

[1] To establish. [2] Plural form of *criterion.* [3] Characterized by opposing views and dispute. [4] Constantly.

consideration of your thesis or central point will almost always guide you in the selection process. If, for instance, your subject were "the energy crisis," a thesis like "With the current high cost of oil and gas, environmentalists[1] may have to relax the pollution standards they insist on for coal as a source of energy," would guide you in choosing, from the available material, which facts, statistics,[2] and arguments would be most relevant to the development of that subject. That thesis might make you decide to include, for instance, material you discovered about the current prices of domestic and imported oil, estimates of the future price of oil, the comparative costs of oil and coal, figures showing the plentiful reserves[3] of coal in this country—and to exclude the less relevant material about working-conditions in the mines, the hazards[4] of lung disease for miners, the politics of the coal-mining unions, the increasing educational opportunities for middle-class children in Arab lands, the sharp rise in sales of Cadillacs and Mercedes-Benzes in Arab oil-producing countries. Some of this latter material might be usable if you were allotted 10,000 words to argue your case, but it becomes dispensable[5] when you are confined to 1200, and your thesis is helpful in discriminating[6] the more usable from the more dispensable material.

Rhetoric is the art of making judicious[7] choices. One of the choices to be made in the writing process is the choice of material that has been turned up by the discovery process. Considerations like the six outlined above should help you make judicious choices.

The next judicious choice you have to make is the choice of ways in which to arrange the material you have discovered

---

[1] Persons actively concerned about the human environment. [2] Facts (often numerical) gathered and arranged in an orderly way for reference and study. [3] Stocks; supplies kept in reserve. [4] Sources of danger. [5] Capable of being omitted or dispensed with. [6] Distinguishing; differentiating. [7] Having or using good judgment.

Selecting and Organizing

and selected. **The proper arrangement of what you have to say can be of crucial importance for the effectiveness of your communication.** The wrong choice of order for the parts of your writing could blur, if not completely obscure, the message you have to convey to your readers.

The basic structure of any extended piece of writing is, as Aristotle pointed out in his *Poetics,* a beginning, a middle, and an end. That view of basic structure is philosophically sound, but it is too general to be of much help to the writer who has to make hard decisions about how he will marshal[1] the parts of his paper. He needs some more specific[2] guidelines. The Aristotelian structure of beginning, middle, and end must become functional—that is, in terms of *what* must be done or *what* is typically done in each of the three basic parts of an extended discourse.

The beginning

A more common term for *beginning* is *introduction,* used for that section of a paper that "leads into" the main part (the middle). In his *Rhetoric,* Aristotle observes that an introduction is not an *essential* part of a persuasive oration.[3] What is essential is that you state your case and then prove it. Get right to the point, Aristotle seems to be suggesting. Being a realist, however, Aristotle had to concede[4] that readers or listeners cannot always be plunged abruptly[5] into the main part; they have to be eased into it. Just as the orchestra at an opera or a musical plays a prelude[6] or overture[7] before the

---

[1] Arrange in order or position. [2] Definite; exact. [3] A formal speech. [4] To admit (the truth of something). [5] Suddenly. [6] Introductory performance or composition before the main performance or piece. [7] Orchestral introduction to a musical drama.

curtain goes up, a writer often has to prepare his audience for what he is about to say. **An introduction thus *prepares* the audience to receive the message that will be delivered in the middle section of the paper.**

But what does that *preparation* entail?[1] It all depends on a number of circumstances: on the nature of the subject and the extent of your readers' familiarity with it; on the attitude of your readers toward the subject; on their attitude toward you. Some subject matter would not require much preparation of the readers—a subject, for instance, that has been much discussed or that has figured[2] prominently[3] in the news. Other subject matter, because of its complexity or its unfamiliarity, might require much preparation. You might have to establish the importance of the subject or give some background information about it. You might have to define some key terms. You might want to state at the outset what point

[1] Include or involve as a result. [2] Been or appeared in some situation or arrangement. [3] Very noticeably; clearly standing out.

Selecting and Organizing

you intend to make about the subject. The introduction is often the place where you announce what the thesis or central point of your paper is.

The presumed[1] attitude of your readers toward the subject or toward you also requires some attention before you launch into the middle section. If your readers harbor[2] some hostility[3] toward the subject or some hostility toward you, you will have to spend some time allaying[4] that hostility. You may have to establish your credentials[5] to talk about the subject or at least reveal your concern about it. As Aristotle put it in his *Rhetoric,* you may have to spend some time in your introduction rendering[6] your audience *attentive* (disposed[7] to listen to you), *benevolent* (well-wishing toward you), and *docile* (willing to be instructed or persuaded by you). In short, you will have to put your audience in the right frame of mind to receive your message.

How much space you can devote to this preparation of your audience will depend partly on how much wordage you are allotted. If you are limited to 500–800 words for the entire essay, you may be able to devote only 150 or even fewer words to orienting[8] and disposing[9] your audience. In that case, you will have to practice extreme economy. For a longer paper, you will be able—in fact, you may be obliged—to devote several hundred words, spread out over three or four paragraphs, to the introduction.

The middle

Once you have *introduced* yourself and your subject, you

---

[1] Taken for granted; assumed. [2] Hold (as a thought or feeling). [3] Unfriendliness.
[4] Reducing the intensity of; putting at rest. [5] Something that establishes credit or confidence. [6] Making or causing to be. [7] Inclined. [8] Familiarizing with a situation or place. [9] Preparing.

have to settle down to the development of your subject. You are ready to get into the "heart of the matter," into the core of your paper. Here you will have to make the most crucial, and sometimes the most difficult, decisions about the order of the parts. Although an introduction always comes first, you may have some minor decisions to make within it, such as whether you will establish your credentials first and then inform your reader about the subject and thesis to be developed or adopt the reverse order. Still, because an introduction is usually short, it does not have many parts that require some "most effective" order. However, even in a paper as short as 800–1000 words, *the middle section may have three, four, or five major divisions that will require a "best" order for maximum*[1] *effectiveness.*

Some kinds of writing have a natural order, requiring no deliberation.[2] For instance, narratives of an event and expositions of a process naturally fall into a *chronological*[3] or *sequential order:* first this happened, then this happened, and then that happened; or, in the case of an exposition of a process, first you do this, then you do this, and then you do that. It is true that sometimes in reporting events or in story-telling, we open with something that happened further ahead in time and then through flashbacks[4] recount[5] happenings that occurred previously. But most often, narratives have a strictly chronological order. So if you're writing a narrative or an exposition, you won't have to spend much time considering the order of the parts. **You simply have to make sure that all the necessary parts are there and that they are in the order in which they occurred.**

The difficult decisions about the most effective ordering of the parts will present themselves when you are dealing with

[1] Characterized by the greatest amount or degree. [2] Careful consideration. [3] Arranged in the order in which occurrence took place in time. [4] Appearances, in a story or other account, of things that happened earlier. [5] Tell, usually in detail.

Selecting and Organizing

those kinds of writing or those subjects that don't have a single, natural order but rather offer a number of different orders. When, for instance, you are writing an argumentative[1] essay, you may have to decide whether you will first refute the opposing arguments and then present your own or adopt the reverse order; or you may have to decide whether to begin with your weakest argument and then present progressively stronger arguments or begin with the strongest and then follow with progressively weaker arguments. If your subject matter is "the causes of the American Civil War," you will have to make some decision about the order in which you discuss the various causes. Will you treat the economic causes first or the political causes? Will you treat the minor causes first or the major causes? Or will you treat the more familiar causes first and then the lesser-known?

Answers to such questions will depend on such considerations as the occasion of your writing, the mood of your audience, the prevailing[2] climate[3] of opinion, the emphasis to be achieved by a climactic[4] order or an anticlimactic[5] order. Presenting the strongest argument first, for instance, will not always be the best order in all situations and for all audiences. Because such decisions will always have to be made in relation to a particular situation or to a great many other circumstances, it is impossible to lay down general principles that will prevail in all cases. What we can do, however, is set forth some of the common patterns of organization that are used in certain kinds of discourse. (See Fig. 4.1 for an outline of these patterns.)

[1] Involving a connected series of statements intended to establish or destroy the case for something. [2] Characterized by being superior in strength or influence; predominant. [3] Environment; condition; state. [4] Increasing in force and power from the first to the last. [5] Decreasing in force and power from the first to the last.

Some Common Patterns of Organization

(A) CHRONOLOGICAL AND SEQUENTIAL[1] ORDER

Time commonly governs[2] the order of the parts in narratives[3] (first this happened, then this, then that, etc.), and sequence does this in expositions[4] of a process (first you do this, then this, then that, etc.).

(B) FROM THE FAMILIAR TO THE UNFAMILIAR

Movement from the more familiar to the less is often used in *explaining* a new or complicated idea, issue, movement, etc. Beginning with what is likely to be more familiar to readers helps to orient them and prepare them for the less familiar or the totally unfamiliar.

(C) FROM THE WHOLE TO THE PART

Giving readers an overview[5] of something before proceeding to the parts is common in descriptive writing, especially in descriptions of a physical object or a scene. If, for instance, you were describing a historic battlefield, it might help to orient your readers by presenting the layout[6] of the battlefield from a bird's-eye view. Sometimes, but perhaps less often, the reverse order—from part to whole—will be the best one to follow.

(D) THE SPATIAL[7] SEQUENCE

Like the chronological sequence, the spatial sequence is a

---

[1] Characterized by one thing following another as in a series. [2] Determines; controls; directs. [3] Accounts; stories. Narrative also refers to the act of narrating, of giving an account. [4] Discourses designed to convey information. [5] Brief survey; summary. [6] Arrangement. [7] Relating to space.

SOME COMMON PATTERNS OF ORGANIZATION

CHRONOLOGICAL ORDER

—In **narrative** prose, takes events in order of **time.** In description of **process,** follows actual **sequence.**

FAMILIAR TO UNFAMILIAR ORDER

—In **explanatory** prose, explains new, complex ideas, issues, etc. by moving from known to unknown.

WHOLE TO PART (OR REVERSE)

—In **descriptive** prose, works from the smaller to the larger, from aspect to whole (or reverse), etc.

SPATIAL ORDER

—In **descriptive** prose, follows a "natural" order, as from top to bottom, right to left, outside to inside, etc.

CLIMACTIC ORDER

—In **narrative** and **argumentative** prose, takes matters in order of increasing importance or intensity.

ANTICLIMACTIC ORDER

—In **argumentative** and occasionally in **expository** prose, takes matters in order of decreasing importance or intensity.

CLEARING THE GROUND BEFORE (OR AFTER) BUILDING	LOGICAL ORDER	ASSOCIATIONAL ORDER
—In **expository** and **argumentative** prose, sets forth the inadequacies of previous accounts, explanations, etc. **or** refutes arguments of opponents **and then** sets forth own account, explanation, or argument.	—In **expository** and **argumentative** prose, employs **inductive** reasoning (from the particular to the general) or **deductive** reasoning (from the general to the specific) or **cause-to-effect** or **effect-to-cause** reasoning.	—In any prose where one thing, person, place, etc. **"naturally suggests"** (in the mind of the writer) some other person, place, thing. In **stream-of-consciousness** prose, follows mind's own erratic, illogical motions. In **episodic narrative** and in accounts of **personal experiences,** events follow one another in no discernible order.

Figure 4.1

Selecting and Organizing

linear[1] pattern that begins at some point and proceeds in natural spatial sequences such as from top to bottom, from left to right, in a circle, around the four sides of a square. In describing a room in an art museum, for instance, you might begin by relating what you see as you stand in the entryway of the room, then describe what you see as you walk up the left-hand side, then describe what you see along the back wall, then describe what you see as you walk down the right-hand side of the room. Of course, you could reverse that order and walk up the right-hand side first and then come back down the left-hand side. The important thing would simply be to adhere[2] to a natural spatial order and not violate it by shifting from right to left to right.

(E) THE CLIMACTIC ORDER

This pattern, common in narrative writing, arranges the parts in an order of increasing importance or intensity. We speak of a story as "building toward a climax"—that is, the incidents are arranged so that the reader becomes increasingly excited or fascinated until the story reaches the height[3] of intensity. But the climactic order is often used also in argumentative writing, where the arguments are arranged in sequence from the weaker to the stronger. As an argumentative writer, you decide to use the order because you want to leave the audience with your strongest argument ringing in their ears.

(F) THE ANTICLIMACTIC ORDER

This order is the reverse of the previous one. It proceeds from the strongest to the weakest. Narrative writing almost never uses this order, but argumentative writing and occa-

---

[1] Consisting of, or relating to, a line. [2] To stick; to cling to. [3] The highest point.

sionally expository[1] writing sometimes follow it. As an argumentative writer, you might conclude that you would win greater acceptance of your weaker arguments if you presented your strongest argument first.

(G) THE PATTERN OF "CLEARING THE GROUND" BEFORE (OR AFTER) "BUILDING"

In expository writing, this pattern takes the form of first pointing out the shortcomings of previous explanations of something before presenting the preferred explanation. In argumentative writing, it takes the form of first refuting the arguments of your opponents before presenting your own. Sometimes, however, it is strategically[2] advisable to reverse this pattern and to do the "building" before the "demolishing."

(H) THE LOGICAL ORDER

This is often the natural order to follow in expository and argumentative writing. It can take a variety of forms. Two basic logical patterns are the **inductive** order and the **deductive** order. In the inductive order, you proceed from a series of *particulars* to a *generalization* (for instance, describing conditions in the ghettos of some of the major cities and then making some generalization about those conditions). In the deductive order, you begin with a *generalization* and then examine a series of *particulars* that support the generalization. For instance, you might begin with the generalization that "the miserable conditions existing in many urban ghettos are dehumanizing"[3] and then present a num-

---

[1] Adjective form of *exposition;* See *A* above. [2] Adverb form of *strategy.* [3] Robbing of human values.

Selecting and Organizing

ber of examples of this dehumanizing process. Two other basic logical patterns are *effect-to-cause* and *cause-to-effect.* For instance, an essay might begin with portraits of a number of mentally disturbed children (the effects) and then proceed to seek out the causes of those pathologies.[1] The cause-to-effect order would simply reverse that sequence.

(I) THE ASSOCIATIONAL ORDER

In some people's view, this order is "no order at all." Although it has the appearance of being chaotic[2] or, at best, arbitrary,[3] it has a "logic" of its own: it follows the sequence that naturally *suggests* itself to you, the writer. One thing follows another because it is *associated* in your mind—and not necessarily in your audience's mind—with what has just been mentioned or discussed.

An extreme form of the associational order is the so-called stream-of-consciousness technique[4] devised by such fiction writers as James Joyce and Virginia Woolf. This technique tries to duplicate the ways in which the mind often moves. If you could observe your own mind, you would discover that it rarely "thinks" in the neat, orderly ways outlined above. It often moves in fits[5] and starts,[6] in stop-and-go patterns. It begins a line of reasoning or reflecting, then suddenly and inexplicably[7] shoots off on a tangent.[8] That tangent may in turn shoot off into another tangent. After entertaining that tangent for a few seconds, the mind might return to the original line of reasoning or reflecting and pursue that line;

---

[1] The abnormal conditions and processes in disease. [2] Marked by disorder and confusion. [3] Determined randomly or by whim. [4] The way in which technical or operational details are handled with care and skill. [5] A sudden motion, as an outburst. [6] A sudden or very brief involuntary motion. [7] In a way that cannot be explained. [8] An abrupt change of course—from one action, thought, etc. to another.

but it might also never return to the original line and instead end up "miles" away from the starting point.

Stream-of-consciousness is an extreme example of associational order. Less extreme instances include episodic[1] narratives (the incidents follow no noticeable principle of order, not even the usual chronological order) and accounts of personal experiences (the events are so arranged simply because one event suggested another that was part of the total experience but that did not necessarily follow the first in the actual experience). Associations of things in your mind dictate the ordering of the parts.

However, you cannot always justify[2] the apparent chaos of your paper by saying, "I'm using an associational order here." There will be occasions when the associational order will not be the appropriate or effective one, and on those occasions it will justifiably be judged as chaotic.

Plotting an Outline

After finding and selecting your material and deciding to arrange it according to one of the patterns outlined above, you may want to plot[3] that order in an outline—a device[4] that you are probably familiar with and that you may have been required to include in papers you wrote for class. The standard format[5] of the major divisions of a paper resembles the outline shown in Figure 4.2 on the following page.

Note that the introduction and the conclusion in Fig. 4.2 are not preceded by Roman numerals; the Roman-numeral divisions outline only the middle section of your paper. Some-

---

[1] Characterized or marked by incidents in a course of events. [2] Prove right, true, or reasonable. [3] To mark, set down, or plan as on a chart. [4] Arrangement; plan; procedure. [5] The general plan or arrangement.

Selecting and Organizing

Introduction: [followed by some statement of what you
will do in this introductory section]

   I [followed by a phrase or a complete sentence that indicates the main topic dealt with in this section]

  II [followed by a phrase or a sentence, grammatically
parallel[1] with the phrase or sentence above, that indicates the main topic dealt with in this section]

 III [followed by a parallel phrase or sentence that indicates
the main topic covered in this section]

Conclusion: [You might state here what your major con-
conclusion is from the study presented in the
Roman-numeral divisions of the paper]

Figure 4.2

times you may be required to preface[2] the entire outline with
a thesis statement, in a format like this:

**Thesis: Stricter laws on the possession and use
of marijuana are not likely to cure the drug
problem.**

Sometimes you have such a clear mental preview of the parts
of the paper that you can prepare a more detailed outline,
with two or three levels of subdivisions under the Roman-
numeral divisions. See Figure 4.3 for the format of a detailed
outline (each of the divisions and subdivisions in Figure 4.3
would be followed by a sentence or phrase or word that
indicated the main topic in that part).

    Many writers confess that they cannot prepare a detailed
formal outline *before* they write their paper. (In fact, many

---

[1] Similar in essential parts.   [2] To introduce (with a statement).

Introduction:
I.
    A.
        1.
        2.
        3.
    B.
        1.
        2.
            a.
            b.
    C.
        1.
        2.
II.
    A.
    B.
    C.
    D.
III.
    A.
        1.
        2.
    B.
        1.
        2.

Conclusion:

(One caution about the format of the outline: if you make any division in your outline, you must have *at least two parts*. Division implies a "breaking into parts," and if you have only one part, no division has been made.)

Figure 4.3

Selecting and Organizing

outlines are put together *after* the paper is written.) **Writers who have difficulty preparing a formal outline often find it helpful to sketch[1] notes for themselves about how their paper is going to proceed.** Such notes might look like this:

> Introduction:
> a brief review of the literature on this subject, followed by a statement of the problem that persists after all this investigation and an indication of how I propose to deal with the problem.

What the previous investigators have failed to notice. The hidden causes that have escaped the attention of other investigators. Why the apparent causes don't get us to the heart of the problem.

Jacob Miller's hang-up on "ethnic origins."

The dead end that Susan Black reached when she pursued "economic predeterminers."[2]

The explosion of Pierre LeClerc's "social implosion"[3] theory.

The do-gooders.

The ultra[4]-conservatives.

The clergy, of all faiths, either barking up the wrong tree or just barking.

Why has no one thought of looking at the psychological traumas[5] of unemployment? Mental depression. Schizophrenia.[6] Loss of dignity. Marital[7] tensions. Alcoholic

---

[1] To make in rough outline form. [2] Factors, elements, etc. that determine something beforehand. [3] A bursting inward. [4] "Extreme." [5] An injury to body or mind, usually by an external force. [6] A mental disorder marked by personality breakup and loss of contact with reality. [7] Relating to marriage.

solace.[1] Withdrawing into a shell. Male menopause.

Back to the womb. At least back to the childhood environment.

Someone picking up these notes wouldn't find them very revealing. (Is this writer investigating the causes of perennial[2] unemployment?) Unlike the formal outline, which can be revealing to the reader even *before* he reads a paper, a set of loose notes is meaningful only to the writer. He knows what they mean. They suggest to him what he is going to cover and the order in which he is going to cover the points. They indicate the stages of the development of his paper.

Somewhere between the detailed formal outline and the set of loose notes is the system that plots the organization of the paper in *blocks.* The size of the blocks might indicate to the writer the relative length of that part of the paper. (See Fig. 4.4 for an example of the block system.)

Some writers find it even more helpful to put blocks within blocks. These blocks-within-a-block (represented by a slight indentation) show the number of paragraphs in the larger block, and each of them has a note indicating what is covered in that paragraph. (See Fig. 4.5 for an example of paragraph blocks within one of the larger blocks.)

These are some of the systems of plotting the organization of the middle section of a paper that have worked for some writers. You might try these systems to find out whether they are helpful to you in organizing your papers.

Other writers, however, are incapable of such systematic planning. When they sit down to write, they have some general idea of the points they want to cover and perhaps a clear idea of how they are going to begin; but they trust that *the writing itself* will suggest the order in which to take up their

---

[1] Comfort. [2] Recurring regularly; permanent.

Figure 4.4

Introduction
one paragraph

First major division of paper
two paragraphs

Second major division of paper
three paragraphs

Third major division of paper
two paragraphs

Conclusion
one long paragraph (100–150 words)

SECOND MAJOR SECTION OF THE PAPER

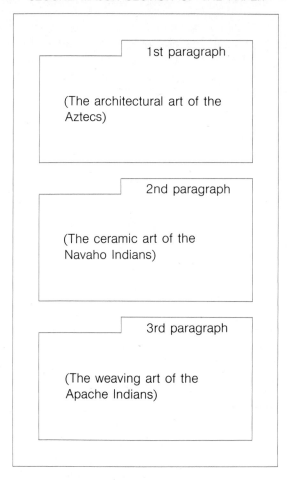

Figure 4.5

1st paragraph

(The architectural art of the Aztecs)

2nd paragraph

(The ceramic art of the Navaho Indians)

3rd paragraph

(The weaving art of the Apache Indians)

transitional[1] paragraph to next major division

[1] That makes a passage from one thing to another.

Selecting and Organizing

points. This "playing it by ear" might be the procedure used by writers who find that the first draft is still part of the discovery process for them. Each writer must find, through trial and error, the system of organization that works best for him. Try one or all of these systems, and see which works best for you.

The end

The more common term for that part of a paper that Aristotle called the *end* is *conclusion.* Just as Aristotle denied that a beginning or introduction was essential, so he denied that a conclusion was essential. But he was realist enough to concede that audiences expected and appreciated having an essay rounded off in a concluding section. Listeners and readers often feel uncomfortable when a speech or an essay comes to an abrupt halt. **They want at least a few parting words that will wrap up the discussion.** Presenting a conclusion is, at least, a courtesy to the audience, much like saying farewell when you take leave of friends or acquaintances. Moreover, a conclusion can render a valuable service for the audience, satisfying them that a discussion has been brought full circle.[1]

What do you normally do in a conclusion? Recall Aristotle's saying that the function of an introduction is to render the audience *attentive, benevolent,*[2] and *docile.*[3] But as the end of an essay approaches, you hardly need to make your readers attentive any longer. In fact, if they have not

[1] To a conclusion.   [2] Well-wishing; desiring the good of others; kindly; charitable.
[3] Easily taught, led, or managed.

already left you at that point, the mere announcement or hint that you are concluding your essay serves to perk them up and revive their attentiveness. Notice the almost palpable[1] sigh of relief you hear when a speaker says, "In conclusion. . . ." You sit up straight in your seat and pay special attention to what (you hope) will be only two or three more minutes of speech.

There is also not much need at the end of an essay to render your audience *docile*—that is, willing to be instructed or persuaded by you. It was important to put your audience in that mood at the beginning, but by the time you reach the conclusion, you have very little instructing or persuading left to do. But you do want to make your audience receptive to a summary of the main points that you made in the middle section of your paper. Your audience will be receptive[2] if in the conclusion you **touch on only the *highlights*[3] of the points made at length in the middle section** and if you **keep the summary as *brief* as possible.** Any unnecessarily elaborate[4] rehashing[5] of the points will weary[6] and perhaps alienate[7] your readers.

There may be a need at the end of a paper—perhaps more than at the beginning—to render the audience *benevolent* toward you. It is especially important to make this effort if you have been espousing[8] an unpopular cause, if you have had to bruise their feelings in any way, or if you have had to discredit[9] anything that they favor. Some conciliatory[10] words, some generous gesture toward your opponents, some acknowledgment[11] of the "right" on the other side of

[1] Capable of being touched or felt; evident. [2] Able or inclined to receive; open to ideas, etc. [3] Main points or events. [4] Complex; in great detail. [5] Presenting in another form without real change or improvement. [6] To tire or make tired. [7] To make hostile, unfriendly. [8] Arguing for; giving active support to. [9] To cause disbelief in the accuracy, value, or authority of someone or something. [10] Gaining the goodwill of; to win over from hostility. [11] Recognition as true or valid.

Selecting and Organizing

the issue—overtures like these at the end of your paper will help to confirm or regain your readers' benevolent attitude.

Another way to secure that benevolent attitude is to make an *emotional* appeal to your audience. On august[1] occasions, orators[2] are inclined to pull out all the emotional stops[3] in the concluding part of their speech. Their sentences shower fire and bombast;[4] figures of speech begin to cascade[5] one after the other; explicit or subtle appeals to emotions of sympathy, fear, or anger begin to appear.

In the written medium, however, emotional appeals are not likely to be as blatant[6] as they are in oratory,[7] particularly oratory on occasions of crisis, such as wartime, or of social importance, such as election time. The written medium demands a tighter rein[8] on emotional appeals. But restrained emotional touches are still common in some kinds of writing, especially in argumentation where you are trying to move your audience to action. Arguments mainly influence the intellect; emotional appeals mainly influence the will. An audience could be intellectually convinced that it should do something—like donating blood to the Red Cross—and still not be moved to action. In that situation, the will of the audience needs to be moved, and the best way to move the will is through the emotions. (A military or football band is an example of this.) In addition, emotional appeals, if skillfully managed, can also dispose an audience to feel *benevolent* toward a speaker or writer. And while it is sometimes necessary to secure that attitude at the beginning of an essay, it can also be necessary, or at least advisable, to secure or reinforce[9] a benevolent attitude in the conclusion.

---

[1] Marked by majesty or great dignity. [2] People skilled in public speaking. [3] Control knobs (for a set of organ pipes). [4] Inflated, wordy speech or writing. [5] To fall in a series or succession of stages. [6] Noisy; offensively or vulgarly obvious. [7] The art of effective public speaking. [8] Check; restraining influence. [9] To strengthen with more or new force.

Another thing that is commonly done in the conclusion is to remind the readers of the importance and the larger dimensions[1] of your subject. If you have done your job properly in the introductory and middle sections, the importance of what you have been discussing should be obvious, but it doesn't hurt to underscore[2] that importance at the end. You can reinforce the audience's sense of that importance by putting the topic or issue in some larger context.[3] You might, for instance, say something like, "The adoption of this policy will restore confidence and lead to a revitalization[4] of faith in the economy." By thus enlarging the dimensions of the subject, you at least reassure your audience that it has not been a waste of their time to listen to you.

Not every piece of writing needs an extensive[5] conclusion, but if it does need to be "concluded" rather than just "ended," it will require more than two or three sentences. You will have to compose at least a substantial[6] paragraph. Here in summary outline are some of the things that are customarily done in the conclusion and that you may also have to do—not all of them always, but certainly some of them sometimes:

---

1 Recapitulate[7] or summarize the main points you have made in the middle section of your paper.
2 Make your readers well disposed toward you.
3 Make some kind of emotional appeal to your readers.
4 Emphasize the crucial importance or the larger dimensions of what you have been talking about.

---

[1] Extent; scope; proportions. [2] To underline; to emphasize. [3] The parts that immediately precede and/or follow a passage or text and that determine its meaning. [4] A giving of new life or energy to. [5] Far-reaching; broad. [6] Of full amount or size. [7] Restate briefly; summarize.

Selecting and Organizing

The functions of the three-part structure of beginning, middle, and end can be summarized in a bit of advice that is sometimes given to speakers: "Tell them what you're going to tell them. Tell them. And then tell them what you've told them."

Chapter 5
Expressing What You Have Discovered, Selected, and Arranged

After the stage of prewriting, you are faced with the task of *putting words on paper*—of verbalizing what you have discovered, selected, and arranged. For you, as for many other writers, this part of the writing process may be the most difficult. But if you have been conscientious[1] in the prewriting process, you will find that the actual writing is easier—although it may never become easy. The writing becomes easier because you know what you want to say and because you have enough ability in your own language to convey[2] your thoughts to other speakers of the same language. You may not always be able to do this clearly, economically,[3] and gracefully, but with your basic ability you can convey the substance of your message. What every serious writer seeks to improve is the effectiveness of written expression—its clarity,[4] conciseness,[5] brevity,[6] and gracefulness.

[1] Guided by a sense of honesty and commitment to a position or task.   [2] To carry over; to transmit.   [3] Thriftily; done with minimum expenditure of money, words, resources, etc.   [4] Clearness.   [5] Expression of much in few words.   [6] Shortness.

Expressing What You Have Put Together

At a very early age, you acquired a basic competence in speaking your native language. You were in command of a minimal vocabulary and of most, if not all, of the basic sentence structures, and you could understand many more words and structures than you yourself used. From that point on, your style matured through your acquiring a larger vocabulary and learning how to use a wider range of sentence structures.

What you *know,* perhaps subconsciously,[1] is that the English sentence is basically a two-part structure, consisting of a subject and a predicate[2] verb. Minimally, this structure can consist of a single word in each position, as in the sentence

Birds/sing.

More often, however, the subject-verb structure consists of a cluster of words, in both positions, as in the sentence

The shiny red apples/pleased me very much.

A child first utters isolated words—*mama, doggie, ball.* Next, the child begins to form phrases—"red ball," "doggie hungry." Finally, the child forms the minimal, two-part structures like those in the sentences above. The maturing[3] of style comes when the child learns how to expand [4] the minimal structures.

By an almost miraculous[5] process, we eventually learn how to expand the minimal sentence "Birds sing" into a sentence like "The huddled gray birds sing forlornly[6] in the bare branches of the tree." This sentence is the result of *embedding,*[7] a process of combining several minimal sentences into a single sentence:

[1] Below the level of consciousness. [2] That makes a statement about a subject.
[3] Bringing to completion or full development. [4] To enlarge; to develop in detail.
[5] Extraordinary in the extreme. [6] As though having been abandoned, left in a pitiful state. [7] Enclosing in a surrounding mass.

The birds sing.

The birds are gray.

The birds are huddled.

The birds sing forlornly.

The birds sing in the bare branches of the tree.

By deleting[1] repeated words ("the birds," for instance) and rearranging the remaining words, a writer combines all of the meaning contained in the series of sentences into the single sentence "The huddled gray birds sing forlornly in the bare branches of the tree."

Because you can do this kind of deleting, rearranging, and combining, you have the basic competence[2] to express what you want to say. But some writers are better at this process than others, partly because they have practiced more and partly because they have acquired a larger vocabulary and a wider range of sentence patterns. In speaking, you can often get by with imprecise diction and with sprawling, awkwardly constructed sentences. *In writing, however, you need more exact words and tighter, neater sentences.* But you can't produce what you don't have in the first place. You can't come up with alternative[3] words if those words are not part of your vocabulary. You won't come up with alternative sentence structures if those structures are not part of your equipment. Rhetoric is an art of making choices, but you can't make choices if you haven't things to choose between.

Your vocabulary will expand as you gain new experiences. You unconsciously absorb new words, but you can also make conscious efforts to expand your vocabulary. One way is to systematically study lists of new words. In his *Autobiography,* Malcolm X tells us that while he was in prison, he

---

[1] Eliminating.　[2] Ability.　[3] Such that one or the other may be chosen.

Expressing What You Have Put Together

prepared himself to become a writer by systematically copying out the definitions of words in a dictionary that he had in his cell.

Studying word lists is one way to expand vocabulary, but it is not the ideal way, because by that method, you learn words in isolation.[1] A much better way is to *look up the meaning of any unfamiliar word that you encounter*[2] *in your reading or listening.* Thumbing through a dictionary each time you meet an unfamiliar word is a nuisance, but a necessary one, if you want to speed up expansion of your vocabularly. You have already noticed the Vocabulary Development System used in this book; among its many numbered words there are bound to be at least some that you need help with, and this book aims at providing that help.

However, it is not enough for you to look up the meanings of unfamiliar words in a dictionary. **New words can be made part of your working vocabularly only if you make a deliberate effort to use them in sentences you write.** At first, you may use the new words awkwardly or inappropriately, but you will eventually gain a more finely tuned sense of their shades of meaning, and then they will become a permanent part of your vocabularly, ready for use when needed.

The advice given here is about all that a text on writing can produce to help you add to your stock of words so that you can make choices from among alternatives. However, a text can do more than merely give advice when it comes to expanding your stock of alternative *sentence structures.* It can present some exercises that will acquaint you with a variety of sentence patterns. You may not want to use all the structures that you have practiced, but you are at least able to produce them if they serve your purpose.

[1] Separation from other (persons, things; in this case, words). [2] Meet.

● Copying Passages of Prose

The following are some exercises that can acquaint you with a variety of sentence patterns and maybe add to your repertory.[1]

●
Copying passages of prose

Copying passages of prose may seem a simpleminded exercise just because it is so simple, but it can pay big dividends[2] if engaged in conscientiously. The system consists of taking a short passage of prose[3] that you admire and copying it by hand. The mere act of writing out the sentences that someone else has written can reveal structures that only the most careful reading might show. Copying passages makes you pay close attention to how a writer has put words together and can acquaint you with sentence patterns that might never otherwise occur to you.

In order to see how this system works, write out the following paragraph:

It is time for the baby's birthday party: a white cake, strawberry-marshmallow ice cream, a bottle of champagne saved from another party. In the evening, after she has gone to sleep, I kneel beside the crib and touch her face, where it is pressed against the slats, with mine. She is an open and trusting child, unprepared for and unaccustomed to the ambushes of family life, and perhaps it is just as well that I can offer her little of that life. I would like to give her more. I would like to promise her that she will grow up with a sense of her cousins and of rivers and of great-grandmother's teacups, would like to

[1] List of skills or devices possessed by someone. [2] An amount to be divided and distributed; a bonus. [3] Ordinary language of writing or speaking.

Expressing What You Have Put Together

pledge her a picnic on a river with fried chicken and her hair uncombed, would like to give her *home* for her birthday, but we live differently now, and I can promise her nothing like that. I give her a xylophone and a sundress from Madeira, and promise to tell her a funny story (Joan Didion, "On Going Home," in *Slouching Towards Bethlehem* [New York: Farrar, Straus & Giroux, 1967]).

Here are some features of the passage that you may have noted and that you may want to make part of your skills:

1 The specific, concrete wording: *a white cake, strawberry-marshmallow ice cream, a bottle of champagne; crib, face, slats; cousins, rivers, great-grandmother's teacups; fried chicken, hair uncombed; xylophone, sundress from Madeira.*

2 The large number of one-syllable words (130 of the 170 words).

3 Variety of sentence length: the number of words in the six sentences is 22, 27, 33, 7, 63, 18 (an average of 29 per sentence). You wouldn't gain so specific an idea of the variations in length from merely copying the passage; you have to do some counting. Even without counting, however, everyone who copied the passage would note the dramatic difference in length between the fourth and fifth sentences.

4 Variety of ways of beginning sentences: Although four of the six sentences begin with the subject followed immediately by the verb (*She is. . . , I would like. . . , I would like. . . , I give. . .*), there is some variety. The first sentence begins with what is called an *impersonal*[1] *structure*

[1] Not referring to any person.

(*It is. . .*). There is another impersonal structure at the beginning of the second clause of the third sentence (*it is just as well that. . .*). The second sentence begins with a prepositional phrase (*In the evening*), followed by an adverb clause (*after she. . .*).

5 Variety of grammatical types of sentence: No two consecutive sentences are of the same grammatical type. But this fact alone does not entirely reveal the variety. These six sentences have nine independent clauses and four subordinate[1] clauses, and in three of the sentences, the predicate verb is compounded.

6 Some notable sentence patterns: (a) the adverb clause in the second member of a compound predicate ("and touch her face, *where it is pressed against the slats,* with mine"); (b) the two parallel phrases placed after the noun that the pair modifies[2] ("She is an open and trusting child, *unprepared for and unaccustomed to the ambushes* of family life"); (c) the three parallel verb-phrase structures beginning with the same words ("I *would like to promise her. . . , would like to pledge* her. . . , *would like to give* her. . ."); (d) the three parallel phrases (*"of her cousins* and *of rivers* and *of great-grandmother's teacups"*).

You may have been struck by some other features in this passage of 170 words. But in whatever passage you copy, you will usually find some feature, either of vocabulary or of sentence structure, that strikes your attention. Later, you will be surprised at how often some feature noted in the act of copying appears in your own writing.

One of the side-benefits of the copy exercise is that you can learn spelling and punctuation by doing it.

---

[1] Of lower rank; secondary.   [2] Relates to by limiting the meaning of.

Expressing What You Have Put Together

Some Advice about the Copy Exercise

1 Don't spend more than fifteen or twenty minutes at any one time on the copy exercise. When your attention wanders, you will only be copying words. It is more fruitful[1] to spend ten minutes a day over a period of several weeks than to spend thirty minutes a day for only a few weeks.

2 Don't concentrate on a single author; copy passages from a variety of authors. The object is not to acquire someone else's style but to acquaint yourself with the variety of vocabulary and sentence pattern that professional writers employ. Concentrate on contemporary[2] writers, especially those that you admire; but you may also profit by occasionally copying a passage written by an eighteenth- or nineteenth-century writer.

3 Choose your passages from a variety of sources—newspapers, magazines, books, collections of essays, ads, business and promotional[3] letters, even some of your textbooks.

4 Read the passage all the way through both *before* and *after* you copy it, to get a sense of the whole.

●

Imitating sentence patterns

This exercise consists of writing out a single sentence, composed by someone else, analyzing its structure, and then writing a sentence of your own on the pattern of that sentence. You must be able to distinguish various kinds of grammatical structures, even if you cannot label them properly. Your own sentence need not have the same number of words

[1] Yielding results; productive. [2] Occurring or existing at the same time. [3] Advancing the fortunes of; contributing to the growth or prosperity of.

84

as the model sentence, but it should have the same pattern. For instance, if a sentence begins with a participial phrase, your sentence should begin with one; if the main verb of the sentence is a transitive verb followed by an object, your sentence should use a transitive verb rather than an intransitive verb or a linking verb.

Here are some examples of analyses and imitations of sentence patterns:

MODEL

We don't encourage animals to come into the house, but they get in once in a while, particularly the cosset lamb, who trotted through this living room not five minutes ago looking for an eight-ounce bottle (E. B. White, "A Shepherd's Life").

ANALYSIS

This sentence consists of two independent clauses and of an adjective clause in the second independent clause. You should observe at least that much of the pattern in the sentence you write, but you may also want to include a participial phrase like the one that concludes White's sentence (*looking for an eight-ounce bottle*).

IMITATION

The police will not allow outsiders to walk across the picket lines, but children stray into the lines occasionally, especially bewildered five-year-olds, who weave in and out of the lines searching for their mothers.

Expressing What You Have Put Together

MODEL

How beautiful he was, with his olive-tinted flesh and dark gold ringlets, his eyes of mingled blue and brown, his perfect limbs, and the soft voluptuous roll which the blood of Africa had moulded into his features (W. E. B. DuBois, "Of the Passing of the First-Born").

ANALYSIS

This sentence begins with the main clause that notes, in a general way, the beauty of the new-born child and then spells out, in a series of prepositional phrases, the particular features that contribute to his beauty. In your own sentence, you might want to employ more phrases than the model sentence does.

IMITATION

How noisy it was, with the scarlet[1]-coated brass band and the bright, ornate[2] steam-calliope,[3] the cages of roaring lions and tigers, the jingling tambourines,[4] the honking horns, the exploding firecrackers, and the comic old-fashioned automobiles that the clowns maneuvered[5] in circles with exaggerated backfirings.

---

[1] Bright red. [2] Highly decorated. [3] A musical instrument made of a series of whistles played by keys. [4] Small, shallow hand-drums with metal sounding-disks built into the circular rim. [5] Moved skillfully, often through or past obstacles.

MODEL

If it is not perfect, it is not love, and if it is not love, it is bound to be hate sooner or later (Katherine Anne Porter, "The Necessary Enemy").

ANALYSIS

This is a balanced sentence: the two sentences on both sides of the conjunction *and* have the same grammatical structure—an adverb clause followed by the main clause.

IMITATION

When you are happy, you are a gentleman, but when you are a gentleman, you are a bore.

Expressing What You Have Put Together

MODEL

From the age of six onward, I constantly polished the enamel with peanut brittle, massaged the incisors twice daily with lollipops, and chewed taffy and chocolate-covered caramels faithfully to exercise the gums (S. J. Perelman, "Dental or Mental, I Say It's Spinach").

ANALYSIS

Try analyzing the structure of the sentence yourself.

IMITATION

After the beginning of the year, his girl friend promptly returned his engagement ring with an ironic[1] thank-you note, canceled three appointments with her hairdresser, and resumed[2] her tennis lessions avidly[3] to improve her game.

---

[1] Characterized by the use of words to express the opposite of what is meant; difference between an actual fact or event and what is expected to be or happen. [2] Returned or begun again. [3] Eagerly; enthusiastically.

MODEL

Four steps past the turnstiles, everybody is already backed up haunch to paunch for the climb up the ramp and the stairs to the surface, a great funnel of flesh, wool, felt, leather, rubber and steaming alumicron, with the blood squeezing through everybody's old sclerotic arteries in hopped-up spurts from too much coffee and the effort of surfacing from the subway at the rush hours (Tom Wolfe, "A Sunday Kind of Love").

ANALYSIS

Try analyzing the structure yourself.

IMITATION

Try writing a sentence of your own on the pattern of the model.

From these examples, you should have an idea of how this exercise works. In order to expand your own range of sentence patterns, you should choose the kinds of sentences that you like but do not normally write. If you exercise yourself in this way, you will soon be using some of the unusual patterns in your own writing.

Expressing What You Have Put Together

Combining and rearranging sentences

In the copy exercise, you merely reproduced a passage of prose, noting unusual features of vocabulary and structure that you might be able to use. In the previous exercise, you took a single sentence, analyzed its structure, and tried to write a sentence on the same pattern. In the exercise that follows, you are asked to combine and/or rearrange groups of whole sentences according to specific directions.

We will begin with some simple exercises in combining and rearranging and move to progressively more complex combinations and rearrangements.

I. BASE SENTENCES

1 I tried to discuss religion with the villagers.
2 I found the villagers reluctant[1] to discuss religion with strangers.

A. DIRECTIONS

Combine sentences (1) and (2) into a single sentence by the conjunction *but.*

RESULT

I tried to discuss religion with the villagers, but I found the villagers reluctant to discuss religion with strangers.

To avoid the repetition of *villagers* and *religion,* you could rewrite the sentence in this way:

[1] Unwilling.

I tried to discuss religion with the villagers, but I found them reluctant to discuss the subject with strangers.

B. DIRECTIONS

Take the same two sentences and combine them into a single sentence with two verbs joined by the conjunction *but.*

RESULT

I tried to discuss religion with the villagers but found them reluctant to discuss the subject with strangers.

After repeated practice of this kind, you will find that you can combine two sentences into a simple sentence with a compound predicate verb only when both sentences have the same subject. If sentence (1) had the subject *I* and sentence (2) had the subject *he,* a simple sentence with a compound predicate would be impossible.

C. DIRECTIONS:

Take the same two sentences and combine them by converting sentence (1) to a dependent clause beginning with the subordinating conjunction *when.*

RESULT

When I tried to discuss religion with the villagers, I found them reluctant to discuss the subject with strangers.

The positions of the *when* clause and the main clause can be reversed, but the words *religion* and *villagers* will also have to be transferred from the *when* clause to the main clause:

Expressing What You Have Put Together

I found the villagers reluctant to discuss religion with strangers when I tried to discuss the subject with them.

D. DIRECTIONS

Combine the same two sentences by turning sentence (1) into a phrase, using the *-ing* form of *try.*

RESULT

Trying to discuss religion with the villagers, I found them reluctant to discuss the subject with strangers.

REMINDER

You will discover a variety of ways in which sentences can be combined and/or rearranged, but you will also find that not all resultant sentences will be equally good stylistically.[1] Faced with a number of *possible* options, you will have to choose the best, or at least the better, option.

II. BASE SENTENCES

1 Craig Beard won the state lottery.
2 Craig Beard is a carpenter.
3 Craig Beard is an electrician.

A. DIRECTIONS

a convert sentence (1) to the passive voice, making *the state lottery* the subject.

---

[1] In terms of style.

b convert sentence (2) to a clause beginning with *who.*

c convert sentence (3) to an adjective clause beginning with *who.*

d combine the two *who* clauses.

e combine all the converted sentences into a single sentence.

RESULTS

a The state lottery was won by Craig Beard (*passive voice*)

b who is a carpenter (clause with *who*)

c who is an electrician (clause with *who*)

d who is a carpenter and an electrician (*combining adjective clauses*)

e The state lottery was won by Craig Beard, who is a carpenter and an electrician. (*combining all converted sentences*)

B. DIRECTIONS

a Using the same three sentences, make no change in sentence (1).

b reduce sentence (2) to an appositive.[1]

c reduce sentence (3) to an appositive.

d combine the appositives with sentence (1) to form a single sentence.

RESULTS

a Craig Beard won the state lottery (*no change*)

[1] A word that explains or illustrates another word.

Expressing What You Have Put Together

b a carpenter (*appositive*)

c an electrician (*appositive*)

d Craig Beard, a carpenter and an electrician, won the state lottery. (*combining and rearranging converted sentences*)

III. BASE SENTENCES

1 The team of engineers uses sophisticated[1] electronic equipment.

2 The team inspects power-plant boilers.

3 The team inspects power-plant smokestacks.

A. DIRECTIONS

a leave sentence (1) unchanged.

b change the verb in sentence (2) to the infinitive form (*to . . .*)

c change the verb in sentence (3) to the infinitive form (*to . . .*)

d combine the two infinitives into a single infinitive phrase.

e combine all the converted sentences into a single sentence.

RESULTS

a The team of engineers uses sophisticated electronic equipment (*no change*)

b to inspect power-plant boilers (*infinitive form*)

c to inspect power-plant smokestacks (*infinitive form*)

---

[1] Complex (of persons); worldly-wise.

d to inspect power-plant boilers and smokestacks (*combining infinitives*)

e The team of engineers uses sophisticated electronic equipment to inspect power-plant boilers and smokestacks. (*combining converted sentences*)

IV. BASE SENTENCES

1 Maggie Miller wrote the manifesto.[1]

2 Maggie Miller was one of the leaders of the committee.

3 Maggie Miller said SOMETHING.

4 The time has come for a revolution.

A. DIRECTIONS

a convert sentence (1) to the passive voice, making *manifesto* the subject.

b reduce sentence (2) to an appositive phrase.

c convert sentence (3) to a dependent clause beginning with *who*.

d convert sentence (4) to a dependent clause beginning with *that*.

e combine all four converted sentences into a single sentence, substituting the converted sentence (4) for the SOMETHING in converted sentence (3).

RESULTS

a The manifesto was written by Maggie Miller (*passive voice*)

b one of the leaders of the committee (*appositive phrase*)

[1] A public statement of actions and motives.

Expressing What You Have Put Together

c who said SOMETHING (*adjective clause*)

d that the time has come for a revolution (*noun clause*)

e The manifesto was written by Maggie Miller, one of the leaders of the committee, who said that the time has come for a revolution. (*combining all converted sentences*)

V. BASE SENTENCES

1 They intended SOMETHING.

2 They buy groceries.

3 They came home from work.

4 They saw the rain.

5 The rain was falling.

6 The rain was heavy.

7 The rain was cold.

8 They decided SOMETHING.

9 They take a taxi.

10 The taxi was standing on the corner.

A. DIRECTIONS:

a leave sentence (1) unchanged.

b reduce sentence (2) to the infinitive form (*to . . .*)

c convert sentence (3) to a dependent clause beginning with *when.*

d convert sentence (4) to a dependent clause beginning with *when.*

e reduce sentence (5) to a participle.

f reduce sentence (6) to an adjective.

g reduce sentence (7) to an adjective.

h leave sentence (8) unchanged.

● Exercise in Combining and Rearranging

i convert sentence (9) to the infinitive form (*to . . .*)

j convert sentence (10) to a dependent clause beginning with *which.*

k combine all of these transformed sentences into a single compound-complex sentence joined by *but,* substituting the infinitive phrase in (b) for the SOMETHING in (1) and substituting the infinitive phrase in (i) for the SOMETHING in (8).

RESULT*

They intended to buy groceries when they came home from work, but when they saw the heavy, cold rain falling, they decided to take a taxi, which was standing on the corner.

●
Exercise in combining and rearranging

Now that you have seen several examples of combining and rearranging groups of sentences, try to combine and/or rearrange each of the following groups of base sentences into a single sentence. If you see more than one way of combining and rearranging, write out all the alternatives you can devise.

A (1) Primitive[1] societies depend on human memory for the retention[2] of knowledge.

    (2) Primitive societies depend on the human voice for the transmission[3] of knowledge.

* (a) through (j) as combined in (k).

[1] Early, simple, and elemental in development. [2] The act of keeping in a fixed place; to hold in possession or use. [3] The act of passing something on.

Expressing What You Have Put Together

B (1) Undercoating does two things.
    (2) Undercoating prevents rust.
    (3) Undercoating deadens sound.

C (1) The decisive event may have been the oil embargo.
    (2) The oil embargo began about 1973.

D (1) Some of the guests were uncomfortable.
    (2) Some of the guests were restless.
    (3) Others enjoyed the chitchat.[1]
    (4) Others enjoyed the gossip.

E (1) The polls tell us SOMETHING.
    (2) The American people want honesty in government.
    (3) The American people want a reduction in federal spending.

F (1) He walked cautiously.
    (2) He skirted the rain puddles.
    (3) He slipped on a banana peel.

G (1) One of the eight bodies was found near a culvert.[2]
    (2) The culvert was in a farm community near Philadelphia.
    (3) The body was identified as that of the wife of one of the three men.
    (4) The three men are being held in the county jail.

H (1) I was leaving the party.
    (2) I heard the host say SOMETHING.
    (3) Everyone should drive carefully.

I (1) This week we received a letter from a friend.
    (2) Our friend is a close observer of the national scene.
    (3) Our friend monitors[3] violations of regulations.
    (4) The regulations govern environmental pollution.

---

[1] Casual conversation; light, familiar chat. [2] A drain running beneath and across a road, canal, or railroad embankment. [3] Watches or observes for a special purpose.

J (1) This country is like an addict.
    (2) An addict can't kick his drug habit.
    (3) This country finds itself more and more dependent on the importation[1] of foreign oil.

●
Varying sentence patterns

A variation on the exercise in the previous section is to take a sentence and try to express the same meaning in a variety of other ways—by changing some of the words or by altering[2] the order of words or by using different grammatical structures. Take the following sentence, for instance:

> They refused to attend the concert, for they thought that the price of admission was exorbitant.[3]

Here are some other ways to express approximately[4] the same meaning:

1 They refused to attend the concert because they thought that the price of admission was exorbitant.

2 Because they thought that the price of admission was exorbitant, they refused to attend the concert.

3 The reason they refused to attend the concert was that the price of admission was exorbitant.

4 The reason they gave for refusing to attend the concert was that the price of admission was exorbitant.

5 Their reason for refusing to attend the concert was simple: the price of admission was exorbitant.

---

[1] The act of bringing into a country from a foreign or external source. [2] Making different. [3] Beyond what is usual or proper. [4] Almost; nearly.

Expressing What You Have Put Together

6 Thinking that the price of admission was exorbitant, they refused to attend the concert.

7 They registered[1] their objection to the exorbitant price of admission by refusing to attend the concert.

8 The exorbitant price of admission made them refuse to attend the concert.

9 "We refuse to attend the concert because we think the price of admission is exorbitant."

10 The price of admission was exorbitant, so they refused to attend the concert.

11 Since the price of admission was exorbitant, they refused to attend the concert.

●
Exercise in varying patterns

See in how many different ways you can express the meaning of the following sentences:

1 Many of the assembled stories, of course, can be dated quite definitely, but all of them were recited for live audiences by traveling bards[2] for at least a hundred years before they were written down.

2 Those who are genuinely concerned about the energy shortage, about environmental pollution, and about worldwide malnutrition[3] will be following with great interest the astronomers'[4] studies of the sources of energy in interstellar[5] space.

---

[1] Indicated; recorded. [2] Poets. [3] Faulty and inadequate nutrition. [4] A scientist of the makeup, positions, and motions of the heavenly bodies, including the earth. [5] Among the stars.

● Exercise in Varying Patterns

3 As inheritors[1] of the past, we must both respect and ignore our heritage[2] if we are to make significant advances.

4 It should be conceded that subjecting these problems to the scrutiny[3] of concerned citizens may result in more confusion than enlightenment[4] for the community.

5 There are, according to my judgment, three conflicting stories in the defendant's[5] testimony, including the story about his visit to a friend's house on the night of the murder.

6 She was perturbed[6] by the indifference[7] of the committee to the plight[8] of the refugees,[9] but she felt that she would only jeopardize[10] the relief program if she openly criticized the committee.

7 The supervisors had to decide whether the workers staged[11] the walkout in deliberate defiance of the injunction[12] from the State Supreme Court.

8 If we are to understand the dilemmas[13] that our forefathers[14] confronted, we must do more than just read history books; we must read the newspapers, broadsides,[15] pamphlets, and manifestos published between 1776 and 1783.

9 While searching in the library for some information about sunspots,[16] I discovered a fascinating book about Unidentified Flying Objects.

[1] Those who receive what comes down from those who have gone before. [2] Property or other value that is received by an heir; legacy. [3] Close examination. [4] Insight; mental illumination. [5] A person charged with wrongdoing and required to make answer in a legal proceeding. [6] Disturbed greatly in mind; agitated; upset. [7] Absence of care or concern. [8] Condition; state. [9] People who flee for safety, usually to a foreign country. [10] Expose to death, injury, or loss; Endanger. [11] Performed or produced on, or as though on, a stage. [12] An order by a court to perform or not to perform a certain act. [13] Choices between unfavorable, undesirable alternatives; positions of doubt and puzzlement. [14] Persons of an earlier period in the same culture, history, etc.; ancestors. [15] Large sheets printed on one side only. [16] Dark spots appearing from time to time on the sun's surface.

Expressing What You Have Put Together

10 Founded by missionaries, who were primarily interested in spreading the gospel among the heathen,[1] the Institute has served the people well, bringing medical relief to thousands who might otherwise have died.

Regular practice in some or all of the exercises set forth in the previous sections will build up a store[2] of words and sentence structures to be used in your own writing. What you derive from these exercises may become a permanent part of your own style.

Figures of speech

An expanded vocabularly and range of sentence patterns are not the only resources that make writing easier and more effective. Suitable use of figures of speech can make your prose lively and clear. But in order to use them, you must increase your awareness of the great variety of figures of speech.

Figurative language is an integral[3] part of everyone's speech. Not only do you use hundreds of figures of speech in your own talking and writing—probably unconsciously— but you have even invented some of your own.

Basically, **a figure of speech is the use of a word in a transferred sense. It departs from the common literal meaning of a word and gives the word another meaning.** When we say, "The runner was a bolt of lightning," we obviously do not mean to say that the runner is literally a bolt of lightning. What we want to convey is a notion of the runner's amazing speed. We *could* say, "The runner is

---

[1] Persons whose religion does not acknowledge the God of the Bible. [2] A large quantity. [3] Essential to the completeness of the whole.

amazingly fast,'' and frequently of course we use such literal language. But we convey the same meaning with greater vividness by using the metaphor of *a bolt of lightning.* **Metaphor** is one of several figures of speech that are based on **analogy:** *something is like something else.* When we use a **simile,** we point out the analogy by actually using the words *like* or *as:* ''the runner was like a bolt of lightning.'' By dropping the *like* or the *as* in a metaphor, we *imply*[1] the analogy.

Everyone's speech or writing contains numerous **dead metaphors** or **submerged metaphors**—figures that have been used so often that we no longer think of them as being used in a transferred sense and instead use them quite literally. Words and phrases like ''skyscraper,'' ''leg of a table,'' ''bulldozer,'' ''eye of the storm,'' ''mouth of the river,'' ''glowing words,'' ''stonefaced,'' ''turtleneck sweaters,'' ''ashen[2] complexion'' are examples of dead or submerged metaphors.

There is nothing wrong with using dead metaphors; in fact, use of them is inevitable, because they have become a regular and serviceable part of the vocabularly. *But be on guard against the use of* **trite**[3] **metaphors.** There is a difference between dead or submerged metaphors and trite or tired metaphors, although the line between them is sometimes thin. Dead metaphors have been used so often that they have become an indispensable[4] part of the language. Tired metaphors, on the other hand, have been used so often that we are weary of them and would like to see them go away. There is a significant difference between expressions like ''skyscraper'' and ''the mouth of the river'' and expressions like ''a beacon[5] of hope'' and ''a tower of strength.'' The first two are so apt[6] that it would be hard to find alternative words or

[1] Express indirectly; suggest. [2] Ash-colored; deadly pale. [3] Worn out by constant use; stale. [4] Absolutely essential. [5] A signal mark, fire, or light used for guidance. [6] Suitable.

Expressing What You Have Put Together

phrases to replace them. The latter[1] two expressions are so stale that we wish they would disappear from the language.

Another kind of figurative language that you should avoid is the **mixed metaphor.** *A mixed metaphor results from joining, in one and the same unit of speech, two or more comparisons that clash because their imagery[2] is different.* We mix metaphors when we write, for example, "Now that he's in the saddle, everything will be smooth sailing." Besides being trite, the two metaphors clash: one uses the imagery of horsemanship, the other that of sailing. Unmixing might yield "Now that he's at the rudder,[3] everything will be smooth sailing." A writer can shift metaphors as he moves from one part of his paper to another or even from one sentence to another, but he should not mix *clashing images* in the same expression. Trite metaphors creep into our writing when we unthinkingly use an expression that has been

[1] More recent; final; of or being the second of two things, pairs, etc. [2] The pictures or illustrations that the words present to the mind's eye. [3] A broad, flat piece of metal or wood attached vertically to the sternpost of a ship (or plane) for purposes of steering.

left ringing in our ears from frequent repetition; mixed metaphors come from a conscious but careless effort to "tone up" our writing.

Some of the freshest and most startling figures of speech are those that appear unbidden, in a sudden flash as we write. No one can account for those sudden, apt, vivid images, but they do occur. Spontaneity,[1] however, is not their only source. Writers tell us that some of their best metaphors have resulted from a conscious effort on their part to invent a figurative[2] way of saying what they wanted to say. Both the spontaneous metaphor and the deliberate metaphor must, however, be used with care—care that the spontaneous metaphor is not trite and that the deliberate metaphor is not mixed.

One final bit of advice: **it is better to try using figurative language and make mistakes than not to dare use it at all.** A clumsy or a stale or an inappropriate[3] figure of speech is evidence that the writer is at least moving toward the creation of word-pictures.

Let us summarize the points that have been made about figurative language:

☐ **Figures of speech are not mere decoration; they are an integral and indispensable part of everyone's language.**

☐ **Figures of speech enliven[4] prose by expressing things in vivid, concrete[5] ways.**

☐ **Writers must sensitize[6] themselves to language so that they can avoid both trite and mixed figures of speech.**

---

[1] Spontaneous, natural, voluntary action. [2] Using figures of speech or metaphors; not literal. [3] Not proper, fit, or suitable. [4] Give life, vigor, spirit, or action to. [5] Real; actual; not theoretical or abstract. [6] Make sensitive.

Expressing What You Have Put Together

☐ **Apt, vivid figures of speech can come to us sponta-neously or can be produced deliberately.**

☐ **It is better to risk making mistakes in the use of figures of speech than not to attempt figures of speech at all.**

●

Some common figures of speech

Here are definitions and illustrations of some of the common figures of speech.

METAPHOR

Suggests a comparison between two things of differ-ent nature that nevertheless have something in common.

The colorful display was a *magnet* for all the buyers in the room. (Here the metaphor is in the noun.)

He *knifed* his way through the dense[1] crowd of shop-pers. (Here the metaphor is in the verb.)

His *snail's-paced* crawl toward the sensitive bomb held the onlookers in suspense. (Here the metaphor is in the adjective.)

SIMILE

Directly states a comparison between two things of different nature that nevertheless have something in common.

[1] Thick.

● Some Common Figures of Speech

He raced for the goal-line *like an antelope.* (The sentence "He raced for the goal-line like O. J. Simpson" would be a simple comparison, not a simile, because the things being compared both have the same nature—they are both human.)

Her eyes were as inert[1] *as stone.*

Silence hung in the room *like a ball of lead.*

SYNECDOCHE

A part stands for the whole.

Male teenagers often get caught up in a love affair with their *wheels.* (Here *wheels* stands for the entire car or motorcycle.)

Give us this day our daily *bread.* (Here *bread* stands for food in general.)

The buccaneers[2] raised their *steel* with a resounding[3] shout. (Here *steel* stands for the whole sword.)

METONYMY

A thing stands for the person, position, or state of affairs that uses it.

They dedicated their *pens* to the cause of peace. (Here *pens* stands for writing talent.)

The people maintain[4] an unshakable loyalty for the *crown.* (Here *crown* stands for the king or queen or for royalty in general.)

The women exchanged their *typewriters* for the *key to*

[1] Having no power to act or move; inactive; sluggish. [2] Pirates. [3] Echoing; ringing.
[4] Continue in; keep in an existing state.

Expressing What You Have Put Together

the executive washroom. (Here *typewriters* stands for jobs as secretaries, and the *key to the washroom* stands for positions as business executives.)

PUNS

A play on words, such as repeating a word in two different senses or using words that sound alike but have different meaning.

He was always *game*[1] for any *game.*

That huckster[2] has had *lots* of experience selling *lots* to senior citizens.

If you feel *alone,* come to us for *a loan.*

While the *sun* shines, his prodigal[3] *son* makes hay.[4]

PERIPHRASIS

Substitutes a descriptive word or phrase for a proper name or substitutes a proper name for a quality associated with that name.

The *little old lady from Dubuque* wouldn't approve this movie. (Here the *little old lady from Dubuque* stands for any prim and proper lady from small-town America.)

The *Human Backboard* won her match in straight sets. (Here the *Human Backboard* refers to a tennis player, like Chris Evert, who relentlessly[5] keeps returning the ball over the net.)

They tried to fight *Jim Crow* with legislation. (Here *Jim*

---

[1] Having the spirit or the will. [2] Peddler; hawker. [3] Given to extravagant spending; recklessly wasteful. [4] *To make hay while the sun shines:* to lose no time; to profit from opportunities. [5] In a determined, hard, persistent way.

Crow refers to racial discrimination, especially against blacks.)

What are you going to do about the *Archie Bunkers* in the electorate?[1] (Here *Archie Bunkers* refers to the kind of bigoted[2] middle-class citizens like the character in the TV show *All in the Family*.)

PERSONIFICATION

Assigns human qualities or abilities to abstractions or to inanimate objects.

His naiveté[3] would make *stones weep*.

The thatch-roofed[4] cottages in the valley seemed *to be asleep*.

Integrity[5] *thumbs its nose* at pomposity.[6]

While *vigilance[7] nodded,*[8] *rapacity[9] rampaged*[10] through the streets.

HYPERBOLE

Exaggerates for the purpose of emphasis or heightened effect.

No sooner had I thrown the hamburger away than a *million* flies swarmed over it.

My son's friends tracked a *ton of mud* through my clean kitchen.

---

[1] A body of persons entitled to vote. [2] Stubbornly attached to a belief or organization and intolerant of others. [3] The condition of being sincerely simple and unsophisticated. [4] With a roof made of straw or other plant material. [5] Character of uncorrupted virtue; uprightness; honesty; sincerity. [6] Pretentious dignity; self-importance; "putting on airs." [7] Watchfulness; being on the alert. [8] Was momentarily inattentive or dozing. [9] Grasping or seizing for oneself. [10] Went wildly or violently.

Expressing What You Have Put Together

Her sunny smile would *melt ice.*

I was so embarrassed that I felt about *as big as a peppercorn.*

LITOTES

Understates[1] or downplays for the purpose of emphasis[2] or heightened effect.

She lives in New York City, which, you might say, has a *few* people in it.

"It's only a *slight wound,*" he said, showing me the stump of his leg.

He was a *bit annoyed* about the vandals[3] having set fire to his garage.

You can be sure we were *not unhappy* to see the village after six days of trudging through the waist-high snow.

OXYMORON

Couples two contradictory terms.

He was a *cheerful pessimist*[4] about his chances.

They were stunned by the *loud silence* that greeted their performance.

She revelled[5] in her *luxurious poverty.*

Ralph proclaimed his *wholehearted indifference* to the project.

---

[1] States as being less than is so; states in a reserved way. [2] Stress given, or importance assigned, to something. [3] Those who intentionally or ignorantly destroy or deface important or valuable property. [4] One who habitually takes the worst view of things. [5] Took intense delight in.

IRONY

A word intended to convey a meaning just the opposite of its ordinary or literal meaning.

"Do I love him? Who wouldn't *love* a cheat, a liar and a scoundrel?"[1]

Robbing a widow of her life savings was certainly a *noble* act.

It was one of those *glorious* days—overcast skies, a cutting wind, and sub-zero temperatures.

She wanted him to buy one of those *modest* cars, like a Cadillac or a Mercedes.

You needn't know the names or the definitions of figures of speech to be able to use them in your writing. In fact, you have used dozens of figures already without being aware that you were using them and without knowing what to call them. If, however, you are aware of the various figures of speech, it is probable that you will consciously use them if you see that they serve your purpose. Being able to create fresh figures of your own may also keep you from resorting to trite figures.

●

Some special artistic patterns

The purpose of the imitative exercises presented earlier in this chapter was to make you aware of some patterns of phrasing that are available in the English language but that you may not have used in your own writing. In this section you will meet some special artistic patterns that almost never

---

[1] A person with no moral principle.

Expressing What You Have Put Together

occur in writing unless the writer makes a conscious decision to use them. They are unusual patterns that, like figures of speech, create *special effects*.

When Winston Churchill said in one of his famous speeches during World War II, "We shall fight on the beaches, we shall fight on the landing-grounds, we shall fight in the fields and in the streets, we shall fight in the hills," he was speaking on a special occasion for a special purpose with a special effect. He was addressing the people of Great Britain at a time during the war when their fortunes seemed to be at rock bottom. Hitler's armies had rolled over all opposition in the first nine months of the war, and in May of 1940, the Dutch and the Belgian armies had surrendered to the Germans, leaving the British people in a very precarious[1] position. The speech that Churchill delivered on June 4, 1940 rallied the spirits and the resolve of the British people. The sentence quoted above occurred in that famous rallying speech. By phrasing his message in a series of parallel clauses, all beginning with the same words ("we shall fight"), Churchill drew special attention to this part of his message. The drum-roll of that repeated pattern conveyed the firm determination that it was intended to convey. If sentence after sentence of the *entire* speech had begun with the same words, the pattern would soon have grown monotonous[2] and ultimately ridiculous. But used in the right place at the right time, an artistic pattern like that can produce a stunning effect.

There are two things one needs to learn about these artistic patterns: (1) *what* they are, and (2) *when* they should be used. You can very quickly learn what the special patterns are, and you will be introduced to some of them below. A sense of when they can be used appropriately and effectively

[1] Dangerously unstable or insecure. [2] Dull through repetition.

● Some Special Artistic Patterns

will develop with your growth in the use of language.

Here are definitions and illustrations of some of the special artistic patterns (many of these are based on the principles of parallelism and repetition):

PARALLEL PATTERN
Stringing together a series (three or more) of grammatically similar phrases or clauses.

As Abraham Lincoln said, what this country needs is a government of the people, by the people, and for the people. (*a series of prepositional phrases*)

We will achieve this kind of government when our legislative[1] bodies are representative of all segments of society, when elected officials are responsive to the needs and desires of their constituencies,[2] and when the laws truly promote[3] the welfare of all the citizens. (*a series of adverb clauses*)

By electing intelligent and dedicated men and women, by insisting on honesty and integrity, by establishing an effective system of checks and balances,[4] and by maintaining a free and vigilant[5] press, we can achieve this kind of government.

REPETITIVE INITIAL PATTERN

Repeating two or more words at the beginning of successive[6] phrases or clauses.

---

[1] Having the power, or nature, of making laws. [2] Groups of those who have the power to elect to a given office. [3] Contribute to the growth and prosperity of; advance the cause or interests of. [4] Checks are limits placed on (governmental) powers; balances are powers that equal other (governmental, opposing) powers. [5] Watchful; alert. [6] Following one after the other in order.

Expressing What You Have Put Together

We must strive relentlessly to foster[1] honest values, to foster honest goals, and to foster honest responsibilities. (*a series of infinitive phrases beginning with the same group of words*)

Why should we promote the interests of unscrupulous[2] mountebanks?[3] Why should we promote the aspirations[4] of impractical[5] visionaries?[6] Why should we promote the schemes of self-aggrandizing[7] entrepeneurs?[8] (*a succession of parallel clauses beginning with the same words*)

REPETITIVE ENDING PATTERNS

Repeating two or more words at the end of successive phrases and clauses.

Nations assume the burdens of responsibility, special-interest groups extoll[9] the burdens of responsibility, and individuals avoid the burdens of responsibilities.

ANTITHETICAL PATTERNS

Joining contrasting ideas in a pair of grammatically similar phrases and clauses.

We advocate[10] social justice, yet we tolerate racial discrimination; we praise merit, yet we reward mediocrity,[11]

---

[1] To promote the growth and development of. [2] Lacking in principles; having no regard for what is right. [3] Bold pretenders, usually those who publicly offer false promises or proposals. [4] Strong desires for something noble. [5] Not practical; idealistic. [6] Those who entertain fantastic ideas or plans; dreamers. [7] Building up (for) oneself. [8] Those who organize and promote an activity, especially a business. [9] Praise; glorify. [10] Plead in favor of. [11] The quality of being of neither much nor little value or goodness; ordinary.

we preach integrity, yet we practice duplicity.[1]

REVERSED PATTERNS

Reversing the normal order of words in a sentence.

Harmony they planted; discord[2] they reaped.[3]

A reliable, affectionate, mild-mannered son he was not.

The struggle, the heartache, the disappointment I cannot claim to be familiar with.

CRISSCROSS PATTERNS

Reversing grammatical structures in successive clauses.

He praises his enemies, but his friends he maligns.[4]
I know what they want; what they would settle for I can't imagine.

CLIMACTIC PATTERNS

Arranging a series of words, phrases, or clauses in an order of increasing importance.

Her way of life was expensive, pointless, and utterly ruthless.

He wanted to educate his children, serve his country, and satisfy his God.

This law should meet with your approval because it is simple, because it is enforceable, and because it is just.

---

[1]Deception by representing oneself in one way and being or acting in another.
[2]Lack of agreement or harmony. [3]Got in return; gathered; obtained. [4]Speaks evil of.

Expressing What You Have Put Together

ALLITERATIVE PATTERNS

Repeating the initial consonant(s)[1] in two or more adjacent[2] words.

Brainless brawn[3] can break the bravado[4] of brittle[5] men.

Try a tasty, tempting tart today.

Although the alliterative pattern is effective occasionally as an attention-getting device or for a humorous effect, writers should use it sparingly.[6] The alliterative pattern is especially conspicuous,[7] but all of the special artistic patterns outlined in this section should be used only occasionally, as when you want to create a special effect or to draw unusual attention to what you have written.

Paragraphing

After the sentence, the paragraph is the next largest unit in a piece of writing. It is a collection of related sentences. Groups of paragraphs, in turn, mark off still larger units in this development.

A good way to regard the paragraph is as a form of visual punctuation marking off stages in the development of thought. By using the visual device of indentation,[8] you indicate the breaks and shifts in the development of your thought. You thereby make it easier for your reader to follow and understand you. To demonstrate this, simply imagine

[1] A letter other than *a, e, i, o,* or *u.*   [2] Situated next to; side by side.   [3] Muscular strength.   [4] Boastful display of courage or boldness.   [5] Easily broken; fragile.   [6] In small and restrained measure; economically.   [7] Attracting attention; highly noticeable.   [8] The blank space made between a (usually the first) line (of a paragraph) and the margin set on the paper.

yourself reading a text that had no paragraph indentations at all. As a reader, you would have to work much harder to follow that text. Indentation is to a text what punctuation marks are to a sentence.

Your own individual way of putting thoughts together and developing them from sentence to sentence within any paragraph reveals a pattern. *Look for this pattern in your writing.* It will reveal itself in the *length* of your average paragraph, and this in turn will govern the *frequency* of paragraphs that occur in your writing. Your own "style" of paragraphing will be influenced partly by the kind of writing you are doing and partly by the subjects you are writing about. If you were writing an instruction manual for assembling an electronic computer, your paragraphs might be only two sentences long—one "paragraph" for each stage of the assembly. If, on the other hand, you were explaining a political concept, you might have to string together six, eight, ten sentences—enough sentences to make the concept clear to your readers. Occasionally, you might use a one-sentence paragraph to emphasize a point or to signal a transition to the next major section of your paper. Despite these variations in length, however, the collection of paragraphs in your paper will reveal an *average* length that is characteristic of your writing.

Now let us look at some of the principles governing the construction of paragraphs.

Unity

We defined the paragraph as *a collection of related sentences.* One of the principles that helps to relate the sen-

---

[1] Something that serves as a part of something else.

Expressing What You Have Put Together

tences in a paragraph is the principle of unity. **A unified paragraph is one in which all of the sentences are talking about the same topic.** The four sentences in the following paragraph seem not to be talking about the same topic:

A chemist is interested in the atomic weights of the elements in a substance. When she heard the explosion, she ran to the telephone to call the police. The cost of education in these inflationary times puts some segments of our population at an extreme disadvantage. Automobiles have begun to roll off the assembly line once again.

Admittedly, this is an extreme example of a disunified paragraph. A more usual kind of breakdown in unity is the one in which the first three or four sentences of a paragraph deal with the same topic, but then suddenly and without warning, a sentence occurs that introduces another topic. The following paragraph is an instance of this:

Bluegrass is a distinct kind of country-and-western music. Associated with the Appalachian regions of the country, it has its roots in the folk culture of the rural people who inhabit the hills and the mountains of these regions. The instruments that are featured in this kind of music are the acoustic guitar, the banjo, the fiddle, the dobro, and the autoharp. The fast-paced, rippling melodies issuing from those instruments are often more important than the lyrics.[1] Nashville is now the capital of the country-and-western industry. Big-name performers can be seen every day driving up to the plush[2] recording studios in their Cadillacs and Continentals.

[1] The words of a piece of popular music. [2] Noticeably luxurious.

The first four sentences of this paragraph deal with some of the characteristics of bluegrass music. But with the appearance of the fifth and sixth sentences, a new topic is introduced. Nashville, of course, has some connection with bluegrass music, but the fifth and sixth sentences do not talk about that connection. Instead, they introduce the notion of Nashville being the capital of country-and-western music, of which bluegrass is only a part. The writer should have begun a new paragraph with the fifth sentence.

Associate unity with *one*. **Each paragraph should deal with only one topic.** Be vigilant. *If you detect that a sentence in a paragraph you wrote shifts to a discussion different from the topic you started out with, either drop that sentence or begin a new paragraph.*

● Coherence

Coherence is another principle that governs the relationship of sentences in a paragraph. It is the principle that ensures the "hanging-together" of all the sentences in a paragraph. Unity also contributes to the "hanging-together" of sentences in a paragraph, but conceivably, a paragraph could be unified and still not be coherent. Coherence governs the *logical and connected flow* of sentences, whereas unity governs the *logical wholeness* of the group of sentences. A *unified* paragraph keeps the focus on a *single topic;* a *coherent* paragraph makes it easy for the reader to *move from sentence to sentence.*

Here are some of the devices that help the reader sense the interconnections between the sentences of a paragraph:

Expressing What You Have Put Together

LOGICAL BRIDGES

1 **The carry-over of the same idea or topic from sentence to sentence.**
2 **Parallel structure of successive sentences** (see p. 113).

VERBAL BRIDGES

1 **Repetition of key words in several of the sentences.**
2 **Use of synonymous[1] words in successive sentences.**
3 **Use of pronouns referring to nouns in previous sentences.**
4 **Use of coordinating conjunctions and conjunctive adverbs.**

Even more than pronouns and repeated and synonymous words, coordinating conjunctions and conjunctive adverbs explicitly tie sentences together and indicate the kind of relationships that exist between sentences. Here is a list of some of the commonly used conjunctions and conjunctive adverbs arranged in categories that indicate the kind of relationships they establish:

ADDITIVE

and/also/besides/moreover/furthermore/in addition/not only . . . but also/both . . . and/first, second . . . finally.

OPPOSING

but / yet / however / rather / nevertheless / instead / on the contrary / on the other hand.

[1] The same or equivalent in meaning.

ALTERNATIVE

or/either . . . or/nor/neither . . . nor.

TEMPORAL[1]

then/next/afterwards/previously/now/meanwhile/
subsequently/later/thereafter/henceforth.

CAUSAL

for/so/therefore/thus/consequently/hence/
accordingly/as a result/otherwise/perhaps/indeed/
surely/clearly.

Observe the use of some of these linking devices in a coherent paragraph:

> The flexibility of a racquet—that is, the amount of "give" in the frame—is important to your game. You can test the flex of a racquet by clamping the handle to the edge of a table with one hand and then pressing down on the end of the frame with the other. Metal racquets are generally more flexible than wood racquets. The more flexible a racquet is, the more power it will add to your shots by its greater whiplash action during a swing. But it provides that extra power at the expense of control. Stiffer racquets thus offer more control, although they can subject your arm muscles to damaging vibrations if you have tennis elbow (Jeffrey Bairstow, "Which Racquet Is Right for Your Game?" *Tennis,* 11 [January 1976], 21–22).

Analysis of the coherence devices in this paragraph:

[1] Of, or related to, time.

Expressing What You Have Put Together

LOGICAL BRIDGES

1 Every sentence in the paragraph is dealing in some way with the "topic" of the paragraph—the flexibility of tennis racquets. The frequent occurrence of comparative phrases—*more flexible, more power, greater whiplash action, extra power, more control, stiffer racquet*—indicates that the major means of development in the paragraph is *comparison and contrast.*

2 There are no instances in this paragraph of the use of parallel structures in successive sentences to promote coherence.

VERBAL BRIDGES

1 Repetition of key words in several of the sentences—*flexible, racquet, power, control, frame.*

2 Use of synonomous words in successive sentences—*flexibility:* flex, amount of 'give'; *greater power:* extra power; antonym of *flexible:* stiffer.

3 Use of pronouns—*racquet:* it; *racquets:* they; *one hand:* other; you, your.

4 Use of coordinating conjunctions and conjunctive adverbs—*But, thus, then, that is.*

Since coherence is so vital to intelligibility,[1] you should never relax in the pursuit of this skill. Another benefit of the copy exercise recommended earlier in this chapter is that you can learn how practiced writers make their prose "hang together."

---

[1] Capability of being understood.

●
Adequate development

No definite rule can be established to help you determine whether a paragraph is adequately developed. A paragraph must be as long as it needs to be, but that is not saying much. Judgments about adequate development must always be made in relation to *particular* paragraphs. Although we cannot specify in the abstract[1] how many sentences a paragraph must have to be adequately developed, we can say that **usually—but only usually—the topic of a paragraph cannot be adequately developed with only one or two sentences.** Most readers would sense that the following two-sentence paragraph, for instance, was not adequately developed:

> There are several questions we must ask when we are buying a new or a used car. Are we getting true value for our money?

Readers readily sense the inadequacy[2] of development here because the first sentence mentions "several questions," and the second sentence poses only *one* question. What are some of the other questions that must be asked?

Even where the inadequacy of development is not as obvious as it was in the paragraph quoted above, most readers can tell when a paragraph does not give them all that they expected or all that they needed to know. They may not be able to specify what is missing; nevertheless, they are quite sure that they have been "cheated" by the skimpy paragraph. Although some paragraphs give readers "too much"

---

[1] As considered theoretically or apart from a real example. [2] The quality of being not adequate or enough; insufficient.

Expressing What You Have Put Together

or, at least, more than is needed, the more common fault is that paragraphs give readers "too little."

Although no definite rules can be laid down about the adequate development of paragraphs, two practical bits of advice can be given:

☐ **Look carefully at all one-sentence, two-sentence, and even three-sentence paragraphs that you find in your paper.** (Do those paragraphs say all that you could say or all that you *should* say on the topic of the paragraph?) **Most of the time you will find that those thin paragraphs need to be fleshed out with a few more sentences.**

☐ **Use the "topic sentence" of your paragraph as a gauge to test whether the paragraph you wrote is adequately developed. This is the commitment-and-response test.** (What did the topic sentence of your paragraph *commit* you to do? Do the other sentences in the paragraph totally or at least *sufficiently* deliver on that commitment?)

Finally, remember that there are some legitimate[1] uses of one- and two-sentence paragraphs:

1 For dialogue: a new paragraph must be started each time the speaker changes, even if the speaker utters only one sentence or a fragment[2] of a sentence or only a single word.

2 For emphasis: an important idea can be given great prominence[3] by being set off in a paragraph by itself. A listing of important points, for instance, might be laid out in a sequence of one-sentence paragraphs.

---

[1] Proper; normal; permissible. [2] A part broken off and so incomplete. [3] The quality or state of being plainly noticeable or conspicuous.

3 For transition: a one- or two-sentence paragraph can sometimes be used effectively to signal the shift from one section of a paper to the next section—e.g. "Now let us consider the disadvantages of this system."

4 For newspaper copy: journalists are encouraged to break up their copy into one- and two-sentence paragraphs so that their paragraphs won't appear to be so formidably[1] dense when they are printed in the narrow columns of the newspaper.

●
Topic sentences

A topic sentence is a sentence that indicates, in a general way, what idea or thesis or subject the paragraph is dealing with. A recent study of paragraphs from some of the nation's most famous newspapers and magazines revealed that professional writers frequently do not include in their paragraphs a sentence that could be regarded as the topic sentence. The absence of a topic sentence, however, does not mean that their paragraphs do not have a central *idea* or *thesis;* it simply means that sometimes writers do not explicitly[2] indicate what the central idea or thesis is but instead allow the reader to infer[3] the topic of the paragraph. In fact, paragraphs of narrative prose and of descriptive prose frequently do *not* have topic sentences.

Nevertheless, a close study of published prose also reveals that many paragraphs *do* have a topic sentence, and **beginning writers should include a topic sentence somewhere in their paragraphs.** The presence of a topic sentence can

---

[1] Alarmingly; in a way to cause fear.　[2] Clearly and precisely.　[3] To derive as a conclusion from facts or statements; to surmise.

Expressing What You Have Put Together

serve as a guideline to ensure the unity, coherence, and adequate development of the paragraph by suggesting to the writer how that unit of the paper might be developed.

Although experienced writers probably do not consciously formulate a topic sentence and then go on to develop it, beginners should try to do so. After a while, the formulation and development of topic sentences will become as instinctive[1] for them as for experienced writers. As models for the formulation of topic sentences, here are some randomly selected from paragraphs published in 1975:

1. Aerosols, in fact, may have a slight edge over other hazards when it comes to danger potential.
2. For some time now, the Boy Scouts have been going to considerable lengths to modernize their image.
3. The toy business has been expanding despite the decline in the birthrate.
4. Social Security is not a pension plan; it is an income-transfer plan.
5. More than most businesses, florist shops are constantly adjusting to new—and unusual—market conditions.
6. In contrast with what I saw years ago, I was struck by the earnest, stolid[2] attitude of the ordinary people on the streets and in the restaurants and department stores of Peking.
7. The field of astronomy is in the midst of what is often called its "golden age."
8. The first version provides two criteria that the critic may use in determining whether a given work justly belongs to science or to literature.

---

[1] Taking place below the conscious level; "natural." [2] Not easily excited; showing little or no emotion.

9 Unlike many modern stories for children, fairy tales present evil as being no less omnipresent[1] than virtue.

10 If there is any one major question posed by the CIA's behavior in Laos and elsewhere, it is that the CIA may have reached the point at which it has itself become a threat to our national security.

See the section on Methods of Development below for suggestions about how some of these topic sentences might be developed.

Although topic sentences theoretically can—and actually do—occur anywhere in the paragraph, *they most often occur first, if they occur at all.* **It will definitely be helpful to you to adopt the practice of beginning most of your paragraphs with the topic sentence.** Placed in that initial position, it will trigger the development and suggest the direction that the development must take.

Here is a summary of the points made about topic sentences:

☐ **Not all paragraphs have a clear-cut topic sentence; sometimes the topic of a paragraph is *implied* rather than stated.**

☐ **However, many paragraphs do have an explicit topic sentence.**

☐ **You should make it a practice consciously to formulate a topic sentence for your paragraphs.**

☐ **Although the topic sentence can occur anywhere in the paragraph—the first sentence, the last sentence, or somewhere in the middle—you should begin most of your paragraphs with the topic sentence.**

---

[1] Present everywhere at the same time.

Expressing What You Have Put Together

Methods of development

Just as experienced writers probably do not *consciously* formulate a topic sentence for their paragraphs, they also probably do not *consciously* decide how they will develop their paragraphs. Most professional writers just put down one sentence after the other, without any preconceived[1] plan, but because of frequent practice in writing, their paragraphs are usually unified, coherent, and adequately developed. And although they may not have paused to ask themselves *how* they would develop a particular paragraph, their method of development seems to be not only appropriate[2] but inevitable.[3]

But when you closely study the paragraphs of published prose, you discover that the paragraphs *were* developed by one or another of the methods recommended in Chapter 2 for discovering something to say about a subject. There are only a limited number of ways in which the human mind operates. So when you face the task of writing a sentence or a paragraph or a whole essay, you go about it in one or another of these set ways.

Here is a list of the common ways in which writers develop their paragraphs—develop, that is, the implied central idea or the clearly stated topic sentence.

☐ **They present examples or illustrations of what they are discussing.**

☐ **They cite data[4]—facts, statistics, evidence, details, precedents—that corroborate[5] or confirm what they are discussing.**

[1]Conceived beforehand. [2]Proper; fit; suitable. [3]Bound to be or happen; unavoidable. [4]Facts. [5]Support with evidence; confirm.

- [ ] They quote, paraphrase, or summarize the testimony of others about what they are discussing.

- [ ] They relate[1] an anecdote[2] that has some bearing on what they are discussing.

- [ ] They define terms connected with what they are discussing.

- [ ] They compare or contrast what they are discussing with something else—usually something familiar to the readers—and point out similarities or differences.

- [ ] They explore the causes or reasons for the phenomenon or situation they are discussing.

- [ ] They point out the effects or consequences of the phenomenon or situation they are discussing.

- [ ] They explain how something operates.

- [ ] They describe the person, place, or thing they are discussing.

A consideration of the topic sentence will often suggest not only the direction that the paragraph might take but also one or more ways to develop the paragraph. Let us look at some of the topic sentences listed on p. (126) and see how they might suggest possible lines of development:

[1]Give an account of; tell.   [2]A brief story of a striking or interesting happening or event.

Expressing What You Have Put Together

Aerosols, in fact, may have a slight edge over other hazards when it comes to danger potential.
Possible lines of development:

1 Cite some examples of the hazards of aerosol-spray cans.
2 Compare aerosol-spray cans with other common household hazards and show how aerosols are potentially more dangerous.

Social Security is not a pension plan; it is an income-transfer plan.
Possible lines of development:

1 Define *pension plan* and *income-transfer plan*.
2 Compare the Social Security system with a regular pension plan and show how it differs.

The toy business has been expanding despite the decline in the birthrate.
Possible lines of development:

1 Cite some statistics to confirm the decline in the birthrate and the increasing sales of toys.
2 Explore the causes or reasons for the expansion of the toy business despite the declining birthrate.

In contrast with what I saw years ago, I was struck by the earnest, stolid attitude of the ordinary people on the streets and in the restaurants and department stores of Peking.

Possible lines of development:

1 Describe the current behavior of the Chinese people observed in public places in Peking.

2 Contrast their current behavior with their behavior several years ago.

For some time now, the Boy Scouts have been going to considerable lengths to modernize their image.

Possible lines of development:

1 Describe the dress and the demeanor[1] of the "new" Boy Scouts.

2 Quote some comments about the changing image of the Boy Scouts.

The first version provides two criteria which the critic may use in determining whether a given work justly belongs to science or to literature.

Possible lines of development:

1 Specify the two criteria and show how they operate to discriminate types of literary texts.

2 Point out the beneficial effects of adopting this set of criteria.

---

[1] Conduct; manner of comporting oneself with others.

Expressing What You Have Put Together

As you can see from these examples, careful consideration of the topic sentence can suggest not only *what* you are obliged to do in the paragraph but also *how* you might go about doing what you have to do. This is another instance of the commitment-and-response approach. **Discover what your topic sentence commits you to do, and then make a decision about the kind of response that will best fulfill your commitment.**

One of the benefits of the copy exercise recommended earlier in this chapter is that it reveals how professional writers structure and develop their paragraphs. Among other things, you can learn how to pick out the topic sentence—if the paragraph has one—and see the variety of positions that the topic sentence can occupy in a paragraph; finally, you can become acquainted with the variety of ways of developing topic sentences. From observations based on copying, you discover the *choices* of means available for structuring and developing paragraphs. Discovery of the variety of ways of writing paragraphs may eventually make this task less of a mechanical exercise and more of an art. Then you will have acquired a *style.*

Chapter 6
Putting It All Together

Having reviewed the several steps involved in the writing process, you will now see what it is like to run through the whole sequence, from original assignment to final product, and see how all our theory works out in practice. By taking an assignment and running it through the stages of

1 **settling on a subject**
2 **deciding on a thesis**
3 **discovering something to say on the subject**
4 **selecting from what you have found**
5 **organizing what you have selected**
6 **writing the first draft**
7 **revising the first draft**
8 **writing the final draft**

you will realize the series of *choices* you have to make at every stage. In facing and making those choices, you will become aware, in a concrete way, of what the art of rhetoric is all about.

Putting It All Together

Assignment

As you saw in Chapter 2, most of the time when you have to write something, you do so in response to an assignment. Only established writers—and mainly those who write poetry, fiction, or drama—initiate[1] their own writing projects. Your assignment to write something will usually designate[2] the general subject and the length of the paper. You may be allowed to decide *what aspect* of the general subject to treat and *how to treat it.*

Let us suppose that in a sociology class you are assigned to review a continuing series on television and to write a 1200–1500–word paper on the social implications[3] of that series. There is the general assignment: the subject that you are to deal with and the length of the paper are set for you. What is left to your decision is the particular series that you will review and write about—and of course dozens of subsequent[4] decisions.

From among the continuing TV series, you can make a choice of talk shows, game shows, news broadcasts, situation comedies,[5] detective dramas, etc. About any one of those, you might be able to write an interesting and significant paper. But recently, you have become hooked on watching some of the daytime soap operas. Almost despite yourself, you, like millions of other viewers, have been fascinated by these slow-paced, crisis-packed domestic dramas. And yet you think you can still be somewhat objective in evaluating the social significance of these sometimes tawdry[6]

[1] Set into motion; start; begin. [2] Indicate; specify. [3] Those things that are involved or implied in something else. [4] Following after or later. [5] Weekly TV comedies involving the same characters in new (mis)adventures. [6] Cheap and gaudy in appearance and quality.

tales of American life. So you make your first decision: you are going to review and write about daytime soap operas.

●
Settling on a subject

Having decided on the particular kind of television series to write about, you now have to make some further decisions that will narrow your subject to manageable size. You have only 1200–1500 words in which to treat your subject. Having to put 1200–1500 words together might chill you at first, but when you stop to think about it, an allotment[1] of 1200–1500 words really doesn't give you very much room in which to work—somewhere between four and five double-spaced typed pages. So you conclude[2] that while you may be able to

[1] A share; something portioned out. [2] Decide; judge.

Putting It All Together

say something in general about soap operas, you will have to concentrate on a *single* soap opera, preferably one that is fairly representative.

You are faced then with another decision: *which* soap opera to focus on. From the three or four that you have regularly watched, you decide to concentrate on *Days of Our Lives,* an hour-long NBC soap opera that deals, in a rather daring way, with some of the controversial social issues of the day. You realize that there is something arbitrary about that choice, because you could just as easily write about *All My Children* or *As the World Turns.* But you make this choice anyway, perhaps for the simple reason that *Days of Our Lives* is the soap opera that most captures your interest.

Deciding on a thesis

You have chosen a particular soap opera for your paper, and yet you feel that you still have some further narrowing to do if you are to treat your subject adequately in 1200–1500 words. There are many *aspects* of this soap opera that you could deal with—the kinds of characters that figure in the drama, the quality of the acting, the pace[1] of the show, the kinds of social issues dealt with. Which of these—or others—will you carve out of the larger subject to deal with?

You sense that you might be better able to make that decision if you could formulate a *thesis* for your paper. Sometimes, writers are not able to formulate a thesis until they have explored the subject. But you are familiar enough now with soap operas in general, and with *Days of Our Lives* in particular, to formulate at least a *tentative* thesis. You might

[1] Rate of movement or progress.

decide later to modify or refine or even change it but you are prepared at this point to attempt a thesis—one that might help you decide which aspect of *Days of Our Lives* to treat in 1200–1500 words.

You know that **a thesis should be formulated in a single declarative sentence**—basically, a sentence in which something about the subject is asserted[1] or denied, a sentence like "War is hell" or "An increase in taxes will not by itself solve the problem of welfare."

What thesis sentence could you formulate about soap operas in general or about *Days of Ours Lives* in particular? Your sociology teacher specified[2] that your paper should deal with the *social* implications of some television series. That specification considerably narrows the range of your choices. The specified length of the paper also sets some limits for the choice of a thesis. Some theses that you can think of in connection with this soap opera would need at least 10,000 words for adequate treatment.

With those considerations in mind, you make a stab at[3] formulating a thesis sentence. What has particularly intrigued you as you watched *Days of Our Lives* from day to day is the way in which men and women experience seemingly endless conflicts based on blind sexual desire. On the surface, the conflicts revolve around such situations as a crumbling marriage, an interracial[4] romance, a miscarriage,[5] someone's wavering faith, a decision about artificial insemination.[6] But at the root of most of these situations, one can detect impetuous[7] sexual motivation.[8] One could view this drama as a good example of the old wisdom that when men and women don't come together out of love and respect for each other,

---

[1]Stated; declared; affirmed.   [2]Stated definitely; indicated firmly.   [3]Make a brief or quick attempt at.   [4]Of or for members of different races.   [5]Giving birth before the fetus can survive on its own.   [6]Introduction of semen into the genital tract (of a female).   [7]Acting with sudden, often rash, energy.   [8]A force, idea, or reason that makes someone act.

Putting It All Together

they get burned. This last sentence has the air and ingredients of a thesis sentence. You decide on it as the tentative thesis for your paper, which you formulate in these terms:

Soap operas, like *Days of Our Lives,* show that sex without genuine love, mutual respect, and firm commitment[1] leads to frustration,[2] exploitation,[3] and unhappiness.

That thesis sentence may later have to be rephrased,[4] but at this point it can at least give a tighter focus[5] to your subject. For one thing, it will guide you in selecting those features, incidents, and situations that are pertinent to the aspect that you have decided to write about.

●
Discovering something to say: research

Having settled on a narrowed subject and on a thesis, you are faced now with the task of discovering something to say. Your thesis commits you to presenting some evidence that soap operas in general and *Days of Our Lives* in particular demonstrate the misfortunes that arise when unbridled[6] passions rule the mind. *The chief source of material to develop that thesis will be some firsthand[7] research.* This means watching several of the shows and taking notes about episodes[8] that manifest[9] the unbridled sexual motivations of the characters. Of course, you have watched several of the shows already, and you remember several previous episodes

---

[1] The action of committing oneself to; to adhere faithfully and actively. [2] The act of defeating or blocking a wish or an endeavor. [3] Unfair use for one's own advantage. [4] Worded or phrased again. [5] Adjustment of view for the sake of clarity. [6] Unrestrained. [7] Relating directly to the original source or origin. [8] Self-contained units of action in dramas or stories. [9] Make evident; display.

that will be pertinent to your thesis. Watching a few additional shows will provide you with some more material and, more importantly, may confirm the continuing sexual orientation[1] of the dramatic conflicts.

To provide a context for your discussion, you might want to give your readers some background information about soap operas in general and about *Days of Our Lives* in particular. To gather that kind of information, you will have to do some outside reading, but not much, because background information will be only a small part of your 1200–1500-word paper. You might be able to get by with reading only one or two authoritative[2] articles.

A good reference source for finding magazine articles is the *Reader's Guide to Periodical Literature,* which you can find in the reference room of the library. Consulting some recent installments[3] of this reference work, you discover, under the heading "Television, Daytime," that *Time* magazine in its January 12, 1975 issue did a cover story on soap operas, entitled "Sex and Suffering in the Afternoon." You also discover an article by Edith Efron in the March 13, 1965 issue of *TV Guide;* its title, "The Soaps—Anything but 99 44/100 Percent Pure," suggests that it might provide some relevant material for your paper. You recall too that the anthology[4] of essays you used in high school and still have in your library contained a classic article that James Thurber wrote on radio soap operas in 1948 for the *New Yorker* magazine. You also learn from the *Reader's Guide* that there are a number of gossipy fan-magazines about soap operas, like *Daytime TV* and *Afternoon TV Stars* and that there are new periodicals[5] like *Daytime Serial Newsletter* and *Soap Opera Digest,* which provide readers with plot outlines of

[1] The state or condition of being arranged in a certain position or way. [2] Deriving from a competent authority; entitled to acceptance. [3] Parts presented or added at different times. [4] A collection of literary pieces. [5] Publications that come out at regular periods.

Putting It All Together

recent soap-opera shows. Since you won't be able to spend much time in your paper on background material, these three or four articles may supply you with all the information you will need.

Finding something to say: recall

To orient your readers to the particular soap opera of your choice, you can rely mainly on your memory of the show to supply you with some data. (Where your memory does not supply you with the needed information about the show, you can probably get that information from the magazine articles.) In stimulating[1] your memory to recover this kind of background information about the show, you might make use of the journalistic formula of *who, what, when, where, how,* and *why* or Kenneth Burke's pentad of *act, agent, agency, scene,* and *purpose.* The classical topic of *definition* suggests that you ought to provide your readers with a definition of the soap opera. Your definition will be based on conclusions drawn from your experience with soap operas. Since your thesis commits you to demonstrating that there seems to be some connection between the characters' actions and their sexual drives, the classical topics of *cause-and-effect* or *antecedent-consequence* may be relevant in your search for something to say about your subject. The topic of *testimony* should also be useful. It would certainly strengthen your case if you could find some quotations by experts—psychologists, for instance—confirming your thesis. But since you already know much about your subject, perhaps the best system to

---

[1] Making active; arousing.

use in this case would be brainstorming, reinforced perhaps by some quiet meditation on the subject.

At least you now know how to gather something to say on your subject: you must do some brainstorming and meditating; you must do some reading; you must make use of those systems (the journalistic formula, the Burkeian pentad, or the classical topics) most likely to yield some material; and you must watch, and take notes on, some of the episodes of *Days of Our Lives.*

Your subject "notebook"

Let us suppose that over a week's time you do all of the above things and that you end up with a collection of random notes like the following:

Some notes about soap operas in general

(most of these from the *Time* article of January 12, 1975)

More than 20 million Americans watch daytime serials.

Mainly watched by housewives, senior citizens, college students, and the unemployed.

14 soap operas now on the networks.

More revenue from daytime serials than from some prime-time[1] evening shows. (*Time* revealed that an evening show like *Kojak* costs $250,000 to produce but brings in ad[2] revenue of only $200,000, but while it costs NBC $170,000 to produce five days of *Days of Our Lives,* those five showings bring in $600,000 of ad revenue.)

[1] In television, the time from 8 P.M. to 11 P.M., during which the audiences are the largest, and television advertising rates the highest, of the entire day. [2] Abbreviated form of *advertisement.*

Putting It All Together

A few of the more popular shows have been expanded from the usual half-hour to an hour.

In Sept. 1975, *Love of Life* celebrated its 24th anniversary on network TV. *Search for Tomorrow,* the oldest TV soap, has been running for over 25 years.

As the World Turns is the top-rated soap. Ten million viewers every day.

The major script[1]-writers earn annual[2] salaries ranging from $100,000 to $250,000.

Irna Philips, a writer of soap operas for over 40 years, died in 1973 at the age of 70. Three of the four shows she originated[3]—*Days of Our Lives, As the World Turns, Another World*—are the three top-rated shows on daytime TV.

Agnes Nixon is another successful soap-opera writer. Besides writing for most of the soaps, she has created two of her own shows—*One Life to Live* and *All My Children.*

Several magazines about soap-opera personalities are published. A magazine like *Daytime TV* has a circulation[4] in excess of[5] 380,000.

Several prominent[6] people watch soap operas: Supreme Court Justice Thurgood Marshall watches *Days of Our Lives;* entertainer Sammy Davis, Jr. watches *Love of Life;* former governor John Connally and artist Andy Warhol watch *As the World Turns;* novelist Dan Wakefield and literary[7] critic Leslie Fiedler watch *All My Children.*

Soap operas becoming very popular with college students. *Time* magazine reports, "At Princeton, something like a quarter of the student body drops everything to watch *The Young and the Restless* every afternoon."

---

[1] The lines to be recited in plays, radio programs, and television programs. [2] Covering the period of a year. [3] Caused to arise or begin; initiated. [4] The number of copies sold over a given period. [5] That exceeds; that is more than. [6] Readily noticeable; distinguished; famous. [7] Relating to literature.

● Your Subject "Notebook"

Some data about Days of Our Lives

Produced by NBC. #3 in the Nielsen ratings. Recently expanded to an hour-long show.

Portrays[1] the drama in the lives of four generations of the Horton family.

William J. Bell writes the 12-month outline for *DOL*. Patricia Falken-Smith is the head writer.

The show is filmed in Los Angeles. More than 350 actresses recently showed up for an audition[2] for a new part.

Edward Mallory has played the part of Dr. Bill Horton for over ten years.

Susan Seaforth has played the trouble-making Julie Anderson for over seven years. In 1974, Susan married Bill Hayes, who plays Doug Williams, a man who was married to Julie's mother on the show.

More than 26 actors or actresses involved in the show.

Names of some of the characters in Days of Our Lives

Don Craig	Julie Anderson
Robert LeClare	Doug Williams
Alice Horton	Dr. Bill Horton
Laura Horton	Marty Hanson (formerly
Maggie Hanson	Mickey Horton)
Mark Anderson	Michael Horton
Matt Anderson	Phyllis Anderson
Susan Peters	Dr. Greg Peters
Eric Peters	Dr. Neil Curtis
Amanda Howard	Trish Clayton

---

[1] Shows as in a picture.   [2] A trial performance to test a performer's abilities.

Putting It All Together

Some episodes with overtones of sexual conflict that have been portrayed on DOL

Julie Anderson, who has been married twice, is continually frustrated in her love for Doug Williams, her deceased[1] mother's husband.

Julie's son David lives with the Grants, a struggling black family, and is falling in love with their daughter Valerie. David's abandoned[2] girl Brooke tried to commit suicide after she had had an abortion to get rid of David's child.

Johnny Couts got Rebecca pregnant and left for Paris. Rebecca refuses to have an abortion.

Dr. Neil Curtis, married to Phyllis Anderson, is involved in an affair with one of his patients, Amanda Howard, a widow. Dr. Greg Peters, who knows about the affair, wants to marry Amanda.

A constant round of marital infidelities,[3] seductions, fornications,[4] divorces, remarriages, pregnancies, abortions, torrid[5] embraces, secret rendezvous,[6] rivalries, intrigues,[7] broken homes.

Some ideas generated by the use of one or other of the discovery systems

Definition: Soap operas are serial dramatizations of domestic[8] conflicts between married and unmarried men and women. Soap operas derive their name from the fact that in the early days most of them were sponsored by manufacturers of soaps and detergents.[9]

---

[1] Dead. [2] Given up; deserted. [3] Disloyalties; in marriage, acts of adultery. [4] Sex between persons other than husband and wife. [5] Hot; passionate. [6] Meetings at designated places. [7] Secret schemes; secret love affairs. [8] Relating to the household or the family. [9] Cleansing agents, especially those different from soap.

Some characteristics of soap operas: The focal characters are usually women, young or middle-aged. Young or middle-aged men, usually of the professional class (doctors, lawyers) also figure in these dramas, often as the complicating factors in the story. But audiences are more interested in what happens to the women.

The action of the plots is slow-paced and protracted. A simple incident is often strung out over several days. Between Monday and Friday of any week, the plot may have advanced very little.

Five or six plots, involving different characters, are often interwoven in a single show. The scenes tend to be short, and shifts are made from scene to scene abruptly.

Complications are constantly and often artificially introduced into the stories. A show usually ends on a threatening note, and the Friday show usually ends with a "cliff-hanger"[1] in order to entice the audience to tune in on Monday after the long weekend.

Comparison with other kinds of popular dramatizations, like westerns, detective stories, situation comedies: Soap operas are *like* these other forms in that they tend to be melodramatic. Melodramas[2] are sensational, not very believable, have superficial[3] characters, and are often very sentimental.[4] They *differ* from the other forms mainly in the kinds of incidents and characters portrayed. Westerns deal mainly with physical conflicts between "good guys" and "bad guys." Detective stories deal with the solving of a crime and the catching of the criminals. Situation comedies are *like* soap operas in that they deal with the day-to-day conflicts in family life, but they *differ* in that the conflicts are exploited for comedy rather than for the disruptive[5] effect on the family.

[1]Suspenseful ending of an installment of an adventure serial or other drama. [2]Dramas with sensational incidents and strong appeals to the emotions. [3]Of the surface only; shallow. [4]Appealing to sentiment; expressing tender feelings and emotions; determined by feeling rather than reason. [5]Tending to break apart or throw into disorder.

Putting It All Together

Cause-and-effect (or antecedent-consequence): Most of the conflicts in the lives of the characters are produced by something that has a sexual base. There is a constant round of marriages, affairs, remarriages, adulteries,[1] pregnancies, abortions.

Serious illnesses and accidents are frequently complicating factors in the lives of the characters. Frequently these are artificial means of breaking deadlocked[2] plots. The death or terminal[3] illness of some character often frees another character to pursue a romantic interest. A favorite such device is amnesia,[4] often the result of a fall.

Reasons (cause-and-effect) for the appeal of these melodramas

Vicarious[5] sexual excitement.

Relief from the monotony of the audience's humdrum[6] lives.

Audience identification: sometimes the situations are so much like the experiences of the TV audience that the viewers can get pleasure or comfort from watching others cope[7] with similar problems. Sometimes the situations are so different that viewers can vicariously enjoy experiences that they never had themselves but that they are curious about.

Feelings of smugness or superiority in the audience.

Feelings of satisfaction from seeing a nasty character get put down. Feelings of satisfaction from seeing a sympathetic character get a well-deserved reward.

The natural human appetite for stories.

[1] Sexual unfaithfulness of a married person. [2] Brought to a complete stop or standstill. [3] Forming an end or a limit. [4] Abnormal loss of memory. [5] Experienced through sympathetic association with another's condition or activity. [6] Dull; monotonous. [7] Deal successfully.

● Your Subject "Notebook"

Examples from a recent week of DOL incidents that have a troubled sexual basis

Mickey Horton (renamed Marty Hanson after his amnesia) holds his brother Dr. Bill Horton at gunpoint. "Did you have an affair with Laura (Mickey's former wife)?" he asks. "No," says Bill. "Then tell me how she conceived your child."

Trish Clayton wants to go to Phoenix and find the man who is her father and reveal to him that she is his child.

Having learned indirectly that Rebecca is pregnant with his child, Johnny Couts comes back from Paris to confront her with the question of what she is going to do about the child she is carrying.

Scenes between David Anderson and his former girl friend in which they angrily discuss the abortion Brooke had to get rid of David's child.

Pertinent quotations from articles and from authorities

Edith Efron, "The Soaps—Anything but 99 44/100 Percent Pure," *TV Guide,* March 13, 1965.

"Folks squawking about cheap nighttime sex should hearken[1] to the sickly sexuality of daytime soap opera. *Love of Life* details frank affairs between married women and men; *Search for Tomorrow* has a single girl in an affair with a married man, result: pregnancy; *The Secret Storm* has another single girl expecting a married man's child."

"The fundamental theme of soap operas is the male-female relationship."

[1] Give attention; listen.

Putting It All Together

"The act of searching for a partner goes on constantly in the world of soap opera. . . . This all-consuming, single-minded search for a mate is an absolute good in the soap-opera syndrome. Morality—and domestic conflict—emerge from how the search is conducted. Accordingly, there is sex as approached by good people, and sex as it is approached by villains."

Frank Dodge, producer of *Search for Tomorrow:* "These shows are a recognition of existing emotions and problems. It's not collusion[1] but a logical coincidence that adultery, illegitimate[2] children, and abortions are appearing on many shows. If you read the papers about what's going on in the suburbs—well, it's more startling than what's shown on the air." (quoted in the Efron article)

Dr. Harold Greenwald, of the National Psychological Association for Psychoanalysis and the supervising psychologist of the Community Guidance Service in New York: "They're realistic. . . . They're reflecting the changes taking place in our society. There are fewer taboos.[3] The age of sexual activity in the middle classes has dropped, and it has increased in frequency. There is more infidelity. These plays reflect these problems." (quoted in Efron)

Betty Friedan, author of *The Feminine Mystique:* "The image of woman that emerges in these soap operas is precisely what I've called 'The Feminine Mystique.' The women are childish and dependent; the men are degraded[4] because they relate to women who are childish and dependent; and the view of sex that emerges is sick." (quoted in Efron)

---

[1] Secret agreement for purposes of trickery or deceit. [2] Born of parents not married to each other. [3] Prohibitions imposed by unwritten social codes. [4] Reduced or lowered in character, rank, or reputation.

● Your Subject "Notebook"

Edith Efron: "On the basis of these comments, one can certainly conclude that all this sex-based human wretchedness[1] is on the air because it exists in society. And the producers' claims that this is dramatic 'realism' appear to have some validity."[2]

James Thurber, "Ivorytown, Rinsoville, Anacinburg, and Crisco Corners," *The New Yorker,* copyright 1948 (reprinted in *Writing Prose: Techniques and Purposes,* ed. Thomas S. Kane and Leonard J. Peters, 2nd edition (New York: Oxford University Press, 1964), pp. 445–456.

"Thus, a soap opera is an endless sequence of narratives whose only cohesive[3] element is the eternal presence of its bedevilled[4] and beleaguered[5] principal characters."

"Time in a soap opera is now an amazing technique of slow motion. It took one male character in a soap opera three days to get an answer to the simple question 'Where have you been?' If, in *When a Girl Marries,* you missed an automobile accident that occurred on a Monday broadcast, you could pick it up the following Thursday and find the leading woman character still unconscious and her husband still moaning over her beside the wrecked car."

"As for the sexual aspect of daytime morality, a man who had a lot to do with serials in the nineteen-thirties assures me that at that time there were 'hot clinches'[6] burning up and down the daytime dial . . . there has been a profound cooling off, for my persistent[7] eavesdropping[8] has detected nothing but coy[9] and impregnable chastity[10] in the good women."

"'Emotional understanding,' a term I have heard on serials several times, seems to be the official circumlocution[11] for the awful word 'sex.'"

[1] Misery; distress; contemptibility. [2] Foundation in truth or fact. [3] Sticking together.
[4] Tormented. [5] Besieged; harassed. [6] Passionate embraces. [7] Going on, continuing, despite difficulties. [8] Listening secretly. [9] Bashful; shy. [10] Sexual purity. [11] A roundabout way of saying something.

Putting It All Together

●

Selecting and arranging your material

You now have material for your paper, but obviously you have more than you can use. You will have to do some *selecting,* and after you have selected the material, you will have to decide how you are going to *organize* it. Recall from Chapter 4 that what can help you in making the selection is consideration of such things as the specified *length* of the paper, the *occasion* and *purpose* of your paper, the *audience* for the paper, and, above all, the *thesis* of the paper.

The specified length of the paper will be a major factor in the selection process. In your case, you have to work within 1200–1500 words—a relatively short paper—and the four or five pages will quickly fill up. You will have to tightly control the material you incorporate into your paper.

☐ **The occasion of the paper is an assignment for a sociology class.**

☐ **The purpose of the paper is to point out the social implications of some continuing show on television.**

☐ **The audience for the paper will be your sociology teacher, but your teacher may ask you to show or read your paper to your classmates.**

These last three considerations will help you somewhat in deciding which material to select. They will help you at least on the basis of whether the material fits the assignment or the purpose or the interests of your audience.

However, the consideration that will be *most* helpful in the selection process is the thesis you have decided on for your paper: *Soap operas like* Days of Our Lives, *show*

that sex without genuine love, mutual respect, and firm com-
mitment leads to frustration, exploitation, and unhappiness.
Since you have decided to demonstrate that thesis by citing
examples from a single, typical soap opera,

1 You will concentrate on the material having to do with the
   soap opera *Days of Our Lives,*
2 You will concentrate on the material connected with that
   show that best exemplifies the impetuous sexual motivation of the characters' actions.

In the preliminary[1] part of your paper, you will have to say
something about soap operas *in general,* just to provide a
context for the more particular discussion. So you will be able
to use *some* of the material that doesn't deal specifically with
Days of Our Lives or with the sex-conflict basis of the actions
of the show. How much of this *general* material you will be
able to use will be dictated mainly by the limitations on the
length of your paper.

So the next decision you have to make is how much of
your paper will be devoted to preliminary, background material about soap operas. And with that decision, you are into
the next stage—the stage in which you make decisions about
the organization of your paper. At this point, any decisions
you make about organization must involve guesswork and
cannot be final; still, you make these rough estimates:[2]

$1\frac{1}{2}$ pages—introduction (background information
about soap operas in gen-
eral and *DOL* in particular)

2 pages—development of your thesis

1 page—conclusion (summary remarks about the social
implications of soap operas)

[1] Leading up to the main business; preparatory. [2] Approximate calculations based
on probabilities.

Putting It All Together

You decide that your next step will be to make some rough notes of what will go into each of these three sections and of the order in which you will take up the various points. Later, you may be able to turn these rough notes into a formal outline or a block outline. In making these rough notes, you will be accomplishing two things: (1) selecting from your available material in the light of earlier considerations of length, occasion, purpose, audience, and thesis; (2) organizing—at least tentatively—what you select. Since you already have a *full* set of notes, you decide that here you will jot down *very brief* notes that can refer you to the fuller set.

$1\frac{1}{2}$ pages—introduction and general background information

Audience of 20 million.

Mainly housewives, senior citizens, unemployed men, students.

Prominent people who watch: Thurgood Marshall, Sammy Davis, Jr., John Connally, Andy Warhol, Dan Wakefield, Leslie Fiedler. Students at Princeton.

Extremely lucrative.[1] *Kojak* $250,000 to produce, only $200,000 in ad revenue. *DOL* $170,000 to produce five shows, $600,000 in ad revenue.

Salaries of script writers—$100,000 to $250,000. Salaries for performers—$35,000.

Magazine side-industry. Circulation of 380,000.

Viewer-appeal: satisfies appetite for stories, escape, audience identification, vicarious sexual titillation.[2]

Sexual implications of soap operas, using *DOL* as typical example, will be pursued.

[1] Profitable. [2] Pleasing excitement.

● Selecting and Arranging Your Material

Soap operas, like *Days of Our Lives,* show that sex without genuine love, mutual respect, and firm commitment leads to frustration, exploitation, and unhappiness.

2 pages—body of paper (development of thesis)

General information about DOL: 1 hour, produced by NBC, 3rd in ratings, more than 26 actors and actresses.

Deals with the lives of four generations of Hortons and associated people. Treats some bold themes very openly.

Julie Anderson's frustrated love for Doug Williams, her deceased mother's husband.

Doug Williams and the artificial-insemination program.

Julie's son David goes to live with a black family, falls in love with their daughter Valerie.

David's abandoned girl friend Brooke. Her abortion and suicide attempt.

Johnny Couts gets Rebecca pregnant and goes off to Paris. Rebecca won't get abortion.

Dr. Neil Curtis, married to Phyllis Anderson, engaged in affair with wealthy, attractive widow[1] Amanda Howard. Dr. Greg Peters in love with her.

Central incident from recent week of *DOL:* main event of the week, Marty Hanson threatening to shoot his brother Dr. Bill Horton because suspects him of having had affair with his former wife Laura.

Associated and interwoven incidents: Johnny Couts back from Paris, has angry scenes with Rebecca about her pregnancy. Anguished scenes between David and

---

[1] A woman whose husband is dead and who has not married again.

Putting It All Together

his former girl friend Brooke. Trish Clayton wants to go off to Phoenix to find her father, reveal that she is his child. Flashes of brewing[1] affair between Dr. Neil Curtis and Amanda Howard.

1 page—conclusion (summary remarks about general social implications of all this display of sexual motivation).

Edith Efron quote about "searching for a partner" and "domestic conflict."

Dr. Harold Greenwald quote about soap operas as reflections of morals of society.

Dr. William Menaker quote about changing morals of society.

Frank Dodge quote about *why* shows are displaying sex-based conflicts.

Betty Friedan quote about image of women on soap operas.

James Thurber quote about how moral[2] soap operas were in the 1940s.

Reaffirm[3] the thesis of the paper.

Making an outline

Now that you have a set of rough notes recorded in some kind of order and distributed according to the three main divisions of your paper—introduction, body, and conclu-

[1] In process of mixing, concocting, etc. [2] Conforming to a standard of right behavior. [3] To repeat a firm statement.

sion—you decide to sharpen this arrangement of parts by making a more formal outline. Of the kinds of outlines discussed in Chapter 4, the one that you find it easiest to work with is the *paragraph outline,* arranged in blocks. So you decide to arrange your selected material in a sequence of blocked paragraphs, with some labeling that will indicate to you what is covered in each paragraph. Your block outline appears in Figure 6.1.

●
Writing the first draft

With your outline drawn up, you now have a map to follow. **It is important that you not feel locked in by the outline,** no matter how good it is. After you begin writing, you may discover an unexpected detour that you have to take or a shortcut that did not appear on your map. **You must remain flexible at all stages of the writing process.** Your outline points you only in the general direction that you want to go and marks off only the main stages on the way. So if some convenient alternative shows up after you start out, you will be faced with another choice: whether to take that alternative or stick to the route you plotted in your outline.

Often, the first sentence of a paper is the hardest one to write. A blank sheet of paper is facing you, and you have to begin putting words down on that paper. What will that first sentence be? A well-thought-out first sentence can overcome paralysis,[1] get you on your way, and launch a series of other sentences. So it would be well if you could conceive of such an initial sentence. But if after racking[2] your brains you can't come up with one, the next best thing is to **put down the**

[1] Powerlessness; inability to move or act. [2] Stretching or straining.

THE SOCIAL IMPLICATIONS OF SOAP OPERAS

INTRODUCTION 1½ pages

> The great popularity of soap operas.

> Soap operas very lucrative for the producers.

> Why soap operas are popular with viewers. Statement of thesis.

BODY 2 pages

> General information about *Days of Our Lives.*

> Past episodes of *Days of Our Lives* that illustrate the sexual basis of the conflicts.

> Episodes from a recent week of *Days of Our Lives* that illustrate the sexual basis of the conflicts.

CONCLUSION 1 page

> Conclusion: summary remarks about the social implications of soap operas

Figure 6.1

first relevant sentence that occurs to you. Sometimes, just the act of putting some words on paper breaks the logjam.[1] You may later decide to scrap[2] your first sentence, but at least it has served its purpose: it has given you a shove in the direction you want to go. Once you are in motion, don't stop, because if you do, you will just have to overcome the inertia once more. Hang on to the momentum and keep going forward.

Let's see if you can come up with a well-thought-out first sentence rather than rely on a haphazard[3] one. A sentence that immediately grabs the reader's interest or attention is often a good one to begin with. Sometimes, a *provocative*[4] *question* will hook the reader's attention—"Is it true that today's college student is barely literate?"[5] Sometimes, a sentence that poses a *critical*[6] *situation* will gain attention—"Nuclear power plants can save us or doom us." Sometimes, a sentence that stresses the *importance or uniqueness*[7] *of the subject* you are going to talk about will hook the reader—"Since total disarmament[8] of the major nations of the world is improbable,[9] an effective program of arms control is the only measure that can prevent an end-of-the-world global war."

But note the *sometimes* repeated in the previous paragraph. An initial sentence does not always have to be dramatic. Sometimes, a very quiet, unpretentious[10] sentence will do. What is important is that the first sentence lead easily and naturally into the next one.

Now, after much thought, you come up with this initial[11] sentence for your paper: "Between the hours of 11:30 A.M.

---

[1] Deadlock; blockage. [2] To get rid of as useless. [3] Lacking plan or order; occurring or taken up by chance or at random. [4] Having the quality of stirring up, stimulating, or exciting some reaction. [5] Able to read and write. [6] Of the nature of a crisis; crucial. [7] The quality of being the only one of its kind. [8] Reducing the size and strength of armed forces. [9] Unlikely to be true or to happen. [10] Not showy or pompous. [11] First.

Putting It All Together

and 3:30 P.M., Monday through Friday, twenty million Americans sit down at their television sets and watch one or more of the fourteen soap operas now being broadcast on the networks." With the inertia broken, you settle down to write the first draft[1] of your paper. With all of its fumblings and strike-overs,[2] the following represents the first draft of your paper on soap operas.

---

[1] A preliminary sketch or version.   [2] Letters of the alphabet typed over by other letters.

The Social Implications of Soap Operas

Between the hours of 11:30 a.m. and 3:30 p.m., Monday through Friday, some twenty millions Americans sit down before their television sets and watch none or more of the fourteen soap operas now being broadcast on the networks. Who are these Americans who have th leisure and the desire to watch these melodramas about domestic life in this country? Mainly they are housewives, senior citizens, unemployed men, and college students. Usually, they are not just casual drop-ins on the program; they are regular, loyal watchers of the show. They may knit or drink cokes or muchx munch pretzels or smoke or do physical exercises while they are watching, but for all their casualness they are following the story with great intensity. The characters portrayed in the dramas are familar to them, sometimes more familiar than members of their own family, and often the viewers are vitally concerned about what happens to the characters. The viewers resent the interruptions of the flow of the story by the commercials, but very few of them will abandon their watching of a program show before it is completed

What is the reason for the appeal of soap operas for many Americans/ It is easy to understand the appeal from the standpoint of the producers. Soap operas are constitute a very lucrative business. In a recent cover story in Time about soap operas (January 12, 1976), _Time_ magazine pointed out that while it costs NBC $170,000 to produce five days of _Days of Our Lives_, those five showings bring in $600,000 of ad revenue. The major script-writers earn annual salaries ranging from $100,000 to $250,000. Many of the actors and actresses on the shows

Putting It All Together

financially rewarding
earn $35,000 a year. Soap operas have created a/satellite industry
for the publication of fan magazines about the personalities appearing on the shows. One of these, <u>Daytime TV</u>, has a circulation in
excess of 380,000.

The financial rewards explain the appeal of soap
operas for the producers. But what accounts for the appeal of
soap operas for the producers viewers? The simplest explanation
is that soap operas appeal to the natural human appetite for
stories. But why do soap operas draw larger audiences than
other kinds of popular dramas, like Westerns and detective
stories? For one thing, they permit more audience identification.
Sometimes the situations are so much like the experience of the
TV audience that the viewers can derive pleasure and comfort
from watching others cope with similiar problems. On the
other hand, the situations are sometimes so different from the
humdrum experiences lives of people that viewers can participate
vicariously in experiences that they have never had themselves
but that they are curious about. Because of their closer
identification with the characters on the show, viewers can
get more satisfaction from seeing nasty characters get their
comeuppance or sympathetic characters getting their deserve
reward. But we should not underestimate the appeal of the
subtle or blatant sexual titillation of the shows. The conflict
in soap operas is ultimately based on the romantic entanglements
between male and female characters. It is this sexual orientation of the soap operas that I would like to discuss. I contend
that soap operas show that sex without genuine love, mutual respect,
and firm commitment leads to frustration, exploitation, and unhappiness. I can best demonstrate this thesis by considering

a soap opera that is typical of the shows, <u>Days</u> <u>of</u> <u>Our</u> <u>Lives</u>.

<u>Days</u> <u>of</u> <u>Our</u> <u>lives</u> is an hour-long show, produced by NBC,
which deals with the lives of four generation of the Horton
family and the other men and women closly associated with
that family. Dr. Tom Horton is the patriarch of a family
who are notable for messing up th~~k~~eir own lives and the lives
of ~~people~~ those associated with ~~it~~ them. After more than
ten years on the air, the relationships of the twenty-five
or so characters who appear on the show have been so hopelessly scrambled by a succession of courtships, marriages,
divorces, affairs, and remarriages that a chart made of
these relationship would be as complicated as the circuit
design for a solid-state television set.

Many of the situations that have been dramatized in
past shows and that continue to spark the drama in the lives
of the intermeshed characters illustrate the sexual bases of
this domes~~s~~tic melodrama. Julie Anderson, the siren character
in the show, has been married twice already, and for some time
now has been frustrated by her passion for Doug~~h~~ Williams,
an older man who had been married to Julie's mother, now dead.
Doug~~h~~ recently entered into an artificial-insemination program
so that his child by Julie's mother could have a playmate, and
unbeknowst to him, his housekeeper has arranged to be the
child's mother. Julie's son David has gone to live with the
Grants, a black family and is ~~following~~ falling in love with
their daughter Valerie. David's abandoned girl friend, Brooke,
tried to commit suicide after she had had an abortion to get
rid of David's child. Dr. Neil Curtis, married now to Phyllis
Anderson, is currently involved in an affair with one of his

Putting It All Together

patients, a wealthy widow named Amanda Howard. Dr. Greg Peters
wants to marry Amanda, even though he knows of her romantic
interest in Dr. Neil. Johnny Couts got Rebecca pregnant, and
then left for Paris, but Rebecca, unlike Brooke, refused to
have an abortion.

The episodes on a recent week of the <u>Days</u> <u>of</u> <u>Our</u> <u>Lives</u>
show reveal how the consequences of some of these past situa-
tions come home to roost. The central incident during the
week was the one in which Mickey Horton (who sometime ago
assumed the new name of Marty Hanson after a long bout of
amnesia) threatens to shoot his brother Dr. Bill Horton.
Obviously suffering from some kind of mental derangement,
while his son Michael is undergoing a critical operation
for a crushed chest suffered in a freak accident, Mickey
locks himself in a room with Bill, pulls a gun on him, and
asks him point-blank, "Did you have an affair with Laura
(Mickey's former wife)?" "No," says Bill emphatically.
"Then tell me how she conceived your child?" Despite all
his protestations of innocence, Bill finds that he can't
reason with his mentally disturbed brother. At the typical
snail's pace of the action in soap operas, Mickey holds Bill
at bay with the guns over a three-day period. In the
meanwhile, in the typical interweaving pattern of incidents,
we get flashes of the drama going on in the lives of other
characters outside that locked room. Having heard indirectly
that Rebecca is pregnant with his child, Johnny returns unexpectedly from Paris and accuses the weeping Rebecca of
using him as a stud to generate a child in her womb. "You're
just in love with motherhood," he snarls. David shows up

too and has some angry scenes with Brooke about her abortion.

He reminds her that he had offered to marry her, but she had

refused. She tells him that she refused and went ahead with

the abortion because he didn't manifest that he was genuinely

~~loved~~ in love with her. We get flashes of the brewing affair

between Dr. Neil and his patient Amanda. Michael emerges from

the operating room and asks/why his father Marty has not come
                             his mother Laura

to see him in the hospital. Marty is still back in that locked

room with Bill. Bill finally manages to seize ~~Michael's~~ Marty's

gun-h~~a~~nd, the two men struggle, a shot goes off, and after a

fifteen-second pause, during which we are uncertain which one

of them has been shot, Bill crumples to the floor. . . . As

the week ends, we learn that Bill has been wounded only super-

ficially, that Dr. Tom Horton has brought Marty to the psychia-

tric ward of the hospital, and that Marty, who is a lawyer,

reminds his father that he can be legally restrained there for

only seventy-two hours and that when he gets out, he is going

to "get" Bill and Laura.

    The central and the surrounding conflicts in this week of

episodes are typical not only of <u>Days of Our Lives</u> but also

of most of the episodes on daytime soap operas. If one looks

only at the surface of many of the dramatic conflicts, one can

posit jealousy, rivalry, misunderstanding, selfishness, or

resentment as the motive powers of the actions of the characters,

but if one looks deeper one can detect sexual instincts as the

mainspring. All of the characters in some way and to some

degree seem to be motivated by their libido. If the characters

could somehow get a tight rein on their sexual drives, life in

soapland would be much more harmonious. <u>Time</u> magazine entitled

Putting It All Together

its cover story on soap operas "Sex and Suffering in the Afternoon."
And one gets the impression that if it weren't for the ~~sx~~ sex there
would·be no suffering. In 1965, in an article in <u>TV</u> <u>Guide</u> entitled
"The Soaps--Anything ~~a~~bout 99-44/100 Percent Pure," Edith Efron
remarked that/~~it~~ ^{the theme of} nine out of ten daytime shows was "the mating-
marital-reproductive cycle set against a domestic background. . . .
This all-consuming, single-minded search for a mate is an absolute
good in the soap-opera syndrome. Morality--and dramatic conflict--
emerge from how the search is conducted." Apparently, the sexual
undertone of the daytime shows is a fairly recent development. In
the article "Ivorytown, Rinsoville, Anacinburg, and Crisco Corners"
that he wrote about radio soap operas in 1948 for the <u>New</u> <u>Yorker</u>,
James Thurber remarked about "the coy and impregnable chastity" of
the characters on these shows. Edith Efron quoted some prominent
psychologists to back up ~~the~~ her claim that this "sex-based human
wretchedness is on the air because it exists in society." Dr.
Harold Greenwal. the supervising psychologist of the Community
Guidance Service in New York City, maintains that soap operas
"reflect the changes taking place in our society. There are
fewer taboos. The age of sexual activity in the middle classes
has dropped, and it has increased in frequency. There is more
infidelity. These plays reflect these problem." Dr. William
Menaker, Professor of Clinical Psychology at New York University,
says, "Increasing frankness in dealing with these problems isn't
a symptom of moral decay but rather reflects the confused values
of a transitional period of sociosexual change." These soap operas
seem to be reflecting the increasing public frankness about sexual
matters and the growing rejection of society's taboos about sex.

—7—

The implications of what we are seeing portrayed on the television
screen are that there is more unbridled sex in our society and
consequently more frustration, exploitation, and unhappiness. If
he were alive today, Dr. Sigmund Freud might say, "I told you so."

Putting It All Together

Revising and polishing the rough draft

You have the first draft of your paper written now, and if time permits, you can put it aside for a day or two and then come back to it to revise and polish it. In the *revision,*[1] you may have to do some cutting or some expanding or some shifting. In *polishing* the essay, you may be able to smooth out the phrasing, tighten up some of the sentences, substitute more precise wording. Writing the first draft is usually the hardest part; revising and polishing that draft can actually be enjoyable. Let us look at the first draft again and make notes of the changes you may want to make in the next draft.

[1] A new and improved version.

● Revising and Polishing the Rough Draft

Get more precise title
Possibilities: Sex in Soap Operas
The Sexual Basis of the Conflicts in Soap Operas

The Social Implications of Soap Operas

(EST)

Between the hours of 11:30 a.m. and 3:30 p.m., Monday
through Friday, some twenty millions Americans sit down before
their television sets ~~and~~ to watch ~~n~~one or more of the fourteen
soap operas now being broadcast on the networks. ~~Who are these~~
~~Americans who have th leisure and the desire to watch these~~
~~melodramas about domestic life in this country? Mainly they~~
The size of the audience is even more remarkable when one considers that the only people who have the leisure to watch these shows during the daytime
~~are housewives,~~ senior citizens, (unemployed men,) and college
students. ~~Usually, they are not just casual drop-ins on the~~
~~program; they are regular, loyal watchers of the show.~~
Because of this huge and loyal audience, soap operas have become a very lucrative business for the producers. They

Cut

may knit or drink cokes or ~~xxxx~~ munch pretzels or smoke or do
physical exercises while they are watching, but for all their
casualness they are following the story with great intensity.
The characters portrayed in the dramas are familar to them,
sometimes more familiar than members of their own family, and
often the viewers are vitally concerned about what happens to
the characters. The viewers resent the interruptions of the
flow of the story by the commercials, but very few of them will
abandon their watching of a ~~program~~ show before it is completed

What is the reason for the appeal of soap operas for many
Americans/ It is easy to understand the appeal from the standpoint of the producers. Soap operas ~~are~~ constitute a very
lucrative business. In a recent cover story ~~in Time~~ about
soap operas (January 12, 1976), *Time* magazine pointed out that
~~while it costs NBC $170,000 to produce five days of Days of Our~~
~~Lives, those~~ five showings bring in $600,000 ~~of ad~~ revenue. The
major script-writers earn annual salaries ranging from $100,000
to $250,000, Many of the actors and actresses on the shows

the weekly of a soap opera can in advertising as much as
but cost only about $170,000 to produce, that
and that appearing in
m

167

Putting It All Together

/

Cut

earn $35,000 a year. Soap operas have created a/ *financially rewarding* satellite industry for the publication of fan magazines about the personalities appearing on the shows. One of these, <u>Daytime TV</u>, has a circulation in excess of 380,000.

New ¶

Although intellectuals tend to look down their noses at the taste of the millions of people who watch these shows daily and to disparage the ~~XXXXXX The financial rewards explain the appeal of soap operas for the producers. But what accounts for the appeal of soap operas for the producers viewers? The simplest explanation~~ *commercialism of the sponsors, soap operas represent* ~~is that soap operas appeal to the natural human appetite for~~ *a cultural phenomenon that is not likely to disappear* ~~stories. But why do soap operas draw larger audiences than~~ *from the American scene. What are the social implications* ~~other kinds of popular dramas, like Westerns and detective~~ *of this phenomenon? One doesn't have to watch many* ~~stories? For one thing, they permit more audience identification.~~ *soap operas to become aware that most of the dramatic* ~~Sometimes the situations are so much like the experience of the~~ *conflicts portrayed on the "soaps" are based ultimately* ~~TV audience that the viewers can derive pleasure and comfort~~ *on the romantic entanglements between the male and* ~~from watching others cope with similar problems. On the~~ *female characters. In 1965, in an article in TV Guide*

Insert Edith Efron quote here

~~other hand, the situations are sometimes so different from the~~ *entitled "The Soaps—Anything but 99-44/100 Percent* humdrum ~~experiences~~ *lives of people that viewers can participate* ~~Pure," Edith Efron referred to "the sickly sexuality~~ vicariously in experiences that they have never had ~~themselves~~ ~~of daytime soap opera," calling it a "sex-based human~~ but they are curious about. ~~Because of their closer~~ *wretchedness." She went on to quote a number of* ~~identification with the characters on the show, viewers can~~ *commentators on the soap opera phenomenon, including*

Add quote from Betty Friedan

~~get more satisfaction from seeing a nasty characters get their~~ *Women's Lib author Betty Friedan (The Feminine Mystique),* ~~comeuppance or sympathetic characters getting their deserve~~ *who says that "the view of sex that emerges* ~~reward. But we should not underestimate the appeal of the~~ *[from the soaps] is sick."* ~~subtle or blatant sexual titillation of the shows. The conflict~~

~~in soap operas is ultimately based on the romantic entanglements~~ ~~between male and female characters.~~ It is this *unhappy* sexual orienta-

New ¶

tion of the soap operas that I would like to discuss. I contend that soap operas show that sex without ~~genuine~~ love, ~~mutual~~ respect, and ~~firm~~ commitment leads to frustration, exploitation, and un-

drop the adjectives

happiness. I ~~can best demonstrate~~ *could support* this ~~thesis by considering~~ *thesis by citing*

● Revising and Polishing the Rough Draft

—3—

broadcast, but
in the interest ^ *incidents from a number of the soap operas now being*
of brevity, I soap opera that is typical ~~of the shows,~~ Days of Our Lives.
will confine
my attention to ~~which~~ Days of Our Lives ~~is~~ an hour-long show, produced by NBC,

deals with the lives of four generations of the Horton

family and the other men and women closly associated with

~~that~~ *the* family. Dr. Tom Horton is the patriarch of a family

whose members
~~who~~ are notable for messing up their own lives and the lives

of ~~people~~ those associated with ~~it~~ them. After more than

ten years on the air, the relationships of the twenty-five

or so characters who appear on the show have been so ~~hope-~~

and intertwined
~~lessly~~ scrambled by a succession of courtships, marriages,

divorces, affairs, and remarriages that a chart made of

these relationships would be as complicated as the circuit

design for a solid-state television set.

on
Many of the situations that have been dramatized ~~in~~
the *in recent years*
~~past shows, and that continue to spark the drama in the lives~~
Insert here
something about ~~of the intermeshed characters~~ illustrate the sexual bases of
Mickey Horton, this domestic melodrama. Julie Anderson, the ~~siren~~ character *"wicked woman"*
who had a long
bout of amnesia ~~in~~ *on* the show, has been married twice already, and for some time
after openly *the indifference of*
but unknowingly now has been frustrated by ~~her passion for~~ Doug Williams,
lusting after
his sister an older man who had been married to Julie's mother, now dead.
Marie and who Doug recently entered into an artificial-insemination program
changed his *secretly*
name to so that his child by Julie's mother could have a playmate, and
Marty Hanson; ~~unbeknowst to him,~~ his housekeeper has arranged to be the
divorced his child's mother. Julie's son David has gone to live with the
wife Laura, ~~Grants, a black family,~~ and is ~~following~~ falling in love with
and married
Suzanne. their daughter Valerie. David's abandoned girl friend, Brooke,

tried to commit suicide after she had had an abortion to get

rid of David's child. Dr. Neil Curtis, married now to Phyllis

Anderson, is ~~currently~~ involved in an affair with one of his

Putting It All Together

patients, a wealthy widow named Amanda Howard. Dr. Greg Peters
wants to marry Amanda, even though he knows of her romantic
interest in the handsome Dr. Neil. Johnny Couts got Rebecca pregnant, and
then left for Paris, but Rebecca, unlike Brooke, refused to
have an abortion.

The episodes on a recent week of ~~the~~ Days of Our Lives
~~show~~ reveal how the consequences of some of these past situations come home to roost. The central incident during the
week was the one in which Mickey Horton (~~who sometime ago~~ now known
~~assumed the new name of~~ as Marty Hanson) ~~after a long bout of
amnesia)~~ threatens to shoot his brother Dr. Bill Horton.
Obviously suffering from some kind of mental derangement,
while his son Michael is undergoing a critical operation
for a crushed chest suffered in a freak accident, ~~Mickey~~ Marty
locks himself in a room with Bill, pulls a gun on him, and
asks him point-blank, "Did you have an affair with Laura?"
~~(Mickey's former wife)?"~~ "No," says Bill emphatically.
"Then tell me how she conceived your child?" Despite all
his protestations of innocence, Bill finds that he ~~can't~~ cannot
reason with his mentally disturbed brother. At the typical
snail's pace of the action, ~~in soap operas,~~ ~~Mickey~~ Marty holds Bill
at bay with the gun over a three-day period. *New ¶* / In the
meanwhile, in the typical interweaving pattern of incidents, (soap operas
we get flashes of the drama going on in the lives of the other sometimes have as many
characters outside that locked room. Having heard indirectly as seven plots going
that Rebecca is pregnant with his child, Johnny Couts returns un- o. concurrently))
expectedly from Paris and accuses the weeping Rebecca of
using him as a stud to generate a child in her womb. "You're
just in love with motherhood," he snarls. Elsewhere, David ~~shows up~~

—5—

~~too and~~ has some angry scenes with Brooke about her abortion.
He reminds her that he had offered to marry her, but ^that^ she had
refused. ^the offer^ She tells him that she ~~refused and~~ went ahead with
the abortion because he ~~didn't manifest~~ ^she was convinced^ that he ~~was~~ ^didn't^ genuinely
~~loved in love with~~ ^love^ her. We get flashes of the brewing affair
between Dr. Neil and his patient Amanda. Michael emerges from
the operating room and asks/why his father Marty has not come ^his mother Laura^
to see him in the hospital. Marty is still ~~back~~ in that ~~locked~~
room ~~with~~ Bill. ^holding the gun on his brother^ Bill finally manages to seize ~~Michael's~~ Marty's
gun-hand, the two men struggle, a shot goes off, and after a
fifteen-second pause, during which we are uncertain which one
of them has been shot, Bill crumples to the floor. . . . As
the week ends, we learn that Bill has been wounded only superficially, that Dr. Tom ~~Horton~~ has brought Marty to the psychiatric ward of the hospital, and that Marty, who is a lawyer,
reminds his father that he can be legally ~~restrained~~ ^held^ there for
only seventy-two hours and that when he ~~gets out~~ ^is released^, he is going
to "get" Bill and Laura.

The central and the surrounding conflicts in this week of
episodes are typical not only of <u>Days</u> <u>of</u> <u>Our</u> <u>Lives</u> but also
of most ~~of the episodes on~~ daytime soap operas. If one looks
only at the surface of ~~many of~~ the ~~dramatic~~ conflicts, one ~~can~~ ^sees^
~~posit~~ jealousy, rivalry, misunderstanding, selfishness, or
resentment as the motive powers of the ^characters'^ actions ~~of the characters~~,
but if one looks deeper, one ~~can detect~~ ~~sexual instincts~~ ^blind and selfish sexuality^ as the
mainspring. ^of the actions^ All of the characters, in some way and to some
degree, seem to be motivated by their libido. ^And they seem^ If the characters
^unable, or at least unwilling,^ could somehow get a tight rein on their sexual drives, life in
^to harness their^ Soapland would be ~~much~~ more harmonious, ^-- and apparently duller^ <u>Time</u> magazine entitled
^sex urges to love, respect, and commitment.^

Putting It All Together

its cover story on soap operas "Sex and Suffering in the Afternoon."
a
And one gets the impression, *from reading the article* that if it weren't for the ~~of~~ *unbridled* sex, there

would be no suffering. In 1965, in an article in <u>TV Guide</u> entitled

Cut
Quote
Edith Efron
in the
introduction

"The Soaps--Anything ~~about~~ 99/44/100 Percent Pure," Edith Efron
the theme of
remarked that/~~in~~ nine out/of ten daytime shows was "the mating-

marital-reproductive cycle set against a domestic background. . . .

This all-consuming, single-minded search for a mate is an absolute

good in the soap-opera syndrome. Morality--and dramatic conflict--

emerge from how the search is conducted." Apparently, the sexual
relatively
undertones/of the daytime shows ~~is~~ *are* a ~~fairly~~ recent development. In

Now all the taboos on the mention of sex on the airwaves have been lifted.

the article "Ivorytown, Rinsoville, Anacinburg, and Crisco Corners"

that he wrote about radio soap operas in 1948 for the <u>New Yorker</u>,

James Thurber remarked about "the coy and impregnable chastity of
In her article *a*
the characters on these shows. Edith Efron quoted ~~some~~ prominent
and a TV producer *the*
psychologists, to back up ~~the~~ her claim that ~~this~~ "sex-based human

new ¶
wretchedness is on the air because it exists in society." Dr.

Harold Greenwald, the supervising psychologist of the Community

Guidance Service in New York City, maintains that soap operas

"reflect the changes taking place in our society." There are
" // he goes on to say.
fewer taboos, /"The age of sexual activity in the middle classes

has dropped, and it has increased in frequency. There is more

Insert here: Frank Dodge producer of Search for Tomorrow says, 'It's not collusion but a logical coincidence

infidelity. These plays reflect these problems." Dr. William

Menaker, Professor of Clinical Psychology at New York University,

says, "Increasing frankness in dealing with these problems isn't

a symptom of moral decay but rather reflects the confused values

of a transitional period of sociosexual change." These soap operas

seem to be reflecting the increasing public frankness about sexual

matters and the growing rejection of society's taboos about sex.

Cut. Replace with a quote from Frank Dodge

that adultery, illegitimate children, and abortions are appearing on many shows. If you read the papers about what's going on in the suburbs — well, it's more startling than what's shown on the air."

● Revising and Polishing the Rough Draft

Cut. Replace with new concluding paragraph

The implications of what we are seeing portrayed on the television screen are that there is more unbridled sex in our society and consequently more frustration, exploitation, and unhappiness. If he were alive today, Dr. Sigmund Freud might say, "I told you so."

Interestingly, none of these authorities denies the wretchedness, suffering, confusion, and other problems. The soap operas are viewed by them as reflections of existing individual and social ills based on "sick sex." And the sex is sick, not because sex in itself is evil or wrong, but because, as exemplified here, it is compulsive, unbridled, and selfish. It clearly lacks appropriate restraint, real commitment, mutual respect and responsibility, and intelligent love. Instead, as Betty Friedan further asserts, the men are "degraded," the women "childish and dependent." The result can only be bitter: real love is frustrated, people are shamelessly "used," and unhappiness is almost always everybody's share of the prize. Meanwhile, the struggling has produced a lot of subtle and blatant excitement for the millions of daily viewers of soap operas. All the soap in Soapland has not been able to wash away the soiled sex. <u>Mary Hartman</u>, <u>Mary Hartman</u>, Norman Lear's spoof of soap operas, may be the needed detergent.

Putting It All Together

As is clear from the notes written on the first draft, you saw that it was taking you too long to get into the main part of your paper. Your introduction took up as many paragraphs (three) as the body of the essay did. When one has turned up a lot of interesting material on a subject, one is tempted to include it all in the paper. When you made your rough outline, you should have noticed that your introduction was taking up a disproportionate amount of space, but it was only after you had written your first draft that you saw that the "tail was wagging the dog." Then you recognized the need to condense[1] the introductory section so that you could get down to the main point of your paper sooner.

Cutting out big chunks from the introduction not only will get you into the main part of your paper sooner but will bring the paper as a whole down below the specified maximum length of 1500 words. (The first draft ran to about 1650 words.) You also made some readjustments in the arrangement of the paper. You saw, for instance, that a quotation from the conclusion would be more effective if shifted to the introduction. Knowing that you are not obliged to keep the paragraph divisions used in your rough outline, you also saw the possibility of breaking up some of the long paragraphs in the body of the paper into shorter paragraphs. And you saw the need to round off your conclusion by adding a few more sentences at the end.

When you type up another draft from your annotated[2] first draft, you may discover the need for further additions, subtractions, rearrangements, and revisions. If this second draft gets to be too messy because of those further changes, you will have to type up a third and final draft. That third draft, however, may not be the final one. The *final* draft of a paper is the one that represents your best efforts under the circumstances.

[1] To make more compact; to reduce in volume; to concentrate. [2] Furnished with notes.

● Writing the final draft

Here is the draft that you finally turned in to your sociology teacher.

```
                The Sexual Basis of the Conflicts in Soap Operas

        Between the hours of 11:30 a.m. and 3:30 p.m. (EST), Monday
   through Friday, some twenty million Americans sit down before their
   television sets to watch one or more of the fourteen soap operas
   now being broadcast on the networks.  The size of the audience is
   even more remarkable when one considers that the only people who
   have the leisure to watch these shows during the daytime are house-
   wives, unemployed men, senior citizens, and college students.  Be-
   cause of this huge and loyal audience, soap operas have become a
   very lucrative business for the producers.  In a recent cover story
   about soap operas (January 12, 1976), Time magazine pointed out that
   the five weekly showings of a soap opera can bring in as much as
   $600,000 in advertising revenue but cost only about $170,000 to
   produce, that the major script-writers earn annual salaries ranging
   from $100,000 to $250,000, and that many of the actors and actresses
   appearing in the shows earn $35,000 a year.

        Although intellectuals tend to look down their noses at the
   taste of the millions of people who watch these shows daily and to
   disparage the commercialism of the sponsors, soap operas represent
   a cultural phenomenon that is not likely to disappear from the
   American scene.  What are the social implications of this phenomenon?
   One doesn't have to watch many soap operas to become aware that most
   of the dramatic conflicts portrayed on the "soaps" are based ulti-
   mately on the romantic entanglements between the male and female
   characters.  In 1965, in an article in TV Guide entitled "The
   Soaps--Anything but 99-44/100 Percent Pure," Edith Efron referred
   to "the sickly sexuality of daytime soap opera," calling it a
```

Putting It All Together

"sex-based human wretchedness." She went on to quote a number of commentators on the soap-opera phenomenon, including Women's Lib author Betty Friedan (The Feminine Mystique), who says that "the view of sex that emerges [from the soaps] is sick."

It is this unhappy sexual orientation of the soap operas that I would like to discuss. I contend that soap operas show that sex without love, respect, and commitment leads to frustration, exploitation, and unhappiness. I could support this thesis by citing incidents from a number of the soap operas now being broadcast, but in the interest of brevity, I will confine my attention to a soap opera that is typical, Days of Our Lives.

Days of Our Lives, an hour-long show produced by NBC, deals with the lives of four generations of the Horton family and the other men and women closely associated with the family. Dr. Tom Horton is the patriarch of a family whose members are notable for messing up their own lives and the lives of those associated with them. After more than ten years on the air, the relationships of the twenty-five or so characters who appear on the show have been so scrambled and intertwined by a succession of courtships, marriages, divorces, affairs, and remarriages that a chart made of those relationships would be as complicated as the circuit design for a solid-state television set.

Many of the situations that have been dramatized on the show in recent years illustrate the sexual bases of this domestic melodrama. Mickey Horton, Dr. Tom's eldest son, at one time openly but unknowingly lusted after his sister Marie, finally driving her to a convent. After recovering from a long stretch of amnesia, he divorced his wife Laura, changed his name officially to Marty Hanson,

and married a younger woman named Suzanne, who was on the rebound
from a disastrous teenage marriage that she entered into because
of an unwanted pregnancy. Julie Anderson, the "wicked woman"
character on the show, has been married twice already and for
some time now has been frustrated by the indifference of Doug
Williams, an older man who had been married to Julie's mother,
now dead. Doug recently entered into an artificial-insemination
program so that his child by Julie's mother could have a playmate,
and his housekeeper has secretly arranged to be the child's mother.
Julie's son David has gone to live with the Grants, a black family,
and is falling in love with their daughter Valerie. David's abandoned girl friend, Brooke, tried to commit suicide after she had
had an abortion to get rid of David's child. Dr. Neil Curtis,
married now to Phyllis Anderson, is involved in an affair with one
of his patients, a wealthy widow named Amanda Howard. Dr. Greg
Peters wants to marry Amanda, even though he knows of her romantic
interest in the handsome Dr. Neil. Johnny Couts got Rebecca pregnant and then left for Paris, but Rebecca, unlike Brooke, refused
to have an abortion.

The episodes on a recent week of Days of Our Lives reveal how
the consequences of some of these past situations come home to
roost. The central incident during the week was the one in which
Mickey Horton (now known as Marty Hanson) threatens to shoot his
brother Dr. Bill Horton. Obviously suffering from some kind of
mental derangement, while his son Michael is undergoing a critical
operation for a crushed chest suffered in a freak accident, Marty
locks himself in a room with Bill, pulls a gun on him, and asks
him point-blank, "Did you have an affair with Laura?" "No," says

Putting It All Together

Bill emphatically. "Then tell me how she conceived your child." Despite all his protestations of innocence, Bill finds that he cannot reason with his mentally disturbed brother. At the typical snail's pace of the action, Marty holds Bill at bay with the gun over a three-day period.

In the meanwhile, in the typical interweaving pattern of incidents (soap operas sometimes have as many as seven plots going on concurrently), we get flashes of the drama going on in the lives of the other characters outside that locked room. Having heard indirectly that Rebecca is pregnant with his child, Johnny Couts returns unexpectedly from Paris and accuses the weeping Rebecca of using him as a stud to generate a child in her womb. "You're just in love with motherhood," he snarls. Elsewhere, David has some angry scenes with Brooke about her abortion. He reminds her that he had offered to marry her but that she had refused the offer. She tells him that she went ahead with the abortion because she was convinced that he didn't genuinely love her. We get flashes of the brewing affair between Dr. Neil and his patient Amanda. Michael emerges from the operating room and asks his mother Laura why his father Marty has not come to see him in the hospital. Marty is still in that room, holding the gun on his brother Bill. Bill finally manages to seize Marty's gun-hand, the two men struggle, a shot goes off, and after a fifteen-second pause, during which we are uncertain which one of them has been shot, Bill crumples to the floor. . . . As the week ends, we learn that Bill has been wounded only superficially, that Dr. Tom has brought Marty to the psychiatric ward of the hospital, and that Marty, who is a lawyer, reminds his father that he can be legally

—5—

held there for only seventy-two hours and that when he is released, he is going to "get" Bill and Laura.

The central and the surrounding conflicts in this week of episodes are typical not only of Days of Our Lives but also of most daytime soap operas. If one looks only at the surface of the conflicts, one sees jealousy, rivalry, misunderstanding, selfishness, or resentment as the motive power of the characters' actions, but if one looks deeper, one detects blind and selfish sexuality as the mainspring of the actions. All of the characters, in some way and to some degree, seem to be motivated by their libido. And they seem unable, or at least unwilling, to harness their sex urges to love, respect, and commitment. If the characters could somehow get a tight rein on their sexual drives, life in Soapland would be more harmonious--and apparently duller. Time magazine entitled its cover story on soap operas "Sex and Suffering in the Afternoon," and one gets the impression from reading the article that if it weren't for the unbridled sex, there would be no suffering. Apparently, the sexual undertones of the daytime shows are a relatively recent development. In the article "Ivorytown, Rinsoville, Anacinburg, and Crisco Corners" that he wrote about radio soap operas in 1948 for the New Yorker, James Thurber remarked about the "coy and impregnable chastity" of the characters on those shows. Now, all the taboos on the mention of sex on the airwaves have been lifted.

In her article, Edith Efron quoted a prominent psychologist and a TV producer to back up her claim that the "sex-based human wretchedness is on the air because it exists in society." Dr. Harold Greenwald, the supervising psychologist of the Community

Putting It All Together

Guidance Service in New York City, maintains that soap operas "reflect the changes taking place in our society." "There are fewer taboos," he goes on to say. "The age of sexual activity in the middle classes has dropped, and it has increased in frequency. There is more infidelity. These plays reflect these problems." Frank Dodge, producer of <u>Search for Tomorrow</u>, says, "It's not collusion but a logical coincidence that adultery, illegitimate children, and abortions are appearing on many shows. If you read the papers about what's going on in the suburbs--well, it's more startling than what's shown on the air."

Interestingly, none of these authorities denies the wretchedness, suffering, confusion, and other problems. The soap operas are viewed by them as reflections of existing individual and social ills based on "sick sex." And the sex is sick, not because sex in itself is evil or wrong, but because, as exemplified here, it is compulsive, unbridled, and selfish. It clearly lacks appropriate restraint, real commitment, mutual respect and responsibility, and intelligent love. Instead, as Betty Friedan further asserts, the men are "degraded," the women "childish and dependent." The result can only be bitter: real love is frustrated, people are shamelessly "used," and unhappiness is almost always everybody's share of the prize. Meanwhile, the struggling has produced a lot of subtle and blatant excitement for the millions of daily viewers of soap operas. All the soap in Soapland has not been able to wash away the soiled sex. <u>Mary Hartman</u>, <u>Mary Hartman</u>, Norman Lear's spoof of soap operas, may be the needed detergent.

●
Summary

In "Putting It All Together," you have gone through the following series of steps:

(1) GETTING THE ASSIGNMENT

It is important that you pay close attention to, and clearly understand, the assignment. If there is something about the assignment that you do not understand, ask for a clarification.[1]

(2) SETTLING ON A SUBJECT

Although the general subject may be assigned, you will usually have some choice of the part or aspect of that general subject to write about. It is important that you narrow the subject to fit the length, occasion, purpose, audience, and thesis.

(3) DECIDING ON A THESIS

Sometimes you may not be able to formulate a precise thesis until after you have gone through the search process. But even a tentatively formulated thesis at the outset will guide you in what to look for in your search for something to say.

(4) DISCOVERING SOMETHING TO SAY

Discovering something to say is the most important step

---

[1] The action or process of making clear.

in the composition process. If you engage conscientiously in this step, your paper will almost write itself later on.

(5) SELECTING AND ARRANGING THE MATERIAL

Because the previous step will usually turn up more material than you can use in your paper, you will have to select the material you are going to use and make some decisions about organizing the material that you have selected.

(6) MAKING AN OUTLINE

You will frequently find it helpful to draw up some kind of outline before you begin to write your paper.

(7) WRITING THE FIRST DRAFT

In writing the first draft, you should not be concerned about the correctness of your grammar, punctuation, spelling, and style. It is more important at this stage to get your thoughts written out.

(8) REVISING AND POLISHING THE FIRST DRAFT

After you have written the first draft, you can come back to it and correct the faulty grammar, punctuation, spelling, and style, and you can cut or expand or shift passages.

(9) WRITING THE FINAL DRAFT

The final draft is the one that you submit. It may represent the second or the third or the twelfth rewriting of the paper. But it should be as well wrought[1] and as flawless[2] as time and your talents permit.

This sequence of steps is the one that many serious writers follow, either consciously or unconsciously, whenever they write a paper. As you gain more practice in writing, you may be able to shorten or even omit some of the steps. But during your training as a writer, you may find this sequence—or some modification[3] of it—extremely helpful to you. This sequence of steps can at least serve you until you have devised your own method of composing.

---

[1] Fashioned; formed.   [2] Without faults or imperfect parts.   [3] Change; alteration.

Chapter 7
Special Kinds of
Writing Assignments

This chapter will deal with the rhetoric of three special kinds of writing assignments—writing about *literature,* writing *essay examinations,* and writing *reports.* Like the kind of writing assignment dealt with in the previous chapter, these also involve the processes of **finding, selecting, arranging,** and **expressing.** What makes them ''special'' is either that they deal with a particular kind of subject-matter or that they follow certain rules of style and form.

Whole courses are devoted to two of these kinds of writing—writing about literature and writing reports—and this little book cannot deal with all of their details and technicalities. However, it will show the highlights of these special kinds of writing assignments. In connection with writing about literature, it will explain some of the techniques of fiction, drama, and poetry and suggest questions you can ask yourself as you search for something to say about a literary text. In connection with writing essay examinations, it will give practical advice about how to improve your performance in this kind of writing under pressure. And in connection with writing reports, it will discuss some of the special considerations governing this kind of writing and will discuss the parts and organization of a typical formal report.

●
Writing about literature

In a literature course, you will certainly be asked to write papers about literary texts that you have read—poems, plays, essays, short stories, novels. The course will acquaint you with various ways of reading and discussing literary texts. Some of the classroom discussions will deal with the **content** of the text—*what is said? what is implied? what happens? what does it mean? is it worth our attention?* Other discussions will be concerned with the **form** of the text—*what type of literature are we dealing with?* (poem? play? short story? novel? essay?); if a *poem,* for instance, *what kind of poem?* (lyric? epic? narrative? descriptive? didactic? satirical?); if a *lyric* poem, for instance, *what special form of lyric?* (sonnet? ode? ottava rima?); *what special verse form is the lyric written in?* (iambic pentameter? blank verse? free verse?).

Whether you talk about the content or the form, your principal reference will be the text itself. You can supplement[1] what the text tells you with what your other reading or experience tells you about the history of the text, about the type of literature, about the author, about the period when the text was written, about the original audience.

Classroom lectures and discussions are designed to teach you how to read, understand, appreciate, and evaluate[2] a

[1] Add to; fill up the deficiency of. [2] To estimate the value of; to rate in terms of worth of content, qualities, etc.

Special Kinds of Writing Assignments

literary text. But eventually, you will be asked to write out your response to a literary text. You will not be expected—in fact, you may be forbidden—to do any research (that is, to read what others have said about the text). (That kind of response to a literary text will be dealt with in the next chapter, in the section on writing the research paper.) Instead, you will be expected to present, in a well-organized essay, your *own* response out of your *own* literary awareness. You will be asked to give the kind of response—but more fully and more coherently[1]—that you give to a friend who asks you, "How did you like the movie last night?" Your immediate response to that question might be, "It was great." But then you might go on to tell your friend what the movie was about or to comment on the unusual way in which the movie was put together or on some of the special effects created by the photography or on the acting or on the theme of the movie.

In writing about literature, you will be engaged in one or more of the following activities:

☐ **analyzing the work**

☐ **interpreting the work**

☐ **evaluating the work**

In **analyzing the work,** you will be answering one or both of these general questions: *what is the work about? how is the work put together?* In **interpreting the work,** you will be answering these general questions: *what did the author mean? what does the work mean to you?* In **evaluating the work,** you will be answering one or both of these general questions: *how well did the author accomplish what he set out to do? was the work worth your time and attention?*

---

[1] Consistently; with parts hanging together.

● Analyzing a Literary Work

A series of questions will be given in this section, questions that could give you some ideas of what to say in a paper about a literary text. You might be able to write a 3–4-page paper in response to a single question. Or you might make use of five or six (or more) questions in writing your paper. You might find that some questions yield more material when applied to one kind of literary work (a short story, for instance) than they do when applied to other kinds. Or you might find that it is easier for you to write in response to questions about the *what* of a work (the content) than it is to write about the *how* of the work (the form). Use the questions that work best for *you*. Eventually,[1] you may be able to invent questions that work better for you than any of those in the text. Whatever questions you use, think of them as devices to help you *find something to say* about a literary text.

● Analyzing a literary work

> General Questions to Be Answered in *Analyzing a Literary Work*
> **What is the work about? (content)** and/or
> **How is the work put together? (form)**

What kind of work is it?

One way to respond to that question is to classify the work as to its literary type: *poem, short story, novel, essay, play.* But once you determine the general type, you may want to classify it more particularly. For instance, if you are dealing

[1] Ultimately; finally.

Special Kinds of Writing Assignments

with a novel, you may want to indicate what kind of novel it is: a detective story (Agatha Christie's *Who Murdered Roger Ackroyd?*), an adventure story (Mark Twain's *Huckleberry Finn*), a ghost story (Henry James's *The Turn of the Screw*), a war story (Ernest Hemingway's *A Farewell to Arms*), a political novel (George Orwell's *1984*), a social novel (John Steinbeck's *The Grapes of Wrath*), a novel about "growing up" (J. D. Salinger's *Catcher in the Rye*).

If you are dealing with a poem, you may want to indicate whether it is a narrative poem (an epic like Homer's *Iliad* or a ballad like "Bonnie Barbara Allan") or a didactic poem (a poem that "teaches," like Alexander Pope's *An Essay on Criticism* or Karl Shapiro's *Essay on Rime*) or a descriptive poem (a poem that pictures a scene, like Matthew Arnold's "Dover Beach"), a satirical[1] poem (John Dryden's "Mac-Flecknoe"), a poem of social protest (William Blake's "The Chimney Sweeper" or Allan Ginsberg's "Howl"), a lyric poem (any one of a wide variety of poems in which the "voice" in the poem gives vent[2] to thoughts or emotions about an intense[3] personal experience).

If you are dealing with a play, you may want to say whether it is a tragedy (Shakespeare's *Hamlet* or Arthur Miller's *Death of a Salesman*), a comedy (Oliver Goldsmith's *She Stoops to Conquer* or Eugene O'Neill's *Ah, Wilderness!*), or a historical play (Shakespeare's *Richard III* or Robert Sherwood's *Abe Lincoln in Illinois*).

There are, of course, more types of poems, plays, and fiction than are named above, and there are many variations of the types that are named. Your literature courses will acquaint you with these additional types and variations.

---

[1] Characterized by the use of ridicule, sarcasm, or irony to expose or denounce vice, folly, abuses, or evils. [2] Outlet; expression. [3] Deeply felt; strong.

● Analyzing a Literary Work

What happens or what is said?

If you are dealing with a short story, novel, play, or narrative poem, one way to respond to this question is to give a **summary of the plot.** The *plot* is the sequence of actions or events in a story—first this happened, then this happened, then this happened, etc. If you ever wrote a school "book report," one of the things you may have been asked to do, in order to prove that you read the book, was to retell the story in your own words. In college, a paper in which you gave only a summary of the plot would probably be unacceptable. But you might be allowed to give a brief summary of what happened as the basis for your discussion of some other aspect of the work. And you certainly would be allowed to cite incidents from the story as examples of, or support for, some point you were making about it.

If you are dealing with a poem other than a narrative poem, you can't respond to this question by summarizing the plot, because there is no plot to summarize. What you do in that case is talk about the *what is said* part of the question. You *paraphrase* the poem—that is, you tell in your own words what the poet said in the verse lines. Let's look at a short poem, a sonnet by John Keats, and then at a paraphrase of it:

On First Looking into Chapman's Homer

Much have I travell'd in the realms of gold,
And many goodly states and kingdoms seen;
Round many western islands have I been
Which bards in fealty to Apollo hold.
Oft of one wide expanse had I been told
That deep-brow'd Homer ruled as his demesne;
Yet did I never breathe its pure serene

Special Kinds of Writing Assignments

Till I heard Chapman speak out loud and bold:
Then felt I like some watcher of the skies
When a new planet swims into his ken;
Or like Cortez when with eagle eyes
He star'd at the Pacific—and all his men
Look'd at each other with a wild surmise—
Silent, upon a peak in Darien.

PARAPHRASE

In this sonnet, the poet tells us how he felt when he read Homer's *Odyssey* for the first time in Chapman's English translation. He could have told us how he felt in straightforward literal language ("I was excited, awestruck"[1]), but instead he tells us how he felt by using the two metaphors of *travel* and *discovery.* In the first eight lines, under the metaphor of travel, he tells us that he had read many of the Greek and Roman poets in translation but because he couldn't read Greek, he never read Homer's epic until he came across Chapman's translation. In the last six lines, using the metaphor of discovery, he tells us what the effect of that experience was. It was like the excitement that an astronomer feels when he sees a new planet through his telescope. It was like the astonishment that Cortez (actually it was Balboa) and his men felt when they stood on a mountain in Mexico and caught their first glimpse of the Pacific ocean.

What is the source of conflict?

The basic element in all story-telling—what holds our attention and keeps us turning the pages—is **conflict.** Conflict

---

[1] Filled with respectful and possibly fearful astonishment.

results from some kind of problem, struggle, or tension facing the characters in the short story, the novel, or the play. The conflict may take the form of physical action (a fight, a shoot-out, a race, a journey). Or it may take the form of a verbal[1] contest between two or more characters (an argument, a clash of opinions or ideologies,[2] a debate about values). Or it could take the form of some kind of psychological struggle (a character debating with himself or herself about a crucial decision, a character struggling to solve some kind of problem or mystery). **Whatever form the conflict takes, it is basically a struggle between two forces,** and the more nearly the opposing forces are equal, the greater the drama, the more eager we are to read on in order to find out how the struggle comes out.

Conflict is an element you discuss when you are dealing with fiction and drama, but in dealing with some poems, you could talk about how the speaker in the poem resolved the psychological or spiritual *tension* he was experiencing.

What kind of characters appear?

You could write an entire paper in response to this question. Often it is the characters, rather than the plot, that most interest us. If a storyteller is especially skillful, the characters become even more *real* to us than people we know in our daily lives, and we can talk about them as though they were *real* people. They are men or women, young or old, noble or base,[3] aggressive[4] or timid,[5] likable or hateful, intelligent or stupid. We can picture what they look like, how they dress, how they carry themselves. We hear their voices and what

[1] Related to, or consisting of, words. [2] Ideas, assertions, and aims that constitute the political, social, or economic program of a person or group. [3] Of low (moral) quality. [4] Making unprovoked attacks; of hostile, harmful behavior. [5] Fearful.

they say, and sometimes we are even allowed inside their heads to find out what they are thinking. We care about what happens to them. If they are sympathetic characters, we want to see them succeed or survive; if they are "wicked" characters, we want to see them defeated, shamed, or routed.[1]

Such an infinite number of things could be said about characters in a story, a play, or even a poem that it is hardly necessary to suggest specific aspects that could be discussed. Just talk about characters as you would about people in real life.

How does the author characterize the people in the work?

We spoke in the previous section about how lifelike people in stories become for us. How does an author create lifelike people and give us an idea of what kind of people they are? Here are the principal means of characterization:

☐ **By actions**—*what people do and how they do it.*

☐ **By speech**—*what people say and how they say it.*

☐ **By description**—their *physical appearance* (facial features, weight, height, stature,[2] carriage[3]) and their *manner of dress.*

☐ **By testimony**—*what others say about a person.*

☐ **By thoughts**—*what a person thinks and feels* (all those *interior* reactions that reveal so much about a person—speculations, dreams, rationalizations,[4] reveries,[5] emotions, etc.).

---

[1] Put to flight; forced to flee. [2] A person's quality or status especially as seen by others. [3] Manner of carrying oneself; deportment; behavior. [4] Reasons or justifications for ideas or behavior that one cannot face, justify, or explain in a more accurate or honest way. [5] Daydreams.

☐ **By exposition**—*a summary sketch by the author.*

An author may use all of these means to give us an idea of what kind of people his characters are, but he will probably use two or three of them more than others.

What is the setting?

Every story is acted out in a particular place and time. You may want to talk about that setting, either for its own sake or for its function in the story. You may find the setting interesting for its own sake because it transports you to a faraway place and a long-ago time; or you may find the setting interesting simply because it is familiar and contemporary. In either case, the author's descriptions help you to visualize[1] the scene. But sometimes you are interested in the setting because it plays an important part in the drama of a story. The setting becomes more than just a place and time in which the action occurs; it becomes *atmosphere,* helping to set the mood and the tension in the story. Recall how important setting and atmosphere are in a ghost story or an adventure story. Setting and atmosphere usually play a dominant role, for instance, in the stories of Edgar Allan Poe and Joseph Conrad. In the following description of a bridal chamber in Poe's story "Ligeia," the reader gets not only a vivid picture of the scene and atmosphere but also a strong sense that something tragic will happen in that room (as indeed it does later in the story):

> The room lay in a high turret of the castellated abbey, was pentagonal in shape, and of capacious size. Occupying the whole southern face of the pentagon was the

[1] To see mentally.

Special Kinds of Writing Assignments

sole window—an immense sheet of unbroken glass from Venice—a single pane, and tinted of a leaden hue, so that the rays of either the sun or moon passing through it fell with a ghastly lustre on the objects within. Over the upper portion of this huge window extended the trellis-work of an aged vine, which clambered up the massy walls of the turret. The ceiling, of gloomy-looking oak, was excessively lofty, vaulted, and elaborately fretted with the wildest and most grotesque specimens of a semi-Gothic, semi-Druidical device. From out the most central recess of this melancholy vaulting depended, by a single chain of gold with long links, a huge censer of the same metal, Saracenic in pattern, and with many perforations so contrived that there writhed in and out of them, as if endued with a serpent vitality, a continual succession of parti-colored fires.

Descriptions of setting can also tell us something about the characters. A messy room, for instance, tells us something about the habits of the occupant of that room; a room with floor-to-ceiling bookshelves laden with leather-bound volumes tells us something about the interests of the occupant of that room. The next time you see a movie or a television drama, make a special effort to study the setting. Try to figure out what part that setting is playing in the drama you are watching and what that setting tells you about the characters associated with it.

What is the style of the work?

Although you may not have paid much attention to the *style* of a literary work, the style does exert a subtle[1] influ-

---

[1] Scarcely noticeable; delicate.

ence on you. If you have ever remarked about the style, you may have said things like the following.

The author's style is easy to understand.

The sentences flow smoothly and gracefully.

I felt the power of the author's style.

She uses lots of short, vivid, sensory words.

Metaphors keep tumbling at you so fast you can't absorb them all.

I was so bored by the heavy, plodding sentences that I skipped over dozens of pages at a time.

Except for the two statements that mention *words* and *metaphors,* the statements are rather general and impressionistic.[1] In your paper, you may want to give only your *general impressions* of the author's style, but if you want to be *more specific* in your commentary on the style, you can do some counting and tabulating of features like the following:

☐ **The average sentence-length in number of words**
    (you get this average by dividing the total number of words by the total number of sentences; if, for instance, you counted 150 sentences and found a total of 3678 words, you would have an average sentence-length of 24.5 words per sentence).

☐ **The average paragraph-length, figured either in average number of words per paragraph or in average number of sentences per paragraph**
    (if there were 20 paragraphs in the 3678-word sample, you would have an average of 183.9 words per paragraph and an average of 7.5 sentences per paragraph).

☐ **Percentage of single-syllable words in a 200-word sample**

[1] Giving rather rough, scattered details and highlights; creating an overall *impression* rather than depicting exactly.

Special Kinds of Writing Assignments

(you get this average by dividing the total number of single-syllable words by 200; if you found 136 single-syllable words in 200 words, the percentage would be 68%).

☐ **The number or percentage of nouns and pronouns in a 200-word sample**

(you could also determine the number and percentage of verbs, adjectives, and adverbs in the same 200-word sample, although it might be more significant to determine the relative proportions[1] of active verbs and passive verbs or of concrete nouns and abstract nouns).

☐ **The number and kinds of figures of speech in a selected passage**

(see the list and definitions of figures of speech on pp. 102–111 in Chapter 5).

There are some finer points of style that you might look at, like sentence rhythms, parallel structures, symbols, imagery, but the five features listed above are the easier features to find and catalogue, *if* you want to say something specific about an author's style in a short story, novel, play, or poem.

How is the work organized and structured?

The basic organizing principle in narratives (short stories, novels, plays, narrative poems) is **time** (*chronology*)—first this happened, then this happened, then that happened; in other words, the incidents in a story are arranged in the order in which they happened. But sometimes stories depart from a straight time-sequence. An author may halt the forward movement of the story to give us a *flashback*—something that took place before the time when the story begins. Or the

---

[1] The relation of one part to another (or to the whole) in respect to size or number.

author may give us a *foreshadowing*—a hint of something that will happen later in the story.

The basic structure of a story follows this pattern:

1 Posing the basic conflict of the story.

2 Complicating or intensifying[1] the basic conflict—making the situation get worse.

3 Reaching the climax—the point of highest dramatic intensity in the story, the point in the story where the conflict is finally resolved.

4 Winding down the story, usually very short—sometimes called the *anticlimax* or *denouement* ("the unknotting").

But some stories depart from this basic structure. A story might begin with the "end," for instance—a man being stood up before a firing squad—and then it would go back to the "beginning" to show you the sequence of events that brought the man to that critical moment. Television dramas often begin with an exciting incident that occurs later on in the story; the TV producers want to "hook" the viewers and prevent them from turning to another channel.

A number of typographical[2] devices are used to mark off the parts of literary works. Novels are likely to be broken up into chapters. The parts of short stories are sometimes marked with Roman numerals (I, II, III, etc.) or simply with extra space on the page between parts. Plays are usually marked off into Acts and Scenes (often with two or more scenes in each act). Poems are often marked off in stanzas—groupings of lines with extra space between each group. The thought structure of a sonnet, a fourteen-line poem, often observes one of these patterns:

[1] Making more intense; heightening; making sharper or more acute. [2] Relating to the art, style, arrangement, or appearance of printing from type.

197

Special Kinds of Writing Assignments

1 The **Italian** or **Petrarchan sonnet:** a two-part structure composed of the *first eight lines,* called the *octave,* and the *concluding six lines,* called the *sestet.* (John Keats's "On First Looking into Chapman's Homer" has this structure.)

2 The **Shakespearean** or **Elizabethan sonnet** has the structure of *three quatrains* (three groups of four lines) and a *concluding couplet* (a group of two lines).

There are many other stanzaic[1] patterns, which you will meet in literature courses that study poetry.

You probably won't feel the need to comment on the organization and structure of a narrative unless the story presents interesting variations of the basic time-sequence. There are some other interesting variations of structure besides *flashbacks* and *foreshadowing.* Sometimes a novel that involves several groups or families of interrelated people will use an *alternating* or *interweaving* pattern—one chapter will present an incident involving one group, the next chapter the second group, the next chapter the third group, and then the next chapter will resume the story of the first group, etc. Sometimes authors interrupt the forward movement of the novel by throwing in an *interchapter* every now and then—a chapter that deals with something other than the story. In *Tom Jones,* Henry Fielding has interchapters that deal with the art of fiction; in *Moby Dick,* Herman Melville frequently interrupts his narrative with interchapters dealing with whales and the whaling industry; in *The Grapes of Wrath,* John Steinbeck throws in interchapters that deal with the larger social implications of the poverty of the sharecroppers[2] during the dust-bowl[3] years in the 1930s. It is variations like these that you may want to comment on in your paper.

---

[1] Relating to the grouping of lines that mark off a unit or division of a poem. [2] Farmers who work the land of others for a share of the crops. [3] An area afflicted with prolonged drought and dust storms.

● Analyzing a Literary Work

What is the point of view from which the story is told?

The point of view is the consciousness, the filter, through which the events in a story come through to the reader. Another way to get at the point of view is to ask yourself "Who is telling the story?" or "Through whose eyes do we see the action of the story?" Point of view is a factor only in short stories, novels, and narrative poems. There is no point of view involved in a play, a movie, or a television drama, because there is no one standing between us, the viewers, and the events being acted out.

There are four points of view from which a story can be told—two of them *interior* points of view, two of them *exterior* points of view:

(1) INTERIOR (told by a character *in* the story)

(A) First-Person Point of View

This is the easiest of the points of view to distinguish. It is a major or minor character in the story who is referred to in the narrative parts (that is, the non-dialogue parts) of the story by the pronoun *I* (hence[1] the term *first-person*). This first-person narrator can report anything that the *I* can see or hear or know, can give us the *I*'s thoughts, but cannot give us the thoughts or inward reactions of any other characters in the story.

Here is an example of the first-person point of view. The *I* (*me*) here is Huck Finn, the hero of Mark Twain's novel *Huckleberry Finn:*

---

[1] Therefore; consequently.

Special Kinds of Writing Assignments

After supper she got out her book and learned me about Moses and the Bulrushers, and I was in a sweat to find out all about him; but by and by, she let it out that Moses had been dead a considerable long time; so then I didn't care no more about him, because I don't take no stock in dead people.

Pretty soon I wanted to smoke, and asked the widow to let me. But she wouldn't. She said it was a mean practice and wasn't clean, and I must try to not do it any more. That is just the way with some people. They get down on a thing when they don't know nothing about it. Here she was a-bothering about Moses, which was no kin to her, and no use to anybody, being gone, you see, yet finding a power of fault with me for doing a thing that had some good in it. And she took snuff, too; of course that was all right, because she done it herself.

(B) Third-Person Point of View

This is a major or minor character in the story, who is referred to, in the narrative parts of the story, by his or her name (James Stokes, Nancy Reems) or by the pronoun *he* or *she* (hence the term *third-person*). This narrator can report anything that he or she can see or hear or know, can give us his or her thoughts, but cannot give us the thoughts or inward reactions of any other characters in the story.

In the following example of the third-person point of view, the *he* (*his, him*) is a high-school boy named William, who is the main character of John Updike's short story "A Sense of Shelter":

When he emerged into the hall it was not empty: one girl walked down its varnished perspective toward him, Mary Landis, in a heavy brown coat, with a scarf on her head and books in her arms. Her locker was up here, on the second floor of the annex. His own was in the annex basement. A ticking sensation that existed neither in the medium of sound nor of light crowded against his throat. She flipped the scarf back from her hair and in a conversational voice that carried well down the clean planes of the hall said, "Hi, Billy." The name came from way back, when they were both children, and made him feel small but brave.

[From *Pigeon Feathers and Other Stories* (New York: Alfred A. Knopf, 1962), pp. 94–95]

(2) EXTERIOR (told from a consciousness or vantage-point *outside* the story)

(A) Omniscient Point of View

This is an all-knowing, godlike consciousness outside the story that is unlimited in what it can report. In addition to being able to tell us anything that is taking place or has taken place, the omniscient[1] narrator can give us the thoughts and inward reactions of all of the characters but may choose to give us the thoughts and reactions of only one of them. If the thoughts of more than one character are exposed, you know for sure that the story is being told from the omniscient point of view.

If the thoughts of only one character are exposed, you can distinguish the omniscient point of view by noting whether you are given information that a first-person or third-person narrator could not or would not give you. For instance, if a story is being told by a first-person or third-person narrator,

---

[1] All-knowing.

Special Kinds of Writing Assignments

you will not get a description of the physical appearance of that narrator (unless he or she is looking in a mirror and reporting the image seen there). So if you get a physical description of a character in addition to an exposure of his or her thoughts or if you get some information that the narrator would not or could not supply, you know that the story is being told by an omniscient narrator.

In the following example of the omniscient point of view, from Edith Wharton's short story "Roman Fever," note the information or commentary we get about the two women from some *outside* source ("the two ladies, who had been intimate since childhood"; "Mrs. Ansley was much less articulate than her friend") and the exposure of the thoughts of *both* women:

> Mrs. Slade drew her lids together in retrospect; and for a few moments the two ladies, who had been intimate since childhood, reflected how little they knew each other. Each one, of course, had a label ready to attach to the other's name; Mrs. Delphin Slade, for instance, would have told herself, or any one who asked her, that Mrs. Horace Ansley, twenty-five years ago, had been exquisitely lovely—no, you wouldn't believe it, would you? . . . though, of course, still charming, distinguished. . . . Mrs. Ansley was much less articulate than her friend, and her mental portrait of Mrs. Slade was slighter, and drawn with fainter touches. "Alida Slade's awfully brilliant; but not as brilliant as she thinks," would have summed it up; though she would have added, for the enlightenment of strangers, that Mrs. Slade had been an extremely dashing girl; much more so than her daughter, who was pretty, of course, and clever in a way, but had none of her mother's—well, "vividness,"

someone had once called it.
[from *The World Over* (New York: D. Appleton-Century, 1936), p. 219]

(B) Objective or "Camera-eye" Point of View

Think of this point of view as a motion-picture camera equipped to record sound. This point of view is restricted to reporting only what can be recorded on film and on sound-tape. It cannot, and does not, report the thoughts of any of the characters. The camera-eye point of view relays to the reader only what is done or said or can be seen, without any commentary or background information.

Outside of the script for a play or a movie, it is difficult to find a *pure* example of the objective[1] or camera-eye point of view. Occasionally, authors will use the objective point of view in parts of their story but then shift to one of the other three points of view. In the first half of his long short story "Big Boy Leaves Home," Richard Wright uses the objective point of view, but after Big Boy kills the white man at the swimming-hole, Wright shifts to the third-person point of view of Big Boy. Most of Ernest Hemingway's famous short story, "The Killers," is told from the objective point of view, but after the scene shifts from Henry's lunchroom to Ole Anderson's rooming-house, we see and hear things from Nick Adams's point of view, although the story continues to be told largely through dialogue.

The objective point of view that we observe in these paragraphs of George Milburn's novel *Catalogue* prevails throughout the story:

---

[1] Dealing with facts without the element of distortion by feelings or prejudices.

Special Kinds of Writing Assignments

The sun was blistering the sanded green paint on the M. K. & T. railway station. A gray farm wagon drawn by two mousy mules turned up the dust-cushioned road and came gritting along the graveled platform. It stopped on the shady east side of the depot. The driver eased his blue hulk to the ground and went into the waiting room for Whites.

He gaped a moment at the empty slat benches. Flies droned against the paint-sealed windows. There was a muffled chatter of telegraph in the room beyond. The ticket window was shut; so he lumbered on through to the sunny side of the station. He went round and stuck his head in at the Negro waiting room, off which the office door opened.

"Hello, Mr. Conklin! Hello!" he bawled.

[from *Catalogue* (New York: Harcourt, Brace, 1936), pp. 194–195]

Why did the author choose this point of view from which to tell the story?

The previous question could be answered in a single sentence—e.g. "Mark Twain tells his story from the first-person point of view of the main character, Huck Finn." A more important question and one that would take you at least a full paragraph to answer adequately is the question, "Why did the author choose this particular point of view for his story?"

The choice of point of view determines not only *what* can be narrated to us but also *what effect* the story will have on us. A change in point of view results in a different story and a different effect. Some authors have experimented with telling the same story from a variety of points of view. In *The Sound and the Fury,* for instance, William Faulkner tells the same story four times, each time from the perspective[1] of a different character in the story—Benjy, Quentin, Jason, and Dilsey.

Perhaps the most important decision that a fiction writer makes is the choice of point of view, because that point of view determines what can, and what cannot, be told to us and what effect the story will have upon us. A detective story, for instance, cannot be told from the omniscient point of view, because an all-knowing narrator would know "whodunit" right from the outset and could not withhold[2] that information from the reader. Detective stories are usually told from the third-person or the first-person point of view, and that first-person or third-person narrator is usually the detective who is trying to solve the mystery. Detective stories can also be told—and sometimes have been told—from the objective or camera-eye point of view. (In that case, the story would be told in much the same manner as it is told in a movie or in a television drama.)

An author will choose the omniscient narrator when the drama of his story depends on the exposure of the thoughts of more than one character, because omniscience is the *only* point of view that allows the thoughts of more than one character to be exposed. Or he might choose the omniscient point of view if he has to supply vital background information about characters or situations that could not or would not come naturally from a character within the story.

If an author has a tale of strange and exotic[3] adventure to tell, he will often choose the first-person point of view, because readers more easily believe a tale of adventure told by an eyewitness. If an author wants to gain some distancing from the intensely personal tone of the / point of view, he will

[1] The aspect from which a subject or its parts are viewed.   [2] Hold back.   [3] Strikingly unusual or different.

Special Kinds of Writing Assignments

adopt the third-person point of view. If an author wants to tell a story from a completely impersonal point of view, without any interpretive[1] or influencing commentary by a narrator, he will adopt the objective point of view.

One of the ways in which to approach the answer to the question, "Why did the author choose this point of view from which to tell this story?" is to **imagine what the story and its effect might have been if the author had told the story from one of the other three points of view.**

A word needs to be said here about the *psychological viewpoint* of the narrator. Sometimes the narrator in the story gives the events *as* they are happening or *shortly after* they happened; at other times, he narrates events from a perspective many years removed from the time when they actually took place. In a story about childhood, for instance, it makes a big difference whether the story is being told as the child is experiencing it or whether it is being told by an adult looking back upon an experience he or she had as a child. A child and an adult are bound to have a different perspective on what happened, and this *difference in perspective* can make a profound difference in what is reported to the readers and in the effect the narrative has on them.

●
Interpreting a literary work

General Questions to Be Answered in *Interpreting a Literary Work*

What did the *author* mean? (*objective* interpretation)
and/or
What did the work mean to *you*? (*subjective* interpretation)

[1] Relating to understanding according to personal belief, judgment, or interest.

206

● Interpreting a Literary Work

The *analysis* of a literary work tries to discover *what is there*—either in the content or in the form. The *interpretation* of a literary work seeks to discover the *meaning or significance of what is there.* Obviously, analysis must precede interpretation. You don't have to analyze the work *totally* before you can proceed to interpretation, but at least you must first discover that portion of the work that you are going to interpret.

Sometimes when you are assigned to write a paper on a literary text, you are not expected to analyze the work—at least not in the paper itself—but instead you are asked to interpret the work or a part of the work. What you are being asked to do is explain *what the author meant* **(objective interpretation)** and/or *what the work means to you* **(subjective interpretation).** The two meanings do not *necessarily* differ; the meaning you derive from the work could be the same meaning that the author intended.

But usually when you are asked to discuss what the work means to you, you are being asked to discuss a different kind of meaning from the meaning of the text itself. You are being asked for your *personal response* to the work: how does the work relate to your life, your experiences, your views, your values. Presumably, there is *one* objective meaning to the text—or at least the author intended one meaning—and we should be able to discover what that one meaning is. But there could be as many *subjective* meanings as there are readers of the text, because the significance of a work for various readers will differ because of different experiences, education, attitudes, values, etc. For that reason, the subjective interpretations cannot be judged *right* or *wrong,* or *good, better, best;* they can only be viewed as *different.*

In order to focus your interpretation, the teacher, in making the assignment, may pose a question or questions to guide you. Listed below are some typical questions that could

Special Kinds of Writing Assignments

guide you in writing an interpretive paper on a short story, novel, play, or poem. They are grouped under two main headings: Author's Meaning (*objective*) and Meaning to You (*subjective*). Some of the questions, especially those mentioning *characters* and *incidents,* apply only to narratives (short stories, novels, and plays). (Regard the parentheses in some of the questions as *blanks* in which could be put the names of particular characters, incidents, objects, etc.)

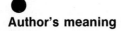

Author's meaning

What is the theme of the work?

As in the case of expository and argumentative writing, so too does imaginative writing have a theme. This theme may not be formally stated in the work, as it often is in expository or argumentative writing, but it is there just the same. **You may have to *deduce*[1] *the theme from the work.*** This theme enunciates[2] a "truth about life" that the reader has learned from reading the literary work. The theme, for instance, of a story about young love might be this: "When two people are head over heels in love, they are not likely to heed[3] the advice of parents, relatives, or friends"; or it might be this: "A man in love will strive relentlessly to overcome every obstacle that separates him from his loved one." Those are only two of dozens of themes that a story about young love could have. Think of the theme as a general statement about the *meaning* or *significance* of a work.

---

[1] To infer; to draw as a conclusion.   [2] Announces; proclaims.   [3] To pay attention to.

In what way is (a particular incident or passage) related to the theme of the work?

If a theme is a summary statement of what the parts of a work add up to, individual incidents or passages should be somehow related to that theme. If, for instance, a story about young love had as its theme, "When two people are head over heels in love with one another, they are not likely to heed the advice of parents, relatives, and friends," a particular incident in that story could be a concrete illustration of two young lovers ignoring the advice of the girl's father. Other incidents or passages in the story could be illustrations of the same theme but in a different way.

What did (a particular character) mean when he/she said, "(quotation of the statement)."

Sometimes you will be asked to interpret the meaning of a particular sentence or sentences. Usually, it will be a passage in which the meaning is not apparent but which has an important bearing on the theme or on the relationships of the characters or on the course of the action. You will have to derive the meaning from the context—who was saying what to whom for what purpose?

What is the symbolism of (a particular event or object in the work)?

Sometimes an author intends certain events or objects to have a larger meaning than their surface meaning. For instance, a ticking clock that keeps getting mentioned at cru-

Special Kinds of Writing Assignments

cial moments in a story could become something more than just a ticking clock: it could symbolize that time is running out for a particular character and could foreshadow[1] the death of that character. There's danger, of course, in "symbol-hunting." If a reader is on the lookout for symbols, he begins to see symbols everywhere—even when an author didn't intend any symbolism. But when an author intends something to be symbolic, he usually gives us hints, such as frequent occurrence or unusual prominence of the symbolic event or object.

What patterns do you find in the (incidents, characters, diction,[2] figures of speech)?

Sometimes an author deliberately arranges various elements in patterns or motifs.[3] For instance, he might set up incidents in his story in a counterpointing[4] pattern: scenes of hope alternating with scenes of despair; scenes of hectic urban[5] life alternating with scenes of placid[6] rural[7] life. Characters too fall into balancing groups: male and female, achievers and failures, idealists and pessimists, intellectuals and nonintellectuals, and (the common grouping in westerns) "good guys" and "bad guys" or "white hats" and "black hats." Patterns or motifs of language frequently appear in literary texts—the images of disease in *Hamlet;* the variations on the words *nothing* and *nature* in *King Lear;* the motif of *light* in Wordsworth's "Ode on Intimations of Immortality" (*glory, sunshine, starry, gleam, radiance, moon, splendor*). It is usually easier to find and demonstrate patterns of this kind than to detect and interpret symbols.

[1] Give a hint or suggestion beforehand. [2] Choice of words, especially with regard to clearness or effectiveness. [3] Distinctive features of design or composition. [4] Employing complementing or contrasting elements that interplay. [5] Relating to or constituting a city. [6] Undisturbed; peaceful. [7] Of or relating to the country, to country people, or to agriculture.

How is the ending of the work related to other parts of the work?

What this question is asking you to do is to show that the ending follows naturally, plausibly,[1] or inevitably from the other events in the work. Sometimes we are left unsatisfied with the ending of a story because it seems arbitrary, contrived,[2] unexpected. In other stories, even in those that end unhappily (like the tragic death of Cordelia in *King Lear*), we are satisfied because the story ended in the way that the previous incidents dictated that it *must* end.

Why did (a particular character) do what he/she did?

This question concerns motivation. When we observe characters in action in a story, we are interested not only in what they do and how they do it but also in *why* they do what they do. Were they motivated by some circumstance? by what some other character did? by some trait[3] in their character? Because the motivation of a character is not always made apparent by the author, we have to arrive at the motivation by interpretation of character and situation. We must be satisfied that the motivation we discover through interpretation is psychologically sound—that is, that it gives a plausible explanation for the character doing what he or she does.

What kind of person is (a particular character in a story or the persona[4] that speaks in a poem)?

In the section on analyzing a literary work, we saw the

---

[1] In an apparently acceptable or believable way. [2] Achieved with difficulty. [3] A distinguishing quality; characteristic. [4] An imaginary person or voice.

various ways by which an author characterizes the people who appear in his work—by *action, speech, description, thoughts,* and *exposition.* We form our idea of what kind of person the character is from whichever of those means the author uses. One way to answer this question is to write a character sketch which summarizes the traits of that "created" person. It is a bit more difficult to get an idea of the persona that speaks in a poem, because our only source of information about the speaker in a poem is what the speaker says in the poem. We gain our notion of the persona from *what* he or she says and *how* he or she says it. We formulate our image of the persona from the views, values, tone, and attitude revealed through his or her speech.

What attitude does the narrator have toward (a particular character) and how is this attitude revealed?

Usually, the attitude that the narrator has toward a particular character is the attitude that the author of the story wants the reader to have too. But sometimes the attitude of the narrator may differ from the reader's. The narrator may admire a character that the reader despises; or the narrator may despise a character that the reader admires. Usually, when there is that kind of difference in attitude, we can be sure that the author planned it that way. The author deliberately tells the story through the eyes of an obviously *unreliable narrator* so that the reader will form an attitude toward the character that is quite the opposite of the narrator's.

A good example of this unreliable narrator is the gabby small-town barber in Ring Lardner's short story "Haircut." The story is one long, uninterrupted monologue in which the barber tells a stranger who comes to his shop about Jim Kendall, a salesman who had lost his job for incompetence[1]

[1] Lack of required ability, power, or qualification.

and ended up being murdered by the town's idiot boy. It is obvious from the tales the barber tells that he considered Jim to be the funniest man he had ever met. But we the readers cringe[1] at the tales of the cruel, "sick" jokes that Jim played on his family, friends, strangers, and the idiot boy, and we are glad to see Jim get his just deserts[2] in the end. The barber's admiration for Jim constantly clashes with our disgust. The author intended that our reaction to Jim be the natural one and that the barber's reaction be an *un*natural one. Ring Lardner reveals his attitude toward Jim Kendall through the outrageousness of his narrator's admiration for the man.

Of course, in most instances, the narrator's attitude toward some character in the story will be the same as ours. But we must be aware that in those cases our attitude toward the character, whether favorable or unfavorable, has been subtly[3] influenced by the narrator. The narrator shapes our attitude by the things he chooses to tell us about the character, by the comments he makes about the character, by the reactions of other characters toward the character. If we trust the narrator, if we find him *reliable,* we will accept his estimate of the character.

●
Evaluating a literary work

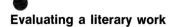

> General Questions to Be Answered in *Evaluating a Literary Work*
> **How well does the author accomplish what he set out to do?** and/or
> **Was the work worth your time and attention?**

---

[1] Shrink back from or at the sight of.   [2] Those things that are deserved, whether good or bad.   [3] In a way hardly noticeable; delicately.

Special Kinds of Writing Assignments

Once you have *exposed* what is in the text through analysis and once you have *discovered* the meaning of the text through interpretation, you can legitimately proceed to *evaluate* the text—that is, express your estimate of the author's accomplishment and your personal reaction to the text. You have progressed from the most objective part of the process, the analysis, to the most personal part, the evaluation. In evaluating the text, you will be expressing your *opinion,* and your opinion is likely to be a mixture of your *taste* and your *judgment.* Your taste reflects your *personal preferences;* your judgment reflects your *reasoned estimate.* For instance, you might not like a particular novel simply because you don't like tales of violence. In that case, your evaluation is based mainly on your taste. But if you said that you didn't like a particular novel because the characters were not believable people, your estimate is probably based on a reasoned judgment. Of course, you are still expressing an opinion (other readers may find the characters perfectly believable), but at least you could present some arguments to support your opinion.

Here are some questions that can guide you in evaluating the literary text. They are divided into two main groups: questions about the author's accomplishment and questions about your personal reactions.

Questions about the author's accomplishment

Was the work true-to-life?

We expect a literary work to reflect life as we know it. We can, of course, read stories set in a distant time or place or

● Questions about the Author's Accomplishment

we can read fantasies (fairy tales, science fiction) and still find them true-to-life if they are consistent[1] with the conditions that the author has set up. If we feel that a story violates the author's own terms, we reject it as being "untrue" or "unrealistic." We are willing to accept Superman's being able to roll a 1000-pound boulder up a steep hill in order to let it roll down on his pursuers, but we are not willing to accept that same action in a western where the "good guy" is trying to escape from the "bad guys."

Was the action plausible?

This question is similar to the previous one. But the previous question is concerned with what is *possible;* this question is concerned with what is *probable.* There is a subtle but real difference between the possible and the probable. The possible refers to what *could* happen; the probable refers to what is *likely* to happen. Strange things happen occasionally, and because they are strange, they usually merit a story in the newspaper. Somebody falls out of a five-story window and escapes with only a bruised shoulder. It is *possible* for a person to survive a fall like that, but it is not *probable.* In at least nine cases out of ten, the person would be killed.

One of the ways in which fiction differs from real life is that events have to be made to seem probable, plausible. The reader must be made to feel that something happened because of something that took place previously or because of the nature of the characters or circumstances involved. Things that happen by chance are possible but not probable. Those stories are most satisfying where we feel that there is a cause-and-effect relationship between events: what happened in this scene *caused* what happened in the next

[1] In agreement or harmony.

Special Kinds of Writing Assignments

scene. When we point out that an event is not plausible or probable, we are pointing out a serious flaw[1] in the author's art.

Were the characters believable and consistent?

This question too is concerned with the true-to-life, but it is concerned with characters rather than with actions. When we ask whether a character is *believable,* we are asking whether that character behaves as a person of that nature could be expected to behave. Strange as a character may be, we still expect him or her to be recognizably human. A character will strike us as being recognizably human when his or her thoughts, words, and actions seem to be properly and plausibly motivated. If we can't figure out *why* a character did, said, or thought something or if the reason given is an unlikely explanation, the character will cease to be believable to us.

We also expect characters in novels, short stories, and plays to be *consistent.* In real life, of course, all of us occasionally behave inconsistently, but except for those occasional lapses,[2] we behave most of the time in a fairly predictable way. And we expect characters in fiction to be more consistent than people in real life. Once the author has clearly established what kind of person a character is, we expect that character to behave consistently with the traits that have been fixed. If a person has been shown throughout the story to be very tightfisted in spending money, we don't expect that character suddenly to turn into a wild spender—not unless we are given some good reason for the sudden,

---

[1]Fault; defect. [2]Slips or deviations from something that is usual or necessary.

surprising change.

It is surprising how often a negative estimate of an author's accomplishment is prompted by his or her failure to create believable, consistent characters.

Was the author's style clear and pleasing?

The danger with this question is that your answer to it could be purely a matter of taste. You may not like an author whose style demands close attention. In order to justify your displeasure, you could accuse the author of having a heavy, plodding[1] style, when really what you should be saying is that you don't like any style that is so packed with meaning that you have to pay close attention to every sentence. Your judgment that the style was heavy and plodding would be more impressive if you could show that the author uses an unusually high percentage of difficult, abstract words, that he writes sentences that are unusually long and involved, that he does not vary the length or pace of his sentences, that he spins out sentence after sentence about a relatively minor point. All those charges might still not add up to a "heavy, plodding style," but at least you are presenting some concrete evidence of what *you* think constitutes a heavy, plodding style.

The important point here is that you cannot get by with mere assertions, favorable or unfavorable, about the clarity and attractiveness of an author's style. You must back up your assertions with some specific evidence from the text. If that evidence is convincing, you will have made a responsible judgment about the failure of the author's style.

---

[1] Slow, laborious, or monotonous.

Special Kinds of Writing Assignments

What changes would improve the work?

Obviously, if the author is deficient in any of the matters raised by the previous four questions, the right changes made in those matters will improve the work. But you might be able to suggest other changes too that would improve the work:

☐ Use a different point of view to tell the story.

☐ Add a scene or character to take care of a "missing link" in the story.

☐ Shift a scene from its present position to a later position to delay the climax and intensify the suspense.

☐ Cut out some material that is unnecessary and that slows the pace of the story.

☐ Correct errors of fact in the story (e.g. types of gun used in a murder story).

☐ (if you are dealing with a poem) Substitute less hackneyed[1] images or use a more appropriate verse form.

Suggesting changes is a form of evaluating a work, because the suggestions imply that the author made the *wrong choices* for his purposes. But you should be aware that the danger in such suggestions is that you may be proposing to the author the kind of work you think he *should* have written, instead of telling him how to improve the work he intended to write.

---

[1] Lacking freshness or originality.

●

Questions about your personal reactions

Did the work capture and hold your interest?

This is an important question to ask about any literary work. The answer to that question represents, of course, only *one* reader's response to the work, and it may be based solely on the reader's taste. But if we are convinced that the critic has given a careful and sensitive reading to the text, we do pay attention to such individual responses. The evaluations of reviewers of new books in the mass media[1] have some influence on sales, and often we are moved to read a work simply on the recommendation of a friend. You can strengthen your answer to this question by explaining *why* the work captured and held your interest.

How does the work compare with other literary works you have read or with some movie, play, or television drama you have seen?

Comparison is another way of evaluating a work. In the act of comparing, you point out *similarities* and *differences,* and eventually you make judgments about which is *better.* Sometimes, you have the opportunity to compare a work produced in two different media. For instance, you might compare the novel *Jaws* with the movie made from the novel. You probably liked one version better than the other, and you could write a whole paper in which you give the reasons for your

---

[1] Channels of communication (as broadcasting, publishing, motion pictures).

Special Kinds of Writing Assignments

preference. You should make allowances, however, for the different media. Some things can be done in the written medium (for instance, reproducing the thoughts of characters) that cannot be done in a pictorial medium. On the other hand, the pictorial medium can present some scenes more dramatically and vividly than written words can. Allowances must also be made for the fact that you may be more familiar with one medium than with another.

Do you agree or disagree with what other critics have said about the work?

Other critics' judgments about a work can serve as a springboard for your own evaluation. If you have done a careful job of analyzing and interpreting the work, you should be able to state the grounds for your agreement or disagreement with other critics. But remember that you cannot just assert your contrary judgments. You have to present arguments to support your judgments.

If you were writing a review of the work for a newspaper, what would you say to encourage others to read or not read the work?

This question suggests a good way in which you might approach the writing of a short paper on a literary work. It offers you a wide range of things that you could talk about—the plot, the characters, the theme, the ideas, the style. Knowing the audience for, say, a college newspaper, you can concentrate on those aspects of the work that are likely to interest such readers and that are most likely to induce them to read (or not read) the work.

What have you learned from reading this work that could make your life better or different?

We read literature mainly to be entertained. But there is a *teaching* function to literature also. Frequently, literature gives us a taste of experiences that we might never have in real life. It can transport us imaginatively to distant times and places; it can introduce us to types of people that we never meet in real life; it can plunge us into experiences that are much more exciting than our humdrum lives. In short, literature can extend our range of experiences. And the sensitivity of the author's vision can make us *see* more, *realize* more, even in the familiar experiences of our lives. Whether we are aware of it or not, the reading of literature can affect our lives, for better or for worse. You could write an entire paper in which you talk about how a particular work has affected you.

Special Kinds of Writing Assignments

The sets of questions grouped under Analyzing Literature, Interpreting Literature, and Evaluating Literature are intended to suggest, but not exhaust, the things you might say in a paper you are asked to write about a literary text. Your paper might deal with all three processes of analysis, interpretation, and evaluation, but it might confine itself to only one of those processes. The advantage of writing about literature is that you have a definite subject to write about. All the material you need is right there in the words of the text. The questions are intended as a device to *discover* what is there to talk about in your paper.

Examples of comments about literary texts

Here are some excerpts from essays about literary texts. Some of them were written by students; others were written by professional critics. They do not illustrate answers to all of the *particular* questions posed in this section, but they do illustrate answers to all of the *general* questions. They are grouped under the three headings of Analyzing Literature, Interpreting Literature, and Evaluating Literature.

Analyzing Literature

In this excerpt from a book, a professional critic analyzes the function of the "double plot" in Shakespeare's play *King Lear:*

> Consider next the double action. It has certain strictly dramatic advantages and may well have had its origin in purely dramatic considerations. To go no further, the

secondary plot fills out a story which would by itself have been somewhat thin, and it provides a most effective contrast between its personages[1] and those of the main plot, the tragic strength and nature of the latter being heightened by comparison with the slighter build of the former.[2] But its chief value lies elsewhere and is not merely dramatic. It lies in the fact—in Shakespeare without a parallel—that the sub-plot simply repeats the theme of the main story. Here, as there, we see an old man ''with a white beard.'' He, like Lear, is affectionate, unsuspicious, foolish, and self-willed.[3] He, too, wrongs deeply a child who loves him not less for the wrong. He, too, meets with monstrous[4] ingratitude from the child whom he favours, and is tortured and driven to death. This repetition does not simply double the pain with which the tragedy is witnessed: it startles and terrifies by suggesting that the folly of Lear and the ingratitude of his daughters are no accidents or merely individual aberrations,[5] but that in that dark cold world some fateful malignant[6] influence is abroad,[7] turning the hearts of the fathers against their children and of the children against their fathers, smiting[8] the earth with a curse, so that the brother gives the brother to death and the father the son, blinding the eyes, maddening the brain, freezing the springs of pity, numbing all powers except the nerves of anguish and the dull lust of life.

from A. C. Bradley, *Shakespearean Tragedy* (New York: Meridian, 1955), pp. 210–211.

In the following example of analysis, the student attempts to

---

[1] Persons of rank; distinction, or importance. [2] Of two things, the first or earlier; the second is called *the latter*. [3] Governed by one's own will; obstinate. [4] Of an unusually large size or extent. [5] Deviations from the usual or normal. [6] Harmful; evil. [7] Over a wide area. [8] Striking heavily.

define the basic conflict in William Golding's novel *Lord of the Flies:*

What is the source of conflict in Golding's haunting tale about a group of twelve-year-old English choir-boys marooned[1] on a tropical island? On the surface level—on the level, that is, of the plot—the basic conflict stems from the struggle for leadership between the group typified[2] by Ralph and Piggy and the group typified by Jack and Roger. Ralph and Piggy represent the rational,[3] democratic group that think they can survive only if they make plans and follow them. "We've got to have rules and obey them," Ralph says. "After all, we're not savages. We're English." The first strategy that Ralph proposes for survival is to maintain a fire, night and day. Impressed by Ralph's commonsense, the boys take a vote and elect Ralph as their leader. But gradually, moved by their fears of the unknown and of the "beast" that dropped onto their island out of the skies, the boys turn to the leadership of Jack, the instinctive hunter. Jack gains more and more followers, and before long, Jack and his followers, who represent the forces of primitivism[4] and savagery,[5] kill Piggy and Simon and pursue Ralph to kill him. On the surface level, then, the novel portrays a struggle between rival groups for "political" power.

But it soon becomes obvious that Golding's novel is an allegorical[6] fable—a story that has larger symbolic meaning. On the allegorical level, the conflict results from the struggle between man's civilized, rational na-

---

[1] Left ashore in isolation. [2] Represented as by a model or resemblance. [3] Characterized by reason or understanding. [4] The ways of primitive people, of people in early stages of development or civilization. [5] An act of cruelty or violence; an uncivilized state. [6] Expressing generalizations or truths through symbolic figures and actions.

● Examples of Comments about Literary Texts

ture and his innate[1] depravity.[2] For a while, the boys' civilized nature holds sway, but gradually their animal instincts get the better of them, and they revert[3] to the savagery that typifies mankind untamed[4] by civil laws and moral codes. As Golding himself has said of the novel, "The theme is an attempt to trace the defects of society back to the defects of human nature." This is the opposite of Rousseau's notion that it is civilization which has corrupted mankind. Golding's view of mankind is based on the notion of Original Sin.

In the following excerpt, Lionel Trilling analyzes the structure and organization of William Blake's poem "Tyger! Tyger!":

The dominant, the single, emotion of the poem is amazement, and perhaps no poem has ever expressed an emotion so fully—it is as if the poem were amazement itself. The means by which it achieves this effect is in part very simple: in the course of twenty-four lines it asks fourteen astonished questions. Up through Stanza IV, the tempo of the questions is in continuous[5] acceleration,[6] generating[7] an intense excitement. At Stanza V, the speed of the questions diminishes[8] and the excited wonder modulates[9] to meditative awe.[10]

But not only does the tempo[11] of the poem change at the fifth stanza; its point of reference, its very subject, alters.[12] Up to Stanza V, the poem has undertaken to define the nature of the Tyger by the nature of God—such is the beauty and strength and wildness of the

---

[1] Belonging to a person from birth. [2] Moral corruption. [3] Go back (to some state or condition). [4] Not subdued, softened, or humbled. [5] Continuing without interruption; unbroken. [6] Increase of speed. [7] Producing; causing to exist. [8] Makes or becomes less or smaller. [9] Changes in measure or proportion. [10] Profound respect. [11] Rate of speed, action, or motion. [12] Becomes different; changes.

Special Kinds of Writing Assignments

Tyger that he must be thought to have been created by God's greatest exercise of power, a power put forth against resistance and even with some risk of failure. But at the fifth stanza, the Tyger is no longer defined by the nature of God; now, in the two remaining stanzas, it is God who is defined by the nature of the Tyger. The amazement first evoked by the Tyger is now directed to God, as God reveals himself through his wonderful and terrible[1] creature. And what the poem finds most amazing about God is not his power but his audacity—not the fact that God *could* (as in the first stanza) but that he *dared* (as in the last stanza) create the Tyger!

from Lionel Trilling, ed., *The Experience of Literature* (New York: Holt, Rinehart, and Winston, 1967), pp. 858–859.

In the following example, the student tells us what he learned about a character in a short story simply by looking at *one* of the means of characterization, *action:*

Just from observing the actions of the mother in Ernest Gaines's story "The Sky Is Gray," we learn a lot about what kind of woman she is. For one thing, she's very shrewd. This trait is revealed in the incident in the hardware store. While walking the streets of the Louisiana town with her young son on a winter day, she realizes that her son is very cold. But being a black, she knows that she can't go into the white man's store and just stand around soaking up the heat from the potbellied stove. So she pretends that she wants to buy an ax-handle. Although she didn't buy the ax-handle, she stalled just long enough for her son to get warm.

In the incident in the cafe, we discover two other traits of her character: her unselfishness and her fearlessness.

[1] Filling (an individual) with terror or dread.

Knowing that her son is hungry, she spends one of the few spare quarters she has to buy him some chocolate cake and buys herself only a cup of coffee, even though she's hungry too. She shows her fearlessness when the man in the cafe propositions her. Facing him like a snarling tiger, she forces him to back off.

Her strong sense of pride is the trait revealed in the incident in the grocery store at the end of the story. Knowing that the mother doesn't have much money, the well-meaning white lady who owns the store wants to give her a bigger piece of salt-pork than the quarter's worth that was ordered. But the mother doesn't want charity; she wants only what she can afford to pay for. So she thanks the kindly lady but orders her to cut off only a quarter's worth.

Just from the mother's *actions* in these three incidents, we learn that she is shrewd, unselfish, courageous, and proud.

This student analyzes some of the distinctive features of Eudora Welty's style in a passage from the short story "Livvie":

The passage that I have closely analyzed has several striking stylistic features. For one thing, there is an unusually high number of concrete and monosyllabic[1] nouns. By actual count, I found that 87 percent of the nouns are concrete and that 80 percent of them are one-syllable words. The simplicity of the words can be viewed as a reflection of the kind of people Welty is describing. I also found a great number of compounded structures and a remarkably frequent occurrence of coordinating conjunctions (the figure of *polysyndeton,*

[1] Having one syllable only.

Special Kinds of Writing Assignments

''deliberate overuse of conjunctions''). These features give the passage a drawn-out, slow-paced quality and contribute to our sense of the monotony and plodding-ness of Livvie's lifestyle. The tropes[1] in this passage are also strikingly simple; 68 percent of them are similes, the most easily recognized of the figures, and they use common everyday objects for comparisons. This simplicity on the figurative level is in keeping with the simple language and the simple compounding structures used so often in the passage. When the mood and pace of the passage change toward the end, the author uses a lot of strong active verbs, many of them in their *-ing* form, and the nouns become more earthy and vital too. What further contributes to our sense of simplicity is that almost a third (32.8%) of the sentences are grammatically *simple* sentences and that 43 percent of her sentences are only 20 words long. It wasn't until I did some actual counting of stylistic features like these that I discovered *why* I got such a strong sense of the simplicity of Eudora Welty's descriptions of Livvie's simple way of life.

Interpreting Literature

In the following excerpt from a longer essay, the student offers his interpretation of something that a character said at a crucial moment in a short story:

When Kurtz was about to die in Conrad's ''Heart of Darkness,'' he uttered the words ''The horror! The horror!'' Marlow, who heard these words, regarded them as Kurtz's ''judgment upon the adventures of his soul on earth.'' Kurtz was acknowledging the corruption of his

[1] Figures of speech.

original idealism and his degeneration into pride, greed, and lust for power. He had come out to the African jungle hoping to "civilize" the natives. But he had been so caught up in the quest for ivory and in the lure of the power he had gained over the natives that he began to exploit them. In becoming a god to the natives, he had lost his humanity.

Marlow regarded the utterance of those words as a "moral victory" for Kurtz, because those words revealed Kurtz's recognition of guilt and his remorse over what he had done and what he had become. Kurtz had looked into his own "heart of darkness" and had seen the horror of it all. That is what Kurtz meant by the words "The horror! The horror!"

In the following passage, a professional critic offers his interpretation of a much-debated point about the Epitaph (the last three stanzas) of Thomas Gray's famous eighteenth-century poem "An Elegy Written in a Country Churchyard": whom is the Epitaph talking about?

Clearly, the character and history of Richard West fit closely into the description and epitaph of the Youth to Fortune and to Fame Unknown. He was Gray's dearest friend. He was solitary,[1] "crazed with care," and a poet. His real promise was cut short by an early death. Fair Science certainly did not frown upon him, for he was said by Bryant, a school-fellow of both, to have been more learned than Gray. Although his birth was not humble—he was a grandson of Bishop Burnet and son of a vice-chancellor of Ireland—neither was it noble. The phrase "humble birth," indeed, gives no more trouble in

---

[1] Being apart from others; alone.

interpreting the Epitaph with references to West than it does when considering the Epitaph as written by Gray for himself. The person commemorated[1] in the Epitaph is characterized by a line very similar to one in which West characterized himself. We have seen the difficulties into which the view that the Youth stands for Gray necessarily leads. There is nothing in the description and Epitaph which does not harmonize with the theory that the Youth stands for Richard West.

from Odell Shepard, "'A Youth to Fortune and to Fame Unknown,'" *Modern Philology,* 20 (May, 1923), 371–372.

In the following passage, we are offered an interpretation of *why* Oedipus does what he does in Sophocles' play *Oedipus Rex:*

Knowing, then, is a form of action. The gaining of knowledge can be the most important thing which happens to a character, and like other happenings, either it may be stumbled upon by the weak and essentially passive[2] character or it may be striven for heroically and tragically. Oedipus strives actively for the damning knowledge; he does not bury his head in the sand. It is his glory that he *must* know. But if his striving for knowledge is his glory, it is also his weakness. He is not only confident of his own powers to unriddle[3] what is obscure: he cannot conceive what the implications of full knowledge of any event may be for the human being. Life for the successful Oedipus is rational and has no mysteries that lurk in dark corners. Oedipus cannot comprehend, as indeed few human beings ever can (Faustus, as we have seen, is another example), that

---

[1] Recalled to mind; celebrated in memory. [2] Acted upon and not active; submissive.
[3] To work out the riddle of; to solve.

human eyes may be dazzled and blinded by a *complete* illumination of even those things which seem best known and most familiar.

from Cleanth Brooks and Robert B. Heilman, ed., *Understanding Drama* (New York: Holt, 1948), pp. 581–582.

In the following interpretation, the student argues that in a certain sense, the main character of Arthur Miller's play *Death of a Salesman* was never really a salesman:

In a sense, there is no death of a salesman in this play at all. Something must first have lived before it can die. Willy Loman never *was* a salesman. He tramped over New England with his sample cases, he cultivated the hearty laugh and the facile joke, he developed fallen arches, he consorted with women in hotel rooms—all hallmarks[1] of the travelling salesman. But Willy Loman never bore the stamp of the true salesman. Willy's special gift was in his hands, not in his tongue. As his son Biff says at the end of the play, "There's more of him in that front stoop than in all the sales he ever made." Physically and temperamentally,[2] Willy was built to work outdoors. Technology dealt Willy the cruelest blow when it devised windshields that could not be opened to the caresses of the warm, fresh breezes. He protests against the bricks and windows that box him in at home. "There's not a breath of fresh air in the neighborhood," he cries. He reveals his true ambition when he allows his anguished heart to speak: "a little place out in the country, and I'll raise some vegetables, a couple of chickens. . . . Me and my boys in those grand outdoors." It is frequent revelations like these throughout the play that

---

[1] Distinguishing features.   [2] By usual manner of emotional response; in disposition.

convince me that I am right: there is no death of a salesman in this play, for the salesman never existed. What we see in this play is the death of a *man.*

In the following excerpt, the authors point out one of the patterns of imagery or symbolism in John Steinbeck's novel *The Grapes of Wrath:*

We have seen that both machines and animals serve as effective symbolic devices in *The Grapes of Wrath.* Frequently the machine and animal motifs are conjoined[1] to afford[2] a doubly rich imagery or symbolism. Thus the banks are seen as monstrous animals, but *mechanical* monsters: "the banks were machines and masters all at the same time" (p. 43). The men for whom the share-croppers formerly worked disclaim[3] responsibility: "It's the monster. The bank isn't like a man" (p. 45). The tractors that the banks send in are similarly monstrous—"snub-nosed monsters, raising the dust and sticking their snouts into it, straight down the country, across the country, through fences, through dooryards, in and out of gullies[4] in straight lines" (p. 47). And the man driving the tractor is no longer a man; he is "a part of the monster, a robot in the seat" (p. 48). Their inability to stop these monsters represents the frantic frustration of the dispossessed;[5] Grampa Joad tries to shoot a tractor, and does get one of its headlights, but the monster keeps on moving across their land (p. 62). The new kind of mechanical farming is contrasted with the old kind of personal contact with the land. The new kind is easy and efficient: "So easy that the wonder goes out of work, so efficient that the wonder goes out of land and

[1] Joined together. [2] To provide; to furnish. [3] Deny (having connection with or responsibility for). [4] Trenches made on the earth by running water. [5] Removed from possession or occupancy.

● Examples of Comments about Literary Texts

the working of it, and with the wonder the deep understanding and the relation" (p. 157).

from Robert J. Griffin and William A. Freedman, "Machines and Animals: Pervasive Motifs in *The Grapes of Wrath*," *Journal of English and Germanic Philology,* 62 (April, 1963), 577–578]

Evaluating Literature

In this excerpt, the student offers his final estimate of Arthur Miller's achievement:

The many criticisms I have made about *Death of a Salesman* may have created the impression that I consider it a very inferior play. My intention, however, is not to depreciate[1] the play but to put it in its proper place. Although I believe it possible to write a tragedy about a "common man," I do not think that Willy Loman is the sort of "common man" who can lift this play to the stature of "tragedy," in the sense that we speak of *Oedipus Rex* or *Hamlet* as being a tragedy. Willy is too common a "common man." His many weaknesses of character are more than the "tragic flaw" that Aristotle says marks the true tragic hero. Willy doesn't have any heroic virtues to compensate[2] for his general moral flabbiness. When he "falls" at the end of the play, we don't have the feeling that he has fallen from the "great heights" from which other great tragic heroes have fallen; he seems to have fallen from the height of a curbstone.

But although *Death of a Salesman* is not a tragedy in

[1] To lessen in value. [2] To supply something equivalent or offsetting.

the traditional sense of that term, it is still a very moving play. Because Mr. Miller portrays genuine emotions honestly and convincingly, I was deeply touched by this pathetic story of Willy Loman. Maybe that adjective sums up my assessment of this play: *Death of a Salesman* is a *pathetic* drama, not a great tragedy. But a dramatist who can make you choke up and drop an occasional tear over the fate of a fellow human being must be given due credit.

This student discloses her appreciation of one feature of John Keats's style in the poem "Ode on Melancholy"—his choice of vivid, sensory words and images:

Every English teacher I have ever had has recommended the use of vivid, sensory words, especially in descriptive writing. I never realized the value of such diction until I read Keats's poetry. More than any other poet I have ever read, he uses words and images that I can *see* and *hear* and *taste* and *smell* and *feel.* This talent of his was most evident to me in his "Ode on Melancholy." I must confess I didn't understand the classical allusions[1] in the first stanza to Lethe, Proserpine, and Psyche or the references to *wolf's-bane, nightshade, yew-berries, beetle,* and *death-moth* until I read the poem in an edition that explained those in footnotes. But even the first time I read the poem, I delighted in his use of such "picture" words as *ruby grape, droop-headed flowers, globed peonies, downy owl, weeping cloud, green hill.* He even achieves this sensory quality in the strenuous[2] verbs he uses: *"glut* thy sorrow" and "the bee-mouth *sips."* Instead of saying things abstractly, he paints a picture, as in this figure of

[1] Indirect references; references by suggestion. [2] Vigorous; energetic.

speech: "Joy, whose hand is ever at his lips, bidding adieu." But the most startling image is found in the lines,

> Though seen of none save him whose strenuous tongue
> Can burst Joy's grape against his palate fine.

How much is expressed in those few vivid, concrete words! He made me experience the sensation of breaking a grape with my tongue against the roof of my mouth and tasting the gush of sweet juice and then the bitterness of the rind and the seeds. And that, after all, is the theme of the poem: that the melancholy[1] mood (bitterness) can best be fed by contemplating[2] the beautiful (sweetness). Now I am convinced of the value of searching for vivid, concrete diction to describe an experience.

This student suggests two changes that she thinks would improve Doris Lessing's *The Four-Gated City,* the last installment of a five-volume novel in the "Children of Violence" series:

Six hundred and thirteen pages! That says a lot about this novel. In fact, 613 pages say more than I want to hear. I have read longer novels than this one—*Gone with the Wind* for instance—but I don't remember ever being as bored by a long novel as I was by this one. Doris. Lessing seems incapable of sacrificing any words she has written out on paper. Since she is incapable of cutting anything she has written, why didn't her editor use his blue pencil? There are big chunks of this novel that could have been cut out without being missed—endless pages dealing with ho-hum domestic duties like

[1] Depressed. [2] Viewing or considering with continued attention.

frying eggs and bacon in the morning. An example or two of this sort of thing could have been included just to give us a sense of the daily tedium[1] of the lives of the characters, but when I have to plow through example after example of this kind of slow-paced trivia,[2] I'm stunned into boredom.

Much as I liked the science-fiction ending of the novel, in which we are projected into the year 1997, when a colony of people living on a Scottish island are threatened with total destruction by a nerve gas that was released by a nuclear explosion, I think this ending was just tacked on. It just doesn't fit with the mood and tone of the rest of the novel. It jars the reader, not so much because it presents a scene of horror as because it does not harmonize with the matter-of-factness of the rest of the novel.

As I said before, Doris Lessing seems incapable of sacrificing anything she has written out on paper. Her novel would have been vastly[3] improved if she had dropped a lot of the tedious[4] and extraneous[5] passages.

This student compares J. D. Salinger's novel *Catcher in the Rye* to Mark Twain's *Huckleberry Finn* and finds that Salinger's book speaks more meaningfully to him:

There are rather obvious analogies between *Catcher in the Rye* and *Huckleberry Finn.* Both are stories of adventure, of an odyssey[6] by two young boys who are in rebellion against the adult society that wants them to conform to its standards. Both boys cut their moorings to their home port—Huck from his comfortable but repressive life with Aunt Polly, Holden from the haven[7] of

[1] Tiresomeness; boredom. [2] Unimportant matters. [3] Greatly; immensely. [4] Tiresome; boring. [5] Not intrinsic; irrelevant. [6] A long wandering, with changes of fortune. [7] A place of safety.

the prep school—and drift away into the great unknown world—Huck drifting down the Mississippi on a raft with Jim, Holden taking off on his aimless trek to New York City with no more companionship than his red hunting cap. Both boys have frequent encounters with the adult world, and they find much that is "phony" about that world. Of course, in their bewilderment and naivety,[1] they both make mistakes too and display their own phoniness. But that's all part of their "growing up." For the most part, they both have their heads screwed on straight, and we're confident that eventually they're both going to turn out all right.

Both of these books had something to say to me, but *Catcher* affected me more deeply. I could relate more easily to Holden than to Huck. One of the reasons, of course, why I could relate more easily to Holden is that he lives in a world that is more familiar to me and he speaks a language that I understand better. But I think another reason is that Salinger managed to create a more believable, more vivid character than Mark Twain did. Huck is not a cardboard figure, by any means, but there are many layers of his character that Mark Twain never revealed to me. But Holden became as real for me as my own brother.

In this excerpt, the student tells us what she learned from reading three stories by William Faulkner—"The Fire and the Hearth," "Delta Autumn," and "Raid":

Reading these three stories by William Faulkner made me aware, in human terms, of the values and philosophy of Southern society that I had learned only in an abstract way in my history and sociology classes. What all of the

[1] Variant spelling of naiveté.

stories revealed was the Southerners' strong sense of roots in family and in tradition. Although he is only a black tenant farmer on Roth Edmonds's farm, Lucas Beauchamp prides himself on being "the oldest living McCaslin descendant still living on the hereditary land." The Negro woman who brings her infant child into the hunting camp in "Delta Autumn" reminds Uncle Ike of how the bloodlines of the McCaslins, Edmondses, and Beauchamps are intermixed through marriages and miscegenation.[1] In "Raid," a story about the Civil War years, we are constantly reminded of family ties by the use of relationship tags in referring to people—*Granny, Cousin* Drusilla, *Uncle* Dennison, *Father* John Sartoris. This consciousness of family ancestry[2] is part of the general interest of Southerners in tradition and history. The two young boys in "Raid," Ringo and Bayard, are thrilled by Cousin Drusilla's tale of how the Confederate soldiers brought the locomotive through the Union lines in the exciting run from Atlanta to Chattanooga. There are all those respectful mentions of codes and customs in Southern life—the duelling codes in "The Fire and the Hearth," the annual hunting trips every November in "Delta Autumn," Granny's equipping herself with a hat and parasol,[3] as any Southern lady would, before setting out on her long trek to recover the confiscated[4] mules and the family chest of silver from the Union officer Colonel Dick. All of these incidents made me realize for the first time what is distinctive about life in the Old South. I never lived that life myself, but I experienced it in the pages of these stories, and I am somehow the richer for the experience.

---

[1] Mixture of races [2] Line of descent; lineage; ancestors. [3] A lightweight umbrella used for protection from sunlight. [4] Taken possession of by, or as by, some authority.

●
Writing essay examinations

Throughout your college years, you can hardly escape from having to write examinations. Many examinations, of course, simply require you to blacken spaces, fill in blanks, or put down the numbers of correct answers. But inevitably you will take some examinations in which you have to write out your answers in sentences, paragraphs, or essays. This kind of single-draft writing is done under pressure—the pressure of having to present "correct" answers within a time limit. This writing is more than a display of the knowledge you have acquired and retained; it is *also* a display of your ability to recall, select, organize, and express that knowledge.

You should develop some proficiency[1] in this kind of writing-under-pressure, not only because it will help you get passing grades but also because much of the writing you will have to do in real life will be single-draft prose that has to meet a deadline. Leisure for extensive revising and rewriting of that kind of prose is a luxury that few people can afford. At best, the only reworking that a lot of written prose gets in the business and professional world is the retyping that an assistant does of a rough draft. Improving your ability to write essay examinations will prepare you for some of the writing you will have to do in connection with your job.

It is not likely that you have had any formal training in how to write examinations. You are merely thrown into a situation of having to take an essay examination and are expected to know how to perform. If you have learned how to perform passably[2] well in such situations, you have learned mainly from repeated trial-and-error. There are a few bits of advice,

---

[1] Skillfulness. [2] Tolerably.

Special Kinds of Writing Assignments

however, that might help you perform better than you do if you merely muddle[1] through. (But never forget: *there is no substitute for knowing the answer to the question.*)

(1) BE SURE YOU UNDERSTAND THE QUESTION BEFORE YOU BEGIN TO WRITE

You are inviting disaster if you begin to write *before you have a clear understanding of what the question is getting at.* Really *read* the question. If you don't completely understand what the examiner wants from you, the reason may be (1) that your grasp of the subject covered by the question is so weak that you can't even make sense of the question, much less answer it or (2) that your reading ability is so deficient[2] that you read words without really understanding what they are saying or (3) that the question is vaguely or ambiguously[3] phrased. It may be too late to do anything about the first condition, but you certainly can do something about the second or third condition: you can ask the examiner to clarify the question. Don't set out blindly; make sure that you're heading in the right direction *before* you start to write.

(2) ONCE YOU UNDERSTAND THE QUESTION, MAKE SURE THAT YOU ANSWER THAT QUESTION AND NOT SOME OTHER, IMAGINED, QUESTION

The chief cause for failure on written examinations—or at least for the loss of points on a question—is *not meeting the question head-on.* If you are not sure about the answer to the

---

[1] Think or act in a confused way. [2] Lacking in something necessary; defective. [3] In a manner capable of being accepted or understood in more than one way.

question, it is natural for you—and maybe wise—to say everything you know about the subject, even though much of what you say is not entirely relevant[1] to the answer. But if you really know the answer, you should aim directly at the bulls-eye.

Look for certain key words in the question to help you keep your answer on target—words like *who, what, when, where, why, how* or words like *explain, define, identify, enumerate, cite, discuss, account for, trace, compare, contrast, relate, support, refute*. Words like those point you to the core of the question. A question like "Who was mainly responsible for getting the Constitution adopted in New York state in 1789?" is asking you to name the *person* or *group of persons* responsible for that event; any information about *what* was responsible (that is, the *causes*) is beside the point and will not gain you any credits for your answer. The word *explain* gives you a lot of room for your answer, but your explanation had better concentrate on the specified subject (e.g., "the economic situation at the outbreak of the Civil War") and not some imagined or wished-for subject (e.g., "the prevailing mood of the slaves at the outbreak of the Civil War"). If you're asked to *compare and contrast* persons, events, situations, etc., you had better concentrate in your answer on the *similarities* (the *compare* part of the question) and the *differences* (the *contrast* part of the question).

(3) SPEND SOME TIME PLANNING YOUR ANSWER

One way to ensure that you will keep your answer on target is to *spend a few moments planning your answer*. If you're allotted ten minutes for answering a question, you

[1] Pertinent; applicable.

Special Kinds of Writing Assignments

might do well to spend two or three of those minutes scribbling a few notes in the margin about the points you want to cover in your answer. Your answer may end up being shorter than it might have been if you had spent the full ten minutes writing. But it may prove to be more compact, more pertinent, and better organized as a result of your planning than if you had launched into your answer aimlessly. Some kind of sketchy outline is even more important when the question demands a well-developed essay rather than merely a 100-word paragraph.

(4) DEVELOP YOUR ANSWER ADEQUATELY

If failure to meet a question head-on is the chief reason for loss of points in an essay examination, failure to *develop an answer adequately or fully* is the next most common reason. This is a trickier pitfall for you, because "adequate development" is a relative matter. But sometimes the examiner gives you some helpful hints about what would constitute an adequately developed answer. If you must answer a question in *one sentence,* you have a definite guideline: a single, well-phrased sentence, if it hits the nail on the head, will constitute an adequate[1] answer.

"In a paragraph of 100–150 words, explain why . . ."—if a question is phrased in that way, you have an idea of how much you must write to answer the question adequately. Sometimes the examiner will specify the amount of *time* you should devote to a question. If you are allotted twenty minutes for an answer, three sentences probably won't be enough to provide an adequate answer to the question. Sometimes the examiner suggests how much you should

---

[1] Equal to or sufficient for a requirement.

develop your answer by the number of *points* he assigns to a question. A question assigned a value of twenty-five points is obviously going to require a more fully developed answer than a question assigned only five points.

But when hints of this kind are not supplied by the examiner, you will have to rely on your own sense of what constitutes an adequate answer. Just as the topic sentence of a paragraph suggests how much development a writer commits himself to, so the question asked in an examination may suggest how much development there must be in the answer. The question "Cite and discuss five causes for the decline of the dollar on the world market in recent years" offers some suggestions of what will be an adequate answer. Citing and discussing only *three* causes is going to lose you some points; citing five causes but not *discussing* them is going to lose you some points. Those who give essay examinations continually get answers in which everything that is said is true and relevant but in which not *enough* is said.

(5) DON'T PAD YOUR ANSWER

Padding[1] an answer is the opposite of shortchanging it. It is probably better to say too much than to say too little, but the ideal is to say just enough. Students turn to padding either when they want to display everything they know about a subject or when they are not sure enough of the answer they are writing. The student may be thinking, "I'm really going to show everything I know on this one" or "Maybe if I keep piling on sentences, I'll come up with what the teacher is looking for." Both are cases of faking it. Most teachers can see through this kind of thing, and they are more likely to be

---

[1] Filling or expanding with needless or fraudulent matter.

Special Kinds of Writing Assignments

annoyed than impressed by the extra reading they have to do. There's a time to be expansive and a time to be brief. *Being able to stop when he has said enough is one of the last skills a writer acquires.*

Examples of essay answers

Here are some illustrations of adequate and inadequate one-paragraph answers to a question in an American history examination:

QUESTION

What weaknesses in the Articles of Confederation, which were adopted by the Continental Congress in 1777, led to the movement in the 1780s to replace the Articles with the Constitution? (150–200 words, 15 points)

Essentially, this is a *why* question (why did something happen?) that should be answered with an *enumeration*[1] of reasons or causes (in this case, an enumeration of the *weaknesses*). Here is an answer that would probably rate the full number of points allotted to this question:

The basic weakness of the Articles of Confederation was that they allowed the thirteen colonies to retain too much sovereignty[2] and independence and didn't grant the Continental Congress enough power to conduct national and international affairs. All the other weaknesses stemmed from this basic one. The Articles set up only one legislative body and did not make provisions for

---

[1] A listing.   [2] Power to govern without external control.

a President, a Cabinet, or a Court to execute[1] and supervise the laws passed by this body. Each state, depending on its population, sent anywhere from two to seven representatives to the Congress, but each state, regardless of size, was entitled to only one vote. Furthermore, this single arm of the central government could not levy[2] taxes (it could only *request* each state to pay its fair share of the national budget), and it could not collect import duties,[3] regulate commerce, or establish a national currency.[4] As a result, the Confederation could not pay its heavy debts to France and Holland, could not negotiate vital trade agreements with Great Britain, could not maintain a national army or navy, and had no clout[5] in dealing either with its own colonies or with foreign nations. The Articles of Confederation established an alliance of thirteen colonies but not a nation of *united* states.

The following answer is true *as far as it goes,* but it is not sufficiently developed, and does not specify enough of the weaknesses, to merit the full allotment of points:

The Articles of Confederation allowed the colonies to be more concerned about their own welfare than about the interests of the nation as a whole. The states were determined not to let ''big government'' rule them. We see this same selfishness today in all the hullabaloo about states' rights. You can't run a government if all the parties go their own way. Everybody must unite and bear the burden together. Some of the Founding Fathers saw the weaknesses of the Articles right from the start, but

---

[1]To carry out; to do what is called for.   [2]Impose by legal authority.   [3]Taxes.   [4]Something in circulation as a medium of exchange; money.   [5]Influence; effectiveness.

they were powerless to overcome the opposition of the states'-rights advocates. Eventually, they saw that the only way to get rid of those weaknesses was to scrap the Articles of Confederation and replace them with a truly federal constitution.

Either because the following student didn't read the question carefully enough or because she didn't know, or couldn't recall, enough details about the Articles of Confederation, she wrote a rambling answer, filled with a lot of irrelevant material, and never did come to grips with the question:

It was a crucial time in the history of our country. After a hard war with the well-trained British redcoats, the colonists had won their freedom and were proud that their ragtail[1] armies had beat the "superior" British troops. But all their blood, sweat, and tears would have been in vain if they couldn't create a government that was better than the one they had broken away from. So they commissioned[2] some of the best minds in the country to set up the Articles of Confederation—men like James Madison of Virginia, Ben Franklin of Pennsylvania, and Alexander Hamilton of New York. It was quite a challenge, but these men came up with a system of government that was as good as it could be under the circumstances. Sure, it had its weaknesses, but what government doesn't? Do you think we have a *perfect* government right now, even under the Constitution? Any government made up of humans is bound to have flaws in it. But at least it can be said that the Founding Fathers were smart enough to see the weaknesses in the Articles and tried to do something about correcting them. So

[1] Confused with the expression *ragtag and bobtail*, meaning *rabble; ragtag* alone means a *motley group*. [2] Charged with performing (a duty); granted authority and power (to do something).

246

they wrote our famous Constitution. (You'll be hearing a lot about that famous document during our Bicentennial celebrations!) They set up a system of checks and balances, safeguarded by the Bill of Rights and a workable system of passing amendments, like the Equal Rights Amendment we're trying to pass right now. So the thirteen original colonies were finally united, and except for the temporary split during the Civil War and the rebellion of young people during the Vietnam War, they have remained united. Our weaknesses were turned into strengths.

Writing an essay examination is much like other kinds of writing. You have to find something to say (in this case, the precise answer to a specific question), you have to select and arrange what your memory dredges[1] up from what you have learned, and you have to express what you have recalled in well-chosen words and well-fashioned sentences. The major difference, of course, is that the whole process of finding, planning, and expressing has to be speeded up. Observing the following bits of advice, however, might improve the writing you do under the pressure of this situation:

---

1 Read the question carefully.
2 Answer the question asked.
3 Plan your answer.
4 Develop your answer sufficiently.
5 Avoid padding your answer.

None of that advice will do you any good, of course, if you don't *know* the answer.

---

[1] Gathers as if with machinery that removes earth or silt.

Special Kinds of Writing Assignments

●
Report writing

Report writing is one of the commonest forms of writing that people have to do in the real world. In fact, it would be safe to say that if you have to do any writing in connection with your job, you will most likely have to write reports of some kind. And it isn't just people in high-level positions who have to write reports; many salesmen, police officers, clerks, nurses, and supervisors have to write reports every day as part of their jobs.

Since you have probably given oral or written reports in school, the form is not totally unfamiliar to you. But as you progress through college, the reports you are called upon to give will increase in number, length, and complexity. The practice you get in writing reports in school will prepare you to do this kind of writing later on in your job.

The principles governing report writing do not differ basically from those that govern other kinds of expository and persuasive writing. A report is an act of communication—someone saying something to someone else for a specific purpose. All the steps of the process that were discussed in the previous chapters—**finding, selecting, organizing,** and **expressing**—play a part in the writing of reports. What you need to become aware of is some of the special considerations and special formats of report writing.

●
Special considerations

Types of Reports

There is a great variety of reports, and you may have heard

of some of them: accident reports, sales reports, annual reports, research reports, progress reports; reports of events, meetings, trips, investigations, surveys, polls, case studies; feasibility reports, evaluation reports, justification reports, problem-solving reports. For the sake of convenience, the several kinds could be classified into two general types: the **informative** and the **persuasive.**

The main function of *informative* reports is to record and convey to interested parties details about what happened, what was done, or what was discovered. In short, they record and share information. Someone may later do something *with* or *about* the information. For instance, an accident report that a police officer submits to the Accident Bureau may later serve as the basis of a law suit filed by one of the parties involved. But the primary purpose of an informative report is to gather, record, and transmit the "facts" about something. News stories, for instance, are basically informative reports. We read them to satisfy our curiosity about what happened, but most of the time, we don't do anything *with* or *about* the information we read in the newspaper.

The main purpose of *persuasive* reports, on the other hand, is to get someone to *do* something—to lead to action. Persuasive reports contain information too—lots of it—but the information is there not only for the enlightenment of the reader, as it is in an informative report, but also for *action* by the reader. Whether its intent is to solve a problem, propose a policy, or recommend a product, the goal of the persuasive report is to move the reader to action based on the information presented and analyzed in the report. For instance, the writer of an evaluation report about various sources of energy may recommend that a manufacturing firm use a particular fuel for its main source of energy because his study has shown this fuel to be the cheapest and cleanest.

Special Kinds of Writing Assignments

The persuasive report leads to *decision-making.*
Your being able to classify your report as *informative* or *persuasive* will help you define your task.

Commissioning of Reports

Most of the time, reports are commissioned. Rarely does someone decide, on his own, to write a report. One of the consequences of the fact that reports are usually commissioned is that several aspects of the writing assignments are often defined more sharply than they are in other writing assignments:

1 A specific person or team of persons is assigned to write the report.
2 A definite audience is designated for the report.
3 A definite subject-matter is specified for the report.
4 A clear purpose is set for the report.
5 A deadline is set for the completion of the report.

These specifications clearly define the writer's task and help him focus his approach. Furthermore, the person or persons who commissioned the report know what to expect in the report. They cannot know ahead of time, of course, what the findings and recommendations of the report will be, but at least, they know something about the subject, purpose, and scope of the report.

Problem and Purpose

More than any other elements, the statements of the problem and of the purpose define the goal of the report.

● Special Considerations

What often prompts the commissioning of the report in the first place is some *problem,* some *unknown,* that needs to be solved. Solving the problem or the unknown becomes, in turn, the goal of the report. The following examples of problem/purpose show how these two elements sharply define the goal of the report:

PROBLEM

What has caused the breakdown and loss of efficiency[1] in telephone communications between Plant A in one city and Plant B in a city fifty miles away?

PURPOSE

To find out what the snag in telephone communications is and, if the snag cannot be corrected easily and inexpensively, to find an alternate system of communication that will be an improvement over the present system.

PROBLEM

Why has a 38% decline in the sales of Brand X Dog Food occurred in recent months?

PURPOSE

From a survey and evaluation of consumer response to the ten bestselling dog foods, to determine what may be lacking in the appeal of Brand X.

PROBLEM

Why has there been a ten-point decline in students' verbal scores in 1974–75 when the average decline in the previous eleven years was only three points?

[1] Production of desired results without loss or waste.

Special Kinds of Writing Assignments

PURPOSE

To determine the cause or causes of the decline so that the nation's schools can take the necessary steps to stop the decline.

The answer to the problem has to be sought in some kind of research—an experiment, an investigation, a review of the literature on the subject. The report then will tell *what was done to find the answer* and *what the findings of the study were,* and if it is a *persuasive* report, it will recommend *what should be done to solve the problem.*

Completeness and Accuracy of the Report

A report must be as complete and as accurate as it needs to be. That truism[1] may strike you as being so obvious that it hardly needs to be stated. But the general principle governing the length, fullness, and precision of a report cannot be stated in any other way. Each case must be judged on its own terms.

What mainly determines the length, fullness, and precision of the report is the complexity of the problem or the scope[2] of the report. Some reports need to be only one or two pages long and can be presented in a letter or a memorandum.[3] In order to respond to a questionnaire from the federal government about a company's Affirmative Action policy, the vice president of the company might ask the personnel manager to supply him with information about the number and per-

---

[1] A self-evident truth. [2] Range; extent. [3] An informal written communication employed for official notification or instruction.

centage of women and ethnic[1] minorities presently employed by the company. That information could be *completely* presented in a one-page letter. On the other hand, if the vice president of a company wanted to know what cost-accounting[2] procedures were currently being used by the ten largest corporations in the country, the writer might need thirty or more pages in order to supply complete information.

The information supplied in a report should be as accurate as possible under the circumstances. Sometimes accurate information is not available. It may not be possible, for instance, to get accurate statistics about the number of auto thefts across the nation in a given year because an efficient system of reporting auto thefts has not yet been developed in some states. In that case, we have to settle for *approximate* figures. Fortunately, in many cases, round numbers will serve the purpose just as well as numbers figured out to three decimal points. We do expect the chemist to report the exact proportions of chemical elements used in an experiment. We expect the simple arithmetic of any calculations to be checked and double-checked. We expect conclusions to be drawn logically and responsibly from the data. We expect the names of persons, institutions, products, etc. to be accurate and correctly spelled.

Decisions made on the basis of incomplete or inaccurate information *could be* disastrous. Perhaps the test of whether a report is complete and accurate enough is the readers' response to it. Do they feel that some important questions have been left unanswered? Do they have any doubts about the accuracy of the report?

---

[1] Relating to races or to large groups of people classed according to traits or customs held in common. [2] Recording and analysis of costs incurred by production.

Special Kinds of Writing Assignments

The Intelligibility of the Report

Intelligibility is, of course, a relative[1] term. A report that would be perfectly understandable to a group of specialists might not be clear to a general audience. Fortunately, the writer of a report has a more definite idea of the audience that will read his report than other kinds of writers do. Sometimes his report will be read by only *one* person, a person that he knows quite well, or it might be read only by the six electrical engineers in the company. Usually, the more limited and homogeneous[2] the audience is, the easier it will be for him to make his report intelligible. His problem is complicated when he has to write his report for a large, mixed audience. A company's annual report, for instance, will be read not only by employees in various departments of the company but also by the stockholders. For that reason, the annual report must be written so that it will be understandable to all segments[3] of that wide audience. The financial statement in that report cannot be presented in the same detail and complexity that a certified public accountant would require.

Intelligibility depends mainly on the language used and the level of technicality[4] on which the subject is treated. Although even writers of reports intended primarily for experts are encouraged to avoid highly technical language wherever possible, they can use, and they may have to use, *some* technical language. In reports intended for a wider audience, however, *writers should try to explain difficult concepts or processes in ordinary language, and if they find it necessary to use some technical language, they have to define those words.* And in their explanations, they should try to avoid the

---

[1] Having relation to, or dependent on, something else. [2] Of the same or similar kind.
[3] Divisions of a thing; sections. [4] The quality or state of being technical; the extent or degree to which attention is paid to detail in the treatment of a thing.

intricacies[1] that would be understandable only to specialists.

The ideal for the writer is to treat the subject adequately enough to satisfy the experts and yet to use language that is simple and clear enough to be understood by ordinary, intelligent people. He has a right, of course, to expect his audience to make a reasonable effort to understand what he has written.

The Readability of the Report

The *readability* of the report is different from the *intelligibility*. Whereas *intelligibility* has to do with *how easy it is to understand the writing, readability* has to do with *how interesting or attractive the writing is.* Some writers have the knack[2] of making reports on even the most complex and highly technical subjects exciting to read. That kind of readability is mainly a matter of *pacing.*

Pacing is a difficult quality to define, but you have probably experienced the effects of pacing while watching a movie or a play. If you found yourself growing impatient with the movement of the drama, the pacing was probably too slow. You probably told your friends that the movie "dragged" or that it "took too long to get going." On the other hand, if you were bewildered by the movement, the pacing was probably too fast; you couldn't adjust yourself to the rapid movement and the quick changes.

Proper pacing is important in writing too, especially in a lengthy report. If the writer plods along at the same pace page after page, if he lingers[3] over unimportant details, if he becomes repetitious,[4] you will soon become bored. On the

---

[1] Complexities; network of interrelated points and details. [2] Natural ability; clever way of doing something. [3] Stays at a place; is slow in leaving; delays. [4] Marked by (tiresome) repetition.

other hand, if the writer rushes through the explanation of a complicated idea or process, if he doesn't provide helpful transitions between the parts of his report, if he doesn't pause occasionally to point out the significance or relevance of what he has been talking about, if his organization is hopelessly scrambled, you will soon become confused.

Pacing is like timing in athletics. Some people seem to be born with a proper sense of pacing or timing. But if you were not born with that skill, you can improve it with practice and by observing and imitating those who do have it.

There are some physical devices also that can increase the readability of your writing. Leaving lots of white space on the page, marking the parts of the text with headings and subheadings, interspersing the text with charts and graphs and illustrations—typographical devices of this sort will help to make the reading of a long, complicated report less tedious. Even such a simple device as heavy black type produced by a fresh typewriter ribbon helps to make the text more attractive. You should not underestimate the effect of just the physical appearance of the page.

The Matter-of-Factness of the Report

Report writing should maintain an objective, impersonal tone. The writer may have to express opinions occasionally and present his judgments about the "facts," but generally the readers of reports are more interested in the substance of the report than they are in the personality of the writer. **The writer should avoid exaggerated claims, highly emotional language, touches of humor, anecdotes (introduced for their own sake), sarcasm,[1] gossip, wishful**

---

[1] Ironic language used in cutting or contemptuous remarks.

thinking, pet peeves—anything that shifts the attention of the reader from *what is being said* to *who is saying it.* Metaphors are sometimes unavoidable—in fact, sometimes they really help the writer make his meaning clear—but for the most part, *the report writer relies more on literal language than on figurative language.*

Because of the matter-of-fact tone that he has to maintain, the report writer finds it more difficult than other writers do to achieve the *readability* discussed in the previous section. But anybody who has read articles in the magazine *Scientific American* knows that readability can be achieved even in objective, impersonal writing. Like Avis, the report writer just has to "try harder."

Many of the considerations reviewed above are pertinent, of course, to other kinds of writing too. All writers, in some measure, have to strive to be complete and accurate and intelligible and readable, but the *combination* of considerations is especially important for report writers. Good report writing is just as much of an art as good fiction writing. Keeping these special considerations in mind can help the writer master this art.

●
Special formats

The Parts of a Report

As was mentioned at the beginning of the section on report writing, there are many kinds of reports, all of which can be classified as either *informative reports* or *persuasive reports.* There is also a great variety of formats for reports. Short,

Special Kinds of Writing Assignments

informal reports, for instance, are often presented in letters or memorandums or even on printed forms that leave blank spaces to be filled in. Long, formal reports usually follow a set pattern. If you are called upon to write reports in school or later in your job, you will often be given specific instructions about the format that you are to follow. In fact, many companies have prepared special manuals that give directions about the number and arrangement of the parts of different kinds of reports, and they keep a file of various reports that serve as models for the writer.

The following is the *typical* format of a full-fledged[1] formal report. The number and order of the parts may vary slightly from company to company, but most long, formal reports follow this format:

1 A letter of transmittal
2 A title page
3 A table of contents
4 A table of illustrations, tables, charts, and graphs.
5 An abstract of the report
6 An introduction to the report
7 The body of the report
8 A list of conclusions
9 A list of recommendations
10 Appendices
11 Bibliography or List of References
12 Index

(1) LETTER OF TRANSMITTAL

The letter of transmittal, typed in the usual form of a busi-

[1] Having full attainment or status in some quality or category.

ness letter (see next chapter) and often very short, formally transmits the report to the interested parties. The body of the letter might say something like this:

> On February 6, 1974, the Board of Directors of Industrial Nucleonics commissioned me and five other members of the Engineering Department to make a feasibility study of converting from natural gas to electricity as the plant's main source of energy. I am now submitting copies of A Report on the Advantages and Disadvantages of Electricity as the Main Source of Industrial Power to the Board of Directors and the twelve Executive Officers of Industrial Nucleonics.
>
> On behalf of the members of my staff, I apologize for the delay in the delivery of the report. But as you are aware, we were delayed for two weeks while the Commonwealth Electrical Company awaited a ruling from the U.S. Court of Appeals on its application for an increase in rates charged to industrial consumers of electrical energy. We could not complete our financial assessment[1] of the project until Commonwealth got a ruling from the courts.
>
> If my colleagues[2] and I can be of further assistance to you, please do not hesitate to call on us.

Those who are not on the list of people scheduled to receive a copy of the report usually do not see this letter of transmittal. The copy they read has all the other eleven parts but not this letter.

(2) TITLE-PAGE

The title-page contains at least two pieces of information:

[1] Valuation; appraisal.   [2] Associates in (usually professional) work.

Special Kinds of Writing Assignments

(1) the title or the subject of the report and (2) the names of the authors of the report. The amount of additional information included on the title-page varies from company to company, but here is a list of other kinds of information often found on the title-page:

(a) The name of the person or agency to whom the report is addressed
(b) The date of the report
(c) The name of the agency that sponsored or funded the study (this could be the same as [a])
(d) The code number of the report
(e) The publisher of the report

(3) TABLE OF CONTENTS

The table of contents lists the parts of the report, using the headings of major divisions and subdivisions and giving the page numbers of those sections.

(4) TABLE OF ILLUSTRATIONS, TABLES, CHARTS, AND GRAPHS

The table of illustrations, tables, charts, and graphs lists any visual material contained in the report. The items are usually numbered and labeled (e.g., *Figure 2, Classification of Workers according to Occupations*), and the page numbers where they occur are given. Sometimes, especially when there are only one or two graphics, the items are listed in the table of contents rather than in a separate section.

(5) ABSTRACT

The abstract gives the reader a quick overview of the whole

report. Because the abstract is not only an important part of a report but also an increasingly important form of writing aside from the report (especially in information-retrieval systems), it will be discussed at some length here.

Writing abstracts is quite an art, for it demands two skills: skill in reading and skill in writing. Unlike the other kinds of writing dealt with in this book, the abstract does not require the writer to find something to say. Instead, the writer takes what he or someone else has written and reproduces the substance of the text in a considerably shortened version. But that kind of abbreviation[1] of the text is not as easy as it may appear. One must be a skillful enough reader to be able to pick out the important points in a text and a skillful enough writer to set forth those important points in a coherent form and in a limited number of words.

An abstract is in some ways like a sentence outline (see the form of an outline in Chapter 4). A sentence outline sets forth the major points (the Roman-numeral divisions) of an essay or article and at least the first level of subordinate points (the capital-letter subdivisions). *The difference between an outline and an abstract is that whereas the outline is presented in the form of a listing of points, the abstract is written out in a sequence of sentences.* But if you are skillful enough to be able to construct a sentence outline of the main parts of a piece of extended prose, you should be able to pick out the main points that should go into the abstract.

Another way to approach the task of writing an abstract is to develop the skill of picking out the topic sentences of the paragraphs in the body of an essay. But a collection of *all* the topic sentences might make your abstract longer than it needs to be and might obscure[2] the relationships and relative importance of the sentences. You might have to combine two

---

[1] The act or result of making shorter.   [2] Conceal or hide.

Special Kinds of Writing Assignments

or three topic sentences into a broader generalization and provide connecting links between sentences (see the discussion of connecting words in the section on coherence in Chapter 5).

Think of the process of abstracting as a distilling[1] of the essence of a longer piece of prose. You need enough sentences to cover all the major points of the essay, but you have to boil away the supporting details of the longer version. What you are left with is a "concentrate" of the longer essay.

There are two kinds of abstracts: **descriptive** and **informative.** The *descriptive abstract,* which is usually quite short, merely *indicates* what *topics* or *areas* are covered in the longer text. The *informative abstract* actually *gives* readers the *main points* or *ideas* of the longer text. The difference between the two can be illustrated in the following sentences:

Descriptive

The major forms of literature produced in England in each of three consecutive centuries are discussed in this article.

Informative

In England, drama was the prevailing form of literature in the seventeenth century, the prose essay was the chief contribution of the eighteenth century, and the novel was the dominant form in the nineteenth century.

On pp. 264–265 you will see a descriptive abstract and an informative abstract of this chapter of the book.

Although you will find descriptive abstracts in some re-

---

[1] Obtaining as if by extracting drop by drop.

ports, you are more likely to find—especially in lengthy reports—informative abstracts, because the reader wants to get a preview of the main ideas presented in the report rather than merely an indication of the areas covered. As you will discover for yourself, the informative abstract is much harder to write than the descriptive abstract.

In preparing to write an abstract, either of a text you wrote or of a text someone else wrote, you might find these suggestions helpful:

1 Read the text all the way through to get an overall view of it.

2 In a second reading of the text, make a checkmark in the margin opposite sentences or paragraphs that make what you think are major points.

(Aids that can guide you in picking out major ideas in a text: table of contents, introduction or preface, headings and subheadings in the text itself, summaries of sections, the conclusion of the whole text, italicized or boxed sentences and paragraphs.)

3 After marking the main points, try making at least a rough outline of the text.

4 From the outline, decide how many points and which points you should include in your abstract.

(Sometimes a word limit is set for the abstract [e.g., 150 words or less]. If so, that limit will help you decide what points and how many points you can include in your abstract.)

5 Write the first draft of the abstract.

(At this stage, don't worry about how many words you are using. Just get something down on paper.)

6 Revise and trim the first draft, if necessary.

(At this stage, see if you can supply linkages between the

Special Kinds of Writing Assignments

sentences to make the abstract read smoothly.)

7 Write the final draft of the abstract.

If you were to follow these suggestions in preparing to write an abstract of this chapter, for instance, you might write descriptive and informative abstracts like these:

Descriptive Abstract

The three kinds of special writing assignments dealt with in this chapter are writing about literature, writing essay examinations, and writing reports. Sets of questions are proposed to help students generate ideas for an analysis, interpretation, or evaluation of fiction, drama, and poetry. Practical advice is given about how to write satisfactory answers in an essay examination. The special considerations and formats of informative and persuasive reports are discussed, and special attention is paid to the writing of descriptive and informative abstracts.

Informative Abstract

In writing about literature, the student is involved in one or more of these acts: analyzing, interpreting, or evaluating. In an analysis of a literary text, the two general questions to be answered are (1) what is the work about? and (2) how is the work put together? In an interpretation of a literary text, the two general questions to be answered are (1) what did the author mean? and (2) what did the work mean to you? In an evaluation of a literary text, the two general questions to be answered are (1) how well did the author accomplish what he set out to do? and (2) was the work worth your time and attention? Sets of more particular questions can lead the student to more specific answers to these general questions.

In writing answers to essay-examination questions, the student should (1) read the questions carefully, (2) address the questions head-on, (3) plan the answers, (4) develop answers adequately, and (5) avoid padding answers. Examples of answers to an examination question in American history illustrate adequate and inadequate answers.

In writing both informative and persuasive reports, the student should give special consideration to the completeness, accuracy, intelligibility, readability, and objectivity of the report. The twelve parts of a typical formal report are (1) the letter of transmittal, (2) the title page, (3) the table of contents, (4) the table of illustrations, tables, charts, and graphs, (5) the abstract, (6) the introduction, (7) the body of the report, (8) the list of conclusions, (9) the list of recommendations, (10) the appendices, (11) the list of references, and (12) the index. Because of the importance of the abstract, both as a separate form and as a part of a report, procedures for writing descriptive and informative abstracts are discussed, and examples of descriptive and informative abstracts of this chapter of the book are presented.

In the next chapter, in the section on reference books, you will find descriptions of some of the collections of abstracts in the sciences and the humanities. You should consult some of these for further examples of abstracts—an increasingly important form of writing in the modern world.

(6) INTRODUCTION

The *introduction to the report* does not differ substantially

Special Kinds of Writing Assignments

from the introductions to other kinds of writing. In general, the introduction provides the preliminary information necessary for leading readers into the body of the report. It may define the scope and the purpose of the report, indicate the problem that prompted[1] the report, explain the procedures and methodology[2] of the study, and define some key terms. It varies in length from a single paragraph in short informal reports to several pages in long formal reports.

(7) BODY

The body of the report, like the body in other kinds of writing, is the longest part. It might occupy as much as 80 percent of the pages in a report. The body occupies such a large proportion of the report because it is in this section that the subject is treated in elaborate detail. The author (or authors) of the report may have to provide background information, describe procedures, summarize results, and present, analyze, interpret, and evaluate various kinds of supporting data. Some kinds of supporting data can be briefly presented in the form of illustrations, graphs, and statistical charts, but the discussion of that data may take up several paragraphs or several pages.

Because the body of the report is usually very long, the parts are marked with headings of various ranks. These headings serve a number of functions: (1) they alert the reader to the subject of that part; (2) they contribute to the readability of the report; (3) they help the reader see the relationships and relative rankings of the parts. The various ranks of heading are distinguished by different typography and different positions on the page.

---

[1] Gave rise to; served as the cause of. [2] A body of rules and methods employed in a certain undertaking.

Examples of Headings in a Report

<u>THIS</u> <u>IS</u> <u>A</u> <u>HEADING</u> <u>OF</u> <u>THE</u> <u>HIGHEST</u> <u>RANK</u>
 The text follows then, on a separate line and indented as here, and continues as a normal paragraph would.

<u>This</u> <u>is</u> <u>a</u> <u>Heading</u> <u>of</u> <u>the</u> <u>Second</u> <u>Rank</u>
 The text follows then, on a separate line and indented as here, and continues as a normal paragraph would.
 <u>This</u> <u>is</u> <u>a</u> <u>heading</u> <u>of</u> <u>the</u> <u>third</u> <u>rank</u>. The text follows then, on the same line as here, and continues as a normal paragraph would.

Figure 7.1

Headings of the highest rank (those that mark off *major* divisions) are *centered* on the page, *underlined,* and typed all in *capitals.* Headings of the second rank start at the *lefthand margin,* are *underlined* and *capitalized,* and occupy a *separate line* (above what follows). Headings of the next lowest rank are *underlined* but *do not occupy a separate line,* are *indented* from the lefthand margin (usually the same number of spaces as paragraph indentations), and are followed by a *period.* (See Fig. 7.1 for examples of the typography and positioning of the three ranked headings.)

(8) CONCLUSIONS

The *conclusions* summarize the *findings* of the study, research, or experiment. Here, the conclusions are placed right after the *body* of the report, where we normally expect to find them, but in some reports, the conclusions occur right after the *introduction.* The reason why the conclusions are sometimes placed earlier in the report is that for busy executives, who may be involved in decisions about the report, the conclusions and the part that follows (the *recommendations*) are the most important parts, and their reaction to the conclusions and recommendations may determine whether they go on to read all the details in the body of the report. (If the conclusions and recommendations were solidly negative, there would not be much point in the busy executive's going on to read the rest of the report.) But unless you are given specific instructions to place the conclusions right after the introduction, put it where the conclusions normally occur—right after the body of the report.

(9) RECOMMENDATIONS

The *recommendations* section usually occurs only in a persuasive report, the kind of report that calls for some action. This section presents the *suggestions* or *proposals* that the authors make as a result of the findings of the project. The authors might recommend, for instance, a change in company policy or the adoption of a more efficient procedure or the investment of money in some project or purchase. Sometimes the authors present a list of *alternative* recommendations, arranged in descending[1] order of importance and numbered 1, 2, 3, etc. As was mentioned in the previous section (see #8), the *conclusions* and the *recommendations* are sometimes placed earlier in the report, right after the *introduction* and before the *body* of the report.

(10) APPENDICES

The *appendices* section contains all *supporting material* that does not fit conveniently or naturally in the body of the

---

[1] That is, from greatest to least (important).

report—charts, graphs, tables of statistics, letters, affidavits, tabulations of surveys, etc. Sometimes material of that sort would distract the reader from the flow of thought if it were inserted in the body of the report, and often that material is not needed "right now" to support a point being made. The author can say, in parentheses, "(see Appendix B)," and if the reader wants to consult that material right then, he can turn to Appendix B at the end of the report.

(11) REFERENCES

The *list of references* section corresponds to the *bibliography page* of a research paper. In this section, you should list all the written and published sources that you have consulted, cited, or quoted in the report—books, articles, pamphlets, monographs,[1] brochures,[2] letters, memorandums, and even other written reports.

(12) INDEX

The *index* section occurs only in lengthy, complex reports. Like the index of a book, it lists, in alphabetical order, key words or phrases, followed by page numbers where those terms appear. The *table of contents,* of course, lists the headings of major parts of the report, but sometimes a reader wants to track down the exact place in a long report where some term or idea or process is discussed, and only a detailed index can direct him to that place in the report.

It should be said once again that not all the parts reviewed in the previous pages appear in *every* long formal report, nor do they always occur in the order given above. These are

[1] Written accounts of single things; short treatises on narrowly defined topics or areas of study. [2] Booklets.

Special Kinds of Writing Assignments

typical parts of a report, listed in a *typical* order. If you are assigned to write a report, either by your teacher or by your employer, you will be given specific instructions about the format of the report, and you will probably have access to other written reports that can serve as a model for your own report.

Chapter 8
Writing Research Papers,
Letters, and Résumés

The research paper and the letter are specialized forms of writing, too, to which we devote a separate chapter. In dealing with the research paper, we will concentrate on two concerns: (1) *gathering material* for the research paper; (2) the *format*[1] of the research paper, including rnodels for footnotes and bibliography. In dealing with the letter and the résumé, we will be concerned only with the format.

●
Using the library

Unless your research paper is simply a report of a lab experiment, a questionnaire, or a series of interviews that you conducted, it will depend largely on your reading of books and articles. The main source of books and articles is the library—either the public library or the college library. Perhaps the chief benefit that you derive from doing a research

[1] The general plan or arrangement.

paper is that this exercise forces you to become acquainted with the library and its resources:[1] Becoming aware of the wealth of knowledge stored in the library and getting to know *where* the various pockets of that wealth are located in the library and *how* to use them will be a valuable part of your general education.

The best way to get acquainted with the library is to visit it, to look around, to look at the card catalogue, to take some books down off the shelves and open them, and, above all, *to use it.* But if you want to speed up the getting-acquainted process, you can consult a book like Constance M. Winchell's *A Guide to Reference Books* (Chicago: American Library Association, 8th ed., 1967), which you can find on the reference shelves of the library. What follows is an introduction to a few general reference sources and some bibliographical[2] sources, which would be both generally helpful in your pursuit of knowledge and particularly helpful to you in preparing to write a research paper.

General Reference Sources

(A) ENCYCLOPEDIAS

Multivolume[3] encyclopedias are the most familiar and usually the most available source of information on a wide range of subjects. You are already aware that the material in an encyclopedia is arranged alphabetically, as a dictionary is. You also know that the treatment of topics in an encyclopedia varies in length from a few sentences to several pages. What you are probably not aware of is that often you can gather

[1] Sources or funds of supplies or support. [2] Related to a list, history, or description of writings (on a subject or by an author). [3] Of more than one volume.

valuable *additional* information about your topic by consulting the *index volume,* which refers you to other entries[1] where your topic is discussed. You should also be aware that many of the entries, especially the longer ones, list pertinent books and articles that you can consult for further information.

The encyclopedia is a good starting-point for a research project, but ordinarily it should not be the stopping-point. You will have to go on to *more specialized* reference sources. Here are three well-known multivolume encyclopedias and one very useful single-volume encyclopedia. All of them cover a wide range of subjects, are international in their scope, and cover all centuries, but each one is strong in a particular area. The first two publish yearbooks, which cover the main events and topics of the previous year.

Encyclopedia Americana (New York: Americana Corporation, 1927, but frequently updated). 30 volumes. Particularly useful for anything connected with the United States.

Encyclopaedia Britannica (Chicago: Encyclopaedia Britannica Corporation, 1929, but frequently updated). 24 volumes. Strong on both American and British topics.

Chambers's Encyclopaedia (London: G. Newnes, Ltd., 1950, but frequently updated). 15 volumes. Particularly strong on British topics.

The New Columbia Encyclopedia, 4th edition (New York: Columbia University Press, 1975). One volume. More than 50,000 articles on the humanities, social sciences, life and physical sciences, and geography packed into the 3052 pages of a single volume.

---

[1] Headwords followed by definitions, descriptions, or identifications.

(B) ALMANACS AND OTHER GENERAL SOURCES OF FACTS AND STATISTICS

You may not be able to afford a set of encyclopedias, but you certainly can afford to buy one of the annual paperback almanacs, a rich storehouse of factual and statistical information. The almanacs always retain the basic historical, geographical, social, political, and statistical information, but each year, they supply the pertinent factual and statistical information for the previous year. Here are the titles of two inexpensive paperback almanacs and the titles of two other sources of facts and statistics that can be found in the reference room of the library:

Information Please Almanac (New York: Simon and Schuster, 1947–   ). Published annually.

World Almanac (New York: Newspaper Enterprise Association, Inc., 1868–   ). Published annually.

Facts on File (New York: Facts on File, Inc., 1940–   ). Published weekly. A valuable source of information about the important events of the week.

U.S. Bureau of the Census: Statistical Abstract of the United States (Washington, D.C.: Government Printing Office, 1879–   ). Published annually. The most comprehensive source of statistical information about all aspects of American life.

(C) HANDBOOKS

Another source of general information about a particular field is the one-volume reference work that we will label *handbook*. Handbooks contain some of the same kinds of information supplied by multivolume encyclopedias, but the entries are shorter, and they are restricted to a special field, like literature or business. But just because they *are* restricted to a particular field, they often cover topics that are considered too minor[1] or specialized for inclusion in a multivolume encyclopedia. In a handbook, you can expect to find these kinds of information about the field covered: definitions of key terms and concepts[2]; identifications of allusions[3]; accounts of historical or ideological movements; short biographical sketches; summaries of important books; bibliographies. Here is a list of a few important handbooks, one for each of seven different fields.

The Reader's Encyclopedia, ed. William R. Benet, 2nd ed. (New York: Crowell, 1965). A handbook of world literature.

Oxford Companion to the Theatre, ed. Phyllis Hartnoll, 2nd ed. (New York: Oxford University Press, 1957). A handy reference source for information about world drama, from its beginnings in ancient Greece.

Oxford Companion to the Film, ed. Liz-Anne Bawden (London: Oxford University Press, 1976). The newest of the many "Oxford Companions," about an art form that has become a prominent part of contemporary life.

Encyclopaedia of Banking and Finance, 6th ed. (Boston: The Bankers Publishing Co., 1962). An invaluable one-volume reference work for anything connected with business.

The Concise Encyclopedia of Western Philosophy and Philosophers, ed. J. O. Urmson (New York: Hawthorn Books, 1960). Brief but authoritative information about philosophy and philosophers.

[1] Of lesser importance, size, or extent. [2] Thoughts, ideas. [3] Indirect references; references by suggestion only.

Dictionary of Education, ed. Carter V. Good, 2nd ed. (New York: McGraw-Hill, 1959). More than a "dictionary," this reference work supplies the usual kind of handbook information about the field of professional education.

International Cyclopedia of Music and Musicians, ed. Robert Sabin, 9th ed. (New York: Dodd, Mead, 1964). One of a number of very good one-volume handbooks on music.

(D) BIOGRAPHICAL DICTIONARIES

Encyclopedias and handbooks will provide you with brief biographical sketches of prominent men and women. But for fuller accounts of persons, both living and deceased, and for biographical sketches of less prominent people, you will have to go to the more specialized biographical dictionaries. Listed below are five of the best-known and most useful of these specialized biographical dictionaries.

Dictionary of National Biography (sometimes referred to as the *DNB*) (London: Oxford University Press, 1921). 21 volumes (a reissue of the original 66-volume set published in 1885). Lives of about 18,000 *deceased* subjects of Great Britain and Commonwealth dependencies. Supplements bring the coverage up to 1960.

Who's Who (London: A & C Black, Ltd., 1849–   ). Published annually. Biographical information about distinguished *living* men and women of Great Britain.

Dictionary of American Biography (sometimes referred to as the *DAB*) (New York: Scribner's, 1928–1937; Supplement I, 1944; Supplement II, 1958). 22 volumes. The equivalent of the British *DNB*, this multivolume set gives the biographies of prominent and not-so-prominent *deceased* Americans.

Who's Who in America (Chicago: Marquis, 1899–   ).
   Published every second year. The equivalent of the
   British *Who's Who,* this reference source provides bio-
   graphical information about notable *living* Americans.

International Who's Who (London: Europa Publications,
   1935–   ). Published annually. Information about the
   lives of prominent *living* men and women of all nations.

Bibliographical Sources

   The reference works mentioned in the previous section can
give you general information that could be useful for your
personal enlightenment or for your classwork or even for
your research paper. But since a research paper is usually
written about a narrow topic in a specialized field, you will
need more specific information than those general reference
works can provide. You need to track down books and articles and monographs and pamphlets that deal more particularly with the topic of your paper. To track down that more
specific material, you will have to turn to *bibliographical
reference works*—works that list the authors, titles, and publication information of published books, articles, etc. Fortunately, there are a number of general and specialized bibliographical guides. A helpful guide to available bibliographies
is the *Bibliographic Index* (New York: H. W. Wilson Co.,
1937–   ). Supplements of this work are published every
three months; and every four years, these quarterly[1] supplements are gathered together and published in one volume.
This guide to the bibliographies that have been published in
books, pamphlets, periodicals, and bulletins is arranged alphabetically according to subject. If you were doing a re-

[1] Published four times a year (at 3-month intervals).

search paper on the trucking industry and wanted to find out whether any bibliographies of this subject had been published, you could consult several volumes of the *Bibliographic Index* under the main subject-heading of *Transportation.* If you found a bibliography listed there on the trucking industry, you would then have to see whether the library had that bibliography, because it is *that* bibliography, and not the *Bibliographic Index* itself, which will give you the actual list of books and articles on the trucking industry.

Listed below are some general—and perhaps familiar—guides to articles in periodicals (magazines and journals) and then a few specialized bibliographical guides.

(A) INDEXES TO PERIODICAL LITERATURE

Readers' Guide to Periodical Literature (H. W. Wilson Co., 1900–   ). Published every two weeks, with cumulations in a single volume every two years. Perhaps the most familiar of the general guides to articles appearing in American weekly, monthly, and quarterly magazines and journals, this reference work is arranged alphabetically according to *author* and *subject.*

International Index (New York: H. W. Wilson Co., 1907–   ), Volumes 1–18. Beginning with volume 19 in 1965, the title of this work was changed to *Social Sciences and Humanities Index.* Published every three months, with cumulations in a single volume every three years. It indexes, by author and by subject, articles appearing in some of the more learned American, as well as British and Canadian, periodicals.

Nineteenth Century Readers' Guide to Periodical Literature (New York: H. W. Wilson Co., 1944). Indexes about fifty British and American periodicals published during the

last nine years of the nineteenth century. The *Readers'
Guide* picks up the coverage in the year 1900.

In the same section of the library in which you find these
general guides to periodical literature, you will find specialized indexes to periodical literature in such fields as Art,
Music, Business, Education, Psychology, Applied Science
and Technology, Biology and Agriculture.

(B) SPECIALIZED BIBLIOGRAPHIES

In addition to the guides to periodical literature mentioned
above, there are *specialized bibliographies* of the books,
monographs, pamphlets, and bulletins published in most of
the fields in the humanities, the social sciences, and the
physical sciences. When you move into your area of special-
ization, you will be expected to become familiar with the
bibliographical tools of that field. In addition to the standard
bibliographies, sometimes occupying more than one volume,
there are *annual bibliographies,* usually published in the
scholarly journals, which list most of the books and articles
published in the previous year. Scholars and graduate students consult these bibliographical sources when they are
preparing to write books, articles, theses,[1] and dissertations.[2]

Listed below are three of the standard cumulated[3] bibliographies in three different fields:

Cambridge Bibliography of English Literature, ed. F. W.
Bateson (Cambridge: Cambridge University Press,
1957). 5 volumes.

Guide to Historical Literature, ed. George F. Howe and
others (New York: Macmillan, 1961).

---

[1] Plural of *Thesis*. [2] Extended written treatments (of subjects). [3] Increased by
successive additions.

Writing Research Papers, Letters, and Résumés

Sources of Business Information, ed. Edwin T. Coman, Jr., revised edition (Berkeley: University of California Press, 1964).

Abstracts

The general and specialized bibliographies mentioned above will enable you to compile[1] a list of books and articles that might yield material for your research paper. The next step is to *find* some of those books and articles and *read* them.

In recent years, however, with the growth in the number of collections of abstracts in several fields, researchers have been able to get a *preview of the contents of books and articles* even before they get those publications in their own hands. After compiling your list of potentially[2] useful books and articles, you might be able to save yourself some wasted motions by consulting the appropriate *collection of abstracts.* By reading a 150–200–word abstract of any of the books and articles on your list, you should be able to tell whether that book or article is worth any more of your time. Most of the scholarly[3] fields now publish annual collections of abstracts of books and articles published during the previous year. The sciences have been publishing abstracts for a number of years, and recently the humanities have begun to publish annual abstracts.

Listed below are some representative[4] annual collections of abstracts in several fields. (Another benefit of looking at some of these collections of abstracts is that *you will find models for writing abstracts,* a form of writing that

[1] To collect together (from various sources). [2] In a way or condition to become actual. [3] Relating to a student or to the qualities or learning of a student. [4] Being or acting for another; serving to represent.

was discussed in the previous chapter. You can also use the collection of abstracts as a bibliographical source, since every abstract is headed with the name of the author, the title, and the publication information of the text being summarized.)

Historical Abstracts 1775–1945 (Santa Barbara, Cal.: American Bibliographic Center, 1955–   ). Published quarterly. Abstracts articles, from some 1300 journals, on world history of the period from 1775 to 1945.

Journal of Economic Abstracts (Cambridge: Harvard University Press, 1963–   ). Published quarterly. Abstracts articles on various phases of economics from thirty-five periodicals published in various countries.

MLA Abstracts (New York: Modern Language Association, 1971–   ). Published annually. Abstracts of articles on the language and literature of America, Canada, Great Britain, and other European, Asian, and African countries.

Chemical Abstracts (Easton, Penn.: later Columbus, Ohio: American Chemical Society, 1907–   ). Published every two weeks. Abstracts articles from over 7000 periodicals published in more than ninety countries.

Sociological Abstracts (New York: Sociological Abstracts, Inc., 1952–   ). Published eight times a year. Abstracts books and articles published in a wide range of countries.

The Card Catalogue[1]

The card catalogue—the rows of file-drawers in the li-

[1] A systematic list of items with descriptive details.

brary—is a valuable resource. Not only does it indicate whether the library has the particular book or periodical you are seeking and where in the library stacks the book or periodical can be found, but it is also another resource for compiling a bibliography for a research project. A library usually has at least three cards in the files for a single book —an *author* card (usually called the "main entry" card), a *title* card, and one or more *subject* cards. **It is the subject cards that give you the best leads on books pertinent to your research project.** Under the appropriate subject-heading will be grouped all the books that the library has on a particular subject. You can discover the "appropriate subject-heading" from looking at the Library of Congress card for a book that you *know* is pertinent to your study, because on every Library of Congress card, one or more subject-headings are suggested for a book.

Most libraries buy the printed cards prepared by a staff of classification[1] experts at the Library of Congress in Washington, D.C. The Library of Congress (abbreviated L.C.) cards carry a lot of information supplied on the cards. In Figure 8.1, four Library of Congress cards are displayed for a particular book, and the various parts of the card are tagged with letters of the alphabet. Here is the interpretation of those various lettered parts:

A The *name of the author* (last name first). This *author* or *main entry* card will be found in the card catalogue in one of the drawers for the letter *S*.

B The *call number of the book,* typed in by the library staff. This is the number you must copy down if you want to find the book yourself in the stacks or if you want one of the library clerks to get the book for you.

[1] Arrangement or assignment by classes or categories.

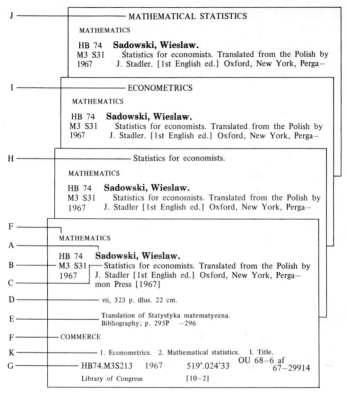

J ———— MATHEMATICAL STATISTICS

MATHEMATICS

HB 74 **Sadowski, Wieslaw.**
M3 S31   Statistics for economists. Translated from the Polish by
1967   J. Stadler. [1st English ed.] Oxford, New York, Perga—

I ———— ECONOMETRICS

MATHEMATICS

HB 74 **Sadowski, Wieslaw.**
M3 S31   Statistics for economists. Translated from the Polish by
1967   J. Stadler. [1st English ed.] Oxford, New York, Perga—

H ———— Statistics for economists.

MATHEMATICS

HB 74 **Sadowski, Wieslaw.**
M3 S31   Statistics for economists. Translated from the Polish by
1967   J. Stadler [1st English ed.] Oxford, New York, Perga—

MATHEMATICS

HB 74 **Sadowski, Wieslaw.**
M3 S31 — Statistics for economists. Translated from the Polish by
1967   J. Stadler [1st English ed.] Oxford, New York, Perga—
       mon Press [1967]

vii, 323 p. illus. 22 cm.

Translation of Statystyka matematyezna.
Bibliography; p. 295P —296

COMMERCE

1. Econometrics. 2. Mathematical statistics.   I. Title.

HB74.M3S213   1967   519'.024'33   OU 68—6 af
                                     67—29914
Library of Congress   [10–2]

Figure 8.1

C The *title of the book and publication information* about the book (e.g. the book was translated from Polish into English by J. Stadler; this is the first English edition of the book; the place of publication was Oxford, New York; the publisher was the Pergamon Press; and the date of publication was 1967).

Writing Research Papers, Letters, and Résumés

D This entry supplies information about the *physical makeup of the book:* there are seven pages of introductory material and 323 pages of text; there are illustrations in the book; and the book measures 22 centimeters[1] in height.

E This entry supplies some additional information about the book: the Polish title of the book and the fact that the book has a two-page bibliography.

F The two entries marked F, which were stamped on the card by the library staff, indicate that there are two copies of the book available—one in the Mathematics Department library, the other in the Commerce Department library.

G This entry carries four bits of information: (1) the Library of Congress call number[2] (notice that this library has used this number as the call number for the book); (2) the suggested Dewey Decimal call number (the other classification system used by some libraries); (3) the order number for the Library of Congress card; (4) a code number, typed in by the library staff, to indicate when the book was acquired by the library.

H The title of the book, typed in by the library staff on the *title* card. If you knew the title of the book but didn't know the author, you could find the book by looking for this title card in the card catalogue.

I The subject-heading for the book, typed in block capitals by the library staff on the first *subject* card for this book. Notice in K after the number 1 that *Econometrics*[3] is the first subject-heading suggested by the Library of Congress staff.

J The subject-heading for the book, typed in block capitals

---

[1] A centimeter (cm) is one one-hundredth of a meter (=0.39 inch).   [2] A combination of letters and numbers assigned to a book to designate its place on a library shelf.   [3] Mathematical forms and statistical methods applied to economic theories and the solution of economic problems.

by the library staff on the second *subject* card for this book. Notice in K after the number 2 that *Mathematical statistics* is the second subject-heading suggested by the Library of Congress staff.

K This entry suggests two subject-headings for the subject cards and indicates that the book can also be filed under its title.

When you are compiling a bibliography for your research project, the most important information for you to copy down from the L.C. card is the *author, title, publication information,* and *call number* of the book.

The Library of Congress has announced that by 1979, it will no longer print cards for new books. Not only is it prohibitively[1] expensive for libraries to insert the thousands of new cards each year into the file drawers of the card catalogue, but it is becoming increasingly difficult for libraries to find space in the card catalogue for the new cards. Libraries, of course, won't dispense with[2] their card catalogues, but many of the larger public and university libraries will computerize[3] their holdings. If you want a particular book, you will go to a computer terminal[4] in the library and give the operator the title or the name of the author of the book. In a matter of seconds, the computer will be able to tell you whether the library has the book and whether it is on the shelves or has been checked out by somebody. You will also be able to request the computer to give you a print-out[5] of all the books the library has on a certain subject.

Although the computer system will facilitate[6] your search

---

[1] In a way that forbids or does not allow to exist or function. [2] Do away with; do without; forgo. [3] Adapt to, or function by means of, a computer. [4] A base where all computer data are directed and stored. [5] A printed record produced by a computer. [6] To make easier.

for the books you need in your research project, it won't make the card catalogue entirely obsolete.[1] Occasionally, you may still want to consult the cards in the file drawers.

Taking Notes: One Student's Project

After you have compiled a bibliography, you must then get your hands on the books and articles you have recorded in it, read this material, and take notes. Under the headings of Gathering Notes and Self-Contained Notecards on pp. 291–293, some practical advice is given about the process of note-taking.

Later on in this chapter, a research paper that Diana Ikenberry wrote on Nathaniel Hawthorne's short story "Young Goodman Brown" is printed. Diana began gathering her bibliography by looking at several of the annual[2] bibliographies published in the scholarly journal *American Literature.* She checked the listings there of books and articles under the heading "Hawthorne" over a ten-year span.[3] Since she couldn't tell from the titles of books listed there which books had sections (or whole chapters) on "Young Goodman Brown," she concentrated at first on those articles whose titles *did* indicate that they dealt specifically with "Young Goodman Brown."

Once she got her hands on some of these articles, she discovered, in footnotes, not only some leads on additional articles on "Young Goodman Brown" but also some leads on chapters in books that dealt specifically with "Young Goodman Brown." One of her most valuable finds was the discovery of a casebook on "Young Goodman

---

[1]No longer in use; antiquated. [2]Occurring once, or covering the period of, a year. [3](Limited) period of time.

Brown" edited by Thomas E. Connolly. This casebook carried the text of the short story and reprinted several of the critical articles that she had listed in her preliminary bibliography.

Once having gathered the books and articles she needed, she began taking notes on 3 × 5 notecards. Since she didn't know at this stage which material would be most useful to her when she came to write her paper, she took at least six times as many notes as she eventually used in the paper. Some of the material she paraphrased in her notecards; other material she copied down verbatim. In Figure 8.2, four of Diana's notecards are reproduced.

Card A represents a *verbatim quotation* from an article by Thomas F. Walsh, Jr. The way that Diana distinguishes notes copied verbatim from notes paraphrased is to enclose verbatim quotations in quotation marks and to leave paraphrased notes *without* quotation marks. Notice the page number between slashes (/335/) to indicate *where the quotation went over* to p. 335. Later, if she uses only part of the full quotation, she will know whether to cite one page or two pages in her footnote. On this and the other notecards, she uses a shorthand[1] system for indicating the source of the note: the last name of the author of the article and the page number(s). On a separate notecard, she has recorded the full bibliographical information for the source. In the upper right-hand corner of each card, she has put the subject-heading she has made up for that note.

Card B represents a *verbatim quotation* from Hawthorne's short story. In a note at the bottom of the card, Diana indicates for her own information that the quotation

[1] Characterized by a rapid writing system using symbols and abbreviations for words and phrases.

CARD A

WALSH, pp 334-5   GOODMAN'S ANCESTORS

The facts concerning the persecution of the quakers and the Indians, Goodman Brown must certainly have known before, although in the past he might never have allowed himself to think of them in relation to sin. But what is most interesting, of all those who are /335/ mentioned and revealed by the devil, his father and grandfather have in their history that which would make one suspect that they were of the devil's party.

CARD B

Hawthorne, p. 21   EFFECT

"Be it so if you will; but, alas! it was a dream of evil omen for young Goodman Brown. A stern, a sad, a darkly meditative, <u>a distrustful</u>, <u>if not a desperate</u> man did he become from the night of the fearful dream."

(quotation from last paragraph of story. Italics added.)

Figure 8.2

CARD C

MATHEWS, pp. 73-74   ANTINOMIANISM

Antinomianism – doctrine espoused by one
group of Calvinists that salvation resulted
from faith, not good works. (p. 73)

Like other Antinomians of his day, Goodman
Brown believed that if his faith was strong,
no evil would be charged against him
for his actions. (p.74)

Perry Miller has written about Antinomians in
Massachusetts in his book "The New England Mind:
The Seventeenth Century (Cambridge, Harvard Univ. Press,
1954), (P.74)

CARD D

Connally, p. 372   CALVINISTIC DOCTRINE

"Calvinism teaches that man is innately
depraved and that he can do nothing to
merit salvation. He is saved only by
the whim of God who selects some,
through no deserts of their own, for
heaven while the great mass of
mankind is destined for hell."

Figure 8.2 (continued)

occurred in the last paragraph of the story and that she, not Hawthorne, underlined some of the words in the quotation ("italics added").

Card C represents three *paraphrased notes* that Diana took from an article on Antinomianism. Even though these notes are set down in her own words, she has put down page numbers at the end of them, because if she uses some of those paraphrased notes in her paper, she may find it necessary to cite in a footnote her authority for the statements.

Card D represents a verbatim *quotation* from one of the articles that she later incorporated in full in her research paper.

The four notecards in Figure 8.2 represent the four kinds of notes that Diana took from her source material. They all have the virtue[1] of being self-contained—that is, they contain all the information she will need to know if she uses the note in her paper; she will not have to go back to the original source to recover any missing information. For that reason, they represent an ideal set of notes.

Format of the research paper

General Instructions

A research paper reports the results of some investigation, experiment, interview, or reading that you have done. Some of the ordinary papers you write are also based on personal

[1] Praiseworthy quality; merit.

investigations, interviews, and reading, and when they are based on external sources, you should acknowledge[1] those sources in the text of your paper. For instance, you can reveal the source of information or quotations by saying in the text, "Mr. Stanley Smith, the director of the Upward Bound project, with whom I talked last week, confirmed the rumor that . . ." or "James Reston said in his column in last Sunday's *New York Times* that . . ." Authors of research papers also use identifying lead-ins like those in the text, but in addition they supply, in footnotes, any further bibliographical information (for instance, the exact date of the newspaper you are quoting from and the number of the page on which the passage occurred) that readers would need if they wanted to check the sources. By revealing this specific information about the source, the author enables his readers to check whether he has been accurate or fair in his reporting, and he also enhances[2] his credibility.[3]

In the pages that follow, we will meet with advice about gathering and reporting material from outside sources, some models for footnote and bibliography forms, and a sample research paper. The instructor or the journal that you write for may prescribe a format that differs from the advice given here, but if no specific instructions are given, you can follow these suggestions and models with the assurance that they conform to the prevailing conventions for research papers.

(A) GATHERING NOTES

Each person eventually discovers a system of gathering

---

[1] Express recognition of; report or imply reliance upon or indebtedness to. [2] Increases the value of. [3] Trustworthiness; ability to be believed.

notes that works best for him. Some people, for instance, just scribble their notes on full sheets of paper or in spiral notebooks. The system that works best for most researchers, however, is to record notes and quotations on 3×5 or 4×6 cards—*one* note or quotation to a card. The advantage of having your notes on cards is that later you can select and arrange the cards to suit the order in which you are going to use them in your paper. It is considerably more difficult to select and arrange notes if they are written out, one after the other, on full sheets of paper.

(B) SELF-CONTAINED NOTECARDS

Each notecard should be self-contained—that is, it should contain all the information you would need to document that material properly if you used it in your paper. A notecard is self-contained if you never have to go back to the original source to recover any bit of information about the note. So each notecard should carry at least this much information:

1 The card should carry some indication whether the note is paraphrased or quoted verbatim. Don't trust your memory to be able to distinguish later whether a note is paraphrased or quoted.

2 If quoted material covers more than one page in the source from which it was copied, you should devise some system of indicating just where the quoted material went over to the next page. If later you use only part of that quotation, you have to know whether to cite one page (p. 189) or two pages (pp. 189–90) in the footnote. Some notation like ($\rightarrow$ p. 190) inserted in the notecard after the last word on the page (in this case, after the last word on p. 189) in the

original source will help you determine later whether you
need to cite one page or two pages.

3 The notecard should contain all the bibliographical information needed to document the note in a footnote of your
paper: name of the author, title of the book or article,
publication information, and page numbers (see Model
Footnotes). If you are taking several notes from the same
source, you can devise some shorthand system so that
you do not have to write out all the bibliographical information on every notecard.

(C) WHAT NEEDS TO BE FOOTNOTED?

You will have to develop a sense for what needs to be
documented with a footnote. Here are some guidelines to
help you:

1 Ordinarily, every direct quotation should carry a footnote.
However, if you were doing a research paper on, say, a
novel, you could be spared having to document every
quotation from the novel by using a footnote like this the
first time you quote from the novel:

> [8]John Steinbeck, The Grapes of Wrath (New
> York: Viking Press, 1939), p. 134. Hereafter,
> all quotations from this first edition of the
> novel will be documented with a page number in
> parentheses immediately after the quotation.

2 Paraphrased material may or may not need a footnote. If
the fact or information that you report in your own words is

generally known by people knowledgeable[1] on the subject, you probably would not have to document that paraphrased material. For instance, if you were writing a research paper on the assassination[2] of Abraham Lincoln, you probably would not have to document[3] your statement that John Wilkes Booth shot Lincoln in Ford's Theater in Washington in April of 1865, because that historical fact is common knowledge. But if one of the arguments in your paper concerned the *exact time of the day* when he was shot, you would have to document your statement that Lincoln was shot at 8:40 P.M. on the evening of April 14, 1865. When, however, you cannot resolve your doubt about whether paraphrased material needs to be documented with a footnote that reveals the source of the information, document it.

3 When you are summarizing, in your own words, a great deal of information that you have gathered from your reading, you can be spared having to document several sentences in that summary by putting a footnote number after the *first sentence* of the summary and using a footnote like this:

> [10]For the biographical information presented in this and the subsequent paragraph, I am indebted to Minnie M. Brashear, Mark Twain: Son of Missouri (Chapel Hill: University of North Carolina Press, 1934), pp. 34–65 and Gamaliel Bradford, "Mark Twain," Atlantic Monthly, 125 (April, 1920), 462–73.

---

[1]Having knowledge or intelligence (about something). [2]Murder by sudden or secret attack. [3]Furnish detailed proof or evidence of.

● Format of the Research Paper

(D) KEEP QUOTATIONS TO A MINIMUM

A research paper should not be just a patchwork of long quotations stitched together by an occasional comment or by a transitional sentence by the author of the paper. You should use your own words as much as possible, and when you do quote, you should keep the quotation brief. Often a quoted phrase or sentence will make a point more emphatically[1] than a long quotation. You must learn to look for the phrase or sentence that represents the kernel[2] of the quotation and to use that extract[3] rather than the full quotation. Otherwise, the point you want to make with the quotation may be lost in all the verbiage.[4] You will be more likely to keep your quotations short if you try to work most of the quotations into the framework of your own sentence, like this:

> Frank Ellis calls such an interpretation "the biographical fallacy, the assumption that an exact, one-to-one correspondence exists between the person who is imagined to be speaking the lines of the poem (the Spokesman) and the historical personage who is known to have written the poem."[12]

Sometimes, however, when you find it difficult to present the essential point in a short extract, you will have to quote something at greater length. Long quotations (two sentences or more) should be *inset*[5] from the left-hand margin and

[1]With stress; with emphasis.   [2]The central or essential part.   [3]A passage (of writing) selected or copied.   [4]Overflow of words; wordiness.   [5]Set in.

single-spaced, with *no quotation marks enclosing the quotation,* like this:

Frank Ellis offers this cogent argument to refute the charge that the Epitaph is not inte-
grated with the rest of the poem:

> The evidence for this is said to lie in the
> fact that there are disparities between the
> two accounts that are given of the Stonecut-
> ter, one by the aged Swain and the other in
> Epitaph. But it has never been pointed out
> that these disparities are deliberate and
> dramatic. The illiterate old rustic is un-
> sympathetic. His disapproval has been soft-
> ened no doubt by death, but it is still ap-
> parent that to him the Stonecutter seemed
> lazy, queer, unsociable, and probably crazy.
> But the Epitaph enables the reader to see
> around this characterization. For the
> Spokesman, who composed the Epitaph, is an
> outlander, a fellow poeta ignotus, and
> therefore unsympathetic.[15]

(E) USE A LEAD-IN FOR ALL QUOTATIONS

Every direct quotation should be accompanied by a lead-in phrase or clause, which at least identifies by name the person who is about to speak. But it further aids coherence if the lead-in also points up[1] the pertinence[2] of the subsequent quotation to what you have been talking about or to what you are going to talk about. Here are some typical identifying and orienting[3] lead-ins:

"It apparently did not occur to any of Wilson's critics," says Oscar Cargill in defense of Wilson's interpretation, "that James might have an adequate motive for disguising his purpose in the tale."

Robert Heilman has this to say about Wilson's interpretation of Henry James's haunting story:

(following this last lead-in would be either a single sentence enclosed in quotation marks or a series of sentences inset and single-spaced, like the extended quotation in [D] *above)*

(F) THE FORMAT OF FOOTNOTES

The first line of every footnote is indented from the left-hand margin (usually the same number of spaces as paragraph indentations in the body of the paper), but any subsequent lines of the same footnote are brought out to the left-hand margin. If footnotes are put at the bottom of the

---

[1] Calls attention to; evidences. [2] Relatedness; relevance. [3] Acquainting with the situation to be met or dealt with.

page, they are single-spaced *within* the footnote and double-spaced *between* footnotes. If footnotes are put on separate pages, they are double-spaced both *within* the footnote and *between* footnotes. See Model Footnotes and Sample Research Paper for further information about the format of footnotes.

(G) PRIMARY AND SECONDARY FOOTNOTES

Primary footnote forms (that is, those giving full bibliographical information) must be used the *first time* a source is cited. Thereafter, that same source can be documented with a secondary footnote form (that is, a shortened form). See Model Footnotes and Sample Research Paper for the format of primary and secondary footnotes.

(H) THE FORMAT OF BIBLIOGRAPHICAL ENTRIES

Bibliographical entries are arranged alphabetically on separate pages at the end of the research paper. The list of entries is alphabetized[1] according to the last name of the author (or, in the case of unsigned articles, according to the first significant word in the title). For that reason, the names of authors are inverted in the bibliography—e.g. Heilman, Robert. The first line of each bibliographical entry begins at the left-hand margin, and any subsequent lines in that entry are indented (just the opposite of the format of footnotes). Bibliographical entries are single-spaced *within* the entry and double-spaced *between* entries. (If, however, the paper is being submitted for publication, the bibliographical entries are double-spaced both within the entry and between en-

[1] Given alphabetical order; arranged from *A* to *Z* according to the first letter of each word or entry.

tries.) See Models for Bibliography (p. 310) for other differences between the format of footnotes and the format of bibliographical entries.

(I) ELLIPSIS PERIODS

Ellipsis[1] periods (three spaced periods) are used to indicate that words or whole sentences have been omitted from a direct quotation:

> The President said last week that "the American people . . . would not tolerate such violence."

(note that there is a space between periods; wrong form: ...)

> Philip Gove said in a letter to the New York Times:
>
>> The paragraph is, of course, a monstrosity, totally removed from possible occurrence in connection with any genuine attempt to use words in normally expected context. . . . A similar artificial monstrosity could be contrived by jumbling together inappropriate words from formal literary language or from the Second Edition.

---

[1] Omission of a word or words obviously intended in the original expression.

Writing Research Papers, Letters, and Résumés

(the fourth *period in this instance is the period used to mark the end of the sentence. Because of this period and the capital letter with which the next group of words begins, we know that at least the end of the first sentence has been omitted and that possibly as much as a whole paragraph has been removed before the next sentence)*

Usually there is no need to put ellipsis periods at the beginning or end of a quotation, because the reader knows that the quotation has been extracted from a larger context. Reserve ellipsis periods for indicating omissions[1] *within* quotations.

(J) SQUARE BRACKETS

Square brackets are used to enclose anything that the author of the research paper inserts into a direct quotation:

```
About this tendency to indulge in scatological
language, H. A. Taine wrote, "He [Swift] drags
poetry not only through the mud, but into the
filth; he rolls in it like a raging madman, he
enthrones himself in it, and bespatters all
passers-by."

The Senator was emphatic in stating his reac-
tion to the measure: "This action by HEW
```

---

[1] Things left out or unmentioned.

[Health, Education, and Welfare] will definitely not reverse the downward spiral [of
prices and wages] that has plagued us for the
last eight months."

We find this entry in the Japanese admiral's
diary: "Promptly at 8:32 on Sunday morning of
December 6 [sic], 1941, I dispatched the first
wave of bombers for the raid on Perl Harber
[sic]."

(sic *is a Latin adverb meaning "thus," "in this manner,"
and is used to let the reader know that the error in logic or
fact or grammar or spelling in the quotation has been
copied exactly as it was in the original source. It is italicized
because it is a foreign word*)

If your typewriter does not have keys that make square
brackets, you will have to draw the brackets with a pen after
you remove the paper from the typewriter.

Format of the Research Paper: Model Footnotes

The models for footnotes and for bibliography follow the forms prescribed in *The MLA Style Sheet,* 2nd ed. (New York: Modern Language Association, 1970), one of the most widely used systems in America.

The models here are single-spaced within the footnote and double-spaced between footnotes, as they would be if they appeared at the bottom of the page in a research paper or a dissertation. For the double-spacing of footnotes, see the Model for Footnotes Entered on Separate Pages on p. 332.

For the bibliography form for each of these model footnotes, see the next section (p. 311).

(K) PRIMARY FOOTNOTES

(the first reference to a source)

(1) A Single Book by a Single Author:

Hozen Seki, <u>The Great Natural Way</u> (New York: American Buddhist Academy, 1976), p. 88.

John W. Landon, <u>Jesse Crawford</u>: <u>Poet of the Organ</u>, <u>Wizard of the Mighty Wurlitzer</u> (Vestal, N.Y.: The Vestal Press, 1974), pp. 75-6.

● Format of the Research Paper

*(Notice that the first line of the footnote is indented and that
subsequent lines of the footnote start at the left-hand margin.
The **p.** is the abbreviation of **page; pp.** is the abbreviation of
pages.)*

(2) A Single Book by More Than One Author:

> Paul A. Baran and Paul M. Sweezy, <u>Monopoly
> Capital</u> (New York: Monthly Review Press,
> 1966), p. 392.

(3) A Book of More Than One Volume:

> William Lee Hays and Robert L. Winkler, <u>Sta-
> tistics</u>: <u>Probability</u>, <u>Inference</u>, <u>and</u> <u>Decision</u>
> (New York: Holt, Rinehart, and Winston, 1970),
> II, 137.

*(Whenever a volume number is cited [here the Roman nu-
meral **II**], the abbreviation p. or pp. is not used in front of the
page number.)*

(4) A Book Edited by One or More Editors:

> <u>Essays</u> <u>in</u> <u>American</u> <u>Economic</u> <u>History</u>, ed.
> Alfred W. Coats and Ross M. Robertson (London:
> Edward Arnold, 1969), pp. 268-9.

> <u>The</u> <u>Letters</u> <u>of</u> <u>Jonathan</u> <u>Swift</u> <u>to</u> <u>Charles</u>
> <u>Ford</u>, ed. David Nichol Smith (Oxford: Claren-
> don Press, 1935), p. 187.

*(Here the abbreviation **ed.** stands for **edited by.**)*

Writing Research Papers, Letters, and Résumés

(5) An Essay or a Chapter by an Author in
     an Edited Collection:

Martin J. Svaglic, "Classical Rhetoric and
Victorian Prose," The Art of Victorian Prose,
ed. George Levine and William Madden (New
York: Oxford Univ. Press, 1968), pp. 268–70.

(6) A New Edition of a Book:

Oswald Doughty, A Victorian Romantic, Dante
Gabriel Rossetti, 2nd ed. (London: Oxford
Univ. Press, 1960), p. 35.

(*Here the abbreviation **ed.** stands for **edition.***)

(7) A Book That Is Part of a Series:

William Heytesbury, Medieval Logic and the
Rise of Mathematical Physics. University of
Wisconsin Publications in Medieval Science,
No. 3 (Madison: Univ. of Wisconsin Press,
1956), p. 97.

(*Here the abbreviation **No.** stands for **Number.***)

(8) A Book in a Paperback Series:

Edmund Wilson, To the Finland Station. An-
chor Books (Garden City, N.Y.: Doubleday,
1955), p. 130.

(9) A Translation:

> Fyodor Dostoevsky, <u>Crime and Punishment</u>, trans. Constance Garnett (New York: Heritage Press, 1938), p. 351.
>
> Jacques Ellul, <u>A Critique of the New Commonplaces</u>, trans. Helen Weaver (New York: Knopf, 1968), pp. 139–40.

*(The abbreviation **trans.** stands for **translated by.**)*

(10) A Signed and an Unsigned Article from an encyclopedia:

> J. A. Ewing, "Steam–Engine and Other Heat–Engines," <u>Encyclopedia Britannica</u>, 9th ed. XXII, 475–7.
>
> "Dwarfed Trees," <u>Encyclopedia Americana</u>, 1948, IX, 445.

(Since encyclopedias periodically undergo revision and updating, the particular edition consulted should be indicated by a date or a number. In the bibliography, unsigned articles are filed alphabetically according to the first significant word in the title—here Dwarfed.)

(11) An Article from a Journal:

Writing Research Papers, Letters, and Résumés

> Nelson Adkins, "Emerson and the Bardic Tradition," PMLA, 72 (1948), 665.
>
> Theodore Otto Windt, Jr., "The Diatribe: Last Resort for Protest," QJS, 58 (1972), 9–10.

(*Well-known scholarly journals are commonly referred to by their abbreviated titles. Here* PMLA *stands for* Publications of the Modern Language Association; QJS *stands for* Quarterly Journal of Speech. *Volume numbers of journals are now designated by an Arabic number [*here 72 and 58*] rather than, as formerly, by a Roman numeral.[1] Because the volume number has been cited, the abbreviations p. and pp. are not used in front of the page numbers.*)

(12) An Article in a Popular Magazine:

> Robert J. Levin, "Sex, Morality, and Society," Saturday Review, 9 July 1966, p. 29.
>
> Charles E. Silberman, "Technology Is Knocking on the Schoolhouse Door," Fortune, Aug. 1966, pp. 121–2.

(*Note that* Saturday Review *is a weekly magazine;* Fortune *is a monthly. Because no volume number is cited, p. and pp. are used in front of the page numbers.*)

---

[1] Roman numerals use I, V, X, etc., for numbers, whereas Arabic numbers are those that, like 1, 2, 3, etc., we most commonly see and use in daily communication.

(13) A Signed and an Unsigned Article in a Newspaper:

> Art Gilman, "Altering U.S. Flag for Politi-
> cal Causes Stirs a Legal Debate" <u>Wall</u> <u>Street</u>
> <u>Journal</u>, 12 June 1970, p. 1.
>
> "Twin Games Bid: Wrestling, Judo," <u>New</u> <u>York</u>
> <u>Times</u>, 9 April 1972, Section 5, p. 15,
> cols. 4–6.

(For editions of a newspaper with multiple[1] sections, each with its own pagination,[2] it is necessary to cite the section in addition to the page number. It is helpful also to give column numbers. Sometimes, if an article appeared in one edition of a newspaper but not in other editions, it is necessary to specify the particular edition of the newspaper—e.g. New York Times, *Late City Ed., 4 Feb. 1972, p. 12, col. 1.)*

(14) A Signed Book Review:

> John F. Dalbor, rev. of <u>Meaning</u> <u>and</u> <u>Mind</u>: <u>A</u>
> <u>Study</u> <u>in</u> <u>the</u> <u>Psychology</u> <u>of</u> <u>Language</u>, by
> Robert F. Terwilliger, <u>Philosophy</u> <u>&</u> <u>Rhetoric</u>,
> 5 (1972), 60–1.
>
> Brendan Gill, rev. of <u>Ibsen</u>, by Michael
> Meyer, <u>New</u> <u>Yorker</u>, 8 April 1972, p. 128

*(The first review appeared in a scholarly journal, the second review appeared in a weekly magazine. The abbreviation **rev.** stands for **review.**)*

---

[1] More than one; several or many.   [2] Numbering of pages.

(L) SECONDARY FOOTNOTES

(shortened forms after a source has once been given in full)

> [15]Seki, p. 80.

(*This is the shortened form of the first footnote given in [1] under Primary Footnotes.*)

> [16]Hays and Winkler, II, 140.

(*This is the shortened form of the footnote given in [3] under Primary Footnotes.*)

> [17]Ibid., I., 87.

(***Ibid.*** *is the abbreviation of the Latin adverb **ibidem**, meaning "in the same place." Ibid. may be used if the source in that footnote is the same as the one cited in the immediately preceding footnote. However, if a reader would have to turn back one or more pages to find the last source cited, it would be better to use the last-name shortened form: Hays and Winkler, I, 87. There must be added to Ibid. only what changes from the previous source. Thus in footnote 17 above, I and 87 were added to Ibid. because both the volume number and the page number changed from the previous footnote. If only the page number changed, footnote 17 would read thus: Ibid., p. 145. If nothing changed, footnote 17 would read thus: Ibid.*)

> [18]Wilson, <u>Finland</u> <u>Station</u>, pp. 220–2.

(*When more than one book or article by the same author has been cited in a paper, you must use an abbreviated title in addition to the surname of the author in order to identify the source. In footnote 18 above,* Finland Station *is an abbreviated form of the full title* To the Finland Station.)

[19]"Rendezvous with Ecology," p. 97.

(*In the case of an anonymous article or book, the title or a shortened form of it has to be used in subsequent references to that source.*)

(M)
Format of the Research Paper: Models for Bibliography

The form of a bibliography entry differs in some ways from that of a footnote reference. The following shows how the two forms handle a citation for the same book.

<table>
<tr><th>BIBLIOGRAPHY</th><th>FOOTNOTE</th></tr>
<tr><td>

Ryan, Edwin. *A College Handbook to Newman*. Washington, D.C.: Catholic Education Press, 1930.

</td><td>

Edwin Ryan, *A College Handbook to Newman* (Washington, D.C.: Catholic Education Press, 1930), p. 109.

</td></tr>
</table>

The first line begins at the left-hand margin, with all subsequent lines indented.

The name of the author is inverted (last name first) for purposes of alphabetizing the list of entries.

The first line is indented, with all subsequent lines brought out to the left-hand margin.

The name of the author is set down in the normal order.

310

The three main divisions of author, title, and publishing data are separated by periods.

The three main divisions of author, title, and publishing data are separated by commas.

Place of publication, name of the publisher, and publication date comprise[1] a separate sentence following the title.

Place of publication, name of the publisher, and publication date are enclosed in parentheses as part of the single sentence making up the entry.

The subtitle, if any, should be included in the citation. See (2) below.

The subtitle, if any, may be omitted in the citation.

There is no page reference unless the entry is for an article or part of a collection, in which case the full span of pages (first page and last page) is cited.

Only a specific page reference is cited.

CORRESPONDING BIBLIOGRAPHY FORMS FOR THE FOURTEEN MODEL FOOTNOTES

(If the research paper is submitted[2] as an assignment in a course, the bibliography entries may be single-spaced within the entry and double-spaced between entries, as in the model for a bibliography page (p. 330). If, however, the paper is being submitted to a journal for possible publication,

---

[1] Make up; constitute. [2] Given over; offered.

the entries should be double-spaced both within the entry and between the entries, as they are in these models.)

(1) A Single Book by a Single Author:

```
Seki, Hozen. The Great Natural Way. New York:
    American Buddhist Academy, 1976.
Landon, John W. Jesse Crawford: Poet of the
    Organ, Wizard of the Mighty Wurlitzer. Ves-
    tal, N.Y.: The Vestal Press, 1974.
```

(2) A Single Book by More Than One Author:

```
Baran, Paul A., and Paul M. Sweezy. Monopoly
    Capital: An Essay on American Economic and
    Social Order. New York: Monthly Review
    Press, 1966.
```

(Only the name of the first author should be inverted.[1] Notice that the subtitle, which was omitted in the footnote, is included here.)

(3) A Book of More Than One Volume:

```
Hays, William Lee, and Robert L. Winkler. Sta-
    tistics: Probability, Inference, and Deci-
    sion. 2 vols. New York: Holt, Rinehart, and
    Winston, 1970.
```

[1] Reversed in position or order (with regard to parts or in relation to something else).

(4) A Book Edited by One or More Editors:

Essays in American Economic History. Ed.

    Alfred W. Coats and Ross M. Robertson. Lon—

    don: Edward Arnold, 1969.

The Letters of Jonathan Swift to Charles Ford.

    Ed. David Nichol Smith. Oxford: Clarendon

    Press, 1935.

(In the bibliography, these books would be filed alphabetically according to the first significant word in the title—**Essays** and **Letters** respectively.)

(5) An Essay or a Chapter by an Author in an Edited Collection

Svaglic, Martin J. "Classical Rhetoric and

    Victorian Prose." The Art of Victorian

    Prose. Ed. George Levine and William

    Madden. New York: Oxford Univ. Press, 1968,

    pp. 268–88.

(Because this essay is part of a collection, the full span of pages is cited in the bibliography.)

(6) A New Edition of a Book:

```
Doughty, Oswald. A Victorian Romantic, Dante
    Gabriel Rossetti. 2nd ed. London: Oxford
    Univ. Press, 1960.
```

(7) A Book That Is Part of a Series:

```
Heytesbury, William. Medieval Logic and the
    Rise of Mathematical Physics. University of
    Wisconsin Publications in Medieval Science,
    No. 3. Madison: Univ. of Wisconsin Press,
    1956.
```

(8) A Book in a Paperback Series:

```
Wilson, Edmund. To the Finland Station. Anchor
    Books. Garden City, N.Y.: Doubleday, 1955.
```

(9) A Translation:

```
Dostoevsky, Fyodor. Crime and Punishment.
    Trans. Constance Garnett. New York: Herit-
    age Press, 1938.

Ellul, Jacques. A Critique of the New Common-
    places. Trans. Helen Weaver. New York:
    Knopf, 1968.
```

(10) A Signed and An Unsigned Article from
an Encyclopedia:

Ewing, J. A. "Steam—Engine and Other Heat—

Engines." <u>Encyclopaedia</u> <u>Britannica</u>. 9th

ed., XXII, 473–526.

"Dwarfed Trees." <u>Encyclopedia</u> <u>Americana</u>. 1948,

IX, 445–6.

(Notice that the full span of pages of these articles is given.)

(11) An Article from a Journal:

Adkins, Nelson. "Emerson and the Bardic Tradi-

tion." <u>Publications</u> <u>of</u> <u>the</u> <u>Modern</u> <u>Language</u>

<u>Association</u>, 72 (1948), 662–7.

Windt, Theodore Otto, Jr. "The Diatribe: Last

Resort for Protest." <u>Quarterly</u> <u>Journal</u> <u>of</u>

<u>Speech</u>, 58 (1972), 1–14.

(Although in footnotes well-known scholarly journals are
commonly referred to by their abbreviated title, it is advisable
to give the full title in the bibliography.)

(12) An Article in a Popular Magazine:

Levin, Robert J. "Sex, Morality, and Society."
    Saturday Review, 9 July 1966, pp. 29–30.

Silberman, Charles E. "Technology Is Knocking
    on the Schoolhouse Door." Fortune, Aug.
    1966, pp. 120–25.

(13) A Signed and An Unsigned Article in
     a Newspaper:

Gilman, Art. "Altering U.S. Flag for Political
    Causes Stirs a Legal Debate." Wall Street
    Journal, 12 June 1970, p. 1.

"Twin Games Bid: Wrestling, Judo." New York
    Times, 9 April 1972, Section 5, p. 15,
    cols. 4–6.

(14) A Signed Book Review:

Dalbor, John B. Review of Meaning and Mind: A
    Study in the Psychology of Language, by
    Robert F. Terwilliger. Philosophy & Rheto-
    ric, 5 (1972), 60–61.

Gill, Brendan. Review of Ibsen, by Michael
    Meyer. New Yorker, 8 April 1972, pp. 126–
    30.

(N)

Format of the Research Paper:
Model Research Paper
(with footnotes at bottom of page)

A Study of the Various Interpretations
of
"Young Goodman Brown"

Diana Lynn Ikenberry
English 302
January 7, 1977

A Study of the Various Interpretations
of
"Young Goodman Brown"

Nathaniel Hawthorne's "Young Goodman Brown" has been subjected to various interpretations. A prime reason for so many different interpretations is the story's extremely ambiguous nature. One critic seldom agrees with another as to why various parts of the story are ambiguous. One question that has engaged many critics is whether Goodman Brown actually went into the forest and met the devil or whether he only dreamed that he did. Richard Fogle is one critic who believes that Hawthorne failed to answer this question definitively, because "the ambiguities of meaning are intentional, an integral part of his purpose."[1] Fogle feels that the ambiguity results from unanswered questions like the one above. And it is just this ambiguity or "device of multiple choice,"[2] as Fogle calls it, that is the very essence of "Young Goodman Brown."

Critic Thomas F. Walsh, Jr. went a step further in analyzing the ambiguity of Brown's journey into the forest.[3] He agreed with Fogle that the reader can never be certain whether the journey was real or imaginary; however, the

[1] Richard H. Fogle, "Ambiguity and Clarity in Hawthorne's 'Young Goodman Brown,'" New England Quarterly, 18 (December, 1945), 448.

[2] Ibid., p. 449.

[3] Thomas F. Walsh, Jr., "The Bedeviling of Young Goodman Brown," Modern Language Quarterly, 19 (December, 1958), 331-6.

reader can be certain "not only of the nature and stages of Goodman Brown's despair, but also of its probable cause."[4] Walsh also points out that the effect upon Brown, once he emerges from the forest, is quite clear: "Goodman Brown lived and died an unhappy, despairing man."[5] It is Walsh's view that the only solution to the problem of ambiguity in relation to what happened in the forest can be found in the story's complex symbolic pattern.

D. M. McKeithan's view of Brown's journey is unlike any of the previously mentioned views. He feels that, in reality, Goodman Brown neither journeyed into the forest that night nor dreamed that he did. What Brown did do, according to McKeithan, was "to indulge in sin (represented by the journey into the forest that night . . .)," thinking that he could break away from his sinfulness whenever he chose to.[6] However, Brown indulged in sin longer than he expected and "suffered the consequences, which were the loss of religious faith and faith in all other human beings."[7]

All of these critics have something to add to readers' notions about the ambiguous nature of "Young Goodman Brown." It is the purpose of this paper to study some of these critics' interpretations, as well as the interpretations of some critics

---

[4] Ibid., p. 332.

[5] Walsh, p. 336.

[6] D. M. McKeithan, "Hawthorne's 'Young Goodman Brown': An Interpretation," _Modern Language Notes_, 67 (February, 1952), 96.

[7] Ibid.

not yet mentioned, to see just exactly what they have to add
to the interpretation of Hawthorne's masterpiece. I will focus primarily on two areas of interpretations: the realizations of Goodman Brown's faith and the over-all implications
of the story itself. These two areas proved to be quite
controversial.

Despite all the ambiguities of meaning mentioned above,
I must conclude that young Goodman Brown did come to some
realizations about his own personal faith. When Brown starts
out on his journey into the forest, he is confident that his
faith will carry him to heaven. As Thomas E. Connolly points
out, "it is in this concept that his disillusionment will
come."[8] I must agree with Connolly's statement, for Brown
thinks that his wife delayed his journey, but when he ar-
rives at the meeting place with the devil, his Faith is already there. Brown's confidence in his virtuous wife has
been shattered, and from this point on, he cannot be at
peace with himself nor with any of those around him.

Not only does Connolly suggest Brown's disillusionment,
but he argues that Brown's Calvinistic religion is a major
cause of his disillusionment.[9] Connolly presents this doctrine of Calvinism to his readers:

> Calvinism teaches that man is innately de-
> praved and that he can do nothing to merit

---

[8] Thomas E. Connolly, "Hawthorne's 'Young Goodman Brown':
An Attack on Puritanic Calvinism," _American Literature_, 28
(November, 1956), 372.

[9] Ibid., p. 375.

> salvation. He is saved only by the whim
> of God who selects some, through no de-
> serts of their own, for heaven while the
> great mass of mankind is destined for hell.[10]

I think Goodman Brown was a Calvinist, in the sense that he
believed himself to be one of God's Elect. I do not think,
however, that Brown found nothing to merit salvation, for
even though he believed himself to be one of the Elect, he
knew he must cling to his faith in order to get to heaven.
One particular group of Calvinists, known as Antinomians,[11]
were quite active during the time Hawthorne was writing "Young
Goodman Brown." It seems quite possible that this Calvinistic
group could have influenced Hawthorne's characterizations.
The Antinomians insisted that salvation was a function of
faith, for even a man's good works were secondary to his faith.
This "mysterious divine grace,"[12] as James W. Mathews calls it,
"was contingent on the degree of the individual's faith,"[13]
while a strong faith was a good indication of predestined
salvation. Extreme Antinomians believed that a man who was
of God's Elect could be confident of salvation, no matter
how the man conducted himself in his daily living. It seems
quite possible, then, that Brown could be classified as an
Antinomian, since he was depending on his faith to carry him

---

[10] Ibid., p. 374.

[11] James W. Mathews, "Antinomianism in 'Young Goodman Brown,'" *Studies in Short Fiction*, 3 (Fall, 1965), 73-5.

[12] Mathews, p. 73.

[13] Ibid.

to heaven.

Mathews makes a strong case for Hawthorne's development
of Antinomianism within young Goodman Brown. Brown himself
does stress the theoretical rather than the practical side
of his religion, as does the Antinomian doctrine. Brown
states at one point in the story that "we are a people of
prayer, and good works to boot, and abide no such wicked-
ness."[14] Later in the story, Brown further adds, "With
heaven above and Faith below, I will yet stand firm a-
gainst the devil!" (p. 15). He is quite confident that
his being one of God's Elect, along with his having Faith
at home, will prevent any of the night's evil doings from
becoming obstacles in his path to salvation.

It seems important at this point to look at Faith's
relationship with her husband. Brown knows that his journey is of a sinful nature: "Poor little Faith! . . . What
a wretch am I to leave her on such an errand!" (p. 10).
Brown clearly manifests a sense of guilt for leaving his
wife, because he seems to think it would "kill her" if she
knew why he was going on his journey. However, I think
Faith does know his purpose, because she says to her husband,

---

[14] This and subsequent quotations from the story
"Young Goodman Brown" are taken from the text of the story
as reprinted in <u>Nathaniel</u> <u>Hawthorne</u>: <u>Young</u> <u>Goodman</u> <u>Brown</u>,
ed. Thomas E. Connolly (Columbus, Ohio: Charles E. Merrill
Publishing Company, 1968), pp. 10-21. Hereafter, quotations from this version of the story will be documented
with page-numbers in parentheses at the end of the quotation.

● Format of the Research Paper

> "Dearest heart," whispered she, softly
> and rather sadly . . . "prithee put off
> your journey until sunrise and sleep in
> your own bed tonight. . . . Pray tarry
> with me this night, dear husband, of all
> nights in the year" (p. 10).

Why would Faith be <u>sad</u> to see her husband leave for just
one night, and why would she <u>beg</u> him to stay home on this
particular evening? Faith not only realizes her husband's
plans but even gives her consent and asks for God's blessing
to be with Brown when he insists that he must go: "'Then God
bless you!' said Faith, . . . 'and may you find all well
when you come back'" (p. 10). I think Faith is particularly
concerned with her husband's state of mind <u>after</u> the night's
experience. Faith does not appear extremely worried about
his leaving, but I think she doubts whether he can accept the
consequences. Faith's ability to see that her husband may
suffer from the results of his journey is Hawthorne's way of
subtly informing his readers that Faith is the wiser and the
more realistic of the two. She knows that her husband will
soon find out the hard way that Faith--both his wife <u>and</u> his
religion--cannot be used at his convenience whenever he is
troubled.

Connolly sheds an even brighter light upon young
Goodman Brown's faith. He points out that Brown did not
lose his faith at all. What Brown did do was not only retain his faith but actually discover "the full and frightening
significance of his faith."[15] Connolly illustrates his point

---

[15] Connolly, p. 371.

-7-

with this line from the story: "And when he had lived long,
and was borne to his grave a hoary corpse, followed by Faith,
an aged woman, and children and grandchildren, . . . they
carved no hopeful verse upon his tombstone, for his dying
hour was gloom" (p. 21). I must agree with Connolly that
Brown's faith--both his wife and his religion--did survive
him. Brown did not lose his wife, even though he did
lose the love and trust that had once linked them together
happily. And Brown did not lose his religion, for I feel
that when Hawthorne wrote this story, he knew that the
Calvinistic faith would outlive Goodman Brown. I think
Hawthorne realizes that many more "young Goodman Browns"
would perish as an indirect result of such a dehumanizing
religion.

Besides the subject of faith in "Young Goodman Brown,"
I would also like to touch upon the over-all implications of
the story. Without a doubt, ambiguity is quite prevalent
throughout the story. For example, one critic asked, "Does
the story have universal significance, or is it merely an
individual tragedy?"[16] Another critic questioned whether
young Goodman Brown represents the majority of the human
race or only a small segment of the human population.[17]
Various critics have asked similar questions and have

---

[16] Paul W. Miller, "Hawthorne's 'Young Goodman Brown':
Cynicism or Meliorism?" Nineteenth-Century Fiction, 14
(December, 1959), 255.

[17] Ibid.

arrived at a variety of answers.

Paul W. Miller is one critic who has struggled with the question of whether Brown should be viewed as an individual or a type, representing either all of mankind or only a segment of it. Miller seems to think that no conclusion can be drawn concerning Brown's representation because the answer depends on "one's understanding of Hawthorne's view of man when he wrote the story, as well as one's interpretation of this enigmatic but nonetheless fascinating tale."[18] Miller contends that if young Goodman Brown is intended to represent all mankind, then Hawthorne must be regarded as a totally cynical man; whereas if Brown represents only a segment of mankind, then Hawthorne could be viewed less pessimistically. Miller brings up an interesting point here. If Brown does not represent all mankind, are men like Brown doomed by their nature alone to be separated from God, or does the society in which they live play a major role in separating them from God?[19] I think that, in Brown's case, the society in which he lives has developed a religion that refuses to acknowledge sin as an inevitable human weakness. Man is responsible for his separation from God, but the Calvinistic religion seems to suggest that a man's reunification with God is unobtainable if he is not one of the

---

[18] Ibid.

[19] Miller, p. 256.

Writing Research Papers, Letters, and Résumés

Elect. Human society ultimately strives to develop a religion to fill man's need for spiritual comfort, but it
appears that the Calvinists developed a religion that tortured man's spirit. What portion of mankind, then, does
Brown represent? Miller contends that

> he represents those weaker members of a
> puritanical society who are traumatized,
> arrested in their spiritual development,
> and finally destroyed by the discovery
> that their society is full of "whited
> sepulchres."[20]

I find Miller's interpretation more acceptable than other
critics' views. Young Goodman Brown's spiritual development has been not only retarded but warped at the same time,
but I do not think Brown himself can be fully blamed.

   I can agree only in part with D. M. McKeithan's opinion
about the over-all implication of the story.[21] He contends
that

> this is not a story of the disillusionment
> that comes to a person when he discovers
> that many supposedly religious and vir-
> tuous people are really sinful; it is,
> rather, a story of a man whose sin led
> him to consider all other people sinful.[22]

I think Brown is extremely disillusioned when he realizes the
sinful nature of Goody Cloyse, Deacon Gookin, and his own wife,
Faith. As I view the story, this disillusionment, which denies
all that Brown had previously believed, is a major factor in

---

[20] Ibid., p. 262.

[21] McKeithan, pp. 93-6.

[22] Ibid., pp. 95-6.

-10-

the over-all meaning of the story. Those persons who had always seemed virtuous, pure, and representative of Brown's religion were suddenly seen in a different light--a definite disillusionment for young Goodman Brown. Contrary to McKeithan's view, the story does seem to imply that Brown is disillusioned when he discovers that certain virtuous people are sinful and that Brown becomes painfully aware of his own sinfulness and of the sinfulness of his fellowmen. However, even with the disillusionment that Brown faces and the realization of his own sinful nature, he still fails to perceive two very important characteristics of sin: its universal and inevitable nature.

I also agree, in part, with Herbert Schneider, who places particular importance on Hawthorne's concern with the sinful side of human nature. He writes of Hawthorne,

> For him sin is an obvious and conspicuous fact,
> to deny which is foolish. Its consequences
> are inevitable and to seek escape from them
> is childish. The only relief from sin comes
> from public confession. Anything private or
> concealed works internally until it destroys
> the sinner's soul.[23]

I strongly agree with Schneider that Hawthorne's denial of sin is foolish and that its consequences are inevitable. However, I question whether Hawthorne feels that a public confession is the sole relief from sin. I think Hawthorne would feel that a private confession could adequately render

_____

[23] Herbert W. Schneider, The Puritan Mind (New York: H. Holt and Company, 1930), p. 260.

Writing Research Papers, Letters, and Résumés

a sense of relief from one's sinfulness. Young Goodman Brown
was unable to bring himself to make either a public or a private confession. He could not accept the sin he saw in others
nor the sin present within himself, primarily because Calvinistic teachings failed to inform him that sin in man is inevitable. Paul Miller sums up my feelings quite well when
he says,

> In "Young Goodman Brown," then, Hawthorne
> . . . is pleading that what survives of
> Puritan rigorism in society be sloughed off
> and replaced by a striving for virtue start-
> ing from the confession of common human
> weakness. Such a society would be based
> upon the firm foundation of humility and
> honesty rather than the sinking sands of
> human pride and the hypocrisy that accom-
> panies it.[24]

I do agree with Miller that even a type like Brown could survive in a society like the one described above. Society can
truly have an adverse effect upon man, as did Goodman Brown's
society. But, at the same time, man must face the realities
of society, as Faith seemed to do, even though the pressures
of society oftentimes seem unbearable.

Doesn't it seem slightly odd that the mere actions of one
character could elicit so many interpretations from critics?
That there should be so many different interpretations seems
quite out of the ordinary to me. Yet when one considers the
questions that Nathaniel Hawthorne was dealing with in "Young
Goodman Brown," the ambiguity present in the story seems as

---

[24] Miller, p. 264.

-12-

inevitable as the sin that is present in man. In "Young
Goodman Brown," Hawthorne found himself dealing with the
mysteries about human nature and the human mind, two mysteries that naturally stimulate man to question. And this
questioning will go on forever, hopefully, because unless
man finds answers to questions concerning his spiritual
being or to questions concerning all the intricacies of
the human mind, life will hardly be worth living.

I think Hawthorne truly valued this questioning when he
wrote this masterpiece. By his dealing with man's faith and
man's society, Hawthorne was able to stimulate man to question
his beliefs and his own personal role in society. Hawthorne
wanted to point out to the Calvinists in a subtle way that
their religious teachings were having an adverse effect upon
certain people. And I think he wanted the Calvinists to see
that the society--not the individual--needed the reform.
Through his characterization of Faith, Hawthorne was able to
show that man could be considered virtuous, even though he
is guilty of some degree of sin. And, finally, I think
Hawthorne wanted his readers to see that man's doubtfulness
concerning his salvation was natural and necessary, for if man
definitely knew that he was one of God's Elect, he would take
love and faith and peace of mind for granted. Young Goodman
Brown lost all doubt concerning his salvation for only one
night, but his experience on that one night caused Brown to
live the rest of his life as an extremely unhappy man.

Writing Research Papers, Letters, and Résumés

BIBLIOGRAPHY

Connolly, Thomas E. "Hawthorne's 'Young Goodman Brown': An Attack on Puritanic Calvinism," <u>American</u> <u>Literature</u>, 28 (November, 1956), 370-5.

Fogle, Richard H. "Ambiguity and Clarity in Hawthorne's 'Young Goodman Brown,'" <u>New</u> <u>England</u> <u>Quarterly</u>, 18 (December, 1945), 448-465.

Hawthorne, Nathaniel. "Young Goodman Brown," <u>Nathaniel</u> <u>Hawthorne</u>: <u>Young</u> <u>Goodman</u> <u>Brown</u>, ed. Thomas E. Connolly. Columbus, Ohio: Charles E. Merrill Publishing Company, 1968, pp. 10-21.

McKeithan, D. M. "Hawthorne's 'Young Goodman Brown': An Interpretation," <u>Modern</u> <u>Language</u> <u>Notes</u>, 67 (February, 1952), 93-6.

Mathews, James W. "Antinomianism in 'Young Goodman Brown,'" <u>Studies</u> <u>in</u> <u>Short</u> <u>Fiction</u>, 3 (Fall, 1965), 73-5.

Miller, Paul W. "Hawthorne's 'Young Goodman Brown': Cynicism or Meliorism?" <u>Nineteenth-Century</u> <u>Fiction</u>, 14 (December, 1959), 255-264.

Schneider, Herbert W. <u>The</u> <u>Puritan</u> <u>Mind</u>. New York: Henry Holt and Company, 1930.

Walsh, Thomas F., Jr. "The Bedeviling of Young Goodman Brown," <u>Modern</u> <u>Language</u> <u>Quarterly</u>, 19 (December, 1958), 331-6.

● Format of the Research Paper

(The bibliography for a paper submitted as a classroom assignment may be single-spaced, as it is in the model above. The bibliography for a paper submitted for publication, however, should be double-spaced, both within the entry and between entries, as in the Models for Bibliography [pp. 312–316].)

(O)
Format of the Research Paper:
Model for Footnotes Entered on Separate Pages

(If footnotes are entered on separate pages at the end of a research paper submitted as a classroom assignment, they may be single-spaced within the footnote and double-spaced between footnotes, just as they are at the bottom of the page in the sample pages of the research paper. If a paper is submitted for publication, however, the footnotes must be entered on separate pages and must be double-spaced both within and between footnotes, as they are in the model below.)

[1]All my quotations from the "Elegy" are taken from the final approved version of 1753, as printed in Herbert W. Starr and John R. Hendrickson, eds., The Complete Poems of Thomas Gray, English, Latin, and Greek (Oxford: Clarendon Press, 1966). Hereafter, quotations from this edition of the poem will be documented by line numbers in parentheses.

[2]Samuel Johnson, "Gray," <u>The</u> <u>Lives</u> <u>of</u> <u>the</u> <u>English</u> <u>Poets</u>, ed. George Birkbeck Hill (Oxford: Clarendon Press, 1905), III, 442.

[3]Odell Shephard, "A Youth to Fortune and to Fame Unknown," <u>Modern</u> <u>Philology</u>, 20 (1923), 347-73.

[4]Ibid., p. 348.

[5]A detailed description of the various manuscript versions is given in Francis G. Stokes, ed., <u>An</u> <u>Elegy</u> <u>Written</u> <u>in</u> <u>a</u> <u>Country</u> <u>Churchyard</u> (Oxford: Clarendon Press, 1929), pp. 23-6. Herbert W. Starr has also presented an illuminating study of the successive versions of the poem in his article "Gray's Craftsmanship," <u>JGEP</u>, 45 (1946), 415-29.

[6]Shephard, p. 366.

[7]Ibid., pp. 371-2.

[8]H. W. Starr, "'A Youth to Fortune and to Fame Unknown': A Re-estimation," <u>JEGP</u>, 48 (1949), 97-107.

Writing Research Papers, Letters, and Résumés

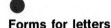

Forms for letters

General Instructions

The one type of writing that most people engage in after they leave school is letter-writing. They will almost certainly write letters to parents, friends, and acquaintances; occasionally they may feel compelled to write a letter to the editor of a newspaper or magazine; and sometimes they may write more formal letters to institutions or officials for such purposes as applying for a job, requesting information or service, or seeking redress[1] of some grievance.[2] Although they do not have to be much concerned about the niceties[3] of form when they are writing to intimate[4] friends, they would be well advised to observe[5] the conventions[6] of form and etiquette[7] in letters to people with whom they are not familiar enough to address them by their first name.

Letters written to acquaintances are commonly referred to as "familiar letters." Although "anything goes" in letters to acquaintances, one should keep in mind that even the most intimate acquaintance is flattered if the author of the letter observes certain amenities of form. A model for a familiar letter appears on p. 338. Here is a list of the conventions for the familiar letter:

☐   Familiar letters may be written on lined or unlined paper of any size, but usually they are written on note-size stationery[8] of some pastel[9] color.

---

[1] Relief; a means of remedy; compensation.   [2] A cause of distress or complaint. [3] The fine points or details.   [4] Very close or familiar.   [5] To conform one's behavior or action to.   [6] Ways approved by social custom; the accepted ways.   [7] Ways of behavior fixed by custom or authority in social, official, or professional situations.   [8] Letter paper and envelopes.   [9] Characterized by paleness or lightness (of color).

● Forms for Letters

☐ Familiar letters may be handwritten and may occupy both sides of the page.

☐ The writer puts his own address and the date at the right-hand side of the heading but does not, as in a business letter, put the name and address of the person to whom he is writing at the left-hand side of the heading.

☐ Depending on the degree of intimacy[1] with the addressee,[2] the writer can use salutations[3] like these: **Dear Mom, Dear Jim, Dear Julie, Dear Mrs. Worth.** The salutation is usually followed by a comma rather than the more formal colon.

☐ The body of the letter may be written in indented paragraphs, single- or double-spaced.

☐ Depending on the degree of intimacy[1] with the addressee,[2] writer may use complimentary closes like these: **Much Love, Affectionately, As ever, Cordially, Fondly.**

☐ Depending on the degree of intimacy with the addressee, the writer may sign his full name or just his first name or nickname.[4]

Formal letters addressed to organizations or strangers or superiors are commonly called "business letters." The form of business letters is more strictly prescribed[5] than that of familiar letters. Models for a business letter appear on pp. (339) and (342). Here is a list of the conventions for the business letter:

☐ Business letters are written on $8\frac{1}{2} \times 11$ unlined paper or on $8\frac{1}{2} \times 11$ paper with a printed letterhead.

☐ Business letters must be typewritten, on one side of the page only.

[1]Closeness of association or familiarity; warmth of relations. [2]Person to whom something is addressed. [3]Expressions of greeting or courtesy. [4]A familiar form of a proper name (e.g. *Gabe* for Gabriel); a descriptive name given in place of, or in addition to, a name belonging to someone or something (e.g. *Slammin' Sammy Snead*). [5]Given as a rule or guide of action.

Writing Research Papers, Letters, and Résumés

☐ In the sample business letter (p. 342) that is typed on printed letterhead stationery, another acceptable format for formal business letters is illustrated. Note that in this format, everything—date, address, greeting, text, salutation, etc.—begins at the left-hand margin. Compare this format with the format of the sample business letter (p. 339) that is typed on plain white paper. All the other directions about format apply to both kinds of formal business letters.

☐ Flush[1] with the left-hand margin and in single-spaced block form, the writer should type the name and address of the person or the organization to whom he is writing. (This is the same form that will be used in addressing the envelope.)

☐ Two spaces below this inside address and flush with the lefthand margin, the writer should type the salutation, followed by a colon. If the writer is addressing an organization rather than a specific person in that organization, he can use salutations like **Dear Sir** or **Gentlemen** or **Dear Madam** or **Ladies.** If the writer knows the name of the person, he should use **Mr.** or **Miss** or **Mrs.** or, if uncertain about the marital status[2] of a woman, **Ms.,** followed by the last name: **Dear Mr. Nelson, Dear Miss Kupferberg, Dear Mrs. Graham, Dear Ms. Bendo.** Women who feel that marital status should be no more specified in their own case than in that of a man (for whom **Mr.** serves, irrespective[3] of whether he is married) prefer **Ms.** to **Mrs.** or **Miss. Messrs.** is the plural of **Mr.; Mmes.** is the plural of **Mrs.; Misses** is the plural of **Miss.** Professional titles may also be used in the salutation: **Dear Professor Buultjens, Dear Dr. Marton** (*Webster's New Collegiate Dictionary* carries a list of the forms of address to various dignitaries[4] [judges, clergymen,[5] bishops, congressman, etc.].)

☐ (The body of the letter should be single-spaced, except for

[1]On a level (with); directly in line (with), adjacent (to). [2]State or condition of a person as seen by the law or society. [3]Without regard to; regardless. [4]Persons of high position or honor. [5]Religious officials (e.g. priests, rabbis, ministers, bhikshus).

double-spacing between paragraphs. Paragraphs are not indented but start flush with the left-hand margin.

☐ The usual complimentary closes[1] for business letters are these: **Yours truly, Very truly yours, Sincerely, Sincerely yours.** The complimentary close is followed by a comma.

☐ The writer should type his name about three or four spaces below the complimentary close. He should not preface his name with his professional title (e.g. **Dr., Rev.**) nor follow it with his degrees (e.g. **M.A., Ph.D.**), but below his typed name he may indicate his official capacity (e.g. **President, Director of Personnel, Managing Editor**). The writer should sign his name in the space left between the complimentary close and his typed name.

☐ If one or more copies of the letter are being sent to someone, that fact should be indicated with a notation like this in the lower left-hand side of the page (**cc.** is the abbreviation of **carbon copy**):

    cc. Mary Hunter
       Robert Allison

☐ If the letter was dictated to, and typed by, a secretary, that fact should be indicated by a notation like this, flush with the left-hand margin and below the writer's signature (the writer's initials are given in capital letters, and the secretary's are given in lower-case letters): WLT/cs or WLT:cs.
See the following models for the text and envelope of a familiar letter and the two styles of business letters.

---

[1] The closing part of a letter that conveys a compliment or expression of esteem or affection.

11 Silver Brook Rd.
Westport, CT 06880
January 5, 1977

Dear Christine,

I'm going back to school tomorrow, and since I didn't get a chance to call you, I thought I'd just write a note.

Did Mom tell you about my dorm's Solar Energy project? The solar collectors we built are in operation on the roof, helping to heat our dorm's water. We'll be calculating the energy savings to the University, and I'll write and tell you the results. New Hampshire winters <u>are</u> cold, but we think it'll work!

Love,
Julie

P.S. Say hi to Arthur!

Sample Typescript Business Letter

239 Riverside Road
Columbus, OH 43210
January 5, 1977

Mr. Thomas J. Weiss
Manager, Survey Division
Acme Engineering Company, Inc.
5868 Fanshawe Drive
Omaha, NB 68131

Dear Mr. Weiss:

Mr. Robert Miller, sales representative of the
Rushmore Caterpillar Company of Columbus and a
long-time friend of my father, told me that
when he saw you at a convention in Chicago recently, you indicated you would have two or
three temporary positions open this summer in
your division. Mr. Miller kindly offered to
write you about me, but he urged me to write
also.

By June I will have completed my junior year
in the department of Civil Engineering at Ohio
State University. Not only do I need to work
this summer to finance my final year of college,
but I also need to get some practical experience
in surveying on a large road-building project

such as your company is now engaged in. After
checking with several of the highway contractors
in this area, I have learned that all of them have
already hired their quota of engineering students for the summer.

For the last three summers I have worked for
the Worley Building Contractors of Columbus as
a carpenter's helper and as a cement-finisher.
Mr. Albert Michael, my foreman for the last
three summers, has indicated that he would write
a letter of reference for me, if you wanted one.
He understands why I want to get some experience
in surveying this summer, but he told me that I
would have priority for a summertime job with
Worley if I wanted it.

Among my instructors in civil engineering, the
two men who know me best are Dr. Theodore Sloan,
who says that he knows you, and Mr. A. M. Slater.
Currently I have a 3.2 quality-point average in
all my subjects, but I have straight A's in all my
engineering courses. For the last two quarters I
have worked as a lab assistant for Professor
Sloan.

I am anxious to get experience in my future
profession and I am quite willing to relocate
for the summer. I own a 1969 Volkswagen that I
could use to commute several miles each day to
the job site, if that is necessary. I am in
good health, and I am willing to work very

hard. If you want any letters of recommendation from any of the men named in my letter, please let me know, but perhaps you will be satisfied by Mr. Miller's testimony about me.

Sincerely yours,

Oscar Jerman

Oscar Jerman

c. Robert Miller

Sample Typescript Business Letter on Letterhead

 JOHN WILEY & SONS, INC., PUBLISHERS
605 THIRD AVENUE, NEW YORK, N.Y. 10016 (212) 867-9800

TELEX 12-7063   CABLE: JONWILE

January 5, 1977

Professor Edward P. J. Corbett
Department of English
The Ohio State University
Columbus, OH 43210

Dear Professor Corbett:

In reply to your query, I can say unequivocally that there are job
opportunities in the publishing industry for liberal-arts graduates
in general and for English majors in particular. In fact, for certain
kinds of jobs, the liberal-arts graduate would have a distinct advantage
over applicants with a more specialized training or education.

I am sure, however, that what your English majors are seeking is specific
information about the kinds of jobs available in publishing, about the
particular competencies and skills we look for in applicants, and about
the process of applying for jobs. I believe that I could offer this
information more clearly in an informal talk. It would also be more
convenient for me as daily office pressures allow little time for writing
the detailed report you need. You mentioned in your letter that the
English Forum regularly schedules a meeting for every third Friday of
the month. It happens that I am planning to visit your campus at a
time that coincides with the next scheduled meeting of that group.
I would be happy to address them and to attempt to answer questions.

If the English Forum is interested in meeting with me to find out about
job opportunities, it would be helpful if you would forward to me specific
questions that the students would like me to answer. I will, of course,
entertain other questions from the floor, but if I have a few questions
in advance, I will be better able to focus my talk.

I would also like to recommend a publication by The Modern Language
Association entitled <u>English: The Pre-Professional Major</u>. This brief
pamphlet by Linwood E. Orange should be read by English majors, prospective
English majors, and your faculty (if they do not already know it).
I think it is a very valuable guide to the employment potential of English
majors, and I recommend it highly.

Sincerely yours,

Thomas O. Gay
Editor

TOG/nb

cc: Mr. William Grant

NEW YORK LOS ANGELES SALT LAKE CITY LONDON SYDNEY TORONTO SOMERSET, N.J.

Forms for Letters:
Models for Addressing Envelopes (reduced size)

FAMILIAR LETTER

Julie Worth
11 Silver Brook Rd
Westport, CT 06880

Ms. Christine Worth
331 Riverside Drive
New York, N. Y. 10025

BUSINESS LETTER

Mr. Oscar Jerman
239 Riverside Road
Columbus, OH 43210

Mr. Thomas J. Weiss
Manager, Survey Division
Acme Engineering Company, Inc.
5868 Fanshawe Drive
Omaha, NB 68131

BUSINESS LETTER

Thomas O. Gay
JOHN WILEY & SONS, INC., PUBLISHERS
605 THIRD AVENUE, NEW YORK, N. Y. 10016

U.S. POSTAGE
24
METER
PB 621227

NEW YORK
JAN-5-'77
N. Y.

Professor Edward P. J. Corbett
Department of English
The Ohio State University
164 West 17th Avenue
Columbus, OH 43210

TWO-LETTER ABBREVIATIONS OF STATES AND OUTLYING AREAS

Here is the U.S. Postal Service list of two-letter abbreviations of the fifty states and the District of Columbia. These abbreviations should be set down in capital letters without a period and should be followed by the appropriate five-digit ZIP code—for example, Tempe, AZ 85281.

Alabama	AL	Montana	MT
Alaska	AK	Nebraska	NB
Arizona	AZ	Nevada	NV
Arkansas	AR	New Hampshire	NH
California	CA	New Jersey	NJ
Colorado	CO	New Mexico	NM
Connecticut	CT	New York	NY
Delaware	DE	North Carolina	NC
District of Columbia	DC	North Dakota	ND
Florida	FL	Ohio	OH
Georgia	GA	Oklahoma	OK
Guam	GU	Oregon	OR
Hawaii	HI	Pennsylvania	PA
Idaho	ID	Puerto Rico	PR
Illinois	IL	Rhode Island	RI

Indiana . . . . IN	South Carolina . . . . . . SC
Iowa . . . . IA	South Dakota . . . . SD
Kansas . . . . KS	Tennessee . . . . TN
Kentucky . . . . KY	Texas . . . . TX
Louisiana . . . . LA	Utah . . . . UT
Maine . . . . .ME	Vermont . . . . VT
Maryland . . . . .MD	Virgin Islands VI
Massachusetts . . . . . . .MA	Virginia . . . . VA
Michigan . . . . MI	Washington . . . . .WA
Minnesota . . . . MN	West Virginia . . . . .WV
Mississippi . . . . .MS	Wisconsin . . . . WI
Missouri . . . . MO	Wyoming . . . . .WY

ABBREVIATIONS OF PLACE DESIGNATIONS IN ADDRESSES

(Note the absence of a period after these and in the two-letter abbreviations given above.)

Alley (Aly); Arcade (Arc); Avenue (Ave); Boulevard (Blvd); Branch (Br); Bypass (Byp); Causeway (Cswy); Center (Ctr); Circle (Cir); Court (Ct); Courts (Cts); Crescent (Cres); Drive (Dr); Expressway (Expy); Extended (Ext); Extension (Ext); Freeway (Fwy); Gardens (Gdns); Grove (Grv); Heights (Hts); Highway (Hwy); Lane (Ln); Manor (Mnr); Parkway (Pky); Place (Pl); Plaza (Plz); Point (Pt); Road (Rd); Rural (R); Square (Sq); Street (St); Terrace (Ter); Trail (Trl); Turnpike (Tpke); Viaduct (Via); Vista (Vis).

●
A Résumé

A résumé (pronounced *réz-oo-may*) is a one- or two-page summary, presented in the form of a list, of a job-applicant's[1] life, relevant[2] personal experiences, education, work experience, extracurricular activities, honors, goals, etc. It is usually submitted, along with such documents as academic[3] transcripts,[4] letters of reference, and specimens[5] of one's writing, as part of a formal application for a job. The résumé is also referred to, and sometimes even labeled with, the Latin phrases *curriculum vitae* (the course of one's life) or *vita brevis* (a short life).

Under the headings of Education, Work Experience, and Extracurricular Activities, items are usually listed in a reverse chronological order, starting with the most recent and ending with the earliest. (See the sample résumé.)

A dossier (mentioned in the sample résumé) is a collection of one's documents (transcripts, letters of reference, etc.), which is kept on file in a school's placement office and which will be mailed out, upon request, to prospective[6] employers. The letters of reference in a dossier are usually confidential—that is, they are letters written by teachers, employers, acquaintances and never seen by the applicant. (According to a federal law passed in 1975, however, applicants must be allowed to see any letters of reference about themselves if the letters were written after the law was passed and if the applicants have not signed a waiver to see the letters.) The names and addresses of other people who have agreed to write letters of reference upon request are often listed in the

---

[1] A person applying for a job. [2] Bearing upon or related to the matter under discussion or consideration; applicable. [3] Relating to institutions of learning. [4] Official copies, usually of a student's academic record. [5] Items or parts that serve as examples of the whole of something. [6] Potential; likely.

Writing Research Papers, Letters, and Résumés

Résumé

Mary Watson Evans
239 E. Torrence Rd.
Columbus, OH 43214
Tel: (614) 267-4819 (home)
     (614) 422-6866 (office)

PERSONAL: Born, Milwaukee, Wisconsin, October 29, 1948

MARITAL STATUS: Married, James Evans, 1973; no children

EDUCATION: 1972-74, MBA (expected in June, 1974), Ohio State University, Columbus, OH
    Major--Accounting
  1969-72, BA, Marquette University, Milwaukee, WI, graduated <u>magna</u> <u>cum</u> <u>laude</u>, 1972
    Major--Economics
    Minor--History
  1966-69, Westside High School, Milwaukee, WI, graduated <u>summa</u> <u>cum</u> <u>laude</u>, 1969

WORK EXPERIENCE: Research assistant for Robert Moberly, Professor of Finance,
    Ohio State University, 1972-74
    Check-out clerk, weekends and summers, A&P grocery store,
    Milwaukee, WI, 1971-72
    Clerk-typist, summer of 1969, Allis Chalmers of Milwaukee
    Clerk, Saturdays and summers, Gimbel's Department Store,
    Milwaukee, WI, 1967-68

EXTRA-CURRICULAR ACTIVITIES: Yearbook assistant editor, Marquette University, 1972
    Freshman representative on Student Council, Marquette
    University, 1969-70
    Reporter, Westside High School newspaper, 1967;
    editorial writer, 1968; editor, 1969

HONORS: $500 Scholarship from Rush Foundation, 1969-70
    Full-tuition Scholarship from Omicron Society, 1971-72
    Quill and Scroll award for Best Reporting, 1967

CAREER GOALS: Position as accountant or editor of in-house journal in a large
    accounting firm or bank in the Chicago area, where my husband,
    who will take his law degree in June, 1974, has accepted a position.
    I plan to take night courses in commercial law.

REFERENCES: My dossier is on file at the Placement Office, Ohio State University,
    164 W. 17th Avenue, Columbus, OH 43210

    Additional letters of reference (besides those in my dossier):

Mr. John Anderson
Personnel Manager
Allis Chalmers Corporation
West Allis, WI 53214

Mr. Hans Schmitz
Manager, A&P Stores (retired)
2841 N. 70th Street
Milwaukee, WI 53210

---

résumé as Additional References.

Depending upon the kind of job being applied for, some of the other categories that could be included in a résumé are Travel, Languages, Community Service, Research, Publications, Teaching Experience.

THE
HANDBOOK

Note to the Writer

You are fortunate if you have an instructor or an editor or a knowledgeable friend who will read what you have written and call attention to the strengths and weaknesses of your prose by writing comments in the margin or at the end of your paper. Comments of that sort, especially when they are judicious and constructive, can be of great help to you in improving your writing. You should value those personal notes, and whenever the correction, question, suggestion, praise, or blame in them strikes you as being well grounded, you would do well to heed it.

To call attention, however, to routine matters of grammar, style, paragraphing, punctuation, or mechanics, your accommodating critic may resort to some kind of shorthand notations. If he knows that you have a copy of this handbook, he may underline or encircle something in your manuscript and write a number in the margin. If, for instance, he scribbles the number 83 in the margin, he is suggesting that you look at item **83** in the section on mechanics. Turning to this item in the handbook, you will find that it has to do with italicizing certain kinds of titles. Perhaps you failed to italicize the title of a book you mentioned, or perhaps instead of italicizing the title of the book, you enclosed it in quotation

Note to the Writer

marks. The principle stated opposite the number **83** may be all that you need to read. But if you need further enlightenment about what you have done wrong, you can look at the graphic diagram of the structure involved (if one is presented for that principle) or at the examples printed below the principle, or you can go on to read the explanation of the principle.

For more complicated matters, the explanation in the handbook may not be sufficient to point out what you have done wrong or to prevent you from making the mistake again. If so, you should arrange to have a conference with the critic of your prose. Although the correction symbols in the margin may strike you as being heartlessly impersonal, it would be a mistake for you to regard them as petulant slaps on the wrist. They are intended to help you discover how to put your written prose in the "proper" form.

This handbook is also intended to serve as a guide to the writer who does not have an instructor or a friend to read and criticize what he has written. Usually, once a writer has completed a Freshman English course or an advanced composition course of some kind, he no longer enjoys the advantage of frequent, expert criticism of his prose. (If he does, he probably has to pay for the service.) If kept at hand, along with such other reference books as a dictionary and a thesaurus, this handbook can be a useful guide for the writer when he sits down to write something that he wants others to read. The reference charts on the endpages will direct him to the section that deals with his particular problem of the moment. For example, "Should the modifying clause in this sentence be enclosed with commas?" Somewhere in its pages, the handbook probably provides a straightforward answer to that query.

Legend

Some of the principles, especially those having to do with punctuation, are illustrated with graphic models, using these symbols:

$$\boxed{}\; = \text{word}$$

A word inside the box designates a particular part of speech, e.g. $\boxed{\text{NOUN}}$

$$\underline{}\; = \text{phrase}$$

The following abbreviations on the horizontal line designate a particular kind of phrase, e.g. $\underline{\text{PREP.}}$:

prep. = prepositional phrase **(on the stagecoach).**
part. = participial phrase **(having ridden on the stage-coach).**
ger. = gerund phrase (**riding on the stagecoach** pleased him).

Legend

inf. = infinitive phrase (he wanted **to ride on the stage-coach**).

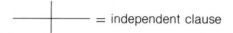 = independent clause

An independent clause, sometimes referred to as a "main clause," can stand by itself as a grammatically complete sentence, e.g. **He rode on the stagecoach.**

 = dependent clause

A dependent clause cannot stand by itself as a grammatically complete sentence. The following abbreviations printed above the first vertical line designate a particular kind of dependent clause, e.g. noun.

 :

noun = noun clause (He claimed **that he rode on the stagecoach**).

adj. = adjective clause (The man **who rode on the stagecoach** was pleased).

adv. = adverb clause (He was late **because he rode on the stagecoach**).

Format of Manuscript

In preparing the final draft of a manuscript, follow the specific directions about format given by your instructor or editor. However, if no specific directions are given, you can be confident that the format of your manuscript will be acceptable if you observe the following conventions:

10
Write on one side of the paper only.

11
Double-space the lines of prose, whether you handwrite or typewrite.

A manuscript submitted to an editor for consideration must be typewritten and double-spaced.

Format of Manuscript

12
Preserve a left-hand and a right-hand margin.

On the left-hand side, leave at least a $1\frac{1}{2}$-inch margin. On the right-hand side, try to preserve about a 1-inch margin. If you are handwriting your manuscript on theme paper, the vertical red line will set your left-hand margin. Try to leave an inch of space between the last line and the bottom edge of the page.

13
Put the title of your paper at the top of the first page of your manuscript—even though you may have put the title on a cover sheet.

See **84** for instructions about how to set down the title of your paper.

14
Number all pages, after the first one, at the top of the page—either in the middle or at the right-hand margin.

Be sure to assemble the pages of your manuscript in the right sequence.

15
Secure your manuscript with a paper clip—*never* with a staple or pin.

Many editors will not even read a manuscript that is stapled together.

16

Use the proper kind of paper.

If you typewrite your manuscript, use white, unlined, opaque paper. If you handwrite your manuscript, use white, lined theme paper. Never submit a formal written assignment on pages torn from a spiral notebook.

Grammar

Grammar may be defined as the study of how a language "works"—a study of how the structural system of a language combines with a vocabulary to convey meaning. When we study a foreign language in school, we must study both **vocabulary** and **grammar,** and until we can put the two together, we cannot translate the language. Sometimes we know the meaning of every word in a foreign-language sentence, and yet we cannot translate the sentence because we cannot figure out its grammar. On the other hand, we sometimes can figure out the syntax of the foreign-language sentence, but because we do not know the meaning of one or more words in the sentence, we still cannot translate the sentence.

If a native speaker of English heard or read this sequence of words

> The porturbs in the brigger torms have tanted the makrets' rotment brokly.

he would perceive that the sequence bears a marked resemblance to an English sentence. Although many words in that sequence would be unfamiliar to him, he would detect that the sequence had the structure of the kind of English sentence that makes a statement, and he might further surmise that this kind of statement pattern was one that said that *porturbs* (whoever they are) had done something to *rotment* (whatever that is), or, to put it another way, that *porturbs* was the subject of the sentence, that *have tanted* was the predicate verb (transitive), and that *rotment* was the object of that transitive verb, the receiver of the action performed by the doer, *porturbs.* How was he able to make that much "sense" out of that sequence of strange words? He was able to detect that much "sense" by noting the following structural signals:

☐ Function words:

The three occurrences of the article **the;** the preposition **in;** and the auxiliary verb **have.**

☐ Inflections and affixes:

The **-s** added to nouns to form the plural; the **-er** added to adjectives to form the comparative degree; the **-ed** added to verbs to form the past tense or the past participle; the **-s'** added to nouns to form the plural possessive case; the affix **-ment** added to certain words to form an abstract noun; and the **-ly** added to adjectives to form adverbs.

☐ Word order:

The basic pattern of a statement or declarative sentence in English is S (subject) + V (verb) + C (complement) or NP (noun phrase) + VP (verb phrase). In the sequence, **The porturbs in the brigger torms** appears to be the S or NP part of the sentence and **have tanted the makrets' rotment brokly** the VP part of the sentence (**have tanted** being the V and **the makrets' rotment brokly** being the C).

☐ Intonation (stress, pitch, terminals, and juncture):

If the sequence were spoken aloud, the native speaker would detect that the sequence had the intonational pattern of a declarative sentence in spoken English.

Grammar

☐ **Punctuation and mechanics:**

If the sequence were written out (as it is here), the native speaker would observe that the sequence began with a capital letter and ended with a period, two typographical devices that signal a statement in written English.

The native speaker of English has been able to read all of this meaning into the string of nonsense words simply by observing the *grammatical* devices of **inflections, function words, word order,** and **intonation** (if spoken) or **punctuation** (if written). Now, if he had a dictionary that defined such words as *porturb, brig, torm, tant, makret, rotment,* and *brok,* he would be able to translate the full meaning of the sentence. But by observing the structural or grammatical devices alone, the native speaker of English has perceived that the sequence of words

The porturbs in the brigger torms have tanted the makrets' rotment brokly.

exactly matches the structure of an English sentence like this one:

The citizens in the larger towns have accepted the legislators' commitment enthusiastically.

What he has been concentrating on is the *grammar* of the sentence, and it is in this sense that we use the term *grammar* in the section that follows.

Almost every child has mastered the fundamentals of this grammatical system of English by the time he starts school. He has "mastered grammar" in the sense that he can form original and meaningful English sentences of his own and can understand English sentences uttered by others. He may not "know grammar" in the sense that he can analyze the structure of sentences and label the parts, but he knows grammar in the sense that he can *perform appropriately* in the language—that is, that he can utter and respond to properly formed sentences.

In a sense, the grammar of a language is a convention. We formulate sentences in a certain way because communities of native speakers of the language, over a long period of time, have developed, and agreed on, certain ways of saying something. The grammar of a language allows some choices but proscribes others. For instance, if you wanted to tell someone that a certain boy kissed a certain girl in a certain manner, grammar would allow you one of these choices of patterns:

> The boy kissed the girl passionately.
>
> The boy passionately kissed the girl.
>
> Passionately the boy kissed the girl.
>
> The girl was kissed passionately by the boy.

Grammar would not allow you to use one of these patterns:

> The girl kissed the boy passionately.
>
> (*this is a grammatical sentence, but because of the altered word order, it does not say what you wanted it to say. Here the girl is the doer of the action, and the boy is the receiver of the action*)
>
> The passionately boy the girl kissed.
>
> Kissed boy the passionately girl the.

The choice of which grammatically acceptable pattern a writer will use is a concern of style, which will be dealt with in the next section.

In this section on grammar, we are dealing with those devices of *inflection, function words,* and *word order* that

Grammar

must be observed if written sentences are to convey the intended meaning to a reader clearly and unequivocally. We do not deal in this section with *intonation,* because this handbook is concerned only with the written language. In a later section of this handbook, we shall deal with the fourth grammatical device of written English, *punctuation.*

20

Use an apostrophe for the possessive, or genitive, case of the noun.

| noun |'s | | noun |s' |

BOY'S   **BOYS'**

Here are some guidelines on forming the possessive, or genitive, case of the English noun:

(a) As indicated in the diagrams above, most English nouns form the possessive case with **'s** (singular) or **s'** (plural). (An alternative form of the genitive consists of an **of** phrase: **the general's commands** or **the commands of the general**.)

(b) The possessive case of nouns that form their plural in ways other than by adding an **s** is formed by adding **'s** to the plural of the noun: **man's/men's, woman's/women's, child's/children's, ox's/oxen's, deer's/deer's, mouse's/mice's.**

(c) Some writers simply add an apostrophe to form the possessive case of nouns ending in **s:**

364

the actress' fame

the alumnus' contribution

Keats' odes

Dickens' death

However, other writers add the usual **'s** to form the possessive case of such nouns: **actress's, alumnus's** (plural, **alumni's**), **Keats's, Dickens's.** Take your choice, but be consistent.

(d) The rules for forming the possessive case of pairs of nouns are as follows: (1) in the case of joint possession, add **'s** only to the second member of the pair: **John and Mary's mother, the brother and sister's car,** and (2) in the case of individual possession, add **'s** to each member of the pair: **the boy's and girl's bedrooms, John's and Mary's tennis rackets, the men's and women's locker rooms.**

(e) Form the possessive case of group nouns and compound nouns by adding **'s** to the end of the unit: **commander in chief's, someone else's, president-elect's, editor in chief's, son-in-law's.** In the case of those compounds that form their plural by adding **s** to the first word, form the plural possessive case by adding **'s** to the end of the unit: **editors in chief's, sons-in-law's.**

(f) Normally the **'s** or **s'** is reserved for the genitive case of nouns naming animate creatures (human beings and animals). The **of** phrase is commonly used for the genitive case of inanimate nouns: not **the house's roof** but **the roof of the house.** Usage, however, now sanctions the use of **'s** with a number of inanimate nouns: **a day's wages, a week's work, the year's death toll, the school's policies, the car's performance, the radio's tone.**

Grammar

21

**Its is the possessive case of the pronoun it;
it's is the contraction of it is or it has.**

More mistakes have been made with the pronoun **it** than with any other single word in the English language. The mistakes result from confusion about the two **s** forms of this pronoun. **It's** is used where **its** is the correct form **(The dog broke it's leg** instead of **The dog broke its leg),** and **its** is used where **it's** is the correct form **(Its a shame that the girl broke her leg** instead of **It's a shame that the girl broke her leg).**

The writer who uses **it's** for the possessive case of **it** is probably influenced by the **'s** that is used to form the possessive case of the singular noun **(man's hat).** He might be helped to avoid this mistake if he would remember that none of the personal pronouns uses **'s** to form its possessive case: **I/my, you/your, he/his, she/her, it/its, we/our, they/their.** So he should write, **The company lost its lease.**

Or the writer might be helped to avoid this mistake if he would remember that the apostrophe has another function in written English: to indicate the omission of one or more letters in an English word, as in contractions **(I'll, don't, he'd).** The apostrophe in the word **it's** signals the contraction of the expression **it is** or **it has.** So he should write, **It's the first loss the company has suffered** or **It's come to my attention that you are frequently late.**

Don't let this little word defeat you. Get **it** right, once and for all.

22
The predicate verb should agree in number with its subject.

SINGULAR NOUN OR PRONOUN	SINGULAR FORM OF VERB
NOUN (no S)	VERB S
boy	runS

PLURAL NOUN OR PRONOUN	PLURAL FORM OF VERB
NOUN S	VERB (no S)
boyS	run

In addition to these differentiated forms of the verb in the third person, present tense, we have to be concerned about the few differentiated forms of the verb **to be (am/is/are; was/were)** and of auxiliary verbs **(has/have; does/do).**

The English verb has been evolving toward a single form for the singular and plural of all three persons (first, second, third)—as witness the **-ed** ending added to the verb in all three persons, singular and plural, of the past tense—and we may yet live to see the day when a totally simplified form of the English verb is achieved. In the meanwhile, the few remaining

Grammar

differentiated forms of the verb will probably continue to give writers some trouble.

Some typical examples of faulty agreement:

1 He **don't** care about anything.
2 The lawyer and his client **agrees** on a fee.
3 If any one of the substations **are knocked** out, we can resort to reserve stations.
4 The jury **has** made up **their** minds.
5 He finds it impossible to live with the ignorance, injustice, poverty, and prejudice that **surrounds** him.
6 Neither the gambler nor Jake **are** really bitter about their bad luck or **blame** anyone for their misfortunes.

Expressions like **He don't care about anything** are not so much "mistakes" in agreement as carry-overs from the dialect that a person speaks, quite acceptably, in his community. Such a person should be made aware of the standard form of the verb in written prose: **He doesn't care about anything** (a singular verb with a singular subject).

Most errors of agreement in written prose are the result of carelessness, inadvertence, or uncertainty. The writer often knows better; he merely slips up. Errors in agreement often occur when several words intervene between the simple subject of the sentence and the predicate verb, as in our third example above: **If any one of the substations are knocked out**. . . . The simple subject of the **if** clause here is **one,** but because the plural noun **substations** (the object of the preposition **of**) intervened between that singular subject and the verb, the writer was influenced to use the plural form of the verb **(are knocked out)** instead of the correct singular form **(is knocked out).** Careful proofreading will often catch such inadvertent errors of agreement.

Errors due to uncertainty are another matter. Uncertainty

about whether the verb should be singular or plural arises in cases where (1) the subject is compound; (2) the subject is a collective noun; (3) the subject of the sentence follows the expletive structure **there is** or **there are;** and (4) the subject takes the form of structures like **one of those who** and **this man as well as.** Here are some guidelines for these puzzling cases:

(a) Compound subject

(1) Singular subjects joined by **and** usually take a plural verb.

John and his sister **were questioned** by the police.

(2) Singular subjects joined by **or** or by the correlative conjunctions **either . . . or, neither . . . nor** take a singular verb.

John or his sister **runs** the store during the week.

Neither the gambler nor Jake **is** really bitter about his bad luck or **blames** anyone for his misfortunes.

(3) When both subjects are plural, the verb is plural.

The detectives and the insurance agents **have expressed** their belief in the innocence of the brother and sister.

Neither the detectives nor the insurance agents **have expressed** any doubts about the innocence of the brother and sister.

(4) When one subject is singular and the other subject is plural and the subjects are joined by **or** or by the correlative conjunctions **either . . . or, neither . . . nor, both . . . and, not only . . . but also,** the verb agrees in number with the closest subject.

Grammar

Either John or his parents **have agreed** to cooperate with the police.

Neither the brothers nor the sister **appears** to be cooperative.

(b) Collective noun as subject

(1) If the collective noun is considered as a **group,** the verb is singular.

The jury **has made up** its mind.

The committee **was elected** unanimously.

The number of students drafted last month **was increased** by 50 percent.

(2) If the collective noun is considered as **individuals** of a group, each acting on his own, the verb is plural.

The jury **have made up** their minds.

The committee **wish** to offer their congratulations to the new chairman.

A number of students **have petitioned** the draft board for a deferment.

(c) Expletive structure **there is/was, there was/were**

(1) If the delayed or real subject following the expletive **there** is singular, the verb is singular.

There **is** a remarkable consensus among the committee members.

(2) If the delayed or real subject following the expletive **there** is plural, the verb is plural.

There **were** ten dissenting votes from the stockholders.

(d) Special structures

(1) In the structure **one of the** (plural noun) **who,** the predicate verb of the **who** clause is plural, because the antecedent of the subject **who** is the plural noun rather than the singular **one.**

> Matilda is one of the women who **refuse** to accept the ruling.

> (*here the antecedent of **who** is the plural noun **women***)

(2) Exception: if **the only** precedes **one of the** (plural noun) **who,** the predicate verb of the **who** clause is singular, because the subject **who** in that case refers to the singular **one** rather than to the plural object of the preposition **of.**

> Matilda is the only one of the women who **refuses** to accept the ruling.

(3) A singular subject followed by structures like **as well as, in addition to, together with** takes a singular verb.

(A plural subject, of course, followed by any of these structures, would take a plural verb. See the third example below.)

> The sergeant as well as his superior officers **praises** his platoon.

> Gill Dougal along with his roommate **has denied** the charges.

> The students together with their counselor **deny** that there has been any distribution of hash in the dorms.

23

A pronoun must agree in person, number, and gender with its antecedent noun.

Grammar

Examples of faulty agreement between a pronoun and its antecedent:

1 A **family** cannot go camping these days without a truckload of gadgets to make **your** campsite look just like home.

2 The crew threw some floatable **items** overboard for the sailor, even though they knew that **it** would probably not save him.

3 The **university** did not live up to **his** promise to the students.

Pronouns, which are substitutes for nouns, have, in common with nouns, **number** (singular and plural) and **gender** (masculine, feminine, and neuter). What nouns and pronouns do not share in common is the full range of **person.** All nouns are **third person** exclusively; but some pronouns are **first person (I, we),** some are **second person (you),** and some are **third person (e.g. he, she, it, they, one, some, none, all).**

A firm grammatical principle is that a pronoun must correspond with whatever of those three aspects of person, number, and gender it shares with its antecedent noun. A second-person pronoun cannot be linked with a third-person noun (see the first example above); a singular pronoun cannot be linked with a plural noun (see the second example above); a masculine pronoun cannot be linked with a neuter noun (see the third example above).

Simple as the grammatical principle is that governs the relationship of a pronoun with its antecedent, there are a few tricky problems for the writer in making a pronoun agree in person, number, and gender with its noun. For one thing, the English language has no convenient pronoun for indicating masculine-*or*-feminine gender. When a noun could be either masculine or feminine, a writer is tempted to use an awkward pronoun form like **his or her, his/her,** or **his (her),** as in the following sentence: "The student should bring **his or her** schedule cards to the bursar's office.'' One way around that awkward locution is to use a plural noun: "**Students** should bring **their** schedule cards to the bursar's office.'' Another way is to settle for one gender in the pronoun, with the implication that the other sex is included in the reference if applicable: ''The student should bring **his** schedule cards to the bursar's office.''

Another problem stems from the ambiguity of **number** of such pronouns as **everyone, everybody, all, none, some, each.** Although there are exceptions, the following guidelines are generally reliable:

(a) **Everyone, everybody, anybody, anyone** invariably take singular verbs and, in formal usage at least, should be referred to by a singular pronoun.

Everyone brings **his** schedule cards to the bursar's office. (*formal usage*)

Everyone brings **their** schedule cars to the bursar's office. (*informal usage*)

(b) **All** and **some** are singular *or* plural according to the context. If the **of** phrase following the pronoun specifies a *mass* or *bulk* of something, the pronoun is singular; if the **of** phrase specifies a *number of things or persons,* the pronoun is plural.

Some of the fabric lost **its** coloring.

Some of the young men turned in **their** draft cards.

All of the draftees registered **their** complaints about the exemption procedure.

(c) **None** is singular or plural according to the context (the distinction in particular cases is sometimes so subtle that a writer could justify either one).

Grammar

None of the young men **was** willing to turn in **his** draft card. (*but* ***were . . . their*** *could also be justified in this case*)

None of the young men in the hall **were** as tall as **their** fathers. (*here it would be harder to justify the singular forms* ***was . . . his***)

(d) **Each** is almost invariably singular.

Each of them declared **his** allegiance to democracy.

If you match up your pronouns in person, number, and gender with their antecedent nouns, you will make it easier for your reader to figure out what the pronouns refer to.

24

A pronoun should have a clear antecedent.

Examples of no antecedent or an unclear antecedent for the pronoun:

1 He retraced his steps to the bedroom, but **it** appeared to be hopeless.

(*what appeared to be hopeless?*)

2 John told his father that **his** car wouldn't start.

(*whose car? the father's or John's?*)

3 The word **deer** originally meant a wild animal, **which** first appeared in the twelfth century.

(*what first appeared in the twelfth century? the word* ***deer?*** *a wild animal? or* ***meaning?***—*a word that is not in the previous clause*)

4 The league's first major step was to sponsor a cleanup day, but **it** could not enlist enough volunteers.

(*a pronoun should not refer to a noun functioning as a possessive or as a modifier—here **league's***)

5 He is a strictly passive character, buffeted by fate, driven hither and yon, the unwilling pawn of forces stronger than himself. **This** makes him resent all offers of help.

(***this** refers to an idea or a situation in the previous sentence, not to some noun in that sentence; but it is not even clear **which** idea or situation is being referred to*)

Careless handling of the pronoun often blocks communication between a writer and his reader. The writer always knows what he meant the pronoun to stand for, but if there is no noun in the previous group of words to which the pronoun can refer, or if it is difficult to find the noun to which the pronoun refers, the reader will not know—and will have to guess—what the pronoun stands for.

A good piece of advice for the apprentice writer is that whenever he uses a pronoun, he should check to see whether there is a noun in the previous group of words that he could put in the place of the pronoun. Let's apply this advice to the sentence "Mayor Worthington, acting on the advice of his physician, resigned the office of the president of the council, and the council, responding to a mandate from the voters, was swift to accept it." There are three neuter, singular nouns in the previous group of words to which the final pronoun **it** could refer: **advice, office, mandate.** But when we put each of these nouns, successively, in the place of **it,** we see that none of them names what the council accepted. If we pondered the sentence long enough, we might eventually figure out that what the council accepted was the mayor's **resignation.** But since there is no such noun in the previous group of words, the writer could avoid even a momentary vagueness if he would use the noun phrase **his resignation** instead of the pronoun **it.**

Grammar

The use of the pronouns **this** and **that** to refer to a whole idea in a previous clause or sentence has been a common practice for a long time in spoken English, and this use is now becoming common in written English as well. Although the practice is gaining the approval of usage, a writer should be aware that by using the demonstrative pronouns **this** or **that** to refer to a whole idea in the previous clause or sentence he runs the risk that the reference of the pronoun will be vague or ambiguous for his readers. If he doesn't want to run that risk, he can use the **this** or **that** (or their corresponding plurals, **these** and **those**) as a demonstrative adjective modifying some summary noun. Thus, instead of saying, "I enjoyed the mountains, but this revealed to me that I really prefer a vacation at the beach," the writer may decide to protect his meaning by saying, "I enjoyed the mountains, but this experience revealed to me that I really prefer a vacation at the beach."

The use of the relative pronoun **which** to refer to a whole idea in the main clause rather than to a specific noun is also becoming more common and acceptable. But there is a risk in this use similar to the one that attends the use of **this** or **that** to refer to a whole idea. The writer who worries about whether his reader may be even momentarily baffled by the sentence "I decided to break the engagement with my girlfriend, which distressed my parents very much" will supply a summary noun to serve as the antecedent for **which:** "I decided to break the engagement with my girlfriend, a decision which distressed my parents very much."

The writer who has mastered the use of the pronoun has mastered a good part of the craft of writing lucid prose.

25

An introductory verbal or verbal phrase must find its "doer" in the subject of the main clause.

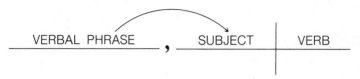

VERBAL PHRASE , SUBJECT | VERB

Examples of "dangling" verbal phrases:

1 Walking on the sidewalk, the Volkswagen ran over me.
2 By returning evil for evil, no permanent good can be accomplished.
3 Refusing to be inducted into the army, the World Boxing Association stripped Muhammad Ali of his title.
4 To accomplish this end, it is necessary for us to study grammar and usage.

In English, an introductory verbal or verbal phrase (participles, gerunds, and infinitives) naturally adheres to the subject of the main clause. When the subject of the main clause is not the "doer" of the action indicated in the verbal, we say that the verbal **dangles**—that it is not attached to the proper agent. By ignoring this basic principle of English grammar, a writer often produces a ludicrous sentence, like the first example above, and in all cases says what he did not intend to say.

To prevent dangling verbals, the writer should make sure that the subject of the main clause is the *doer* of the action specified in the preceding verbal. If the writers of the sample sentences above had observed this caution, they would have revised their sentences to read:

Grammar

1 Walking on the sidewalk, I was run over by a Volkswagen. **OR:** A Volkswagen ran over me while I was walking on the sidewalk.

2 By returning evil for evil, one can accomplish no permanent good.

3 Refusing to be inducted into the army, Muhammad Ali was stripped of his title by the World Boxing Association. **OR:** The World Boxing Association stripped Muhammad Ali of his title for refusing to be inducted into the army.

4 To accomplish this end, we must study grammar and usage.

26

Misplaced modifiers lead to a misreading of the sentence.

Examples of misplaced modifiers:

1 Anyone who reads a newspaper **frequently** will notice that many people are now concerned about pollution.

2 The author seems to be saying that people who refer to the past **constantly** follow the same ritual themselves.

3 He has **only** a face that a mother could love.

4 The teacher distributed examinations to the students **covered with splotches of ink.**

5 **After you entered the park,** the sponsors of the Summerfest decided that you would not have to spend any more money at the concession stands.

6 The plot of the story is a simple one, but there is little chance of the reader's becoming bored **because the author uses many clever devices to advance the plot.**

Because English is a language that depends heavily on word order, related words must often be placed as close as possible to one another. Adverbial and adjectival modifiers especially must be placed as close as possible to words that they modify. Failure to juxtapose related words often leads to a misreading, to a reading different from what the writer intended.

In the first two sample sentences above, we have examples of what are called **squinting modifiers,** modifiers that look in two directions at once. In the first sentence, the adverb **frequently** is sitting between two verbs that grammatically and semantically it could modify—**reads** and **will notice.** If the writer intends the adverb to modify the act of reading rather than the act of noticing, he should shift the position of **frequently** so that the sentence reads as follows: **Anyone who frequently reads a newspaper will notice that many people are now concerned about pollution.** If, however, the writer intends the adverb to modify the act of noticing, he should shift **frequently** to a position between **will** and **notice** or after **notice.**

In the second sample sentence, the adverb **constantly** is likewise sitting between two verbs that it could modify—**refer** and **follow.** Shifting the adverb to a position before the verb **refer** will make the sentence say what the writer probably meant it to say: **The author seems to be saying that people who constantly refer to the past follow the same ritual themselves.**

Because **only** in the third sample sentence is placed in the wrong clause in the sentence, it modifies **a face.** The writer of that sentence could avoid eliciting chuckles from his readers if he would put **only** in the clause where it belongs and make his sentence read as follows: **He has a face that only a mother could love.**

Notice how shifting the position of the modifiers in the fourth, fifth, and sixth sample sentences makes the sentences say what they were intended to say:

Grammar

The teacher distributed to the students examinations covered with splotches of ink.

The sponsors of the Summerfest decided that after you entered the park you would not have to spend any more money at the concession stands.

The plot of the story is a simple one, but because the author uses many clever devices to advance the plot, there is little chance of the reader's becoming bored.

Reading sentences aloud will sometimes reveal the misplacement of modifying words, phrases, and clauses.

27

Preserve parallel structure by using units of the same grammatical kind.

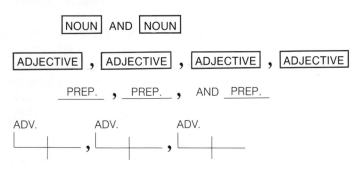

Examples of breakdown in parallelism:

1 The old beliefs about theft have been rejected as **superstitions** and **detrimental** to one's prestige.

   (*noun and adjective*)

2 He was a **miser,** a **bachelor,** and **egotistical.**

   (*noun, noun, adjective*)

3 John was **healthy, wealthy,** and an **athlete.**

(*adjective, adjective, noun*)

4 First of all, Daisy was an **adult, married,** and **had a young daughter.**

(*noun, adjective, verb phrase*)

5 Lincoln was a man **of the people, for the people,** and **loved by the people.**

(*prepositional phrase, prepositional phrase, participial phrase*)

6 The President commended the steelworkers **for their patriotism** and **because they did not ask for a wage increase.**

(*prepositional phrase, adverb clause*)

7 I enjoy reading simply **for personal enlightenment** and **to develop mental sharpness.**

(*prepositional phrase, infinitive phrase*)

8 The admen **not only** convince the reader that the Continental is a luxury car **but also** that the car confers status on its owner.

(*violation of parallelism with correlative conjunctions*)

The principle governing parallel structure is that a pair or a series (three or more) of coordinate units should be of the same kind—nouns with nouns, adjectives with adjectives, not a mixture of nouns and adjectives. A breakdown in parallelism wrenches coherence because it disrupts the expectation that is set up for a reader when a series starts out with one kind of unit and then suddenly shifts to another kind.

The obvious way to correct a breakdown in parallelism is to convert all the members of the pair or the series to units of the same grammatical kind. Sometimes a writer has an either/or choice for the conversion, as in the second sample sentence above: **He was a miser, a bachelor, and egotistical** (noun, noun, adjective). Here the writer has the option of converting all the units of the series into nouns **(He was a miser, a bachelor, and an egotist)** or into adjectives **(He**

was miserly, single, and egotistical). Likewise, the writer of the sixth sample sentence above can convert both units of the pair into prepositional phrases (**for their patriotism** and **for their restraint** in not asking for a wage increase) or into adverb clauses **(because they were patriotic** and **because they did not ask for a wage increase).**

In the third sample sentence above, however, the writer does not have an either/or choice. He can convert the three predicate complements into adjectives (He was **healthy, wealthy,** and **athletic**), but since there is no noun equivalent of the adjective **healthy** (**a valetudinarian** is not quite right) nor a single-word noun equivalent of the adjective **wealthy** (he would have to use **a rich man**), he cannot convert all the complements into nouns.

It should be pointed out that although grammatical options are frequently available, one of the options will usually be stylistically preferable to the other. The writer has to exercise his judgment in making the better stylistic choice.

The breakdown in parallelism in the eighth sample sentence above is of a slightly different kind. This sample sentence illustrates a violation of parallelism when correlative conjunctions are used: **either . . . or; neither . . . nor; not (only) . . . but (also).** The principle operating with correlative conjunctions is that **the same grammatical structure must be on the right-hand side of both conjunctions.** We can more easily see the breakdown in parallelism if we lay out the eighth sample sentence in two layers:

The admen **not only** convince the reader that the Continental is
      a luxury car

        but also that the car confers status on its owner.

On the right-hand side of **not only** the writer has this grammatical sequence: a verb **(convince),** a noun **(the reader),** and a noun clause **(that the Continental is a luxury car).** On the right-hand side of **but also,** however, he has only the noun clause **(that the car confers status on its owner).** He can fix up the parallelism in either of two ways:

> The admen **not only** convince the reader that the Continental is a luxury car
>> **but also** convince the reader that the car confers status on its owner.

>> **OR** (probably preferable stylistically):

> The admen convince the reader **not only** that the Continental is a luxury car
>> **but also** that the car confers status on its owner.

In both revisions we now have the same grammatical structures on the right-hand side of both correlative conjunctions.

Note how parallelism is preserved in the following two sentences using correlative conjunctions:

> **Either** he will love the one and hate the other, **or** he will hate the one and love the other.

> He will **either** love the one and hate the other **or** hate the one and love the other.

The principle governing parallelism: **like must be yoked with like.**

Grammar

28

Use the subordinate conjunction that if it will prevent a possible misreading.

Examples where it would be advisable to insert **that**:

1 My father believed‸his doctor, who was a boyhood friend, was wholly trustworthy.

2 A more realistic person would probably assert‸these statements about the ad were frivolous and sentimental.

3 He discovered‸the radio and the tape recorder in his roommate's closet had been stolen.

4 The author reported‸as soon as a Jew became intensely depressed in camp and lost all purpose for living, death came shortly after.

5 Professor Clements maintained‸Communism rejected capitalism and democracy rejected collective ownership.

The tendency of any language is toward economy of means. So we elide syllables in such contractions as **he's, she'll, we'd, won't,** and we resort to such common elliptical expressions as **not all (of) the men; he is taller than I (am tall); when (I was) in the fourth grade, I went to the zoo with my father.** We also frequently omit the conjunction **that** which introduces a noun clause serving as the object of a verb, as in "He said he was going" and "He announced I was a candidate for office."

Whether to use the conjunction **that** in written prose will be a problem only when a noun clause is being used as the direct object of a verb—but not in every instance of such use. If there is no chance that the syntax of a sentence will be misread, it is all right, even in written prose, to omit **that.** But if there is a chance that a noun phrase following the verb may be read as the object of the verb rather than as the subject of the subsequent clause, then the writer should prevent even a momentary misreading by inserting **that** at the head of the noun clause. What follows may make all of this clearer.

In a sentence like **He said he was going,** it is safe to omit **that** after **said** because **he,** being a pronoun in the nominative case (see GLOSSARY), cannot possibly be read as the object of **said.** But in a sentence like the first sample sentence above, it is not only possible but likely that the noun phrase **his doctor** will momentarily be read as the object of **believed (he believed his doctor).** Of course, as soon as the reader comes on the predicate **was wholly trustworthy,** he realizes that he has misread the sentence, and he has to back up and reread the sentence as the writer intended it to be read. But the writer could have prevented that initial misreading by inserting **that** after **believed—My father believed that his doctor, who was a boyhood friend, was wholly trustworthy.** Then the sentence can be read in only one way—the way in which the writer intended it to be read.

Note how the insertion of **that** where the caret ($\wedge$) is in the other sample sentences prevents an initial misreading of the sentences. Whenever a reader has to reread a sentence in order to make sense of it, the writer is usually the one to blame. Inserting **that** where it is necessary or advisable will save the reader from having to reread a sentence.

29

Avoid the careless or indefensible use of sentence fragments.

Examples of questionable sentence fragments:

1 **The reason for this reaction being that people are flattered by courtesy.**

Grammar

2 I shall not try to defend myself on the grounds that I did not violate the regulation. **Although I could offer the excuse that I didn't know that such a regulation existed.**

3 Both men are alike in that they try to help people only if the effort does not result in too much trouble for themselves. **Herenger, in his idea that it is good to help someone with "so little trouble to himself," and the Baron, who believes in giving money to someone as long as there is no further responsibility involved.**

4 The bond between Gretta and Michael was strong enough to make him face death rather than be separated from her. **The tragedy here that such a love could not be consummated and that one so young should be cut off just at the dawn of life.**

5 Much information about a topic can be brought forth by poetry. **The topic of science, in particular, because science is basically factual.**

A sentence fragment can be defined as a string of words, between an initial capital letter and a period or question mark, that lacks a subject or a finite-verb predicate (or both) or that has a subject and a finite-verb predicate but is made part of a larger structure by a relative pronoun **(who, which, that)** or by a subordinating conjunction **(because, if, when,** etc.).

The string of words in the first example above is a sentence fragment because the subject **reason** lacks a finite-verb predicate. Changing the participle **being** to the finite verb **is** would make that string of words a complete sentence.

The boldface string of words in the second example is a sentence fragment because the subordinating conjunction **although** makes the clause that follows it a part of, or dependent on, a larger structure. The adverb clause introduced by **although** "depends on" the independent clause in the previous sentence, and therefore the adverb clause cannot stand by itself. This example may be more the result of carelessness in punctuating the sentence than the result of ignorance of what constitutes a complete sentence, for the sentence fragment here can be eliminated simply by changing the period after **regulation** to a comma and reducing the first letter in **Although** to lowercase **(I shall not try to defend myself on the grounds that I did not violate the regulation, although I could offer the excuse that I didn't know that such a regulation existed).**

The boldface string of words in the third example is a sentence fragment because it lacks an independent clause. It lacks an independent clause because neither **Herenger** nor **Baron,** which appear to be "subjects," has a predicate verb. Likewise, **The tragedy** in the fourth example and **The topic of science** in the fifth lack predicate verbs.

Whether a string of words constitutes a complete sentence or only a sentence fragment is a grammatical concern; whether the use of a sentence fragment is appropriate in a particular context and is therefore justifiable is a rhetorical or stylistic concern. It is a fact of life that sometimes we communicate with one another in sentence fragments. Take for instance the following exchange:

Where are you going tonight?
The movies.
With whom?
Jack.
Where?
The Palace.
What time?
About 8:30.
By car?
No, by bus.
Can I go along?
Sure.

Grammar

Once the context of that dialogue was established, both speakers communicated with one another in fragments. Notice, though, that the dialogue had to be initiated by a complete sentence (the question **Where are you going tonight?**) and that later the first speaker had to resort again to a complete sentence **(Can I go along?)** because there was no way to phrase that question clearly in a fragmentary way.

Native speakers of a language can converse in fragments because each of them is capable of mentally supplying what is missing from an utterance. When in response to the initial question the second speaker answers, "The movies," that phrase conveys a meaning because the first speaker is able to supply, mentally and perhaps subconsciously, the missing elements in the fragmentary reply: **(I am going to) the movies.**

All of us have encountered sentence fragments in the written prose of some very reputable writers. Predicateless sentences are most likely to be found in mood-setting descriptive and narrative prose, as in this first paragraph of Charles Dickens's novel *Bleak House:*

> London. Michaelmas Term lately over, and the Lord Chancellor sitting in Lincoln's Inn Hall. Implacable November weather. As much mud in the streets, as if the waters had but newly retired from the face of the earth, and it would not be wonderful to meet a Megalosaurus, forty feet long or so, waddling like an elephantine lizard up Holborn Hill. Smoke lowering down from chimney-pots, making a soft black drizzle, with flakes of soot in it as big as full-grown snow-flakes—gone into mourning, one might imagine, for the death of the sun. Dogs, undistinguishable in mire. Horses, scarcely better; splashed to their blinkers. Foot passengers, jostling one another's umbrellas, in a general infection of illtemper, and losing their foothold at street-corners, where tens of thousands of other foot passengers have been slipping and sliding since the day broke (if

this day ever broke), adding new deposits to the crust upon crust of mud, sticking at those points tenaciously to the pavement and accumulating at compound interest.

In that paragraph, there are a few clauses (that is, groups of words with a subject and a finite-verb predicate), but the paragraph is composed predominantly of nouns and noun phrases, some of them modified by participial phrases. But although the passage is largely lacking in predications made by finite verbs, the sequence of sentence fragments creates effects that Dickens could not have achieved—or could not have achieved as well—with complete sentences.

The point of citing these examples of spoken and written discourse is that sentence fragments are a part of the English language (in that sense they are "grammatical"), that in certain contexts they do communicate meaning, and that in some circumstances and for some purposes they are appropriate and therefore acceptable, effective, and even stylistically desirable. But the writer should be aware of what he is doing. He should know that he is writing a sentence fragment rather than a complete sentence; otherwise he will be guilty of a *careless* use of a sentence fragment. And he should have some purpose or effect in mind when he uses a sentence fragment; otherwise he will be guilty of an *indefensible* use of a sentence fragment.

30

Independent clauses cannot be spliced together simply with a comma.

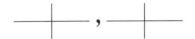

Grammar

Examples of comma splices:

1 We are not allowed to think for ourselves, that privilege is reserved for administrators.

2 Last summer my family saw the whole United States from the inside of an air-conditioned trailer, outside the weather ranged from cool to hot, from dry to muggy.

3 Our minds are never challenged by the television set, it is just so much easier to sit there than to read a book.

4 You will have to choose your vocation yourself, however, you should consider what others have told you about the hazards of various jobs.

A comma splice is the joining of independent clauses with a comma. It occurs only in compound sentences—that is, in sentences composed of two or more independent clauses. A comma splice is an error in punctuation, but since punctuation is, for the written language, the equivalent of vocal intonation in the spoken language, this error in punctuation can also be considered an error in grammar.

Independent clauses must be joined either by a coordinating conjunction **(and, but, or, for, nor, yet, so)** or by a semicolon. In addition to these two ways of properly splicing independent clauses, there are two other ways of fixing up the comma splice: by making separate sentences of the two clauses and by subordinating one of the clauses. Using each of these methods in turn, let us correct the comma splice in the first sample sentence above.

(a) Insert the appropriate coordinating conjunction after the comma:

We are not allowed to think for ourselves, **for** that privilege is reserved for administrators.

(b) Substitute a semicolon for the comma:

We are not allowed to think for ourselves **;** that privilege is reserved for administrators.

(c)   Subordinate one of the independent clauses:

We are not allowed to think for ourselves, **because** that privilege is reserved for administrators.

(d)   Put a period at the end of the first independent clause and begin a new sentence with the first word of the second independent clause:

We are not allowed to think for ourselves**.** **T**hat privilege is reserved for administrators.

Although these four ways of fixing up a comma splice are always available, one of these options will usually be better in a particular instance. In the case of the first sample sentence, splicing the two clauses together with a semicolon would probably be best: **We are not allowed to think for ourselves; that privilege is reserved for administrators.** The semicolon here effects the closest union of the two related clauses and best points up the irony between the thoughts in the two clauses. We have made our choice of the semicolon on stylistic grounds; grammatically, the other three options are equally correct.

See **66** and **67** in the punctuation section for the proper use of the semicolon.

Grammar

31

Do not run independent clauses together without a conjunction or the proper punctuation.

Examples of independent clauses run together:

1 Why am I qualified to speak on this subject I just finished three dreadful years of high school.
2 Those shiny red apples sitting on my desk pleased me very much they were tokens of affection from my students.
3 Two suspects were arrested last week one of them was a cripple.
4 Leggatt was blackballed for having killed a man thus he would never be able to work on a ship again.

The term commonly used to label two or more independent clauses that have been run together without any conjunction or punctuation is **fused sentence** or **run-on sentence.** Fused sentences are not as common in writing as comma splices, but when they do occur, they are even more of a stumbling block for a reader than comma splices are. If the writers of the sample sentences above had read their string of words aloud, they would have detected a natural stopping place—a place where the expression of one thought ended and the expression of another thought began.

Fused sentences can be corrected in the same four ways that comma splices can be corrected:

(a) Join the independent clauses with the appropriate coordinating conjunction:

Those shiny red apples sitting on my desk pleased me very much, **for** they were tokens of affection from my students.

(b) Splice the independent clauses with a semicolon:

Two suspects were arrested last week**;** one of them was a cripple.

(c) Subordinate one of the independent clauses:

Because Leggatt was blackballed for having killed a man, he would never be able to work on a ship again.

(d) Make separate sentences of the independent clauses:

Why am I qualified to speak on this subject**?** I just finished three dreadful years of high school.

As in the case of comma splices, all four of these ways are usually available for correcting a fused sentence, but in a particular instance, one of them will usually be better than the others. Some of the sample sentences do not readily lend themselves to correction by all four means. For instance, because the first sample sentence fuses a question and a statement—**Why am I qualified to speak on this subject** (question) and **I just finished three dreadful years of high school** (statement)—it lends itself to correction only by the fourth method, that of making separate sentences of the two clauses.

Reading one's prose aloud will usually disclose instances where independent clauses have been run together.

Grammar

32

Choose words and put them together so that they make sense.

Examples of confused or puzzling sentences:

1 This same technique of philosophical truths expressed tersely and lyrically, which we often see in Johnson's works, is very prevalent in *Rasselas*.

2 Much later in the story, the dinner conversation the function of the "small talk" seems to be about the old times.

3 The youth, rejected by his parents, by the world, by God, and tragically and ultimately he has rejected himself.

4 William Faulkner presents in his short story "Barn Burning" a human character that is as nonhuman as is feasible to a person's mind.

5 Now in the third stanza, the poet starts his descent. He brings about his conclusion of the boy, which can be paralleled to mankind.

6 Of course, this situation of rundown houses is not always the case, but instead the high rent that the tenants have to pay, which leaves little money for anything else.

A confused or puzzling sentence is one that because of some flaw in the choice or disposition of words reveals no meaning or only a vague meaning. We could say of such a sentence that it is a "non-English" sentence—a sentence that is semantically or grammatically impossible in the English language. A sentence like "The ice cube froze" is a non-English sentence because the meanings of **ice cube** and **froze** are incompatible. We can say, "The water froze," but we are uttering "nonsense" if we say, "The ice cube froze." The phrase **his conclusion of the boy** in the fifth sample sentence above is an instance of a choice of incompatible words. A sentence like "Harshly me teacher scolded the yesterday" is a non-English sentence because English grammar does not allow that order of words. To make sense, those words have to be disposed in an order like this: **The teacher scolded me harshly yesterday.** Each of the first, second, third, and sixth sample sentences has some flaw in syntax that prevents the writer's meaning from getting through to the reader.

If the reader cannot figure out what the writer meant to say, he often cannot even analyze what went wrong with the sentence, and he certainly cannot suggest to the writer how the bewildering sentence might be fixed up. He can only point out to the writer that the sentence makes no sense and urge him to try again to say what he meant to say.

What were the writers of the sample sentences trying to say?

Style

Style is the result of the choices that a writer makes from the available vocabulary and syntactical resources of a language. A writer may not choose—or should not choose

☐ **Words and structures that are not part of the language:**

The defendants have **klinded** the case to the Supreme Court.
(*no such word in the English language*)

All gas stations **have being closed** for the duration of the emergency.
(*no such verb structure in the English language*)

☐ **Words and structures that make no sense:**

The mountains lucidly transgressed sentient rocks.
(*a grammatical but nonsensical sentence*)

☐ **Words and structures that do not convey a clear, unambiguous meaning:**

The teacher gave the papers to the students that were chosen by the committee.
(*was it the **papers** or the **students** that were chosen by the committee?*)

   Aside from these unavailable or inadvisable choices, however, the rich vocabulary and the flexible syntax of the English language offer the writer a number of alternative but
synonymous ways of saying something. One may choose to
use an active verb or a passive verb:

   He reported the accident to the police.

   OR: The accident was reported by him to the police.

or one may shift the position of some modifiers:

   He reported the accident to the police when he was ready.

   OR: When he was ready, he reported the accident to the
   police.

or one may substitute synonymous words and phrases:

   He informed the police about the accident at the intersection.

   OR: John notified Sergeant James Murphy about the colli-
   sion at the corner of Fifth and Main.

A number of other stylistic choices may be open to the writer.
For instance, he may have to decide whether to write a long
sentence or to break up the sentence into a series of separate short sentences; whether to write a compound sentence
or to subordinate one of the clauses; whether to modify a
noun with an adjective clause or with a participial phrase or
with merely an adjective: whether to use literal language
or figurative language; whether to use a ''big'' word or a
simple word (*altercation* or *quarrel*), a specific word or a
general word (*sauntered* or *walked*), a formal word or a colloquial word (*children* or *kids*).
   Grammar will determine whether a stylistic choice is *correct*—that is, whether a particular locution is allowable by the
conventions of the language. Rhetoric will determine whether

Style

a stylistic choice is *effective*—that is, whether a particular locution conveys the intended meaning with the clarity, economy, emphasis, and tone appropriate to the subject matter, occasion, audience, and desired effect.

This section on style asks the writer to consider whether he has made the best choice of words and arrangement of words. Questions about style are not so much questions about *right* and *wrong* as questions about *good, better, best.*

40

Choose the right word for what you intend to say.

Examples of wrong words:

1 The typical surfer has long **ignominious** hair bleached by the **torpid** sun.
2 By the time we reached Phoenix, we had spent our food allotment and were faced with the gloomy **aspect** of starving to death.
3 If you do not **here** from me within three weeks, give me a call.
4 The shortstop played very **erotically** in the first game of the doubleheader.

A word is labeled "wrong" when its meaning does not fit the context, does not express the intended meaning. The most obvious instance of a "wrong word" is the substitution, usually due to carelessness, of a homonym (a like-sounding word) for the intended word, like **here** for **hear** (see the third example above), **through** for **threw, there** for **their, sole** for **soul.**

Another kind of "wrong word" is what is called a **malapropism,** after Mrs. Malaprop in Sheridan's play *The Rivals.*

40 Wrong Word and Faulty Predication

Mrs. Malaprop would say things like "as headstrong as an *allegory* on the banks of the Nile." There is a malapropism in the fourth example above. The writer has heard the expression "he played erratically," but by using the approximate-sounding word **erotically,** he has produced a "howler." **Aspect** in the second example above makes some sense, but *prospect* would come closer to expressing what the writer probably had in mind.

The most common kind of "wrong word" is usually the result of a writer's using a word that is new and somewhat unfamiliar to him. In the first example above, the denotative meaning of **ignominious** is "disgraceful, shameful," but although we can speak of "an ignominious act," the word is inappropriate when attached to **hair.** In the same sentence, if the writer meant to say that the sun was sluggish, **torpid** is the right word; but "torrid sun" comes closer to what he probably meant to say.

Another common instance of "wrong word" can be designated by the term **faulty predication.** A faulty predication occurs when the predicate of a clause (either the verb itself or the whole verb phrase) does not fit semantically or syntactically with the subject of a clause. In other words, the predicate of a clause must fit *grammatically* with the subject (e.g. see sample sentences 8, 9, and 10 below) and must be compatible *in meaning* with the subject (e.g. see sample sentence 1 below). Here are some examples of incompatible predicates:

1 A thief and a liar **are vices** that we should avoid.

2 His purpose **was a ridicule and exposure** of the business mentality.

3 The first section of the poem **is** nothing more than Dryden's reasons for liking Mr. Oldham.

Style

4 He cited an article that **was a dual authorship.**

5 Edgar Lee Masters is saying that the shootings and the hangings are indefensible and that justice **seems** only for the rich.

6 Abused children **should not be tolerated** in our society.

7 The source of Hemingway's title **is taken** from a sermon by John Donne.

8 The reason why she did not come to class **is because she was sick.**

9 The beach **is where I get my worst sunburn.**

10 An example of honesty **is when someone finds a wallet and brings it to the police.**

Faulty predications often occur when some form of the verb **to be** serves as the predicate verb, as in the first four examples and in the last three. Because the verb **to be** is setting up an equation between the subject and the complement, the complement part of the sentence must fit semantically and syntactically with the subject part of the sentence. In the first example, for instance, the complement **vices** does not fit semantically with the subject **a thief and a liar** (thieves and liars are not vices). The adverb clauses following the verb **to be** in the eighth, ninth, and tenth examples do not fit syntactically, because adverb clauses cannot serve as complements for the verb **to be** (no more than a simple adverb could serve as the complement for the verb **to be:** "he is swiftly"). The fifth, sixth, and seventh examples above are instances of faulty predication with verbs other than the verb **to be.**

Revisions of the faulty predications:

1 A thief and a liar exemplify (or practice) vices that we should avoid. (Or: Thievery and lying are vices that we should avoid.)

2 His purpose was to ridicule and expose the business mentality.

3 The first section of the poem presents nothing more than Dryden's reasons for liking Mr. Oldham.

4 He cited an article that had a dual authorship. (Or: He cited an article that was written by two authors.)

5 Edgar Lee Masters is saying that the shootings and the hangings are indefensible and that justice seems to be reserved only for the rich.

6 Abused children should be removed from their parents. (Or: The abuse of children should not be tolerated in our society.)

7 The source of Hemingway's title is a sermon by John Donne.

8 The reason why she did not come to class is that she was sick.

9 The beach is the place where I get my worst sunburn.

10 Honesty is exemplified when someone finds a wallet and brings it to the police.

But now we must point out an important exception to the principle of semantic compatibility between the subject and the predicate. Whenever a metaphor is used, there is, in a sense, a semantic incompatibility between the subject and the predicate. On the literal level, it is nonsense to say "That man is a lion in battle," because, strictly speaking, we cannot predicate lionhood of a human being. But we soon develop enough sophistication in language to recognize that in instances like this the predicate term is being used in a transferred or figurative sense. We understand that the man is not being literally equated with a lion—that is, the man is not really a lion—but that he is being compared to a lion—that is, the man has certain ferocious qualities that remind us of a ravaging lion. Recognizing the metaphorical use of the word *lion,* we do not feel that this complement is semantically incompatible with the subject.

Until a writer gains the assured familiarity with words that will prevent the choice of the wrong word for what he intends to say, he will have to be unusually cautious in his choice of words, and he may have to consult a dictionary frequently.

Style

41

Choose the precise word for what you want to say.

Examples of imprecise words:

1 I liked the movie *Love Story* because it was **beautiful.**
2 What most impressed me about the poem was the poet's **descriptive** language.
3 Has-been athletes always have a **sore** look on their face.
4 To prevent her from catching a cold, he insisted that she wear the **gigantic** galoshes.
5 Honesty is a **thing** that we should value highly.
6 Jane sold her car, **as** she was planning to take a trip to Europe.

Whereas a "wrong word" misses the target entirely, an "imprecise word" hits all around the bull's-eye but never on dead center.

The word **beautiful** in the first example above is too general to convey a precise meaning. A reader's response to a general word like that would be to ask, "In what way was the movie beautiful?" If the writer had said "poignant" or "believable" or "edifying" or "inspiring" or "visually pleasing," the reader might want some more particulars, but at least he would have a clearer idea of why the writer liked the movie.

The word **descriptive** in the second example is too vague. Expressions like "the poet's vivid, sensory diction" or "the poet's simple, concrete words" or "the poet's specific adjectives for indicating colors" would give the reader a more exact idea of the kind of descriptive language that impressed the writer of the sentence.

Sore in the third example is ambiguous—that is, it has more than one meaning in the context. If the writer wants to convey the notion that the former athletes were disgruntled, let him say that "they have an angry look on their face" or simply that "they look angry," but if he wants to convey the notion that the former athletes exhibited physical discomfort, let him say that "they have a painful look on their face"—or in some other way say that their faces reflect their aching wounds.

Gigantic in the fourth example is hyperbolic, or exaggerated. Unless the writer of that sentence deliberately used the hyperbolic **gigantic** for humorous effect, he should use a more proportionate word like *big* or *heavy* or *ungainly.*

In the spoken medium, we often do not have the leisure to search for the precise word; we utter the first word that offers itself. In response to the question "How did you like him?" we might say, "Oh, I thought he was nice enough." If the person with whom we are speaking is not satisfied by our general word of approval, *nice,* he can ask us to be more specific. In the written medium, however, the situation is quite different: we do have the leisure to search for a precise word, and we are not available to the reader who may want more specific information. While we may be able to get by in the oral medium with a catchall word like **thing,** as in the fifth sample above, we should strive for more precision in the written medium and say something like **Honesty is a *virtue* that we should value highly.** Consulting a thesaurus or, better yet, a dictionary that discriminates the meanings of synonyms will frequently yield the exact word for our intended meaning.

The subordinating conjunction **as** carries a variety of meanings, and it is not always possible to tell from the context which of its many meanings it carries in a particular sentence. In the sixth sample sentence above **(Jane sold her car, *as* she was planning to take a trip to Europe),** we cannot tell whether **as** is being used in its sense of "because'' or ''since'' or in its sense of ''when'' or ''while.'' So we should use the conjunction that exactly expresses our intended meaning: **because** she was planning; **when** she was planning; **while** she was planning. We should reserve the conjunction **as** for those contexts in which there is no possibility of ambiguity, as in sentences like ''In that situation, he voted exactly **as** he should'' and ''Do **as** I say.''

42

Choose words that are appropriate to the context.

Examples of inappropriate words:

1 Before the unbelieving **orbs** of the other players, he advances his piece on the board, arresting his **manual appendage** only when he sees that he is going to land on Boardwalk.

2 With **mendacious sangfroid,** he remarked, ''You don't have to apologize. I've known lots of people who have done it,'' and in the same **prevaricating** tone, he **asseverates,** ''Virtue is as virtue does.''

3 The conclusion that I have come to is that **kids** should not have to suffer for the sins of their fathers.

4 My senator tries to act **real groovy and all,** but despite all the **mod rags** he affects, he still gives out with all that graybeard **jive** about the importance of getting a good education so that you can get a good job so that you can afford to maintain a prestigious **pad** and **wheels.**

A word is inappropriate to its context if it does not fit, if it is out of tune with, the subject matter, the occasion, the audience, or the personality of the speaker or writer. It is conspicuous by its inharmonious presence.

No word in isolation can be labeled ''inappropriate''; it

must be seen in the company of other words before it can be declared "inappropriate." Although one would feel safer in making a judgment if one had a larger context, the boldfaced words in the first two examples above seem to be inappropriate because they are too elegant or inflated for the subject matter—a game of Monopoly in the first sentence, a reporting of a remark made at a cocktail party in the second sentence. There seems to be no good reason for the writer of the first sentence not to use the simpler, less pretentious *eyes* for **orbs** and *hand* for **manual appendage.** Young writers consciously striving to enlarge their vocabulary often produce sentences like the second example. Instead of using a thesaurus to find an accurate or precise word for what they want to say, they use it to find an unusual or a polysyllabic word that will make their prose sound "literary." The one hopeful thing that can be said about such writers is that if they are ambitious enough to want to expand their working vocabulary, they will very soon develop enough sophistication about language to know when it is appropriate, and when it is inappropriate, to use "big words."

The more common fault of inappropriateness, however, is diction that is too colloquial, too slangy, for its formal context. Although there are contexts where the colloquial **kids** would be more appropriate than the word *children,* the third example above seems not to be one of those contexts. There are contexts where slang and even the jargon of particular social groups will be perfectly appropriate, but the slang in the fourth sample sentence above seems to be out of tune with the subject matter and with the majority of the other words in the sentence. Even if the writer of that sentence could justify the use of such terms as **groovy, mod rags,** and **jive** as being appropriate to his personality, he could not justify the use of **pad** and **wheels** in that part of the sentence where apparently he is paraphrasing the pious platitudes of his senator. Even if the senator had been addressing a group of hippies, he would not have used **pad** for *home* or **wheels** for *automobile.*

Since dictionaries, thesauruses, and handbooks will not be of much help in telling a writer when a word is appropriate, the writer will have to rely on the criteria of subject matter, occasion, audience, desired effect, and personality of the author. Another way to put the precept is to say that the writer's "voice" must remain consistent with the overall tone he has established in a particular piece of writing.

43

Use the proper idiom.

Examples of lapse of idiom:

1 Although I agree **to** a few of Socrates' principles, I must disagree **to** many of them.
2 Conformity has been a common tendency throughout **the** American history.
3 Blake then **differs** the two introductory pieces by contrasting the simplicity and innocence of the child with the maturity and sophistication of the adult.
4 Harold and the star quarterback from Steuben High also **compared** in being able to throw a clothesline pass.
5 It's these special characters and their motives that I intend **on concentrating** in this paper.
6 Abner had no interest or respect **for** the boy.

To label a locution "unidiomatic" is to indicate that native speakers of the language do not say it that way—in any dialect of the language. Unidiomatic expressions are one of the commonest weaknesses to be found in the prose of unpracticed writers. Why do lapses of idiom occur so frequently? They occur often because many writers have not paid close enough attention—have not attuned their ears—to the way native speakers of the language, including themselves, say something. In trying to express themselves on paper, they put down expressions that they would never use in the spoken medium and that they have never heard any other native speaker use.

No native speaker of the English language, for instance, would use the article **the** in the phrase **throughout the American history** (see the second example above). However, an American speaker would say "He was in the hospital," whereas a British speaker would say "He was in hospital." Some Asian speakers have trouble with the English article, because their language does not use a part of speech like our article.

Lapses of idiom frequently occur with prepositions. A number of prepositions fit idiomatically with the verb **agree,** but the writer must attune his ear to the proper idiom in the proper place. He can say **agree to** in an expression like "He agreed to the conditions we laid down." He can say **agree on** in an expression like "They can't agree on the wording of the proposal." The preposition that fits idiomatically with the sense of **agree** and **disagree** in the first example above is **with:** "I agree **with** a few of Socrates' principles" and "I disagree **with** many of them."

Unidiomatic prepositions often appear in compounded phrases, as in the sixth example above. The preposition **for** does fit with **respect** ("respect for the boy"), but it does not fit with **interest** ("interest for the boy"). In such cases, the idiomatic preposition must be inserted for both members of the compound, e.g. "Abner had no interest **in,** or respect **for,** the boy."

In phrasing the third, fourth, and fifth sentences above, native speakers would say "Blake then **differentiates between** the two introductory pieces . . ." and "Harold and the star quarterback from Steuben High were also **comparable** in their ability to throw . . ." and ". . . that I intend to **concentrate on** in this paper."

What prevents a handbook from setting reliable guidelines for proper idioms is the fact that logic plays little or no part in establishing idiom. If logic played such a part, we would say "He looked *down* the word in the dictionary" instead of "He looked *up* the word in the dictionary." Although the eye normally runs down the columns of a dictionary when searching for a word, native speakers say "look up" a word simply because that is the way people have always phrased that locution. An editor or an instructor can call your attention to an unidiomatic expression and insert the correct idiom, but he cannot give you any rule that will prevent other lapses of idiom. You simply have to learn proper idioms by reading more and by listening more intently.

44

Avoid trite expressions.

Examples of trite expressions:

1 I returned from the picnic **tired but happy,** and that night I **slept like a log.**
2 My primary objective in coming to college was to get a **well-rounded education.**
3 The construction of two new hotels was a **giant step forward** for the community.

4 In the last few years, the popularity of ice hockey has grown **by leaps and bounds.**

5 Convinced now that drugs are a temptation for young people, the community must **nip the problem in the bud** before it **runs rampant.**

There is nothing grammatically or idiomatically wrong with a trite expression. A trite expression is *stylistically* objectionable—mainly because it is a *tired* expression. Whether or not an expression is "tired" is, of course, a relative matter. What is a cliché for some readers may be bright-penny new for others. But it would be surprising if the expressions in the examples above were not jaded for most readers.

Trite expressions are combinations of words that have been used so often that they have lost their freshness and even their meaning for most readers. Metaphors are especially prone to staleness. Metaphors like "nip in the bud," "slept like a log," "giant step" were once fresh and cogent; they are now wilted.

Overworked combinations like "a well-rounded education" should be banished from the language, partly because they are boring and partly because they no longer convey a precise meaning. Someone should be daring enough to mint the expression "a well-squared education" and see whether it gains currency.

Be wary of weary words.

45

Rephrase awkwardly constructed sentences.

Examples of awkward sentences:

1 You could get a dose of the best exercise a person could

Style

undertake, walking. I believe a person should walk at a leisurely pace, with no set goal on distance.

2 The football player has had many broken noses, with which he ends up looking like a prizefighter.

3 I and probably everybody else who started drinking beer in their sophomore year of high school thought the only thing to do was get drunk and go to school activities where we could meet and have a good time.

Awkward sentences are sentences so ineptly put together that the resultant jumble of words is difficult to read or understand. An awkward sentence is often the result of a writer's saying something in a wordy, roundabout way rather than in a terse, direct way. The problem is that the one who writes an awkwardly constructed sentence is usually not aware that he has done so; he has to be told that his sentence is awkward.

The ear, however, is a reliable resource for detecting awkward sentences. If a writer adopts the practice of reading his sentences aloud, he will often detect clumsy, odd-sounding combinations of words. Alerted by his ear, he should look for the usual causes of awkwardness: excessive verbiage, words and phrases out of their normal order, successions of prepositional phrases ("the president of the largest chapter of the national fraternity of students of dentistry"), pretentious circumlocutions ("the penultimate month of the year" for "November"), split constructions ("I, chastened by my past experiences, resolved to never consciously and maliciously circulate, even if true, damaging reports about my friends"), successions of rhyming words ("He tries wisely to revise the evidence supplied by his eyes"). In his effort to rephrase the sentence, the writer should try expressing the same thought in the way he would if he were *speaking* the sentence to someone.

The sample sentences above are awkward for a variety of

reasons, but what they all have in common is excessive verbiage. Pruning some of the deadwood, rearranging some of the parts, using simpler, more idiomatic phrases, we can improve the articulation of those clumsy sentences:

1 Walking is the best exercise. A person should walk at a leisurely pace and only as far as he feels like going.
2 The football player has broken his nose so often that he looks like a prizefighter.
3 Like everybody else who started drinking beer in his sophomore year of high school, I thought that getting drunk was the best way to have a good time at school activities.

46
Cut out unnecessary words.

Examples of wordy sentences:

1 He was justified in trying to straighten out his mother on her backward ideas about her attitude toward Negroes. (19 words)
2 In this modern world of today, we must get an education that will prepare us for a job in our vocation in life. (23 words)
3 In the "Garden of Love," the poem relates the sad experience of a child being born into a cruel world. (20 words)
4 The meaning, at least in my own eyes, that he is trying to convey in the poem "Arms and the Boy" is of the evilness of war in that it forces innocent people to take up the instruments of death and destruction and then tries to teach them to love to use them to kill other human beings. (58 words)
5 These rivers do not contain fish, due to the fact that the flow of water is too rapid. (18 words)

A "wordy sentence" is one in which a writer has used more words than are needed to say what he wanted to say. A writer would soon learn to cultivate restraint if he were charged for every word used, as he is when he sends a telegram. He should not, of course, strive for a "telegraphic" style or a "headline" style, but he should value words so much that he spends them sparingly.

Let us see if we can trim the sample sentences without substantially altering their meaning:

1 He was justified in trying to straighten out his mother's attitude toward Negroes. (13 words)

2 In the modern world, we must get an education that will prepare us for a job. (16 words)

3 The "Garden of Love" relates the sad experience of a child being born into a cruel world. (17 words)

4 As I see it, the poet's thesis in "Arms and the Boy" is that war is evil because it not only forces people to take up arms but makes them use these weapons to kill other human beings. (38 words)

5 These rivers do not contain fish, because they flow too rapidly. (11 words)

Notice that each of the revised sentences uses fewer words than the original. The retrenchment ranges from three words to twenty words. If the writers were being charged a quarter a word, they could probably find other superfluous words to prune. The writer of the fourth sentence, for instance, would probably lop off **As I see it** and **in 'Arms and the Boy,'** and he would condense **to kill other human beings** to **to kill others.**

One should not become obsessed with saving words, but one should seize every opportunity of clearing out obvious deadwood. As Alexander Pope said,

Words are like leaves, and where they most abound,
Much fruit of sense beneath is rarely found.

47

Avoid careless repetition of words and ideas.

Examples of careless repetition:

1 Mr. Bucks, a **fellow colleague,** offered to intercede with the dean.
2 He does not rely on the **surrounding environment** as much as his brother does.
3 The objective point of view accentuates the emotional intensity of the love affair and the **impending** failure that will **eventually happen.**
4 **In Larry's mind** he thinks, ''I have never met anyone so absorbed in himself.''
5 There are some striking similarities between Segal and Hemingway, for **both** have studied life and love and found them **both** to be failures.
6 After **setting** up camp, we **set** off to watch the sun **set.**

A ''careless repetition'' refers to the needless repetition of a word in the same sentence (or in adjoining sentences) or to the juxtaposition of synonymous words that produces what is called a **redundancy** or a **tautology.**

The repetition of the pronoun **both** in the fifth example above is especially careless because the repeated pronouns have different antecedents (the first one refers to **Segal** and **Hemingway,** the second to **life** and **love**). The emphasis in this caution about the repetition of a word should be put on the word *needless*. In the sixth sentence above, we have an instance of the same basic verb form **(set)** used in three different senses. Unless the writer here was deliberately playing on words, he would do well to avoid the awkward repetition, saying something like **After preparing camp, we**

went off to watch the sun set. Sometimes it is better to repeat a word, even in the same sentence, than to run the risk of ambiguity or misunderstanding. In a sentence like "She told her mother that her hairdryer was broken," if the ambiguity of the second **her** could not be remedied in some other way, it would be better to repeat the noun—e.g. "She told her **mother** that the **mother's** hairdryer was broken." In this case, however, there is a better way to avoid the ambiguity of the pronoun, namely by putting the sentence in direct discourse: "She told her mother, 'Your hairdryer is broken'" or "She told her mother, 'My hairdryer is broken.'"

The boldfaced words in the first four examples above are instances of redundancy or tautology (needless repetition of the same idea in different words). **Fellow** and **colleague, surrounding** and **environment, impending** and **eventually happen** are examples of repetitions of the same idea in different words. In the first two instances, drop the first boldfaced word; in the third, drop the whole **that** clause. In the fourth example, the phrase **in Larry's mind** is superfluous (where else does one think but in the mind?). Say simply, **Larry thinks, 'I have never met anyone so absorbed in himself.'**

Repetition of key words can be an effective means of achieving coherence (see **51,** dealing with paragraph coherence, in the next section). What you are here being cautioned about is the redundant and therefore unnecessary expression of words and ideas.

48

Avoid mixed metaphors.

Examples of mixed metaphors:

1 Sarty finally comes to the point where his inner turmoil reaches its **zenith** and **stagnates in a pool** of lethargy.
2 In ''The Dead,'' James Joyce uses small talk as an effective **weapon** to **illustrate** his thesis.
3 He tried to **scale the wall** of indifference between them but found that he couldn't **burrow** through it.
4 For as long as Poe could remember, a **shadow** of guilt **hovered** over his head.
5 Billy was **living in a dream world** that was **wrapped up in his thoughts.**

A mixed metaphor is the result of a writer's failure to keep a consistent image in his mind. All metaphors are based on the perceived likenesses between two things that exist in a different order of being—as for instance between a *man* and a *greyhound* (''The lean shortstop is a greyhound when he runs the bases''), *fame* and a *spur* (''Fame is the spur to ambition''), *mail* and an *avalanche* (''The mail buried the staff under an avalanche of complaints''). Whenever any detail is incompatible with one or other of the terms of the analogy, the metaphor is said to be ''mixed.''

Zenith, as in the first example above, connotes something skyrocketing, and therefore that detail is incompatible with the detail of stagnation. It is also difficult to reconcile the notion of **turmoil** with a **stagnant pool;** turmoil connotes violent movement, but a pool is static.

A **weapon** is not used to **illustrate** something. If one were climbing **(scaling)** a wall, one could not dig **(burrow)**

through it at the same time. And anyone who has ever observed a **shadow** knows that it never **hovers** over a person's
head. There is a similar confusion of images in the fifth
example above: Billy is living *in* a dream world, but that
dream world is, in turn, wrapped up in Billy's thoughts.

Forming and maintaining a clear picture of the notion one
is attempting to express figuratively will ensure a consistent
metaphor.

49

**Consider whether an active verb would be
preferable to a passive verb.**

Examples of questionable use of the passive voice:

1 Money **was borrowed** by the couple so that they could pay off
  all their bills.
2 His love for her **is shown** by his accepting her story and by his
  remaining at her side when she is in trouble.
3 From these recurrent images of hard, resistant metals, it **can be
  inferred** by us that he was a mechanical, heartless person.
4 Talking incessantly, he **was overwhelmed** by the girl.

The passive voice of the verb is a legitimate and useful part of
the English language. A sentence using a passive verb as its
predicate is a different but synonymous way of expressing
the thought conveyed by a sentence using an active verb.
The basic formula for a sentence using an active-verb construction is as follows:

NOUN PHRASE$_1$	+	VERB	+	NOUN PHRASE$_2$
The judge		**pronounced**		**the verdict**

The formula for transforming that active-verb construction into a passive-verb construction is as follows:

$$\text{NOUN PHRASE}_2 \quad + \quad \text{AUXILIARY} \quad + \quad \text{VERB (past participle form)} \quad + \quad \textbf{by} \quad + \quad \text{NOUN PHRASE}_1$$

The verdict   was   pronounced   by   the judge

Notice the changes that have taken place in the second sentence: (1) Noun Phrase$_1$ and Noun Phrase$_2$ have switched positions, and (2) two words have been added, the auxiliary **was** and the preposition **by.** Although the second sentence expresses the same thought as the first sentence, it is longer, by two words, than the first sentence.

If the use of a passive verb is questionable, it is questionable only stylistically; that is, one can question the *choice* of a passive verb rather than an active verb in a particular instance. When someone does question the use of the passive verb, he is merely asking the writer to consider whether the sentence would not be more emphatic, more economical, less awkward, and somehow "neater" if he used an active verb. Challenged to consider the options available in a particular case, the writer still has the privilege of making the choice that seems better to him.

The writers of the first three sample sentences above should consider whether their sentences would be improved by the use of an active verb, as in these revisions:

1 The couple **borrowed** money so that they could pay off all their bills.
2 He **shows** his love for her by accepting her story and by remaining at her side when she is in trouble.

3 From these recurrent images of hard, resistant metals, we **can infer** that he was a mechanical, heartless person.

The writer of the first sentence might argue that he wanted to give special emphasis to **money,** and so he made **money** the subject of the sentence and put the word in the emphatic lead-off position in the sentence (**money was borrowed** . . .). A writer can also justify his use of a passive verb when he does not know the agent of an action or prefers not to reveal the agent or considers it unnecessary to indicate the agent, as in the sentence "The story was reported to all the newspapers."

Dangling verbals often result from the use of a passive-verb construction in the main clause (see **25** on dangling verbals). The writer of the fourth sentence in the examples above **(Talking incessantly, he was overwhelmed by the girl)** may not have a choice available to him. The context of that sentence suggests that the lead-off participial phrase **(talking incessantly)** may be dangling—that is, that it was not the boy **(he)** but the girl who was talking incessantly. If that is the case, the writer may not choose the passive verb instead of the active verb; he *must* use the active verb:

4 Talking incessantly, the girl overwhelmed him.

Paragraphing

One way to regard paragraphing is to view it as a system of punctuating stages of thought presented in units larger than the word and the sentence. Paragraphing is a means of alerting readers to a shift of focus in the development of the main idea of the whole discourse. It marks off for the reader's convenience the discrete but related parts of the whole discourse. How paragraphing facilitates reading would be made dramatically evident if a whole discourse were written or printed—as ancient manuscripts once were—in a single, unbroken block.

Like punctuation and mechanics, paragraphing is a feature only of the written language. Some linguists claim that speakers of connected discourse signal their ''paragraphs'' by pauses and by shifts in the tone of their voice. (The next time you hear a speech being delivered from a written text, see if you can detect when the speaker shifts to another paragraph of his manuscript.) But speakers are not conscious—especially in extemporaneous stretches of talk—of paragraphing the stream of sound as writers must be when they are writing their manuscripts.

The typographical device most commonly used to mark off paragraphs is *indentation*. The first line of each new para-

Paragraphing

graph starts several spaces (usually five or six spaces on the typewriter) from the left-hand margin. Another convention for marking paragraphs in printed texts is the block system: beginning every line at the left-hand margin but leaving double or triple spacing between paragraphs.

In this section, only three aspects of the paragraph are treated: unity, coherence, and adequate development. The traditional means of developing the central idea of a paragraph are mentioned in the section on adequate development, but they are not discussed at length as they are in most of the rhetoric texts. However, if writers take care of unity, coherence, and adequate development, they will be attending to the three most persistent and common problems that beset the composition of written paragraphs.

50

Preserve the unity of the paragraph.

Examples of paragraphs lacking unity:

1 The eminence of Samuel Johnson inclines modern scholars to study his thoughts and opinions. His multifarious knowledge intrigued his contemporaries. Although he manifested his interest in the drama by editing Shakespeare, he did not enjoy the theater. He was envious too of his former pupil David Garrick, the greatest actor of the eighteenth century.

2 "The Cradle Song" from the *Songs of Innocence* has internal rhyme. In this poem, the child is quiet and happy. It has a heavenly image, and throughout the poem, the mother sheds tears of joy. It has a persona—that is, one who speaks for the poet—who is naive and innocent. The poem "Infant Sorrow" contrasts with "The Cradle Song," and this contrast is very distinct. One can see a screaming and devilish child. The piping

is a harsh sound, and the child, who's against restrictions, is looking back and realizing that there is no paradise on earth.

3 Dr. Rockwell let his feelings be known on only one subject: the administration. He felt that the administrative system was outdated. Abolishing grades, giving the student a voice in administration, and revamping the curriculum were three steps he felt should be taken to improve the system. Dr. Rockwell taught in this manner. In class, a mysterious aura surrounded him. He was "hip" to what was going on, but he preferred to hear the members of the class rather than himself. He was quiet and somewhat shy. His eyes caught everything that went on in class. His eyes generated a feeling of understanding.

The principle governing paragraph unity is that a paragraph should develop a single topic or thesis, which is often, but not always, announced in a topic sentence. Every sentence in the paragraph should contribute in some way to the development of that single idea. If the writer introduces other ideas into the paragraph, he will violate the unity of the paragraph and disorient the reader.

In a sense, all three of the sample paragraphs discuss a single idea or topic: the first one talks about Samuel Johnson; the second one talks about William Blake's poetry; the third one talks about a teacher, Dr. Rockwell. But in another sense, all three paragraphs present a confusing mixture of unrelated ideas.

The first sentence of the first sample paragraph, which has the air of being a "topic sentence," talks about what Samuel Johnson means to modern scholars. Instead of the second sentence going on to develop that idea, it mentions what Dr. Johnson meant to his contemporaries. The third sentence talks about his attitude toward the drama and the theater. The fourth sentence mentions his envy of his former pupil David Garrick. What we have in this paragraph is four topics. A

Paragraphing

whole paragraph or a whole paper could be devoted to the development of each of these four topics, but here they are packed into a single paragraph.

We have observed that the second sample paragraph has a certain unity: each sentence is saying something about a poem by William Blake. But notice that the paragraph talks about *two* poems by Blake. Even though the paragraph is about two poems, however, we could still detect some unity in the paragraph if we viewed it as developing a contrast between two poems by the same author. But even if we were generous enough to concede that much unity to the paragraph, it would be difficult for us to perceive a unifying theme among the many disparate things said about the two poems.

The third sample paragraph also has a certain unity: each sentence in the paragraph is talking about the teacher, Dr. Rockwell. And there is a tight unity in the first three sentences: each of these sentences talks about Dr. Rockwell's attitude toward the administration. But with the fourth sentence of the paragraph, the writer introduces another and unrelated topic: a description of how Dr. Rockwell conducted himself in the classroom. If the writer had broken up this stretch of prose into two paragraphs, each of the two paragraphs would have had its own unity.

A paragraph will have unity, will have "oneness," if every sentence in it has an obvious bearing on the development of a single topic. If the writer senses that he has shifted to the discussion of another topic, he should begin another paragraph.

51

Compose the paragraph so that it reads coherently.

Examples of incoherent paragraphs:

1 The first stanza of "The Echoing Green" does not correspond with any other poem by Blake. The glory of nature's beauty is presented in vivid details. Emotional intensity is the overall effect of the poem. Blake resents the mechanization which has been brought about by the Industrial Revolution. The rhythm of the verses contributes to the meditative mood.

2 The preceding account illustrates all the frustrations that a beginning golfer experiences. The dominant philosophy is that the golfer who looks the best plays the best. He complicates the game by insisting on perfection the first time he sets foot on the course. More time and money are spent on clothes and equipment than on the most important aspect, skill. Winning is the only goal. Where is the idea of recreation? Try playing without a caddy sometime, and see how much exercise you get.

3 After the program has been written, each line is punched onto a card. The deck of cards is known as the "program source deck." The next step is to load the program compiler into the computer. The compiler is a program written in machine language for a particular computer, which reads the source deck and performs a translation of the program language into machine language. The machine language, in the form of instructions, is punched onto cards. This machine-language deck of cards is known as the "object deck." After the object deck has been punched, the programmer is then able to execute his program. The program is run by loading the object deck into the computer. The run of the program marks the end of the second step.

Paragraphing

Coherence is that quality which makes it easy for a reader to *follow* a writer's train of thought as it moves from sentence to sentence and from paragraph to paragraph. It facilitates reading because it ensures that the reader will be able to detect the relationships of the parts. It also reflects the clear thinking of the writer because it results from the writer's arrangement of his thoughts in some kind of perceivable order and from his use of those verbal devices that help to stitch thoughts together. In short, as the roots of the Latin word suggest (*co,* "together," + *haerēre,* "to stick"), coherence helps the parts of a discourse "stick together."

Here are some ways in which to achieve coherence in a paragraph (not all of these devices, of course, have to be used in every paragraph):

(a) Repeat key words from sentence to sentence or use recognizable synonyms for key words.

(b) Use pronouns for key nouns. (Because a pronoun gets its meaning from the noun to which it refers, it is by its very nature one of those verbal devices that help to stitch sentences together.)

(c) Use demonstrative adjectives, "pointing words" (**this** statement, **that** plan, **these** developments, **those** disasters).

(d) Use conjunctive adverbs, "thought-connecting words" **(however, moreover, also, nevertheless, therefore, thus, subsequently, indeed, then, accordingly).**

(e) Arrange the sequence of sentences in some kind of perceivable order (for instance, a **time order,** as in a narrative of what happened or in an explanation of how to do something; a **space order,** as in the description of a physical object or a scene; a **logical order,** such as cause to effect, effect to cause, general to particular, particular to general, whole to part, familiar to unfamiliar).

The third of the sample paragraphs above attempts to describe computer programming, a process that most readers would find difficult to follow because it is complicated and unfamiliar. But the process will be doubly baffling to readers if it is not described coherently. What makes this description of computer programming doubly difficult for the reader to follow is that the writer is doing two things at once: (1) designating the chronological sequence of steps in the process, and (2) defining the technical terms used in the description of the process. It would have been better if the writer had devoted one paragraph to defining such terms as **program source deck, compiler, program language, machine language, object deck.** Then he could have devoted another paragraph exclusively to the description of the process of "running a program"—first you do this, then you do that, after that you do this, etc. In the present paragraph, the reader gets lost because he is kept bouncing back and forth between definition of the terms and description of the process.

It is more difficult to suggest ways of revising the first two sample paragraphs; they are so incoherent that it is almost impossible to discover what the principal points were that the writers wanted to put across in them. If we could confer with the writers and ask each what the main idea of his paragraph was, we could then advise him about which of the sentences contributed to the development of that idea (and which sentences had to be dropped because they threatened the unity of the paragraph), about the order of the sentences in the paragraph, and about the verbal devices that would help to knit the sentences together.

Coherence is a difficult writing skill to master, but until the writer acquires at least a measure of that skill, he will continue to be frustrated in his efforts to communicate with

Paragraphing

others on paper. He must learn how to compose paragraphs so that the sequence of thoughts flows smoothly, easily, and logically from sentence to sentence. He must provide those bridges or links that will allow the reader to pass from sentence to sentence without being puzzled about the relationship of what is said in one sentence to what is said in the next sentence. Note how a skillful writer like Thomas Babington Macaulay stitches his sentences together by repeating key words and by using pronouns, connecting words and phrases, and parallel structures:

> It will be seen that we do not consider Bacon's ingenious analysis of the inductive method as a very useful performance. Bacon was not, as we have already said, the inventor of the inductive method. He was not even the person who first analyzed the inductive method correctly, though he undoubtedly analyzed it more minutely than any who preceded him. He was not the person who first showed that by the inductive method alone new truth could be discovered. But he was the person who first turned the minds of speculative men, long occupied in verbal disputes, to the discovery of new and useful truth; and by doing so, he at once gave to the inductive method an importance and dignity which had never belonged to it. He was not the maker of that road; he was not the discoverer of that road; he was not the person who first surveyed and mapped that road. But he was the person who first called the public attention to an inexhaustible mine of wealth, which had been utterly neglected and which was accessible by that road alone. By doing so, he caused that road, which had previously been trodden only by peasants and higglers, to be frequented by a higher class of travellers.

52

Paragraphs should be adequately developed.

Examples of inadequately developed paragraphs:

1 Wilfred Owen combines many types of imagery to get his point across. Most of his imagery is either ironic or sentimental.

2 The young people now growing up in this drug-oriented atmosphere should be made aware of the disadvantages of their indulging in drugs, just as the young people of the previous generation were cautioned about the disadvantages of their engaging in premarital sex. In both cases, responsibility for one's actions is the chief lesson to be taught.

3 The other ways in which these two men differ were that Richard was content with his life, while the Baron was bored with his. Richard was once married, while the Baron was never married but had a son as a result of an affair.

Generally, one- and two-sentence paragraphs are not effective, except for purposes of emphasis, transition, or dialogue.

The preceding one-sentence paragraph can be justified on the grounds that the writer wanted to give special emphasis to a principle by setting it aside in a paragraph by itself. Separate paragraphing for emphasis is a graphic device comparable to italicizing (underlining) a word or a phrase in a sentence for emphasis. Set aside in a paragraph by itself, an important idea achieves a prominence that would be missed if the idea were merged with other ideas in the same paragraph.

A one- or two-sentence paragraph can also be used to mark or announce a transition from one major division of a discourse to the next major division. Transitional paragraphs facilitate reading because they orient the reader, reminding him of what has been discussed and alerting him to what is

Paragraphing

going to be discussed. They are like signposts marking the major stages of a journey. Note how the following two-sentence paragraph helps to orient the reader:

> After presenting his Introduction to *Songs of Experience,* William Blake apparently feels that his readers have been sufficiently warned about their earthly predicament. Let us see now how he uses the poems in *Songs of Experience* to illustrate what the people might do to solve their problems.

One of the conventions in printing is that in representing dialogue in a story we should begin a new paragraph every time the speaker changes. A paragraph of dialogue can be one sentence long or ten sentences long (any number of sentences really). A paragraph of dialogue may also consist of only a phrase or a single word:

> "It's a beautiful day, isn't it?" Melvin asked.
> "Yup," Hank muttered.
> "Remember yesterday?"
> "Yup."
> "I thought it would never stop raining."
> "Me too."

Once an exchange like that gets going, the author can dispense with the identifying tags, because the separate paragraphing will mark the shift in speakers.

But except for the purposes of emphasis, transition, or dialogue, a one- or a two-sentence paragraph can rarely be justified; it is almost a contradiction in terms. There can be little if any development in a single sentence. In a two-sentence paragraph, one of the sentences is likely to be the topic sentence; the remaining sentence is hardly enough to develop the topic idea adequately.

Judgment about whether a paragraph is adequately developed is, of course, a relative matter. Because some ideas need more development than others, no one can say absolutely how many sentences a paragraph needs to be satisfactorily developed. But a topic sentence does set at least a general commitment that a writer must fulfill. When the writer of the first sample paragraph above says, in what is obviously the topic sentence, **Wilfred Owen combines many types of imagery to get his point across,** we have every right to expect that he will specify and discuss several, if not many, types of imagery. But when he develops that topic idea with only one sentence, which is only slightly less general than his first sentence, we can feel quite safe in pronouncing that *this* paragraph is inadequately developed. An obvious way for him to develop the ideas contained in his two sentences is to cite examples, first of ironic imagery, then of sentimental imagery. To flesh out the mere cataloguing of these examples, he could go on to show how these images help the author "get his point across."

Even if the second sample paragraph were a summary paragraph that followed a paragraph (or several paragraphs) in which the writer had discussed the disadvantages of indulging in drugs, the reader could reasonably expect the writer to say something more about the notion presented in his second sentence. What kind of legal or moral responsibilities does an addict have to himself? What kind of responsibilities does he have to his family and to society in general? Once an addict has been "hooked," can he still be held responsible for his actions? What are the consequences, for himself and for society, of his refusing to be responsible for his actions? These questions suggest ways in which the writer might have expanded his thinly developed paragraph.

The writer of the third sample paragraph might have been able to justify his two-sentence paragraph if there were only *two* "other ways" in which Richard Harenger and the Baron Mordiane differed. But if you knew the stories he was discussing (Somerset Maugham's "The Treasure" and Guy de

Paragraphing

Maupassant's "Douchoux") and if you had seen the differences he discussed later on in the paper, you would realize that there were other, even more significant, differences that he might have mentioned and discussed in this paragraph. The topic sentence commits the writer to developing an extensive contrast between the two characters; by citing only two rather superficial differences, he has clearly not delivered on his commitment.

A topic sentence will suggest how long a paragraph has to be in order to create an impression of being adequately developed. Some sentences commit a writer to more development than others. A sentence like "There was only one way in which Julie could rouse John out of bed in the morning" obviously entails less development than a sentence like "There were several ways in which Julie could rouse John out of bed in the morning." A writer must train himself to look at a topic sentence and see what it commits him to do in the paragraph. Then of course he must have resources at his command so that he can fulfill his commitment. Sometimes he can draw on examples or illustrations to expand his paragraph; sometimes he can develop his topic idea by stating it in a variety of different ways; sometimes he can expand his paragraph by comparison or contrast or by analogy or by an anecdote; or he can trace out the causes or the consequences of what he is talking about. Invention, discovering something to say, is of course the crucial part of the composition process. Thinly developed paragraphs are the result of a writer's not thinking enough about his subject to discover what he already knows about it and what he needs to find out about it in order to develop it. Almost invariably he knows more about the idea stated in a topic sentence than he puts down in a one- or two-sentence paragraph. He must be made aware, or must force himself to become aware, of all that he really knows about the topic idea.

Punctuation

Graphic punctuation, which is the only kind dealt with in this section, is a feature of the written language exclusively. For the written language, it performs the kinds of functions that intonation (pitch, stress, pause, and juncture) performs for the spoken language. Punctuation and intonation can be considered as part of the grammar of a language because they join with other grammatical devices (word order, inflections, and function words) to help convey meaning. If writers would regard punctuation as an integral—and often indispensable—part of the expressive system of a language, they might cease to think of it as just another nuisance imposed on them by editors and English teachers.

In *Structural Essentials of English* (New York: Harcourt Brace Jovanovich, 1956), Harold Whitehall has neatly summarized the four main functions of graphic punctuation:

☐ **For LINKING parts of sentences and words.**
    semicolon
    colon
    dash
    hyphen (for words only)

Punctuation

☐ For SEPARATING sentences and parts of sentences.
period
question mark
exclamation point
comma

☐ For ENCLOSING parts of sentences.

pair of commas
pair of dashes
pair of parentheses
pair of brackets
pair of quotation marks

☐ For INDICATING omissions.

apostrophe (e.g. **don't, we'll, it's, we've**)
period (e.g. abbreviations, **Mrs., U.S., A.H. Robinson**)
dash (e.g. **John R--, D--n!**)
triple periods (. . . to indicate omitted words in a quotation)

Punctuation is strictly a convention. There is no reason in the nature of things why the mark **?** should be used in English to indicate a question. The Greek language, for instance, uses **;** (what we call a semicolon) to mark questions. Nor is there any reason in the nature of things why the single comma should be a separating device rather than a linking device. Usage has established the distinctive functions of the various marks of punctuation. And although styles of punctuation have changed somewhat from century to century and even from country to country, the conventions of punctuation set forth in the following section are the prevailing conventions in the United States in the second half of the twentieth century. Although publishers of newspapers, magazines, and books often have style manuals that prescribe, for their own editors and writers, a style of punctuation that may differ in some particulars from the prevailing conventions, the writer who observes the conventions of punctuation set forth in this section can rest assured that he is following the predominant system in the United States.

60

Put a comma in front of the coordinating conjunction that joins the independent clauses of a compound sentence.

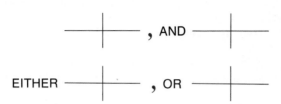

Examples:

1 He disliked this kind of cruel humor, yet when he met the actress at a dinner party, he teased her unmercifully.

2 Alice's embarrassment amused Julian, so he deliberately pursued the conversation with the Dirty Old Man across the aisle.

3 The decision about whether to attend college should be left entirely to the child, and his parents should make every effort to reconcile themselves to his decision.

4 It was snowing outside, and in the building William felt safe.

5 Nick relates all the happenings in his own words, and sometimes his own interpretations of another character or situation are revealed.

6 Either the senators will reject the proposal, or they will modify it in such a way as to make it innocuous.

Pairs of independent clauses joined by one of the coor-

Punctuation

dinating conjunctions **(and, but, or, nor, for, yet, so)** or by one of the correlative conjunctions **(either . . . or, neither . . . nor, not only . . . but)** are the only coordinate pairs that should be separated with a comma (see **62**). The reason why this convention developed is that in many situations, the absence of the comma could lead to an initial misreading of the sentence, as in the third example above or in a sentence like this: "He returned the book for his mother refused to pay any more fines." In the latter sentence, it would be quite natural for us to read **for** as a preposition. Consequently, we might initially read the sentence this way: **He returned the book for his mother** . . . but when we came to the verb **refused,** we would realize that we had misread the syntax of the sentence and would have to back up and reread the sentence. If you read the third, fourth, and fifth sample sentences *without the comma,* you will be aware of the possibility of a misreading of those sentences. A comma placed before the coordinating conjunction that joins the two parts of a compound sentence will prevent such misreadings.

Some handbooks authorize you to omit this separating comma if three conditions prevail: (1) if the two clauses of the compound sentence are short, (2) if there is no punctuation within either of the two clauses, and (3) if there is no chance that the syntax will be misread. (The following sentence satisfies these three conditions: "He said he would go and he did.") However, if you *invariably* insert a comma before the coordinating conjunction that joins the independent clauses of a compound sentence, you never have to pause to consider whether there is a chance that your sentence will be misread, and you can be confident that your sentence will always be read correctly the first time.

The safest practice is *always* to insert the comma before

the coordinating conjunction that joins the main clauses of a compound sentence.

61

Introductory words, phrases, or clauses shoud be separated from the main (independent) clause by a comma.

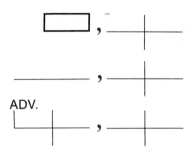

ADV.

Examples:

1 Underneath **,** the papers were scorched.

(*introductory word*)

2 I tiptoed into the house. Inside **,** the front room looked as though it had been recently finger-painted by a group of three-year-olds.

(*introductory word*)

3 In addition to the logical errors **,** Doris had made several miscalculations in addition and subtraction.

(*introductory prepositional phrase*)

4 As we went by **,** the church revealed all of its redbrick Georgian elegance.

(*introductory adverbial clause*)

Punctuation

5 After hurriedly gathering**,** the crowd decided to rush the gates.

(*introductory verbal phrase*)

6 Although he vehemently protested**,** the violence was not as destructive as he predicted it would be.

(*introductory adverbial clause*)

The reason why this convention developed is that the comma facilitates the reading of the sentence and often prevents an initial misreading. Without the "protective" comma in the six examples above, the syntax of those sentences would probably be misread on the first reading. If the comma were left out, most readers would probably read the sentences in this way:

1 Underneath the papers . . .

2 Inside the front room . . .

3 In addition to the logical errors [that] Doris had made . . .

4 As we went by the church . . .

5 After hurriedly gathering the crowd . . .

6 Although he vehemently protested the violence . . .

The insertion of a comma after the introductory element prevents that kind of misreading.

Even in those instances, however, where there is little or no chance of an initial misreading, the insertion of a comma after the introductory word, phrase, or clause will facilitate the reading of the sentence. Put a comma after the introductory word, phrase, or clause in the following sentences, and see whether it isn't easier to read the sentences:

Besides the crowd wasn't impressed by his flaming oratory.

Having failed to impress the crowd with his flaming oratory he tried another tactic.

After he saw that his flaming oratory had not impressed the crowd he tried another tactic.

If a writer *always* inserts a comma after an introductory word, phrase, or clause, he will not have to consider each time whether it would be safe to omit the comma, and he can be confident that his sentence will not be misread.

62

Pairs of words, phrases, or dependent clauses joined by one of the coordinating conjunctions should not be separated with a comma.

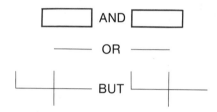

Examples:

1 The **mother AND** the **father appeared** in court **AND testified** about their son's activities.

   (*two nouns and two verbs joined by **and***)

2 There was nothing they could do **to prevent** the gas attack **OR to protect** themselves against the gas once it had been released.

   (*two infinitive phrases joined by **or***)

3 The men **who are able to work BUT who are not willing to work** will not be eligible to receive monthly welfare checks.

   (*two adjective clauses joined by **but***)

The principle behind this convention is that what has been joined by one means (the coordinating conjunction) should not then be separated by another means (the comma, a separating device). The function of the coordinating conjunction is to join units of equal rank (e.g. nouns with nouns, verbs with verbs, prepositional phrases with prepositional phrases, participial phrases with participial phrases, adjective clauses with adjective clauses, adverb clauses with adverb clauses). Once pairs of coordinate units have been joined by the conjunction, it makes no sense to separate them with a comma, like this: **the mother, and the father.** If a coordinating conjunction is not used to join the pair, a comma should be used to separate the pair, like this: "the tall, handsome man" (but not "the tall, and handsome man").

One exception to this convention, as in **60,** is a pair of *independent* clauses joined by a coordinating conjunction. According to **60**, a comma should be inserted before the coordinating conjunction, because in this particular structure the omission of the comma could lead—and often does lead—to an initial misreading of the sentence. But there are almost no instances where the use of a comma would prevent the misreading of pairs of words, phrases, or dependent clauses joined by a coordinating conjunction. As a matter of fact, if the first sample sentence were punctuated in this fashion, it would be harder to read: **The mother, and the father appeared in court, and testified about the son's activities.** If some subtle distinction in meaning were effected by these commas, or if the clarity of the sentence were threatened by the absence of the commas, the writer might be able to justify the use of commas in this sentence; but neither of those conditions seems to prevail here. The commas would only confuse the reader.

Another exception to this convention occurs in the case of suspended structures, as in the following sentence:

62 Pairs (No Comma)

> This account of an author's struggles with, and his anxieties about, his writing fascinated me.

The phrases *struggles with* and *anxieties about* are called "suspended structures" because they are left "hanging" until the noun phrase *his writing,* which completes them grammatically, occurs. If the writer of this sentence could have written "This account of an author's struggles and anxieties about his writing fascinated me," he would not, in accord with the directions in **62**, have put a comma in front of the *and* that joins the pair of nouns *struggles* and *anxieties.* But he saw that although the preposition *about* fitted idiomatically with *anxieties,* it did not fit idiomatically with *struggles.* So he was faced with two choices. He could complete both structures and write "This account of an author's struggles with his writing and his anxieties about his writing fascinated me." But preferring to avoid the repetition of *his writing,* he chose to use suspended structures, and he alerted the reader to the suspended structures by putting a comma after *with* and after *about.* Inserting a comma before the conjunction *and,* which joins the two phrases, makes it easier for us to read the sentence.

Unless you have some compelling reason, like protecting the clarity of the sentence or facilitating the reading of a sentence, do not separate with a comma pairs of parallel elements that have been joined with a coordinating conjunction.

Punctuation

63
**Use a comma to separate a series of coordinate
words, phrases, or clauses.**

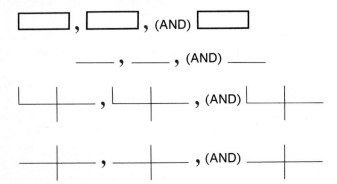

(The parentheses around **and** in the diagrams above indicate
that the coordinating conjunction between the last two members of a series may sometimes be dispensed with. For instance, the phrasing **The tall, robust, gray-haired soldier
rose to speak** is stylistically preferable to **The tall, robust,
and gray-haired soldier rose to speak**.)

Examples:

1 Could he cope with the challenges posed by war, poverty,
pollution, and crime?
(*a series of nouns*)

2 He would have to terminate the war, alleviate the plight of the
poor, arrest the contamination of the environment, and hobble
the criminal.
(*series of infinitive phrases, with **to** understood in the last three
members of the series*)

3 If he is willing to work hard **,** if he is resourceful enough to formulate sensible policies **,** if he subordinates his own interests to the interests of the community, he could rescue the nation from the despair that now prevails.

(*series of adverb clauses*)

4 He wanted to save the nation **,** he knew he could save it **,** and eventually he did save it.

(*series of independent clauses*)

Whereas the convention stated in **62** says that *pairs* of coordinate words, phrases, or clauses should not be separated with a comma, the convention governing a *series* of coordinate words, phrases, or clauses says that these units should be separated with a comma. (A **series** is to be understood as a sequence of **three or more** coordinate units.) Built on the principle of parallelism (see **27**), the series always involves words, phrases, or clauses of a similar kind. So a series should never couple nouns with adjectives, prepositional phrases with infinitive phrases, adjective clauses with adverb clauses, etc.

The convention that will be recommended here follows this formula: **a, b, and c.** Another acceptable formula for the series is **a, b and c**—where no comma is used between the last two members of the series when they are joined by a coordinating conjunction. The formula **a, b, and c** is adopted here because the alternative formula **(a, b and c)** sometimes leads to ambiguity. Consider the following example, which uses the **a, b and c** formula:

Please send me a gross each of **the red, green, blue, orange and black ties.**

The shipping clerk who received that order might wonder whether five gross of ties (red, green, blue, orange, black) were being ordered or only four gross (red, green, blue, orange-and-black). If five gross were being ordered, a comma after **orange** would specify the order unequivocally; if four gross were being ordered, hyphens should have been used to signify the combination of colors.

A more common instance of the ambiguity sometimes created by the use of the **a, b and c** formula is one like the following:

He appealed to **the administrators, the deans and the chairmen.**

In this sentence, it is not clear whether he appealed to three different groups (administrators, deans, chairmen—a meaning that would have been clearly indicated by the **a, b, and c** formula) or to only one group, **administrators,** who are then specified in the double appositive **deans and chairmen.**

Since there is never any chance of ambiguity if you use the **a, b, and c** formula, you would be well advised to adopt this option for punctuating a series.

64

Nonrestrictive adjective clauses should be enclosed with a pair of commas.

Examples:

1 My oldest brother **, who is a chemist ,** was hurt in an accident last week.

2 The shopkeeper caters only to American tourists **, who usually**

have enough money to buy what they want, and to aristo-cratic families.

3 Norman Mailer's book**, which most reviewers considered juvenile in its pronouncements,** was severely panned by the women's liberation groups.

4 The townsmen threaten the strangers**,** who are looking at the young girl.

A nonrestrictive adjective clause is one that supplies infor-mation about the noun that it modifies but information that is not needed to identify the particular person, place, or thing that is being talked about. (The four **that** clauses in the previous sentence, for instance, are **restrictive** adjective clauses—clauses that identify the nouns that they modify.)

In the case of the first example above, the adjective clause **who is a chemist** supplies additional information about **my oldest brother,** but this information is not needed to identify which of the brothers was hurt in the accident, because the adjective **oldest** sufficiently identifies the brother being talked about.

One test to determine whether an adjective clause is nonrestrictive or not is to read the sentence without the adjective clause, and if the particular person, place, or thing being talked about is sufficiently identified by what is left, the adjective clause can be considered nonrestrictive—and, ac-cording to the convention, should be marked off with enclos-ing commas. If, for instance, you were to drop the adjective clause from the first example and say **My oldest brother was hurt in an accident last week,** your readers would not have to ask, ''Which one of your brothers was hurt?'' The brother is specified by the adjective **oldest,** since there can be only one oldest brother. The clause **who is a chemist** merely supplies some additional but nonessential information about the oldest brother.

Punctuation

Another test to determine whether an adjective clause is nonrestrictive or not is the **intonation** test. Read these two sentences aloud:

He caters to American tourists, who have enough money to buy what they want, and to aristocratic families.

He caters to American tourists who have enough money to buy what they want and to aristocratic families.

In reading the first sentence aloud, native speakers of the language would pause briefly after the words **tourists** and **want** (that is, in the places where the commas are in the written form of the sentence) and would lower the pitch of their voices slightly in enunciating the clause **who have enough money to buy what they want.** In reading the second sentence aloud, native speakers would read right through without a pause and would not lower the pitch of their voices in reading the adjective clause. In writing, it makes a *significant* difference whether the adjective clause in that sentence is or is not enclosed with commas. With the enclosing commas, the sentence means this: He caters to American tourists (who, incidentally, usually have enough money to buy what they want) and to aristocratic families. Without the enclosing commas, the sentence means this: He caters only to those American tourists who have enough money to buy what they want (he doesn't cater to American tourists who don't have enough money to buy) and to aristocratic families. Likewise, the presence of the comma before the adjective clause in the fourth sample sentence indicates that the townsmen threaten *all* the strangers, because all of them are looking at the young girl. Without the comma before the **who** clause, the sentence would mean that the townsmen threaten *only* those strangers who are looking at the young girl. So whether the adjective clause is marked off with commas or not makes a real difference in the *meaning* of the sentence.

444

There are some instances in which the adjective clause is almost invariably nonrestrictive:

(a) Where the antecedent is a **proper noun,** the adjective clause is usually nonrestrictive:

Martin Chuzzlewit, who is a character in Dicken's novel, . . .

New York City, which has the largest urban population in the United States, . . .

The College of William and Mary, which was founded in 1693, . . .

(b) Where, in the nature of things, there could be **only one such** person, place, or thing, the adjective clause is usually nonrestrictive:

My mother, who is now forty-six years old, . . .

Their birthplace, which is Jamestown, . . .

His fingerprints, which are on file in Washington, . . .

(c) Where the identity of the antecedent has been clearly established by the **previous context,** the adjective clause is usually nonrestrictive:

My brother, who has hazel eyes, . . . (where it is clear from the context that you have only one brother)

The book, which never made the bestseller list, . . . (where the previous sentence has identified the particular book being talked about)

Such revolutions, which never enlist the sympathies of the majority of the people, . . . (where the kinds of revolutions being talked about have been specified in the previous sentences or paragraphs)

Which is the usual relative pronoun that introduces nonrestrictive adjective clauses. **That** is the more common relative pronoun used in restrictive adjective clauses. **Who** (or its

inflected forms **whose** and **whom**) is the usual relative pronoun when the antecedent is a person; **that,** however, may
also be used when the antecedent is a person and the clause
is restrictive: either "the men whom I admire" or "the men
that I admire."

65

**Restrictive adjective clauses should not be marked
off with a pair of commas.**

Examples:

1 My brother **who graduated from college in June** was hurt in an
   accident last week.
2 The poem is about a boy **who has been in Vietnam and has
   rejoined his family.**
3 The city is obliged to maintain all streets, alleys, and through-
   fares **that are in the public domain.**

A restrictive adjective clause is one that identifies the particular person, place, or thing being talked about. It "restricts"
the noun that it modifies; it "defines"—that is, "draws
boundaries around"—the noun being talked about.

   In the first example above, the adjective clause **who graduated from college in June** is restrictive because it identifies, defines, designates, specifies which one of the brothers
was hurt in the accident. Unlike the nonrestrictive adjective
clause (see **64**), which merely supplies additional but nonessential information about the noun that it modifies, the

restrictive adjective clause supplies information that is needed to identify the noun being talked about.

Whether an adjective clause is restrictive or nonrestrictive makes a substantial difference in the meaning of a sentence. Consider, for instance, these two sentences:

Women who have unusually slow reflexes should be denied a driver's license.

(*restrictive—note the absence of enclosing commas around the* **who** *clause*)

Women, who have unusually slow reflexes, should be denied a driver's license.

(*nonrestrictive—note the enclosing commas around the* **who** *clause*)

The import of the first sentence is that only those women who have unusually slow reflexes should be denied a driver's license. The import of the second sentence is that *all* women should be denied a driver's license, because they have unusually slow reflexes (a claim, incidentally, that is untrue). The presence or absence of commas makes a vital difference in the meaning of the two sentences. For this reason, the punctuation of the sentences is not a matter of option or whim.

If you were speaking those two sentences aloud, your voice would do what the presence or the absence of commas does. In the first sentence, your voice would join the **who** clause with **women** by running through without a pause after **women.** In the second sentence, your voice would pause slightly after **women** and would utter the **who** clause on a slightly lower pitch than the rest of the sentence. In addition to the test of whether the adjective clause is needed to specify the noun referred to, you can use this test of intonation to discriminate restrictive and nonrestrictive clauses.

Restrictive adjective clauses modifying nonhuman nouns

Punctuation

should be introduced with the relative pronoun **that** rather than with **which:**

> Governments, which are instituted to protect the rights of men, should be responsive to the will of the people.
>
> (*nonrestrictive*)

> Governments that want to remain in favor with their constituents must be responsive to the will of the people.
>
> (*restrictive*)

Here is another distinctive fact about the phrasing of restrictive and nonrestrictive adjective clauses: the relative pronoun may sometimes be omitted in restrictive clauses, but it may never be omitted in nonrestrictive clauses. Note that it is impossible in English to drop the relative pronouns **who** and **whom** from the following nonrestrictive clauses:

> John, who is my dearest friend, won't drink with me.
>
> John, whom I love dearly, hardly notices me.

(In the first sentence, however, the clause **who is my dearest friend** could be reduced to an appositive phrase: **John, *my dearest friend,* won't drink with me.**)

In restrictive adjective clauses, we sometimes have the option of using or not using the relative pronoun:

> The man whom I love dearly hardly notices me.
>
> (*with the relative pronoun*)

> The man that I love dearly hardly notices me.
>
> (*with the relative pronoun*)

> The man I love dearly hardly notices me.
>
> (*without the relative pronoun*)

In restrictive adjective clauses like these, where the relative pronoun serves as the object of the verb of the adjective clause, the relative pronoun may be omitted. The relative pronoun in restrictive clauses may also be omitted if it serves as the object of a preposition in the adjective clause: "The man I gave the wallet to disappeared" (here the understood **whom** or **that** serves as the object of the preposition **to**). However, the relative pronoun may *not* be omitted when the relative pronoun serves as the subject of the adjective clause:

> He who exalts himself shall be humbled.
>
> (**who** *cannot be omitted*)
>
> The money that was set aside for scholarships was squandered on roads.
>
> (**that** *cannot be omitted*)

66

If the independent clauses of a compound sentence are not joined by one of the coordinating conjunctions, they should be joined by a semicolon.

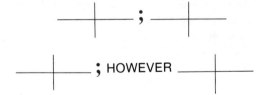

Examples:

1 This refutation is based on an appeal to reason; however, one must remember that an emotional appeal can also move people to reject an argument.

2 All the students spontaneously supported the team; they wanted to show their loyalty, even though they were disappointed with the outcome of the game.

Punctuation

3 He loved his mother **;** in fact, he practically worshiped her.

The coordinating conjunctions are **and, but, or, nor, for, yet, so.** In the absence of one of those words, the independent clauses of a compound sentence should be spliced together with a punctuation device: the semicolon.

Words and expressions like **however, therefore, then, in fact, indeed, nevertheless, consequently, thus, moreover, on the other hand, on the contrary** are not coordinating conjunctions; they are called **conjunctive adverbs.** Conjunctive adverbs provide logical links between sentences and between parts of sentences, but they do not function as grammatical splicers. Unlike coordinating conjunctions, which must always be placed *between* the two elements they join, conjunctive adverbs enjoy some freedom of movement in the sentence. In the first sample sentence above, the word **however** is placed between the two independent clauses, but evidence that this conjunctive adverb is not serving as the grammatical splicer of the two clauses is provided by the fact that **however** can be shifted to another position in the sentence: **This refutation is based on an appeal to reason; one must remember, however, that an emotional appeal can also move people to reject an argument.** The coordinating conjunction **but,** on the other hand, could occupy no other position in the sentence than *between* the end of the first clause and the beginning of the next clause.

Nor can the independent clauses of a compound sentence be joined by a comma, because the comma is a separating device, not a joining device. Compound sentences so punctuated are called **comma splices** (see **30**). As indicated in **60**, if a compound sentence is joined by one of the coordinating conjunctions, a comma should be put in front of the conjunction to mark off the end of one independent clause and the beginning of the next independent clause. But when a coordinating conjunction is not present to join the independent clauses, a semicolon must be used to join them. The semicolon serves both to mark the division between the two clauses and to join them.

It is sometimes advisable to use both a semicolon and a coordinating conjunction to join the independent clauses of a compound sentence. When the clauses are unusually long and have commas within them, a semicolon placed before the coordinating conjunction helps to demarcate the end of one clause and the beginning of the next one, as in this example:

> Struggling to salvage what was left of the semester, he pleaded with his English teacher, who was notoriously softhearted, to grant him an extension of time on his written assignments, quizzes, and class reports **;** **but** he forgot that, even with the best of intentions, he had only so many hours every day when he could study and only a limited reserve of energy.

The coordinating conjunction **but** serves to join the two main clauses of the compound sentence, but the use of the semicolon in addition to the conjunction makes it easier to read the sentence.

67

Whenever you use a semicolon, be sure that you have an independent clause on both sides of the semicolon.

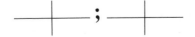

Punctuation

Examples of failure to observe this convention:

1 He played the banjo expertly **;** although he couldn't read a note of music.

2 Americans spend far too many hours as spectators of sports instead of as participants in them **;** watching meaningless drivel on television instead of spending that time reading a book.

3 The two series of poems also differ in style **;** the *Songs of Experience* being more vague and complex than the *Songs of Innocence.*

4 An industry like this benefits everyone, from the poor, for whom it creates employment **;** to the rich, who are made richer by it.

This convention is the corollary of **66**. It cautions against using the semicolon to join elements of unequal rank.

In all of the examples above, a semicolon has been used to join units of unequal rank. In all three sentences, there is an independent clause on the *left-hand* side of the semicolon; however, there is no independent clause on the *right-hand* side of the semicolon in any of those sentences.

In the first example above, there is the independent clause **He played the banjo expertly** on the left-hand side of the semicolon, but on the right-hand side of the semicolon, there is only the adverb clause **although he couldn't read a note of music.** That adverb clause belongs with, depends on, the first clause. Since it is an integral part of the first clause, it should be joined with that clause. The effect of the semicolon is to make the adverb clause part of a new clause that begins after the semicolon. But on the right-hand side of the semicolon, there is no independent clause that the subordinate, dependent adverb clause can be a part of.

The first, third, and fourth examples above can be revised by simply replacing the semicolon with a comma. The second example, however, cannot be revised by a simple change of punctuation. The writer has to supply an independent clause after the semicolon. He can supply that independent clause by adding the words **they spend far too many hours,** so that the whole clause reads, **they spend far too many hours watching meaningless drivel on television instead of spending that time reading a book.** So revised, the sentence has an independent clause on *both* sides of the semicolon.

Like the coordinating conjunction, for which it can serve as a substitute, the semicolon joins parts of equal rank. Therefore, if there is an independent clause on one side of the semicolon, there must be a balancing independent clause on the other side.

68
Use a colon after a grammatically complete lead-in sentence that formally announces a subsequent enumeration, explanation, illustration, or extended quotation.

Examples:

1 The courses I am taking this quarter are as follows: English, sociology, economics, political science, and psychology.

2 His approach works like this: after displaying his product and extolling its virtues, he asks the housewife if she has a small rug that she would like to have cleaned.

3 Examples of the diction used to evoke the horror of the scene include vivid images like these: ''coughing like hags,'' ''thick

> green light," "guttering," "white eyes writhing in his face,"
> "gargling from froth-corrupted lungs."

4 The reaction of the crowd signified only one thing **:** apathy.

5 (*note the use of a colon after a lead-in sentence for an extended quotation in a research paper.*)

> Toward the end of the *Preface,* Dr. Johnson confessed that he abandoned his earlier expectation that his dictionary would be able to "fix the language" **:**

> Those who have been persuaded to think well of my design will require that it should fix our language and put a stop to those alterations which time and chance have hitherto been suffered to make in it without opposition. With this consequence I will confess that I flattered myself for a while; but now begin to fear that I have indulged expectation which neither reason nor experience can justify.

Note that although a word, a phrase, or a clause or a series of words, phrases, or clauses can follow the colon, there must be an independent clause (a grammatically complete sentence) on the left-hand side of the colon.

In accord with this principle, you should not punctuate a sentence in this fashion:

> The courses I am taking this quarter are: English, sociology, economics, political science, and psychology.

That punctuation makes no more sense than punctuating a sentence in this way:

> My name is: John Adams.

In both cases, the words following the colon are needed to complete the sentence grammatically.

What distinguishes the colon from the dash as a symbolic device is that the colon throws the reader's attention *forward,* whereas the dash as a linking device throws the reader's attention *backward.* What the colon signifies is that what *follows* is a specification of what was formally announced in the clause on the left-hand side of the colon.

69

Use a dash when the word or word-group that follows it constitutes a summation, an amplification, or a reversal of what went before it.

Examples:

1 English, psychology, history, and philosophy—these were the courses I took last quarter.

2 If he was pressured, he would become sullen and close-lipped—a reaction that did not endear him to the President or to the Senate.

3 Time and time again he would admit that his critics were right, that he should have realized his mistakes, that he should have read the danger signs more accurately—and then go ahead with his original plans.

Unlike the colon, which directs the reader's attention forward, the dash usually directs the reader's attention backward. What follows the dash, when it is used as a linking device, looks back to what preceded it for the particulars or details that spell out its meaning or invest its meaning with pungency or irony.

The colon and the dash are usually not interchangeable marks of punctuation. They signal a different relationship between the word-groups that precede them and those that follow them. After much practice in writing, one develops a sense for the subtle distinction in relationships that is signaled by the punctuation in the following sentences:

The reaction of the crowd signified only one thing: apathy.

Punctuation

> The crowd clearly indicated their indifference to the provocative speech—an apathy that later came back to haunt them.

In the first sentence, the lead-in clause before the colon clearly alerts the reader to expect a specification of what is hinted at in that clause. In the second sentence, there is no such alerting of the reader in the lead-in clause; but following the dash, there is an unexpected commentary on what was said in the lead-in clause, a summary commentary that forces the reader to look backward. The colon and the single dash are both linking devices, but they signal different kinds of thought relationships between parts of the sentence.

Finally, the writer should be cautioned to avoid using the dash as a catchall mark of punctuation, one that indiscriminately substitutes for periods, commas, semicolons, etc.

70
Use a pair of dashes to enclose abrupt parenthetical elements that occur within a sentence.

— —   — —

Examples:

1 In some instances—although no one will admit it—the police overreacted to the provocation.
2 What surprised everyone when the measure came to a vote was the chairman's reluctance—indeed, downright refusal—to allow any riders to be attached to the bill.
3 One of them—let me call him Jim Prude—is clean-shaven and dresses like an Ivy Leaguer of the early 1950s.
4 Their unhappiness is due to the ease with which envy is aroused

and to the difficulty—or should I say impossibility?—of fighting against it.

5 Yet despite the similarities in their travelogues—for indeed the same trip inspired both works—the two reports differ in some key aspects.

The three devices used to set off parenthetical elements in written prose are commas, parentheses, and dashes. The kind of parenthetical element that should be enclosed with a pair of dashes is the kind that interrupts the normal syntactical flow of the sentence. What characterizes such elements in the examples above is that they abruptly arrest the normal flow of the sentence to add some qualifying or rectifying information. The rhetorical effect of the enclosing dashes is to give the parenthetical element an unusual measure of emphasis.

A pair of parentheses is another typographical device used to mark off parenthetical elements in a sentence. Enclosure within parentheses is used mainly for those elements that merely add information or identification, as in sentences like these:

> All the companies that used the service were charged a small fee (usually $500) and were required to sign a contract (an "exclusive-use" agreement).

> The manager of each franchise is expected to report monthly to NARM (National Association of Retail Merchants) and to "rotate" (take turns doing various jobs) every two weeks.

The typographical device used to set off the mildest kind of interrupting element is a pair of commas. Whether to enclose a parenthetical element with commas or with parentheses or with dashes is more a matter of stylistic choice than a matter of grammatical necessity. There are degrees of interruption and emphasis, and with practice, a writer develops an instinct for knowing when to mark off parenthetical elements with commas (lowest degree of interruption and emphasis), when to mark them off with parentheses (middle degree), and when to mark them off with dashes (highest degree). Consider the degrees of interruption and emphasis in the following sentences:

> That agency, as we have since learned, reported the incident directly to the Department of Justice.

> During the postwar years (at least from 1946 to 1952), no one in the agency dared challenge a directive from higher up.

> When the order was challenged, the attorney general—some claim it was his wife—put a call through to the president.

71

A dash is made on the typewriter with two unspaced hyphens and with no space before the dash or after the dash. (In handwriting, the dash should be made slightly longer than a hyphen.)

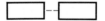

Example:

```
He forgot--if he ever knew--the functions of
the various marks of punctuation.
```

Do not hit the spacebar on the typewriter *before* the first hyphen, *between* the first and second hyphen, or *after* the second hyphen. In short, do not hit the spacebar at all in forming the dash on the typewriter.

Avoid the following kinds of typography in forming the dash on the typewriter:

He forgot–if he ever knew–the functions of
the various marks of punctuation.

He forgot – if he ever knew – the functions of
the various marks of punctuation.

He forgot –– if he ever knew –– the functions
of the various marks of punctuation.

He forgot – – if he ever knew – – the functions of the various marks of punctuation.

Mechanics

The graphic devices dealt with in this section might be, and often are, classified as punctuation. But because such graphic devices as italics, capitalization, and numbers are not correlated—as punctuation marks are—with the intonational patterns of the spoken language, these devices are grouped in a separate section under the heading Mechanics. In the spoken language, a word printed with a capital letter is pronounced no differently from the same word printed with a lower-case letter. Nor is the italicized title of a book pronounced any differently from that same title printed without italics. (Italics used for emphasizing a word or phrase, however, do correspond to stress in the spoken language.) Even quotation marks, which one might regard as correlated with the spoken language, do not correspond to anything the voice does when it quotes direct speech.

But whether one classifies these graphic devices as punctuation or as mechanics is immaterial. What is important to remember is that these devices are part of the written language exclusively and that they facilitate the reading of that language. Most readers would have at least momentary difficulty making sense of the following string of words:

> candy cane replied in the united states people use gas to refer to the liquid propellant that is called petrol in other english speaking countries

If the proper punctuation and mechanics were used with that string of words, readers would be spared the momentary difficulty:

> Candy Cane replied, "In the United States, people use *gas* to refer to the liquid propellant that is called *petrol* in other English-speaking countries."

Deprived of the resources that the human voice has to clarify the meaning of a spoken utterance, the writer should be eager to use all those typographical devices that make it easier for his readers to grasp what he is trying to convey in the written medium.

80

The period or the comma always goes inside the closing quotation mark.

,"   ."

Examples:

1 The author announces at the beginning of his article that he is going to cite only "facts."

2 "I know," she said, "that you are telling me a barefaced lie."

3 Mrs. Robinson's "bearded, sandaled, unwashed hippies," many of whom had traveled over a thousand miles to the festival, represented an aggregation of straight-A students.

Mechanics

This is a clear case where usage, rather than logic, has established the prevailing convention. Many reputable British printers put the period or comma *outside* the closing quotation mark, especially when the quotation marks enclose something less than a complete sentence—e.g. a word or phrase or dependent clause. But American printers almost universally put the period or comma *inside* the closing quotation mark.

The advantage of such consistency is that you never have to pause and ask yourself, "Is this a case where the period goes inside or outside the quotation mark?" Whether it is a single word or a phrase or a dependent clause or an independent clause that is enclosed, the period or comma always goes *inside* the closing quotation mark.

In handwriting, take care to put the period or comma *inside* the quotation mark, not *under* it like this: '' ''. In the case of quotations within quotations, both the single-stroke quotation mark and the double-stroke quotation go *outside* the period or the comma, as in this example:

"I read recently," he said, "that Patrick Henry never said, 'Give me liberty or give me death.' ''

81

The colon or semicolon always goes outside the closing quotation mark.

'';   '':

Examples:

1 He called this schedule of activities his "load": work, study, exercise, recreation, and sleep.

2 He told his taunters, "I refuse to budge"**;** his knees, however, were shaking even as he said those words.

Whereas the period or the comma always goes *inside* the closing quotation mark, the colon or the semicolon always goes *outside* it. If a writer has occasion to use quotation marks with a colon or a semicolon, he has only to recall that the convention governing the relationship of the colon or the semicolon to the closing quotation mark is just the opposite of the convention for the period and the comma.

82

The question mark sometimes goes inside, sometimes outside, the closing quotation mark.

?"   "?

Examples:

1 Who was it that said, "I regret that I have but one life to lose for my country"**?**

2 He asked her bluntly, "Will you marry me**?**"

3 When will they stop asking, "Who then is responsible for the war**?**"

Although a period or a comma always goes inside the closing quotation mark and a colon or a semicolon always goes outside it, you have to consider each case individually before deciding whether to put the question mark inside or outside the closing quotation mark. Fortunately, the criteria for determining whether it goes inside or outside the quotation mark are fairly simple to apply:

Mechanics

(a)   When the whole sentence, but not the unit enclosed in quotation marks, is a question, the question mark goes *outside* the closing quotation mark. (See the first example above.)

(b)   When only the unit enclosed in quotation marks is a question, the question mark goes *inside* the closing quotation mark. (See the second example above.)

(c)   When the whole sentence and the unit enclosed in quotation marks are both questions, the question mark goes *inside* the closing quotation mark. (See the third example above.)

In all cases, the question mark serves as the terminal punctuation for the entire sentence. In (*b*), you do not add a period outside the closing quotation mark, and in (*c*), you do not add another question mark outside the closing quotation mark.

83
The titles of books, newspapers, magazines, professional journals, plays, long poems, movies, radio programs, television programs, long musical compositions, works of art, and ships should be italicized by underlining.

Examples:

1 The critics have always rated Hemingway's *A Farewell to Arms* above his *For Whom the Bell Tolls.*

   (*titles of books*)

2 He has already published three articles in the *Quarterly Journal of Speech.*

   (*title of a professional journal*)

3 To support his contention, he quoted a passage from an anonymous article in *Newsweek.*

(*title of a magazine*)

4 The moonship *Falcon* settled down about 400 yards from the projected landing site.

(*title of the Apollo 15 ''ship''*)

5 My parents insisted on watching *All in the Family.*

(*title of a television program*)

6 The critics unanimously panned the recent performance of *La Traviata.*

(*title of an opera*)

Printers use a special, italic, type, which slants slightly to the right, to set off certain words in a sentence from other words that are printed in regular roman type (upright letters). In handwriting or typewriting, one italicizes words by underlining them.

Although italics are used with the titles of all of the items listed above, the writer most often has occasion to use italics with the titles of book-length or pamphlet-length published materials. Besides being a convention, the use of italics for titles can also protect meaning in some instances. If someone wrote ''I didn't really like Huckleberry Finn,'' a reader might be uncertain (unless the context gave him a clue) whether the writer was revealing his dislike for Mark Twain's novel or for the character of that name in the novel. If the writer intended to indicate that he disliked the novel, he could convey that message unambiguously by simply underlining (italicizing) the proper name.

How does one decide whether a poem is long enough to have its title italicized? As with most relative matters, the extreme cases are easily determinable. Obviously, a sonnet would not qualify as a long poem, but Milton's *Paradise Lost* would. It is the middle-length poem that causes indecision. A reliable rule of thumb is this: if the poem was ever published as a separate book or if it could conceivably be published as a separate book, it could be considered long enough to be set forth in italics. According to that guideline, T. S. Eliot's *The Wasteland* would be considered a long poem, but his "The Love Song of J. Alfred Prufrock" would be considered a short poem and therefore should be enclosed in quotation marks (see **84**). But if you cannot decide whether a poem is "long" or "short," either italicize the title or enclose it in quotation marks and use that system consistently throughout the paper.

84

The titles of articles, essays, short stories, short poems, songs, and chapters of books should be enclosed in quotation marks.

Examples:

1 Thomas Gray's "Elegy Written in a Country Churchyard" is reputed to be the most anthologized poem in the English language.

   (*title of a short poem*)

2 Hollis Alpert's "Movies Are Better Than the Stage" first appeared in the *Saturday Review of Literature.*

   (*title of an article in a periodical*)

3 J. F. Powers's "The Valiant Woman" was reprinted in 1947 in *The Prince of Darkness and Other Stories.*

   (*title of a short story in a collection of stories.*)

4 ''Raindrops Keep Falling on My Head'' set exactly the right mood for the bicycle caper in *Butch Cassidy and the Sundance Kid.*

(*title of a song*)

The general rule here is that the titles of published material that is *part* of a book or a periodical should be enclosed in quotation marks.

The title of a paper that you write should not be enclosed in quotation marks, nor should it be italicized. If your title contains elements that are normally italicized or enclosed in quotation marks, those elements, of course, should be italicized or enclosed in quotation marks.

The right and the wrong formats of a title for a paper submitted for a class assignment or for publication are illustrated here:

WRONG: ''The Evolution of Courtly Love in Medieval Literature''

The Evolution of Courtly Love in Medieval Literature

RIGHT: The Evolution of Courtly Love in Medieval Literature

The Evolution of Courtly Love in Chaucer's Troilus and Criseyde

Courtly Love in Herrick's ''Corinna's Going a-Maying'' and Marvell's ''To His Coy Mistress''

The Shift in Meaning of the Word Love in Renaissance Lyrics

''One Giant Step for Mankind''—Historic Words for a Historic Occasion

Mechanics

85

Italicize (underline) words referred to as words.

Examples of references to words as words:

1 He questioned the appropriateness of *honesty* in this context.
2 *The American Heritage Dictionary* defines *dudgeon* as "a sullen, angry, or indignant humor."
3 Unquestionably, *trudged* is a more specific verb than *walked*.
4 Look, for example, at his use of purely subjective words like *marvelous, exquisite,* and *wondrous.*

"He questioned the appropriateness of honesty in this context."
"He questioned the appropriateness of *honesty* in this context."
Although composed of the same words in the same order, those two sentences carry different meanings. The first sentence signifies that what is being challenged is the appropriateness of the thing (the abstract quality) designated by the word *honesty;* the second sentence signifies that what is being questioned is the appropriateness of the word itself. It is the italics alone that indicate to the reader the difference in meaning between these two sentences.

Italics (underlining) are a graphic device commonly used to distinguish a word being used *as a word* from that same word used as a symbol for an idea. (In handwritten or typewritten copy, you italicize words by underlining them.) An alternative but less common device for marking words used as words is to enclose the words in quotation marks, as in this example:

> The heavy use of such sensory diction as "juicy," "empurpled," "smooth," "creaked," "murmuring" helps to evoke the scene and make it almost palpable to the reader.

468

Since both devices are authorized by convention, the writer should adopt one system and use it consistently. The use of italics is probably the safer of the two systems, however, because quotation marks are also used to enclose quoted words and phrases, as in the sentence, We heard her say "yes." (Here *yes* is not being referred to as a word but is a quotation of what she said.)

86

Italicize (underline) foreign words and phrases, unless they have become naturalized or Anglicized.

Examples of foreign words and phrases:

1 Why does the advertiser, whose mouthpiece is the copywriter, allow himself to be presented before the public as a poet ***malgré lui***?
2 The advice to begin a short story as close to the climax as possible is a heritage of Horace's advice to begin a narrative ***in medias res*** rather than ***ab ovo.***
3 There had been a remarkable revival in the late 1960s of the ***Weltschmerz*** that characterized the poetry of the Romantics.

So that the reader will not be even momentarily mystified by the sudden intrusion of strange-looking words into a stream of English words, printers use italics to underscore foreign words and phrases. The graphic device of italics does not ensure, of course, that the reader will be able to translate the foreign locution, but it does prevent confusion by alerting the reader to the presence of non-English words.

Some foreign words and phrases, like habeas corpus, divorcee, mania, siesta, subpoena, have been used so often in an English context that they have been accepted into the

Mechanics

vocabulary as "naturalized" English words and therefore as not needing to be set forth in italics. Dictionaries have a system for indicating which foreign words and phrases have become naturalized and which have *not* become naturalized. Since dictionaries sometimes differ in their judgments about the naturalized status of certain foreign expressions, the writer should consistently follow the dictates of the dictionary available to him in determining whether a word or phrase needs italics.

An obvious exception to the rule is that proper nouns designating foreign persons, places, and institutions, even when they retain their native spelling and pronunciation, are *always* set forth without italics (underlining).

87
Compound words should be hyphenated.

Examples of compound words:

1 Because I had the normal six-year-old's "sweet tooth," I was irresistibly lured by the candy store.
2 He was attracted to anti-Establishment movements because they lacked policy-making administrators.
3 They scheduled the examinations in three-quarter-hour segments.
4 He preferred eighteenth-century literature because of its urbanity.
5 A five- or six-story building should be all you will need for that kind of plant operation.

87 Hyphen, for Compound Words

English reveals its Germanic origins in its tendency to form compounds—that is, to take two or more existent words and join them together to create a single unit that designates a thing or a concept quite different from what the individual words designate. A familiar example is the word **basketball.** When the two distinct words **basket** and **ball** were first joined to designate an athletic game or the kind of ball used in that game, the words were linked by a hyphen: **basket-ball.** When repeated use had made this new compound familiar to readers, the hyphen was dropped, and the two words were printed as a single word with no break between the two constituent parts.

Dozens of words in English have made this transition from a hyphenated compound to a single amalgamated word (e.g. *postoffice, skyscraper, briefcase, airport*). But hundreds of compounds are still printed with a hyphen, either because they have not been used enough to achieve status as unmarked hybrids or because the absence of a hyphen would lead to ambiguity. A reliable dictionary will indicate which compounds have made the passage and which have not.

With the exception of those words that have become recognized amalgams, a hyphen should be used to link

   (a)   two or more words functioning as a single grammatical unit.

> his **never-say-die** attitude (adjective)
> the junkyard had a huge **car-crusher** (noun)
> the hoodlums **pistol-whipped** him (verb)
> he conceded the point **willy-nilly** (adverb)

   (b)   two-word numbers (from 21 to 99) when they are written out.

> **twenty-one, thirty-six, forty-eight, ninety-nine**

Mechanics

(c) combinations with prefixes **ex-** and **self-.**

ex-chairman, ex-wife, self-denial, self-contradictory

(d) combinations with prefixes like **anti-, pro-, pre-, post-,** when the second element in the combinations begins with a capital letter or a number.

anti-Establishment, pro-American, pre-1929, post-1945

(e) combinations with prefixes like **anti-, pro-, pre-, re-, semi-, sub-, over-,** when the second element begins with the letter that occurs at the end of the prefix.

anti-intellectual, pro-oxidant, pre-election, re-entry, semi-independent, sub-basement, over-refined

(f) combinations where the unhyphenated compound might be mistaken for another word.

re-cover (the chair)
recover (the lost wallet)
re-sign (the contract)
resign (his office)
co-op
coop

With these exceptions, compounds formed with these prefixes now tend to be written as a single word (e.g. *antiknock, preconscious, prodemocratic, postgraduate*). And at least one authority would have all the compounds in (*e*), above, spelled solid. As against this, other authorities make distinctions that allow for *preelection* and *reentry* while prohibiting *antiintellectual*. In adopting any system that makes such distinctions, the writer should consistently follow the conventions of the authority consulted.

Frequently in writing, only a hyphen will clarify ambiguous syntax. If the writer of the third sample sentence had not used hyphens **(They scheduled the examinations in three quarter hour segments),** the reader would not be able to determine whether the examination was divided into three fifteen-minute segments (a meaning that would be clearly signaled by this placement of the hyphen: **three quarter-hour segments**) or whether it was divided into forty-five-minute segments (a meaning that is clearly signaled by this placement of hyphens: **three-quarter-hour segments**). There is a similar ambiguity in the sentence "He was the only new car dealer in town." A speaker would be able to clarify the ambiguous syntax of that sentence by the appropriate intonation of the voice. But in writing, only a hyphen will make clear whether the writer meant to say "He was the only new **car-dealer** in town" or "He was the only **new-car** dealer in town."

The fifth sample sentence shows how to hyphenate when there is more than one term on the left side of the hyphenation **(five-, six-).** In this way, **story** need not be repeated (as in **A five-story or six-story building . . .**). In typing, a space is inserted after the hyphen if it does not immediately precede the word it is meant to join **(five- or;** NOT: **five-or).**

88

A word can be broken and hyphenated at the end of a line only at a syllable-break; a one-syllable word can never be broken and hyphenated.

For the writer, two valuable bits of information are supplied by the initial entry of every word in the dictionary: (1) the spelling of the word, and (2) the syllabification of the word. The word **belligerent,** for instance, is entered this way in the dictionary: **bel·lig·er·ent.** If that word occurred at the end of

Mechanics

a line and you saw that you could not get the whole word in the remaining space, you could break the word and hyphenate it at any of the syllables marked with a raised period. But you could not break the word in any of the following places: **bell-igerent, belli-gerent, bellige-rent.**

Since the syllabification of English words is often unpredictable, it is safest to consult a dictionary when you are in doubt about where syllable-breaks occur. But after a while, you learn certain "tricks" about syllabification that save you a trip to the dictionary. A word can usually be broken

    (a)   after a prefix **(con-, ad-, pre-, un-, im-).**

    (b)   before a suffix **(-tion, -ment, -less, -ous, -ing).**

    (c)   between double consonants **(oc-cur-rence, cop-per, prig-gish).**

One-syllable words, however, can never be divided and hyphenated, no matter how long they are. So if you come to the end of a line and find that you do not have enough space to squeeze in single-syllable words like *horde, grieve, stopped, quaint, strength, wrenched,* leave the space blank and write the whole word on the next line. You have no choice.

Even in the interest of preserving a right-hand margin, you should not divide a word so that only one or two letters of it stand at the end of the line or at the beginning of the next line. Faced with divisions like *a-bout, o-cean, un-healthy, grass-y, dioram-a, flor-id, smok-er, live-ly,* you should put the whole word on that line or the next one. Remember that the hyphen itself takes up one space.

89

Observe the conventions governing the use of numbers in written copy.

Examples of violations of the conventions:

1 **522** men reported to the recruiting center.
2 During the first half of the **20th** century, **28 4**-year colleges and **14 2**-year colleges adopted collective-bargaining agencies.
3 The cocktail party started at **four P.M. in the afternoon.**
4 An account of the Wall Street crash of October **twenty-ninth, nineteen hundred and twenty-nine** begins on page **fifty-five.**
5 About **six and a half %** of the stores were selling a gross of **three-by-five** index cards for more than **thirty-six dollars and thirty-eight cents.**

The most common conventions governing the use of numbers in written copy are as follows:

(a) Do not begin a sentence with an Arabic number; spell out the number or recast the sentence:

Five hundred and twenty-two men reported to the recruiting center.
OR: A total of **522** men reported to the recruiting center.

(b) Spell out any number of less than three digits (or any number under 101) when the number is used as an adjective modifying a noun:

During the first half of the **twentieth** century, **twenty-eight four-**year colleges and **fourteen two-**year colleges adopted collective-bargaining agencies.

(c) Always use Arabic numbers with A.M. and P.M. and do not add the redundant **o'clock** and **morning** or **afternoon:**

Mechanics

The cocktail party started at **4:00** P.M.
OR: The cocktail party started at **four o'clock in the afternoon.**

(d) Use Arabic numbers for dates and page numbers:

An account of the Wall Street crash of October **29, 1919** begins on page **55.**

(e) Use Arabic numbers for addresses (618 N. 29th St.), dollars and cents ($4.68, $0.15 or 15 cents), decimals (3.14, 0.475), degrees (52°F.), measurements (especially when abbreviations are used: 3″ × 5″, 3.75 mi., 2 ft. 9 in., 6′2″ tall, but *six feet tall*), percentages (6% or 6 percent, but always use **percent** with fractional percentages—$6\frac{1}{2}$ percent or 6.5 percent):

About **$6\frac{1}{2}$ percent** of the stores were selling a gross of **3″ × 5″** index cards for more than **$36.38.**

90

Observe the conventions governing the capitalization of certain words.

Examples:

1 **P**resident **G**erald **R**. **F**ord informed the members of **C**ongress that he was appointing **M**s. **S**hirley **T**emple **B**lack as the **U**nited **S**tates ambassador to **G**hana.
2 **T**he title of the article in the *New Yorker* was "**T**he **T**ime of **I**llusion."
3 **D**r. **T**homas **J**. **C**ade, a professor in the **D**ivision of **B**iological **S**ciences at **C**ornell **U**niversity, has been supervising the breeding of peregrines captured in the **A**rctic, the **W**est, and the **P**acific **N**orthwest.
4 **T**he prime vacation time for most **A**mericans is the period between the **F**ourth of **J**uly and **L**abor **D**ay.

476

5 **T**he **K**orean troops resisted the incursion of the **C**ommunist forces.

In general, the convention governing capitalization is that the first letter of the proper name (that is, the particular or exclusive name) of persons, places, things, institutions, agencies, etc., should be capitalized. While the tendency today is to use lowercase letters for many words that formerly were written or printed with capital letters (for instance, *biblical reference* instead of **B***iblical reference*), the use of capital letters still prevails in the following cases:

(a) The first letter of the first word of a sentence.

They were uncertain about which words should be capitalized.

(b) The first letter of the first word of every line of English verse.

Little fly,
Thy summer's play
My thoughtless hand
Has brushed away.

(c) All nouns, pronouns, verbs, adjectives, adverbs, and first and last words of titles of publications and other artistic works.

R*emembrance of* **T***hings* **P***ast* (see **83**)
"**T**he **P**lace of the **E**nthymeme in **R**hetorical **T**heory" (see **84**)
"**A** **T**ent **T**hat **F**amilies **C**an **L**ive **I**n"
The **R***eturn of the* **P***ink* **P***anther*

(d) The first name, middle name or initial, and last name of a person, real or fictional.

H.R. Haldeman   **S**ylvia **M**arie **M**ikkelsen
David **C**opperfield   **A**chilles

Mechanics

(e) The names and abbreviations of villages, towns, cities, counties, states, nations, and regions.

Chillicothe, **O**hio	**F**ranklin **C**ounty
U.S.A.	**S**oviet **U**nion
Indo-**C**hina	**A**rctic **C**ircle
the **W**estern **W**orld	**S**outh **A**merica
the **M**idwestern states	the **S**outh (but: we drove south)

(f) The names of rivers, lakes, falls, oceans, mountains, deserts, parks.

the **M**ississippi **R**iver	**A**tlantic
the **G**rand **T**etons	**Y**ellowstone **N**ational **P**ark
Lake **E**rie	**V**ictoria **F**alls

(g) The names and abbreviations of businesses, industries, institutions, agencies, schools, political parties, religious denominations, and philosophical, literary, and artistic movements.

University of **N**ebraska	**D**emocrats
the **R**epublican convention	**C.I.A.**
Dow **C**hemical **C**orporation	**J**ohn **W**iley & **S**ons, **P**ublishers
Communist(s) (but: a communist ideology)	**S**mithsonian **I**nstitution
Victorian literature	**J**apan **A**ir **L**ines
Thomistic philosophy	the **P**entagon
	Pure **L**and **B**uddhism

(h) The titles of historical events, epochs, and periods.

Renaissance	**T**hirty **Y**ears' **W**ar
World **W**ar II	**I**ce **A**ge
the **M**iddle **A**ges	the **B**attle of **G**ettysburg
Reformation	the **D**epression

(i) Honorary and official titles when they precede the name of the person and when they are used in place of the name of a specific person.

former **P**resident **E**isenhower

the **D**uke of **C**ornwall

Pope **P**aul

His (**H**er) **E**xcellency

Senator **E**dward **K**ennedy

General **P**atton

the **C**hief **J**ustice

Queen **E**lizabeth

Sri **R**amakrishna

(j) The names of weekdays, months, holidays, holy days, and other special days or periods.

Christmas **E**ve

Passover

Lent

Mardi **G**ras

Memorial **D**ay

the **F**ourth of **J**uly

National **B**ook **W**eek

the first **S**unday in **J**une

(k) The names and abbreviations of the books and divisions of the Bible and other sacred books (no italics for these titles).

Genesis

Matt. (**G**ospel of **M**atthew)

Epistle to the Romans

King **J**ames **V**ersion

Talmud

Book of **J**ob

Pss. (**P**salms)

Pentateuch

Acts of the **A**postles

Vulgate

Koran

Scriptures

Bhagavad **G**ita

Lotus **S**utra

Exceptions: Do not capitalize words like the underlined in the following examples:

the African coast (but: the West Coast)

northern Wisconsin

the senator from Wyoming

the municipal library

the river Elbe (but: the Elbe River)

the federal government

the presidential itinerary

the county courthouse

The Tenses of the English Verb

The following paradigms provide models for the tenses of regular verbs, irregular verbs, and the verb **to be** in Edited American English or in what this text calls "public prose."

Regular verbs are those that usually form the past tense by adding **-ed** to the present tense of the verb (e.g. **walk—walked**). A few regular verbs, however, simply add **-d** (e.g. **hope—hoped**) or **-t** (e.g. **deal—dealt**) to form the past tense; and some regular verbs double the final consonant (e.g. **hop—hopped**) or change the final **y** to **i** (e.g. **copy—copied**) before adding **-ed.**

Irregular verbs are those that form the past tense by some change of spelling *within* the verb (e.g. **run—ran; drink—drank; weave—wove**).

A good desk dictionary will indicate which of the regular verbs form the past tense in ways other than simply adding **-ed** and will give the present, the past, and often the past-participle forms of irregular verbs (e.g. **eat, ate, eaten**). Here is the beginning of a typical dictionary entry that lists, in order, the present tense, the past tense, the past participle, and the present participle of an irregular verb. If you are in doubt about any of the forms of an irregular verb, consult your dictionary.

The Tenses of the English Verb

drive (drīv) *vt.* **drove, driv'en, driv'ing** [ME. *driven* < OE. *drifan*, akin to Goth. *dreiban*, G. *treiben*, ON. *drīfa* < IE. base **dhreibh-*, to push] **1.** to force to go; urge onward; push forward **2.** to force into or from a state or act [*driven* mad] **3.** to force to work, usually to excess **4.** *a)* to force by or as by a blow, thrust, or stroke *b)* to throw, hit, or cast hard and swiftly; specif., *Golf* to hit from the tee, usually with a driver **5.** to cause to go through; make penetrate **6.** to make or produce by penetrating [to *drive* a hole through metal] **7.** to control the movement or direct the course of (an automobile, horse and wagon, locomotive.)

With permission. From Webster's New World Dictionary of the American Language, *Second College Edition. Copyright © 1970 by the World Publishing Company, Inc.*

The Verb **To Be**

PRESENT TENSE	PAST TENSE	FUTURE TENSE
I **am** (cold)	I **was** (cold)	I **shall be** (cold)*
you **are**	you **were**	you **will be**
he/she/it **is**	he/she/it **was**	he/she/it **will be**
we **are** (cold)	we **were** (cold)	we **shall be** (cold)*
you **are**	you **were**	you **will be**
they **are**	they **were**	they **will be**

PERFECT TENSE	PAST PERFECT TENSE	FUTURE PERFECT TENSE
I **have been** (cold)	I **had been** (cold)	I **shall have been** (cold)*
you **have been**	you **had been**	you **will have been**
he/she/it **has been**	he/she/it **had been**	he/she/it **will have been**
we **have been** (cold)	we **had been** (cold)	we **shall have been** (cold)*
you **have been**	you **had been**	you **will have been**
they **have been**	they **had been**	they **will have been**

* Current usage also sanctions the use of **will** as the future-tense marker in the first person singular and plural.

The Tenses of the English Verb

ACTIVE VOICE

REGULAR VERBS

PRESENT TENSE
I **select** (the winner)
you **select**
he/she/it **selects**

we **select** (the winner)
you **select**
they **select**

PAST TENSE
I **selected** (the winner)
you **selected**
he/she/it **selected**

we **selected** (the winner)
you **selected**
they **selected**

FUTURE TENSE
I **shall select** (the winner)*
you **will select**
he/she/it **will select**

we **shall select** (the winner)*
you **will select**
they **will select**

IRREGULAR VERBS

PRESENT TENSE
I **drive** (the car)
you **drive**
he/she/it **drives**

we **drive** (the car)
you **drive**
they **drive**

PAST TENSE
I **drove** (the car)
you **drove**
he/she/it **drove**

we **drove** (the car)
you **drove**
they **drove**

FUTURE TENSE
I **shall drive** (the car)*
you **will drive**
he/she/it **will drive**

we **shall drive** (the car)*
you **will drive**
they **will drive**

The Tenses of the English Verb

PERFECT TENSE
I **have selected** (the winner)
you **have selected**
he/she/it **has selected**

we **have selected** (the winner)
you **have selected**
they **have selected**

PERFECT TENSE
I **have driven** (the car)
you **have driven**
he/she/it **has driven**

we **have driven** (the car)
you **have driven**
they **have driven**

PAST PERFECT TENSE
I **had selected** (the winner)
you **had selected**
he/she/it **had selected**

we **had selected** (the winner)
you **had selected**
they **had selected**

PAST PERFECT TENSE
I **had driven** (the car)
you **had driven**
he/she/it **had driven**

we **had driven** (the car)
you **had driven**
they **had driven**

FUTURE PERFECT TENSE
I **shall have selected** (the winner)*
you **will have selected**
he/she/it **will have selected**

we **shall have selected** (the winner)*
you **will have selected**
they **will have selected**

FUTURE PERFECT TENSE
I **shall have driven** (the car)*
you **will have driven**
he/she/it **will have driven**

we **shall have driven** (the car)*
you **will have driven**
they **will have driven**

The Tenses of the English Verb

PASSIVE VOICE

Only transitive verbs (that is, verbs that take a direct object—verbs listed in the dictionary as having **vt.** meanings) have a passive voice. An intransitive verb like *lie, lay, lain* can appear in all the tenses of the active voice, but because this verb cannot be followed by a direct object (one never says "he lies the book on the floor"), it cannot be turned into the passive voice.

REGULAR VERBS

PRESENT TENSE
I **am selected** (as the winner)
you **are selected**
he/she/it **is selected**

we **are selected** (as the winner)
you **are selected**
they **are selected**

PAST TENSE
I **was selected** (as the winner)
you **were selected**
he/she/it **was selected**

we **were selected** (as the winner)
you **were selected**
they **were selected**

IRREGULAR VERBS

PRESENT TENSE
I **am driven** (to school)
you **are driven**
he/she/it **is driven**

we **are driven** (to school)
you **are driven**
they **are driven**

PAST TENSE
I **was driven** (to school)
you **were driven**
he/she/it **was driven**

we **were driven** (to school)
you **were driven**
they **were driven**

The Tenses of the English Verb

FUTURE TENSE
I **shall be selected** (as the winner)*
you **will be selected**
he/she/it **will be selected**

we **shall be selected** (as the winner)*
you **will be selected**
they **will be selected**

PERFECT TENSE
I **have been selected** (as the winner)
you **have been selected**
he/she/it **has been selected**

we **have been selected** (as the winner)
you **have been selected**
they **have been selected**

PAST PERFECT TENSE
I **had been selected** (as the winner)
you **had been selected**
he/she/it **had been selected**

we **had been selected** (as the winner)
you **had been selected**
they **had been selected**

FUTURE TENSE
I **shall be driven** (to school)*
you **will be driven**
he/she/it **will be driven**

we **shall be driven** (to school)*
you **will be driven**
they **will be driven**

PERFECT TENSE
I **have been driven** (to school)
you **have been driven**
he/she/it **has been driven**

we **have been driven** (to school)
you **have been driven**
they **have been driven**

PAST PERFECT TENSE
I **had been driven** (to school)
you **had been driven**
he/she/it **had been driven**

we **had been driven** (to school)
you **had been driven**
they **had been driven**

485

The Tenses of the English Verb

FUTURE PERFECT TENSE

I **shall have been selected** (as the winner)*

you **will have been selected**

he/she/it **will have been selected**

we **shall have been selected** (as the winner)*

you **will have been selected**

they **will have been selected**

FUTURE PERFECT TENSE

I **shall have been driven** (to school)*

you **will have been driven**

he/she/it **will have been driven**

we **shall have been driven** (to school)*

you **will have been driven**

they **will have been driven**

Puzzlers

Each group of sentences shows various treatments of a common problem in phrasing. The letters appearing after the sentences allow you to record your preferred solution and then to compare this with the corresponding number in the KEY at the end of the exercise. Besides testing you, the puzzlers can show very plainly—although without explanation—the preferable way of handling some problems that occur in your writing.

Puzzlers

(1) You believed it to be him (*a*)
You believed it to be he. (*b*)

(2) The reason is because he's sick. (*a*)
The reason is that he's sick. (*b*)

(3) Let you and I do it together. (*a*)
Let you and me do it together. (*b*)
Let's you and I do it together. (*c*)
Let's you and me do it together. (*d*)

(4) We feed children who we think are hungry. (*a*)
We feed children whom we think are hungry. (*b*)

(5) I saw a young girl who I guessed to be Mary. (*a*)
I saw a young girl whom I guessed to be Mary. (*b*)

(6) The paintings were works by an imposter pretending to be he. (*a*)
The paintings were works by an imposter pretending to be him. (*b*)

(7) They should receive with open arms he who comes bearing gifts. (*a*)
They should receive with open arms him who comes bearing gifts. (*b*)

(8) His words seemed to imply that he agreed with her. (*a*)
His words seemed to infer that he agreed with her. (*b*)

(9) The distance between each post is six feet. (*a*)
The distance between posts is six feet. (*b*)

(10) People seem to have been shorter many years ago. (*a*)
People seemed to have been shorter many years ago. (*b*)

(11) He is one of the finest men that has ever lived. (*a*)
He is one of the finest men that have ever lived. (*b*)

(12) What provoke men's curiosity are mysteries. (*a*)
What provoke men's curiosity is mysteries. (*b*)
What provokes men's curiosity are mysteries. (*c*)
What provokes men's curiosity is mysteries. (*d*)

488

(13) Compromise will prevail; no one or no group will be the victor. (*a*)
Compromise will prevail; no one and no group will be the victor. (*b*)

(14) This copy is the best of any I have seen so far. (*a*)
This copy is the best of all I have seen so far. (*b*)

(15) To use a word of Lincoln's, . . . (*a*)
To use a word of Lincoln, . . . (*b*)

(16) Her apple pies are preferable to her custard pies. (*a*)
Her apple pies are preferable than her custard pies. (*b*)

(17) Nobody in their right minds would say such a thing. (*a*)
Nobody in their right mind would say such a thing. (*b*)
Nobody in his right mind would say such a thing. (*c*)

(18) She was very amused. (*a*)
She was very much amused. (*b*)

(19) He had hardly left the room than she got on the phone. (*a*)
He had hardly left the room when she got on the phone. (*b*)

(20) He has dozens of virtues, to which is added a certain pride. (*a*)
He has dozens of virtues, to which are added a certain pride. (*b*)

(1)	*a*	(6)	*b*	(11)	*b*	(16)	*a*
(2)	*b*	(7)	*b*	(12)	*d*	(17)	*c*
(3)	*b*	(8)	*a*	(13)	*b*	(18)	*b*
(4)	*a*	(9)	*b*	(14)	*b*	(19)	*b*
(5)	*b*	(10)	*a*	(15)	*a*	(20)	*a*

Glossary of Grammatical Terms

Some of these terms are defined in the section where they figure prominently. But since many of these terms also occur in other sections where they are not defined, this glossary is provided for the convenience of the curious but puzzled reader.

active verb. See **passive verb.**

adjective clause. An adjective clause is a dependent clause that modifies a noun or a pronoun, much as a simple adjective does.

The relative pronouns **who, which,** and **that** often appear at the head of the adjective clause, serving as the connecting link between the modified noun or pronoun and the clause, which then follows.

The car, **which was old and battered,** served us well.

Those are the houses **that I love best.**

Sometimes the relative pronoun is unexpressed but understood:

The book **I was reading** held my attention. (Here **that** is understood: The book **that** I was reading.)

See **dependent clause, relative pronoun, restrictive adjective clause, nonrestrictive adjective clause, modifier.**

Glossary of Grammatical Terms

adverb clause. An adverb clause is a dependent clause that modifies a verb or verbal, much as a simple adverb does.

The subordinating conjunction (**when, because, so that,** etc.), which appears at the head of the clause, links the adverb clause to the word that if modifies.

When I was ready, I took the examination.
I took the examination **because I was ready.**
To take an examination **when you are not ready** is dangerous.
(Here the adverb clause modifies the infinitive **to take.**)

See **dependent clause, subordinating conjunction, verbal, modifier.**

antecedent. An antecedent is the noun that a pronoun refers to or "stands for."

In the previous sentence, for example, the antecedent of the relative pronoun **that** is **noun.** In the sentence "The mother told her son that his check had arrived," **mother** is the antecedent of the pronoun **her,** and **son** is the antecedent of the pronoun **his.**

See **relative pronoun.**

auxiliary verbs. Auxiliary verbs are those function words—"helping" words (hence, "auxiliary")—that accompany other verb forms to indicate tense or mood or voice.

The following words in boldface are auxiliary verbs:
He **will** walk to work. He **is** walking to work. He **has** walked to work.
He **has been** walking to work. He **could** walk to work. He **must** walk to work.
He **was** driven to work.

See **function words, mood, voice.**

collective noun. A collective noun is a noun that designates a group or class of individuals—e.g. **committee, family, jury, army, faculty** (of a university), **team, crew.** See **summary noun.**

comma splice. A comma splice is the use of a comma, instead of a coordinating conjunction or a semicolon, between the two independent clauses of a compound sentence.

> He could not tolerate noise, noise made him nervous and irritable.

Since the comma is a separating device rather than a joining device, it must be accompanied in this sentence by a coordinating conjunction (here **for**), or it must be replaced with a semicolon.

See **independent clause, compound sentence,** and **coordinating conjunction.**

complement. A complement is the word or phrase, following a verb, that ''completes'' the predicate of a clause.

A complement may be (1) the object of a transitive verb (He hit **the ball**); (2) the noun or noun phrase following the verb **to be** (He is **an honors student**); or (3) the adjective following the verb **to be** or a linking verb (He is **happy**. The milk tastes **sour**.).

See **transitive verb, linking verb, to be, predicate complement,** and **noun phrase.**

complex sentence. A complex sentence is one that consists of one independent clause and one or more dependent clauses.

The following complex sentence has two dependent clauses—the first one an adverb clause, the second an adjective clause:

> **When he got to the microphone,** he made a proposal **that won unanimous approval.**

As used by grammarians, the term has nothing to do with the length or complexity of the sentence.

See **independent clause** and **dependent clause.**

compound sentence. A compound sentence is one that consists of two or more independent clauses.

He was twenty-one, but she was only eighteen.

Young men are idealists; old men are realists.

See **independent clause** and **comma splice.**

compound word. A compound word is a combination of two or more words functioning as a single word.

There are compounds that function as a noun (a **stand-in**), as an adjective (**eighteenth-century** literature), as a verb (they **pistol-whipped** him), or as an adverb (he had to comply **willy-nilly**). Some compounds have been used so often that they are written out with no space and no hyphen between the component parts (e.g. **handbook, postoffice**). Other compounds, especially those used as adjectives, are written with a hyphen (e.g. his **never-say-die** attitude). When in doubt about whether a compound should be hyphenated, consult a dictionary.

coordinate. Words, phrases, and clauses of the same grammatical kind or of equal rank are said to be "coordinate."

A pair or series of nouns, for instance, would be a coordinate unit. An infinitive phrase yoked with a participial phrase would not be a coordinate unit, because the phrases are not of the same grammatical kind. An independent clause would not be coordinate with a dependent or subordinate clause, because the two clauses are not of equal rank. An alternative term for **coordinate** is **parallel.**

See **parallelism** and **coordinating conjunction.**

Glossary of Grammatical Terms

coordinating conjunction. A coordinating conjunction is a word that joins words, phrases, or clauses of the same kind or rank. It joins nouns with nouns, verbs with verbs, prepositional phrases with prepositional phrases, independent clauses with independent clauses, adverb clauses with adverb clauses, etc.

A coordinating conjunction cannot be used to join a noun with an adjective, a prepositional phrase with a gerund phrase, or an independent clause with a dependent clause.

The coordinating conjunctions are **and, but, or, for, nor, yet, so.**

See **coordinate, correlative conjunctions,** and **subordinating conjunction.**

correlative conjunctions. Correlative conjunctions are coordinating conjunctions that operate in pairs to join coordinate structures in a sentence.

The common correlative conjunctions are **either . . . or, neither . . . nor, both . . . and, not only . . . but also,** and **whether . . . or.**

> By this act, he renounced **both** his citizenship **and** his civil rights.

See **coordinate** and **coordinating conjunction.**

dangling verbal. A dangling verbal is a participle, gerund, or infinitive (or a phrase formed with one of these verbals) that is either unattached to a noun or pronoun or attached to the wrong noun or pronoun.

> Raising his glass, a toast was proposed to the newlyweds by the bride's father.

In this sentence, the participial phrase **raising his glass** is attached to the wrong noun **(toast)** and therefore is said to be ''dangling'' (it was not the **toast** that was doing the **raising**). The participial phrase will be properly attached if

the noun **father** is made the subject of the sentence:
See **verbal** and **verbal phrase.**

demonstrative adjective. A demonstrative adjective is an adjective that "points to" its noun.

The singular forms are **this** (for closer objects—**this** book) and **that** (for more distant objects—**that** book); the plural forms are **these** and **those.**

dependent clause. A dependent clause is a group of words that has a subject and a finite verb but that is made part of, or dependent on, a larger structure by a relative pronoun **(who, which, that)** or by a subordinating conjunction **(when, if, because, although,** etc.).

There are three kinds of dependent clause: adjective clause, adverb clause, and noun clause.

A dependent clause cannot stand by itself; it must be joined to an independent clause to make it part of a complete sentence. A dependent clause written with an initial capital letter and with a period or question mark at the end of it is one of the structures that are called *sentence fragments.* An alternative term is **subordinate clause.**

See **independent clause, finite verb, adjective clause, adverb clause, noun clause, subordinating conjunction.**

finite verb. A finite verb is a verb that is fixed or limited, by its form, in person, number, and tense.

In the sentence "The boy runs to school," the verb **runs** is fixed by its form in person (cf. **I run, you run**), in number (cf. **they run**), and in tense (cf. **he ran**). The verbals (participle, gerund, infinitive) are considered **infinite verbs** because although they are fixed by their form in regard to tense (present or past), they are not limited in person or number. The minimal units of a clause, whether it is de-

Glossary of Grammatical Terms

pendent or independent, are a subject (a noun phrase) and a finite verb:

> Bells ring. (but not: Bells ringing)

See **predicate verb, noun phrase, verbals.**

faulty predication. A faulty predication occurs when the verb or verb phrase of a clause does not fit semantically or syntactically with the subject or noun phrase of the clause. It results from the choice of incompatible words or structures.

> The shortage of funds **claimed** more money.
>
> The reason I couldn't go **was because I hadn't completed my homework.**

The verb **claimed** in the first sentence is semantically incompatible with the noun phrase **the shortage of funds** that serves as the subject of the clause. In the second sentence, the adverbial **because** clause is syntactically incompatible as a predicate complement following the verb **was.**

See **predicate complement, predicate verb, noun phrase, verb phrase.**

function words. Function words are those ''little words'' in the language that have very little vocabulary meaning but that perform such vital functions as connecting or relating other words in the sentence.

Sometimes called *particles,* function words comprise all such words in the language as the following:

(1) articles or determiners (in front of nouns): **the, a, an, this, that, these, those, all, some,** etc.

(2) prepositions (for connecting or relating their objects to some other word in the sentence): **of, from, above, on, at,** etc.

(3) coordinating conjunctions (for joining words, phrases, and clauses of equal rank): **and, but, or, for, nor, yet, so.**

Glossary of Grammatical Terms

(4) subordinating conjunctions (for joining clauses of unequal rank): **when, if, although, because, that,** etc.

(5) auxiliary verbs (for indicating changes in tense and mood): **will, shall, have, may, can, would, should,** etc.

(6) conjunctive adverbs (for providing logical links between clauses): **however, nevertheless, moreover, therefore,** etc.

(7) **not** with **do** or **does** or **did** (for negating a verb):

> He **does not** love his mother.
>
> He **did not** love his mother.

fused sentence. A fused sentence is the joining of two or more independent clauses without any punctuation or coordinating conjunction between them.

> He could not believe his eyes mangled bodies were strewn all over the highway.

A fused sentence is also called a **run-on sentence** or a **run-together sentence.**

See **independent clause** and **comma splice.**

genitive case. The genitive case, a term derived from Latin grammar, is the case formed in English by adding **'s** or **s'** to the ending of nouns and some pronouns (e.g. **someone's**) or by using the preposition **of** followed by a noun or pronoun.

The most common use of the genitive case is to indicate possession: the **boy's** book, the arm **of the boy.**

Some of the other uses of the genitive case are as follows:

genitive of origin: **Beethoven's** symphonies

subjective genitive: the **king's** murder (i.e. the murder that the king committed)

objective genitive: the **king's** murder, the murder **of the king** (i.e. the king as the victim of a murder)

genitive of composition: a ring **of gold**

partitive genitive: a piece **of cheese**

Glossary of Grammatical Terms

The personal pronouns form the genitive case by a special spelling: **his, her, its, your, our, their.**

The genitive formed by adding **'s** or **s'** to nouns is often called the **possessive case.**

gerund. A gerund is a word that is formed from a verb but that functions as a noun.

Because of its hybrid nature as part verb and part noun, a gerund may take an object, may be modified by an adverb, and may serve in the sentence in any function that a noun can perform. Since, like the present participle, it is formed by adding **-ing** to the base verb, one can distinguish the gerund from the participle by noting whether it functions in the sentence as a noun rather than as an adjective. The following are examples of the gerund or gerund phrase performing various functions of the noun: As subject of the sentence: **Hiking** is his favorite exercise. As object of a verb: He favored **raising the funds by subscription.**

As complement of the verb **to be:** His most difficult task was **reading all the fine print.**

As object of preposition: After **reading the book,** he took the examination.

The latter sentence would be considered a dangling verbal if it were phrased as follows: After reading the book, the examination had to be taken.

See **verbal phrase** and **dangling verbal.**

independent clause. An independent clause is a group of words that has a subject and a finite verb and that is not made part of a larger structure by a relative pronoun or a subordinating conjunction.

The following group of words is an independent clause because it has a subject and a finite verb:

The **boys tossed** the ball.

The following group of words has the same subject and finite verb, but it is not an independent clause because it is made part of a larger structure by the subordinating conjunction **when:**

When the boys tossed the ball.

The **when** turns the clause into an adverb clause and thereby makes it part of a larger structure—a sentence consisting of a dependent clause (the adverb clause) and an independent clause (which must be supplied here to make a complete sentence).

See **dependent clause, finite verb, subordinating conjunction,** and **relative pronoun.**

infinitive. An infinitive is a word that is formed from a verb but that functions in the sentence as a noun or as an adjective or as an adverb.

Capable of functioning in these ways, the infinitive is more versatile than the participle, which functions only as an adjective, or the gerund, which functions only as a noun. The infinitive is formed by putting **to** in front of the base form of the verb.

Here are some examples of the infinitive or infinitive phrase in its various functions:

As noun (subject of sentence): **To err** is human; **to forgive** is divine.

As adjective (modifying a noun—in this case, **place**): He wanted a place **to store his furniture.**

As adverb (modifying a verb—in this case, **waved**): He waved a handkerchief **to gain her attention.**

The following infinitive phrase would be considered a dangling verbal:

To prevent infection, the finger should be thoroughly washed.

Glossary of Grammatical Terms

(Corrected: To prevent infection, you should wash the finger thoroughly.)

See **verbal phrase** and **dangling verbal.**

inflection.   The inflection of a word is the change of form that it undergoes to show grammatical relation in its context or to express modification of its meaning.

The inflection of the verb *to be* appears in the entry **to be** below.

intransitive verb.   An intransitive verb is a verb that expresses action but that does not take an object.

Intransitive verbs cannot be turned into the passive voice. Most action verbs in English have both transitive and intransitive uses, like **I ran swiftly** (intransitive) and **I ran the streetcar** (transitive). But some verbs can be used only transitively, like the verb *to emit,* and some verbs can be used only intransitively, like the verb *to go.* If in doubt about whether a particular verb can be used both transitively and intransitively, consult a dictionary.

The following verbs are all used intransitively:

He **swam** effortlessly.

They **slept** for twelve hours.

She **quarreled** with her neighbors.

See **transitive verb, passive verb,** and **voice.**

juncture.   Juncture is a grammatical feature only of the spoken language. It concerns the ways in which we divide and articulate the stream of sound to make it intelligible to native speakers of the language.

There is the kind of juncture that operates within and between words to help us discriminate between spoken phrases like "ice cream" and "I scream" or between "great rain" and "gray train." Another group of junctures makes use of various kinds of pauses or lengthening out of syllables to mark off the boundaries and terminations of utterances. This latter kind of juncture is roughly related to the punctuation system—commas, semicolons, periods, and question marks—of the written language.

linking verb. Linking verbs are those verbs of the senses like **feel, look, smell, taste, sound,** and a limited number of other verbs like **seem, remain, become, appear,** that "link" the subject of the sentence with a complement.

Linking verbs are followed by an adjective or a noun or a noun phrase:

The sweater **felt** soft. (adjective as complement)
He **appeared** calm. (adjective as complement)
He **remains** the president of the union (noun phrase as complement)

See **to be, complement, predicate complement,** and **noun phrase.**

modifier. A modifier is a word, phrase, or clause that limits, specifies, qualifies, or describes another word.

In the phrase "the red barn," the adjectival modifier **red** helps to specify or describe the particular barn being talked about. In the phrase "ran swiftly," the adverbial modifier **swiftly** describes the manner in which the action designated in the verb **ran** was done. Phrases and clauses also modify nouns and verbs:

the girl **with the flowery hat** (prepositional phrase modifying **girl**)
the barn **that is painted red** (adjective clause modifying **barn**)
he ran **down the street** (prepositional phrase modifying ran)
he ran **because he was frightened** (adverb clause modifying **ran**)

Glossary of Grammatical Terms

Besides modifying verbs, adverbs also modify adjectives and other adverbs:

It was an **unusually** brilliant color. (modifying the adjective **brilliant**)

He ran **very** swiftly. (modifying the adverb **swiftly**)

See **adjective clause, adverb clause,** and **squinting modifier.**

mood. Mood is that aspect of a verb which indicates the speaker's attitude toward the expressed action or condition. The **indicative mood** is used for statements of fact (The report **is** true); the **imperative mood** is used for commands (**Be** still!); the **subjunctive mood** is used to indicate hope or desire (I pray that they **be** happy), possibility (If it **be** true . . .), or condition (If he **were** here . . .). Except for the verb **to be,** the subjunctive forms of verbs are identical with the indicative forms except in the third-person singular of the present tense—e.g. **if he go** instead of **if he goes.**

nominative case. The nominative case is the form that a noun or pronoun must take when it appears as the subject of a clause or as the complement of a linking verb or of the verb **to be.**

In modern English, however, a writer has to be concerned about the nominative form only of some pronouns, because now nouns change their form only in the possessive case **(boy's, boys')** and in the plural **(boy, boys; man, men)**. The personal pronouns, however, and the relative pronoun **who** are still inflected (e.g. **he, his, him; who, whose, whom**). The nominative case of the personal pronouns are as follows: **I, you, he, she, it, we, they.**

The wrong case (the objective or accusative case) of the pronoun is used in this sentence:

Me hate the smell of burning rubber.

See **complement** and **inflection.**

nonrestrictive adjective clause. A nonrestrictive adjective clause is an adjective clause that supplies information about the noun or pronoun that it modifies but information that is not needed to identify or specify the particular noun or pronoun being talked about.

My father, **who is a college graduate,** cannot get a job.

In this sentence, the adjective clause **who is a college graduate** supplies information about the father, but that information is not needed to identify which father is being talked about. The particular father being talked about is sufficiently identified by the **my.**

A nonrestrictive adjective clause must be separated with a comma from the noun or pronoun that it modifies.

See **adjective clause, restrictive adjective clause,** and **modifier.**

noun clause. A noun clause is a dependent clause that can serve almost every function that a noun or pronoun or noun phrase can serve: as subject of the sentence, as an appositive to a noun, as the complement for a verb, as object of a preposition, but not as an indirect object.

The subordinating conjunctions that most often introduce a noun clause are **that** and **whether**—although **that** is sometimes omitted when the noun clause serves as the object of a transitive verb.

That he would make the grade was evident to everyone. (subject of sentence)
He said **he would not come.** (object of verb; **that** is omitted here, but it is just as correct to say **that he would come**)
The fact **that I had been sick** did not influence their decision.

Glossary of Grammatical Terms

(in apposition to **fact**)

They asked me about **whether I had seen him recently.**
(object of the preposition **about**)

See **dependent clause, noun phrase,** and **complement.**

noun phrase. A noun phrase consists of a noun or a pronoun and all of its modifiers (if any).

In the following sentence all of the words in boldface would be considered part of the noun phrase, which is dominated by the noun **house:**

The big, rambling, clapboard house on the hill belongs to Mrs. Adams.

See **verb phrase** and **verbal phrase.**

parallelism. Parallelism is the grammatical principle that words, phrases, or clauses joined in a pair or in a series must be of the same kind.

Nouns must be coupled with nouns; prepositional phrases must be coupled with prepositional phrases; adjective clauses must be coupled with adjective clauses.

Parallelism breaks down, for instance, when a noun is yoked with an adjective or a prepositional phrase is yoked with a participial phrase. Parallelism has been preserved in the following sentence, because all the words in the series that serves as the predicate complement of the verb **was** are adjectives:

The engine was **compact, durable,** and **efficient.**

See **coordinate** and **coordinating conjunction.**

participle. A participle is a word that is formed from a verb but that functions as an adjective.

Because of its hybrid nature as part verb and part adjective, a participle may take an object, may be modified by an adverb, and may modify a noun or a pronoun.

Glossary of Grammatical Terms

> Pulling his gun quickly from his holster, the sheriff fired a shot before the burglar could jump him.

In that sentence, the participle **pulling** takes an object **(gun)**, is modified by the adverb **quickly** and by the prepositional phrase **from his holster,** and modifies the noun **sheriff.**

The **present participle** is formed by adding **-ing** to the base form of the verb: **pulling, jumping, being.**

The **past participle** is formed by adding **-ed** or **-en** to the base form of the verb or by a special spelling: **pulled, beaten, left, bought.**

The perfect participle is formed with **having** plus the past participle form: **having pulled, having beaten, having left.**

The **passive participle** is formed with **having** plus **been** plus the past participle form: **having been pulled, having been beaten, having been left.**

See **verbal phrase** and **dangling verbal.**

passive verb.   A passive verb is the form that a predicate verb takes when we want to indicate that the subject of the sentence is the receiver, not the doer, of the action.

The form that we use when we want to indicate that the subject is the doer of the action is called the **active verb.**

Only transitive verbs can be turned into the passive form. The passive verb is made by using some form of the verb **to be** (e.g. **am, is, are, was, were, has been**) and the past participle of the base verb.

> The shepherds **tend** the sheep. (active verb)
> The sheep **are tended** by the shepherds. (passive verb)

See **predicate verb, transitive verb, past participle, to be.**

possessive case.   See **genitive case.**

Glossary of Grammatical Terms

predicate complement.   Some grammarians use the term **predicate complement** to refer to any noun, pronoun, or adjective that follows, or "completes," the verb, whether it be a transitive verb, a linking verb, or the verb **to be.** Other grammarians use the term **object** for the noun or pronoun that follows a transitive verb and reserve the term **predicate complement** for the noun, pronoun, or adjective that follows a linking verb or the verb **to be.**

> He is the **president.** (noun following the verb **to be**)
> She became the **breadwinner.** (noun following the linking verb)
> The pie tastes **good.** (adjective following the linking verb)

See **complement, transitive verb, linking verb, to be.**

predicate verb.   A predicate verb is the finite-verb part of the verb phrase that constitutes the whole predicate of a dependent or independent clause.

In the following sentence, the word in boldface is the predicate verb of the independent clause:

> The man **guided** the dogsled through the blinding snowstorm.

See **finite verb** and **verb phrase.**

relative pronoun.   The relative pronouns **who, which, that** serve a grammatical function in an adjective clause (as subject of the clause, as object or predicate complement of the verb of the clause, as object of a preposition in the clause) and also as the connecting link between the adjective clause and the noun or pronoun that the clause modifies.

Who is the only one of these relative pronouns that is inflected: **who** (nominative case), **whose** (possessive case), **whom** (objective case).

See **dependent clause, adjective clause,** and **antecedent.**

restrictive adjective clause. A restrictive adjective clause is an adjective clause that identifies or specifies the noun or pronoun that it modifies, that "restricts" the meaning to a particular person, place, thing, or idea.

> Baseball players who are under contract to a duly franchised professional team are eligible for a pension.

In this sentence, the adjective clause **who are under contract to . . . team** specifies those baseball players who are eligible for a pension. If that adjective clause were enclosed with commas (that is, if it were a **nonrestrictive** clause), the sentence would mean that *all* baseball players are eligible *because* they are under contract to a professional team—a quite different meaning from the sentence that does not have commas enclosing the adjective clause.

A restrictive adjective clause should *not* be separated with a comma from the noun or pronoun that it modifies.

See **adjective clause, nonrestrictive clause,** and **modifier.**

run-on sentence. See **fused sentence.**

sentence fragment. See **independent clause, dependent clause,** and **finite verb.**

squinting modifier. A "squinting modifier" is a metaphorical way of referring to an adverb or an adverbial phrase that is placed between two words that it can modify. Because by position it "looks both ways," it results in an ambiguous sentence.

For example: The candidate whom we favored **enthusiastically** praised our platform.

Since the adverb **enthusiastically** occupies a position between two verbs that it can modify (**favored** and **praised**), we cannot be sure whether it was the favoring or the praising that was done with enthusiasm. Shifting the

Glossary of Grammatical Terms

adverb to a position before **favored** or after **platform** will relieve the ambiguity.

See **modifier.**

subordinating conjunction. A subordinating conjunction is a word that serves as the connecting link between an adverb clause or a noun clause and a word in some other structure.

The most common subordinating conjunctions that connect an adverb clause to the verb or verbal that the clause modifies are **when, whenever, because, since, although, though, while, as, after, before, unless, until, in order that, so that.**

The two subordinating conjunctions that serve as the link between the noun clause and another structure are **that** and **whether.** The conjunction **that** is often omitted when the noun clause functions as the object of a verb:

He said [that] the committee would not accept the proposal.

See **coordinating conjunction, adverb clause, noun clause.**

summary noun. A summary noun is a word that "sums up" an idea or set of particulars presented in the previous sentence. It is usually accompanied by one of the demonstrative adjectives **this, that, these, those.**

He answered telephones, stuffed envelopes, rang doorbells, collected money, and distributed literature. This **work** [or These **activities**] won him a secure position on the candidate's campaign staff.

To avoid the vagueness or ambiguity of reference that may result from beginning a sentence with only a **this** or a **these,** the writer should use a summary noun along with **this** or **these** (or **that, those**).

See **collective noun** and **demonstrative adjective.**

suspended structure. A suspended structure is a phrase whose completion is delayed by an intervening parallel phrase. Both phrases are completed by a common element.

> His financial status is related to, and bolstered by, the vigor of the stock market.
> Weren't you at all fond of, or in the least bit in sympathy with, my stand on this issue?
> Employers are interested in the long-term, as well as the short-term, worth of our graduates.

A comma is usually put at the end of the first arrested phrase in order to signal to the reader that the phrase will be completed later in the sentence. This punctuation represents an exception to the rule stated in **62** that pairs of words, phrases, and dependent clauses joined by one of the coordinating conjunctions should not be separated with a comma.

terminal punctuation. Terminal punctuation is the period or question mark placed after a string of words to signal the end of a sentence or utterance.

Commas, semicolons, and colons—sometimes called **internal punctuation**—are used to mark the boundaries of phrases and clauses within the sentence. An alternative term for **terminal punctuation** is **end punctuation.**

to be. **To be** is the infinitive form of the most frequently used verb in the English language, one that can be followed by a noun, a pronoun, an adjective, an adverb of place (e.g. **there, here, upstairs**), the preposition **like** plus the object of that preposition (e.g. He is **like his father**), a verbal or verbal phrase, or a noun clause.

Here are the various forms of **to be,** as it changes in number, person, and tense: **am, is, are, was, were, shall** be, will be, has been, have been, had been, shall have been, will have been.

Some form of **to be** along with the present participle of the base verb is also used to form the progressive tense of the English verb: He **was going** to the doctor regularly. He **had been going** to the doctor regularly.

Some form of **to be** along with the past participle of the base verb is also used to form a passive verb: He **was struck** on the head. He **has been struck** on the head.

See **linking verb, predicate complement, passive verb,** and **participle.**

transitive verb.   A transitive verb is a verb expressing action that terminates in, or is received by, an object.

The object of a transitive verb can be a noun or noun phrase, a pronoun, a verbal or verbal phrase, or a noun clause.

> They **destroyed** the village. (noun as object)
> They **shot** him. (pronoun as object)
> He **favors** giving me another chance. (gerund phrase as object)
> He **will try** to break the lock. (infinitive phrase as object)
> He **proposed** that everyone in the room be allowed to vote. (noun clause as object)

Only transitive verbs can be turned into a passive verb.
See **intransitive verb** and **passive verb.**

verb phrase.   A verb phrase is a group of words consisting of a verb and all of its auxiliaries (if any), all of its complements (if any), and all of its modifiers (if any).

In the following sentence, all words in boldface would be considered part of the verb phrase (a structure dominated by the verb):

> The army **has been severely restricted in its operations.**

See **noun phrase, verbal phrase, predicate verb, auxiliary verb, modifier.**

verbal. A verbal is the general name applied to participles, gerunds, and infinitives.

These words are called "verbals" because they are formed from verbs; because they are not finite verbs, they cannot by themselves serve as the predicate verb of an independent clause or a dependent clause.

See **participle, gerund, infinitive, finite verb, predicate verb.**

verbal phrase. A verbal phrase is a group of words consisting of a participle or a gerund or an infinitive and all of its complements (if any) and all of its modifiers (if any).

In the following sentence, all words in boldface would be considered part of the verbal phrase, which is dominated by the participle **leaving:**

Leaving behind all of its heavy equipment, the army pressed forward quickly.

voice. Voice is that aspect of a verb which shows the relation of the subject to the action, i.e. whether that of performer or recipient. The former is called **active voice** (I was loving), the latter **passive voice** (I was loved).

See **passive verb.**

Commonly Misspelled Words

accept (cf. except)
accidentally
acquire
acquaintance
address
all right
already (cf. all ready)
arithmetic
athletics
attendance

believe
benign
business

cemetery
changeable
chief
choose (cf. chose)
conscience
correspondent
definite

dependent
design
devise (cf. device)
diminution
disappearance
dispel

effect (cf. affect)
embarrass
environment
exaggerate
existence

familiar
fascinate
flagrant
foreign
forth (cf. fourth)
fragrant
friend
fulfill or fulfil
    (but not *fullfill*)

Commonly Misspelled Words

government

harass
height
hindrance

incredible
independent
irresistible
its (cf. it's)

judgment

library
literature
lose (cf. loose)

maintenance (cf. maintain)
mathematics
minuscule
miracle
miscellaneous
mischief

necessary
neighbor
noticeable
nuisance

occasion
occurrence
occurred
offered
omitted

parallel
peculiar

possess
preceding (cf. proceeding)
preferred
prejudice
principal (cf. principle)
privilege

quite (cf. quiet)

receive
referring
relieve
remuneration
resemblance
reverence
ridiculous

seize
separate
similar
special
stationary (immobile)
stationery (paper)
succeed

than (cf. then)
their (cf. there)
threshold
too (cf. to)
tragedy
truly

usually

whose (cf. who's)
withhold

Index

Index

Index

Index

Index

Index

Index

PROOFREADERS' MARKS

⌒	close up space
℘	delete
⌒℘	delete and close up space
#	separate with a space
∧	insert here what is indicated in the margin
¶	start new paragraph
no ¶	no paragraph; run in with previous paragraph
⊙/	insert period
∧/	insert comma
;/	insert semicolon
:/	insert colon
‖M‖/	insert em dash
‖M‖/‖M‖	insert pair of em dashes
=/	insert hyphen
˅/	insert apostrophe
(cap)	use capital letter here
(lc)	use lowercase letter here
(ital)	set in italic type
(rom)	set in roman type
(sc)	set in small capitals
(bf)	set in boldface type
(tr)	transpose letters or words

FORMAT OF MANUSCRIPT 10–16 (pp. 357–359)

GRAMMAR 20–32 (pp. 360–395)

STYLE 40–49 (pp. 396–418)

PARAGRAPHING 50–52 (pp. 419–430)